1992

BRITISH DESIGN

AND ART DIRECTION

The 30th Annual of the best in
UK and International Advertising
and Graphic Design, including
their respective crafts.

THE DESIGNERS AND ART DIRECTORS ASSOCIATION

Designed by
PEARTREE DESIGN ASSOCIATES

Cover Design & Section Headings
NICK BELL

Cover Photography
ANDY RUMBALL

Image Manipulation
PETER CROWTHER

Jury Photography
ANITA CORBIN & JOHN O'GRADY

Packaging Photography
JOHN SUMMERHAYES

Annual Co-ordination
BEVERLEY PARKER

Assisted by
JAN GAGE

Printed in Hong Kong by
TOPPAN PRINTING COMPANY LIMITED

*The Association would like to thank Lewis Moberly
who designed the original pages of the D&AD Annual*

*All book trade enquiries for Europe and all direct mail enquiries to:
Internos Books, 18 Colville Road, London W3 8BL, England, UK.*

*USA and Canadian book trade rights:
Rizzoli International Publications Inc,
300 Park Avenue South, New York, NY 10010, USA.*

*International trade sales:
Hearst Books International,
105, Madison Avenue, New York, NY 10016, USA.*

ISBN Number 1873968 027

CONTENTS

1992

PRESIDENT

An interesting year. At the outset, it was obvious that changes were necessary. These included a slimming down of the number of categories and a new judging system which took both the advertising and design juries out of London for two days. Expenditure on the dinner was substantially increased to provide members and their guests with an evening that truly reflected D&AD's status. It was also the first year that all the Silvers were sponsored. Many thanks to all those who supported D&AD when they could in this economic climate just as easily refused.

With Anthony Simons-Gooding now installed as Executive Chairman, an even more far-reaching review of D&AD activities has begun. I am sure that the Association will benefit from Anthony's energy and dedication.

All in all, a year that required a lot of hard work for which I would personally like to thank the Committee.

D&AD is hopefully stronger for everyone's efforts.

TIM DELANEY • LEAGAS DELANEY

1992

PRESIDENT'S AWARD

I first encountered Neil Godfrey when I watched him go up to receive two D&AD Silvers for his work at Doyle Dane Bernbach in 1967. As I recall, he was wearing the 60's standard issue white suit, Jimmy Hendrix afro-style hair and his now legendary tan. I was impressed, as one is when confronted by someone who is not only at the top of their profession but also looks like they are.

Since those inspiring days when DDB first arrived in London, advertising has been through all kinds of changes, not least in the area of art direction. The debates about form over content, and about whether originality is more important than either, rage on. Neil Godfrey's work in its simplicity, clarity of purpose and sheer craft stands aloft from those arguments, rendering them, for me at least, rather meaningless and sterile.

Over the years, his work on Tern shirts, Remmington, Bird's Eye, Fiat, Dunn & Co, Albany Life, B&H, to name only a handful of the accounts he has made famous, bears testimony to a talent that must seem infuriatingly effortless to his peers. Yet as we all know the ease with which an ad falls together is totally dependent on an obsession with detail which borders on the neurotic.

Neil Godfrey has won 20 D&AD Silvers and 3 Golds. Most of us feel eternally grateful (and not a little conceited) to have one or two. He has also achieved many things which even he may not be aware of.

I attribute the resurgence of Colletts in the mid 70's to the rise of Frank Lowe and the arrival of Neil and Tony Brignull back from their short stint at Wells, Rich, Greene.

He created a look. 'The Neil Godfrey spread', bold headline across a DPS was copied by every art director in the land. It was, quite simply, the way you put a DPS ad together. Only his worked and 9 times out of 10, everyone else's didn't.

He has also demonstrated that advertising is not about the flame of young talent that somehow burns out. The enduring nature of his skill, displayed with characteristic power in the Amnesty ads last year, should give hope to wrinklies everywhere.

It may seem strange but I have never ever held a conversation with him, even though we have both worked in London for too many years to report accurately. He has always just been 'up there'. And I, like many others, have watched from afar in admiration.

INTRODUCTION

At the time of going to print, I have been at D&AD a mere 6 weeks. It would therefore be inappropriate for me to comment either on activities undertaken during the past year or indeed on this, the 30th Annual.

I would rather share with you my initial thoughts on how I see the future of D&AD, and to tell you why I accepted this assignment.

D&AD holds a world-class position as an organisation that fosters and encourages creative excellence, not just for its own sake but because it is good for business. As a client, I have been lucky enough to have been associated with much award-winning work, and indeed some twenty years ago served on a D&AD jury. As I said on joining, D&AD will be a labour of love.

I am currently in dialogue with the membership to gauge how they see D&AD, and how they would wish to see this great concern developing in the future. Outlined below are topics which are under energetic review.

MORE VALUE FOR MEMBERS

A feeling that apart from the awards, the dinner and the annual, D&AD should be doing more for its members.

ENLARGING THE MEMBERSHIP

The Association has stood at about 750 members for many years. Many people, although qualified for membership, do not take up the opportunity. By offering better value, and more relevance, D&AD has the potential to attract a significantly greater number of members.

OVERSEAS

D&AD is the vehicle by which UK creativity can be promoted abroad, not only throughout the English speaking parts of the world, but also throughout the new Europe.

DESIGN VERSUS ADVERTISING

The Design community feels less well served by D&AD than Advertising. This imbalance needs to be addressed.

FINANCE

D&AD's finances are over-stretched. This inhibits the organisation acting in the way it should. It is difficult to achieve excellence from a position of debt.

EDUCATION

Aimed at two audiences, students and the business community.

D&AD has an important role in capturing the imagination of the young, to ensure that, despite the ravages of recession, an education in the creative disciplines is worthwhile and rewarding. D&AD also has a key role to underline constantly to the business community the commercial value of creative excellence.

ANTHONY SIMONDS-GOODING • CHAIRMAN

DESIGN AND ART DIRECTION

CORPORATE MEMBERS

1991/92

DESIGN AND ART DIRECTION

ADMINISTRATION

EXECUTIVE COMMITTEE

PAST RECIPIENTS OF
DESIGN AND ART DIRECTION
GOLD PENCILS

1992
NO GOLD AWARDS PRESENTED

1991
PAUL ELLIMAN, PETER MILES

1990
ROGER WOODBURN

1989
NO GOLD AWARDS PRESENTED

1988
ALAN STANTON, PAUL WILLIAMS, LESLIE DEKTOR
VERONICA NASH, MARK SHARP, MARY LEWIS, KATHY MILLER

1987
GERT DUMBAR, MICHEL DE BOER, RUHI HAMID

1986
DAVID BAILEY, ALAN PAGE
JEREMY PEMBERTON, NICK THIRKELL

1985
PAUL LEEVES, ALAN TILBY
KEN CARROLL, MIKE DEMPSEY

1984
ANDY ARGHYROU, AXEL CHALDECOTT, CHRIS O'SHEA
JOHN HEGARTY, BARBARA NOKES, RICHARD SLOGGETT
STEVE HENRY

1983
TIM DELANEY, GRIFF RHYS JONES
ROB KITCHEN, MARTIN LAMBIE-NAIRN
BERNARD LODGE, IAN POTTER, MEL SMITH

1982
GERT DUMBAR, DAVID PELHAM, JOHN WEBSTER

1981
MIKE COZENS, JOHN HORTON, SIMON LANGTON
JOHN McCONNELL, DAVID MYERSCOUGH-JONES
KEN TURNER, GRAHAM WATSON

1980
DAVID HORRY, PAUL WEILAND, PETER WINDETT

1979
MIKE COZENS, PAT GAVIN, ALAN WALDIE

1978
GUY GLADWELL, TONY HERTZ

1977
NEIL GODFREY, BOB ISHERWOOD, RALPH STEADMAN

1976
DAVID DRIVER, TERRY LOVELOCK

1975
COLIN CRAIG, JOHN KRISH, DANE KEITH WILSON

1974
GEORGE DUNNING, ALAN FLETCHER
NEIL GODFREY, ALAN PARKER

1973
NANCY FOUTS, DAVID HILLMAN, HUGH HUDSON

1972
DON McCULLIN, TONY MEEUWISSEN
SARAH MOON, ALAN PARKER

1971
JOHN HEGARTY, PETER PHILIPS
CHARLES SAATCHI, PETER WEBB

1970
MICHAEL RAND

1969
MICHAEL RAND

1968
NO GOLD AWARDS PRESENTED

1967
HARRY PECCINOTTI

1966
NO GOLD AWARDS PRESENTED

1965
ROBERT BROWNJOHN

1964
NO GOLD AWARDS PRESENTED

1963
GEOFFREY JONES

AWARDS

GOLD AWARD   SILVER AWARD   NOMINATION

1992

DESIGN AND ART DIRECTION

JURIES

1992

DESIGN JURY

MADELEINE BENNETT • *Madeleine Bennett Design*

BRIAN WEBB • *Trickett & Webb*

MARK WICKENS • *Wickens Tutt Southgate*

MIKE DENNY • *Roundel Design Group*

STEPHEN COATES • *Word Search Publishing*

ALAN HORRI • *Hard Werken Design*

MICHAEL JOHNSON • *Smith & Milton Limited*

MIKE DEMPSEY • *Carroll Dempsey & Thirkell*

MARY LEWIS • *Lewis Moberly*

PETER DAVENPORT • *Davenport Associates*

DAVID ELLIS • *Why Not Associates*

LIONEL HATCH • *The Chase*

MARTIN LAMBIE-NAIRN • *Lambie-Nairn & Co.*

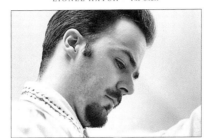

MIKE BENNION • *Blink Productions Limited*

GLEN TUTSSEL • *Michael Peters Limited*

GEORGE HARDIE • *NTA Studios*

MICHAEL WOLFF • *Addison Worldwide*

DAVID STUART • *The Partners*

NANCY WILLIAMS • *Williams and Phoa*

NICK WURR • *Royal College of Art*

MARK FARROW • *Farrow*

HANS BOCKTING • *Una*

HAMISH MUIR • *8vo*

ALEX MARANZANO • *Minale Tattersfield & Partners*

KEREN HOUSE • *The Design Bridge UK Limited*

1992

ADVERTISING JURY

JOHN HORTON • *Abbott Mead Vickers BBDO*

GRAHAM ROSE • *Rose Hackney*

TONY KAYE • *Tony Kaye Films Limited*

NEIL GODFREY • *Collett Dickenson Pearce*

SIMON DICKETTS • *Saatchi & Saatchi*

TIM MELLORS • *GGT*

PAUL WEILAND • *Paul Weiland Film Company Limited*

ALAN WALDIE • *Lowe Haward-Spink*

RICHARD FOSTER • *Abbott Mead Vickers.BBDO*

JOHN BACON • *Ogilvy & Mather*

CHRIS PALMER • *Simons Palmer Denton Clemmow & Johnson*

JOHN O'DONNELL • *Collett Dickenson Pearce*

JOHN HEGARTY • *Bartle Bogle Hegarty*

ADRIAN HOLMES • *Lowe Howard-Spink*

GRAHAM FINK • *GGT*

DAVE WATERS • *Duckworth, Finn, Grubb, Waters*

STEVE HENRY • *Howell Henry Chaldecott Lury*

BARBARA NOKES • *Bartle Bogle Hegarty*

MARK ROALFE • *The Banks Partnership*

MIKE COZENS • *Limelight Commercials*

SUZIE HENRY • *Bairnsfair Sharkey Trott*

TONY COX • *BMP DDB Needham*

CHRIS O'SHEA • *The Banks Partnership*

MALCOLM GASKIN • *Woollams Moira Gaskin o'Malley*

TONY BRIGNULL • *DMB&B*

p

ress adve

—

30 is

t

ng

SILVER AWARD
for the most outstanding
Colour Newspaper
Advertisement

Art Director
JOHN HORTON

Copywriter
RICHARD FOSTER

Typographer
JOE HOZA

Agency
ABBOTT MEAD
VICKERS.BBDO
LIMITED

Managing Director
DAVID GORDON

Client
THE ECONOMIST

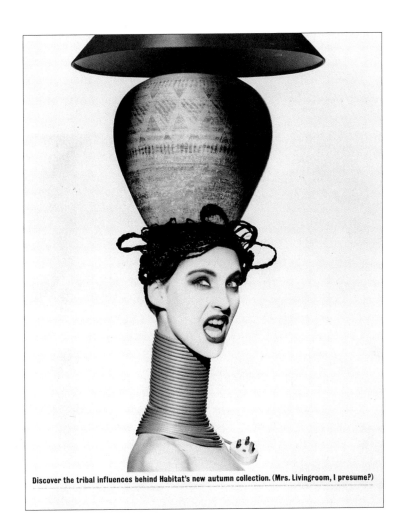

Discover the tribal influences behind Habitat's new autumn collection. (Mrs. Livingroom, I presume?)

We've travelled all over the world for ideas for Habitat's new tribal collection. Drop by if you haven't got too much on your plate.

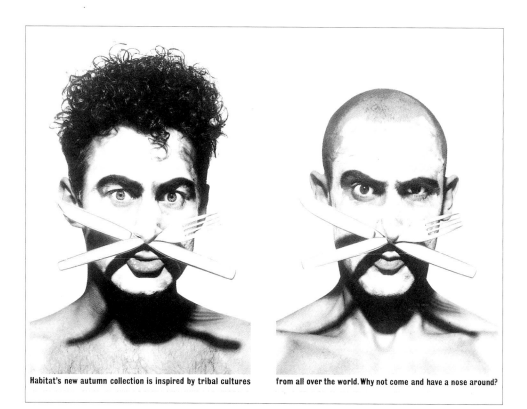

SILVER AWARD
NOMINATION
for the most outstanding
Colour Newspaper
Advertisement

Art Director
DENNIS WILLISON

Copywriter
GERARD EDMONDSON

Photographer
BRUCE FLEMING

Typographer
JEFF MERRELLS

Agency
COLLETT DICKENSON
PEARCE & PARTNERS
LIMITED

General Manager
IAN DICKENS

Client
OLYMPUS

Jeffrey Bernard is unwell.

Jeffrey Bernard is fine.

I used to like my photograph being taken. As a baby I couldn't stop smiling and was a willing target for the Box Brownie.

Now that I am a miserable old man who has lost his looks and has discovered that it takes 120 muscles to make you smile, I have gone off it. I don't like saying cheese and the alternative a showgirl once told me is to have a fixed smile all day long. While she kicked her heels up she kept saying money, pronounced moneee.

But recently I discovered Olympus Cameras and looking through the lens of one of them, I found my friends not to be so ugly as I thought them to be. They suddenly became quite beautiful. I nearly did too.

Known for years as the most bloodshot man on earth, Olympus has cleared my eyes, face and reputation. A miracle of modern science. Physics and optics were never my strong suit but all I know is that when the flash fires, then red-eye has all but vanished. Clever people these Olympic egg heads.

I may be as the title of the play has it "unwell" but I can at last face the birdie. The only trouble is that in my case the birdie is a vulture.

OLYMPUS CAMERAS

The Don McCullin exhibition. Featuring the work of Idi Amin, Pol Pot and Ho Chi Minh.

For over twenty years Don McCullin travelled to the battlefields of the world armed only with a camera.

In Cambodia his pictures bore witness to the work of the Khmer Rouge and their fanatical leader Pol Pot.

In Vietnam he was party to both the horrors of war and the dangers of war coverage. Forty-five journalists and photographers were killed and another eighteen are still missing.

In the Congo he found himself embroiled in a conflict made all the dirtier by the involvement of gun-toting mercenaries.

And he visited places whose names have become synonymous with suffering: Beirut, Biafra and Bangladesh.

But if war and oppression gave us his most powerful pictures then surely peacetime has given us his most appealing ones.

From his travels in the East are photographs of New Guinea tribes, a religious festival on the banks of the Ganges, and scenes from the Sumatra Islands.

From our shores there are dramatic landscapes.

And from his own home there is a series of still lifes.

For this major retrospective includes McCullin photographs that have never been shown before.

McCullin used Olympus cameras for many of these pictures, and Olympus in return are proud to be sponsoring this exhibition.

His work can be viewed at The Royal Photographic Society, Milsom Street, Bath from June 29th to September 1st.

Don McCullin has seen it all. Now so can you. **OLYMPUS**

Consumer Magazines
Black and White

Art Director
PAUL BRIGINSHAW

Copywriter
MALCOLM DUFFY

Photographer
DON McCULLIN

Typographer
KAREN SPINKS

Agency
COLLETT DICKENSON
PEARCE & PARTNERS
LIMITED

General Manager
IAN DICKENS

Client
OLYMPUS

*Consumer Magazines
Colour*

Art Director
BRIAN STEWART

Copywriter
GREG DELANEY

Photographer
PAMELA HANSON

Typographers
BRIAN STEWART
CHRIS DEVONALD

Agency
DELANEY FLETCHER
SLAYMAKER DELANEY
& BOZELL

Marketing Director
ROGER ADAMS

Client
TRIUMPH
INTERNATIONAL

Makes me feel good. Hugs me. Flatters me. (Shame it's only a bra.)

Triumph INTERNATIONAL
The bra for the way you are

The bra designed for the woman's movement.

Triumph INTERNATIONAL
The bra for the way you are

Support. Confidence. Freedom. (Why can't a man give you all that a bra does?)

Triumph INTERNATIONAL
The bra for the way you are

"Thanks to the bank manager we didn't have kittens."

You've settled down, you've saved up, everything is planned for your first baby.

The problem is you don't have one, you have three.

Or you've bought a brand new sofa, which your brand new dog decides to have for lunch.

Or you're trying out the camper van, hit reverse by mistake and knock down your garage.

Unlikely? Well these are some of the real life stories that walked into Lloyds Bank last year.

And in a life that's full of surprises, a Lloyds Bank Personal Loan is one thing you can rely on.

We can lend you the money you need, when you need it, whether it's for three new cots, or

for a whole extra bedroom.

And, rest assured, our rates are extremely attractive: currently 1.85% per month (**APR 24.6%**).

Moreover, we will tailor the loan to suit you, by working out together exactly what your commitments are, and how much you can comfortably afford to pay back each month.

If you'd like to know more, call us on 0800 444210.

Or if you prefer, pop into your local Lloyds Bank branch for an application form.

Then together we can make plans for those little things you never planned for.

PERSONAL LOANS

Lloyds Bank

THE THOROUGHBRED BANK.

Consumer Magazines Colour

Art Director
CHARLES INGE

Copywriter
JANE GARLAND

Photographer
ROLPH GOBITS

Typographer
SIMON WARDEN

Agency
LOWE HOWARD-SPINK

Chief Manager
MIKE BULPITT

Client
LLOYDS BANK PLC

Concentrated Norwegian Formula
Neutrogena® Hand Cream
FOR DRY, CRACKED OR CHAPPED HANDS

Consumer Magazines Colour

Art Director
LYNN KENDRICK

Copywriter
DAVID SHANE

Photographer
RUSSELL PORCAS

Typographer
LYNN KENDRICK

Agency
CHIAT DAY

Managing Director
FRAN MINOGUE

Client
NEUTROGENA UK LIMITED

Consumer Magazines
Colour

Art Director
RUSSELL RAMSEY

Copywriter
JOHN O'KEEFFE

Photographer
ANDREAS HEUMANN

Typographer
MATTHEW KEMSLEY

Agency
BARTLE BOGLE
HEGARTY

Senior Director
DAVID RIST

Client
K SHOEMAKERS
LIMITED

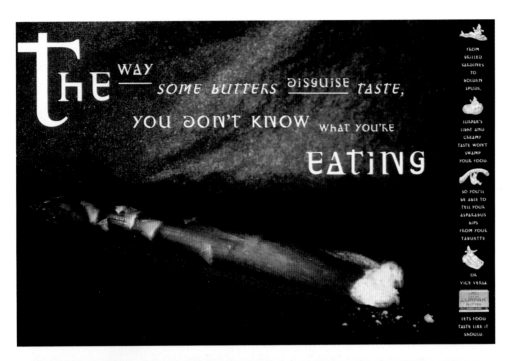

Consumer Magazines
Colour

Art Director
KATE STANNERS

Copywriter
TIM HEARN

Photographer
JOHN PARKER

Typographer
LEN CHEESEMAN

Agency
GGT

Marketing Director
ANNE FREEL

Client
MD FOODS UK
LIMITED

Consumer Magazines
Colour

Art Director
MARK ROALFE

Copywriter
ROBERT CAMPBELL

Photographer
JERRY OKE

Typographer
JOE HOZA

Agency
ABBOTT MEAD
VICKERS.BBDO
LIMITED

Marketing Manager
OLIVER JOHNSON

Client
VOLVO
CONCESSIONAIRES

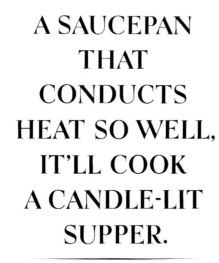

TWO WAYS OF SOLVING A DANDRUFF PROBLEM.

Consumer Magazines
Colour

Art Director
NORMAN ALCURI

Copywriters
JIM AITCHISON
DANNY HIGGINS

Photographer
ALEX KAIKEONG

Typographer
ANDY CLARKE

Agency
THE BALL
PARTNERSHIP
SINGAPORE

Managing Director
HUANG ENG

Client
PACIFIC BEAUTY
CARE

BODDINGTONS. THE CREAM OF MANCHESTER.
Boddingtons Draught Bitter. Brewed at the Strangeways Brewery since 1778.

Consumer Magazines
Colour

Art Director
MIKE WELLS

Copywriter
TOM HUDSON

Photographer
TIF HUNTER

Typographer
NIGEL DAWSON

Agency
BARTLE BOGLE
HEGARTY

Marketing Director
STEVE PHILPOTT

Client
THE WHITBREAD
BEER COMPANY

Consumer Magazines
Colour

Art Director
DENNIS WILLISON

Copywriter
GERARD EDMONDSON

Photographer
CLIVE ARROWSMITH

Typographer
JEFF MERRELLS

Agency
COLLETT DICKENSON
PEARCE & PARTNERS
LIMITED

General Manager
IAN DICKENS

Client
OLYMPUS

Thanks to
Olympus, he's
Mummy's
blue-eyed boy
again.

Consumer Magazines
Colour

Art Director
JOHN HORTON

Copywriter
RICHARD FOSTER

Photographer
GRAHAM FORD

Typographer
JOE HOZA

Agency
ABBOTT MEAD
VICKERS.BBDO
LIMITED

Marketing Manager
OLIVER JOHNSON

Client
VOLVO
CONCESSIONAIRES

INSTEAD OF A COAT OF PAINT, WE GIVE IT A SUIT OF ARMOUR.

If any car can claim to be weatherproof, the Volvo 460 is that car.

It shines come rain, hail, sleet or snow.

(To be honest, we draw the line at 6-inch nails – our picture is intended only as a symbol of the car's durability.)

The 460's resistance to the elements is largely due to an element used in its construction.

Zinc. As any metallurgist will tell you, zinc is the last word in rustproofing. That's why over 60% of the 460's bodyweight is made of zinc-coated steel.

Even then, we spray the entire body-shell (including the zinc-coated parts) with a further layer of zinc phosphate.

We then immerse it in a bath of primer.

We spray exposed parts of the underbody with p.v.c. to protect them from stone chips.

We inject the inner cavities with a special wax-based fluid.

We close off and seal all welded seams, inside and out.

And then we paint it. And then we paint it again. And then, for metallic finishes, we paint it again.

By the time we've finished with it, the Volvo 460 is cocooned in a multi-layered shell of anti-corrosive material.

It's a car that comes in its own garage.

THE VOLVO 460.

TILL DEATH US DO PART.

*Consumer Magazines
Colour*

Art Director
WARREN BROWN

Copywriter
JOHN McCABE

Photographer
ELLIOT ERWITT

Typographer
WARREN BROWN

Agency
BARTLE BOGLE
HEGARTY

Marketing Director
ANDREW KNIBBS

Client
LEVI STRAUSS UK
LIMITED

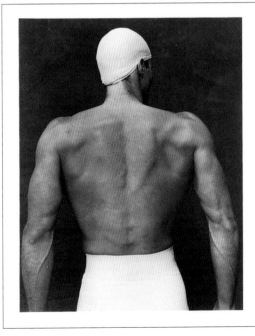

He's spent 21 years 3 months
and 2 days getting here.

But all that matters is the next
48.62 seconds.

SEIKO

Official Timer of the Games of the XXI Olympiad

*Consumer Magazines
Colour*

Art Directors
ROGER PEARCE
BILL GALLACHER

Copywriters
MICK PETHERICK
RICHARD MYERS

Photographers
BRUCE WEBER
GRAHAM FORD

Typographers
ANDY DYMOCK

Agency
SAATCHI & SAATCHI

General Manager
ROBERT WILSON

Client
SEIKO EUROPE
LIMITED

Consumer Magazines
Colour

Art Director
GERARD STAMP

Copywriter
LOZ SIMPSON

Illustrator
ROBIN
HEIGHWAY-BURY

Agency
BSB DORLAND

Marketing Director
LAWRENCE BALFE

Client
H J HEINZ COMPANY
LIMITED

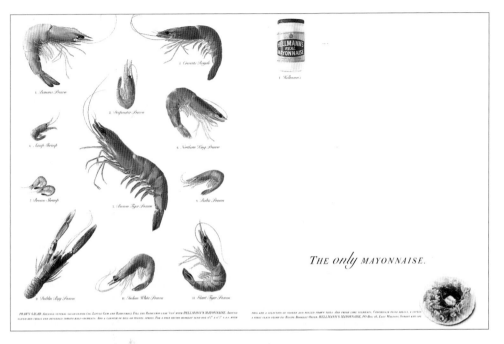

*Consumer Magazines
Colour*

Art Director
BRIAN STEWART

Copywriters
GREG DELANEY
MARTIN LORAINE

Illustrator
OLIVIA BEASLEY

Typographers
BRIAN STEWART
CHRIS DEVONALD

Agency
DELANEY FLETCHER
SLAYMAKER
DELANEY & BOZELL

Marketing Manager
CHIP LLOYD

Client
CPC UK LIMITED

*Consumer Magazines
Colour*

Art Director
DAVE JOHNSON

Copywriter
JONATHAN
KNEEBONE

Photographer
ROBERT
SHACKLETON

Design Group
NICE

Typographer
RICHARD
BONNER-MORGAN

Agency
D'ARCY MASIUS
BENTON & BOWLES
LIMITED

Head of Personal Mail
YVETTE TURNER

Client
ROYAL MAIL

*Consumer Magazines
Colour*

Art Director
NIGEL ROSE

Photographer
NADAV KANDER

Agency
COLLETT DICKENSON
PEARCE & PARTNERS
LIMITED

Marketing Manager
DEREK STOTHARD

Client
GALLAHER LIMITED

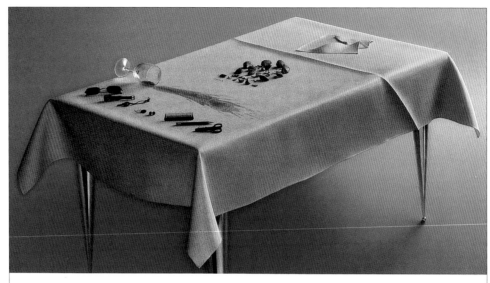

MIDDLE TAR As defined by H.M. Government
Warning: SMOKING CAN CAUSE FATAL DISEASES Health Departments' Chief Medical Officers

*Consumer Magazines
Colour*

Art Director
PAUL BRIGINSHAW

Copywriter
MALCOLM DUFFY

Photographer
BARRY LATEGAN

Agency
COLLETT DICKENSON
PEARCE & PARTNERS
LIMITED

Marketing Manager
DEREK STOTHARD

Client
GALLAHER LIMITED

MIDDLE TAR As defined by H.M. Government
Warning: SMOKING CAN CAUSE HEART DISEASE Health Departments' Chief Medical Officers

Consumer Magazines
Colour

Art Director
WARREN BROWN

Copywriter
JOHN MCCABE

Photographer
ELLIOT ERWITT

Typographer
WARREN BROWN

Agency
BARTLE BOGLE
HEGARTY

Marketing Director
ANDREW KNIBBS

Client
LEVI STRAUSS UK
LIMITED

Consumer Magazines
Colour

Art Director
MITCH LEVY

Copywriter
SEAN TOAL

Illustrator
ANNE SHARP

Typographer
ANNE SHARP

Agency
COLLETT DICKENSON
PEARCE & PARTNERS
LIMITED

Marketing Executive
FIONA PRIOR

Client
BECKS BIER

*Consumer Magazines
Colour*

Art Director
MIKE KEANE

Copywriter
RICHARD SELBOURNE

Photographer
MIKE PARSONS

Agency
COLLETT DICKENSON
PEARCE & PARTNERS
LIMITED

Marketing Manager
DEREK STOTHARD

Client
GALLAHER LIMITED

Nothing should disturb that Condor moment.

*Consumer Magazines
Colour*

Art Director
ROONEY CARRUTHERS

Copywriter
LARRY BARKER

Photographer
JEAN LOUP SIEFF

Typographer
MATTHEW KEMSLEY

Agency
BARTLE BOGLE
HEGARTY

Marketing Director
SIMON ESBERGER

Client
HAAGEN DAZS UK
LIMITED

13mg TAR 1·1mg NICOTINE
PROTECT CHILDREN: DON'T MAKE THEM BREATHE YOUR SMOKE
Health Departments' Chief Medical Officers

BODDINGTONS. THE CREAM OF MANCHESTER.
Boddingtons Draught Bitter. Brewed at the Strangeways Brewery since 1778.

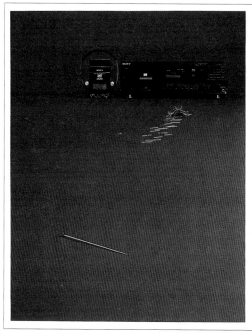

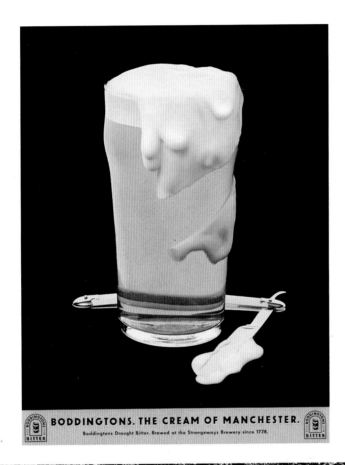

BODDINGTONS. THE CREAM OF MANCHESTER.

Boddingtons Draught Bitter. Brewed at the Strangeways Brewery since 1778.

*Consumer Magazines
Colour*

Art Director
MIKE WELLS

Copywriter
TOM HUDSON

Photographer
TIF HUNTER

Typographer
NIGEL DAWSON

Agency
BARTLE BOGLE
HEGARTY

Marketing Director
STEVE PHILPOTT

Client
THE WHITBREAD
BEER COMPANY

From the front, few small cars are as attractive as our new Polo.

From the back, though, we're tempted to say no small car is as attractive as our new Polo.

Because no other small cars come with a catalytic converter as standard. An advanced 'three-way' catalyst at that.

One capable of reducing by more than 90% the trio of toxic pollutants in exhaust fumes.

It may not be perfect but it's 90% more perfect than no 'cat' at all.

That said, you may be wondering what sort of effect this has on the Polo's performance.

Wonder not. Thanks to the introduction of fuel injection, it's well up to speed.

The brakes are now servo. So stopping suddenly gives you even less of a start.

And not least, the uprated suspension makes for even nimbler handling and an even smoother ride.

All in all, you could say our new Polo leaves the competition behind.

But very little else.

 The new catalytic Polo.

*Consumer Magazines
Colour*

Art Director
MIKE ORR

Copywriter
DAVID DENTON

Illustrator
MEL CALMAN

Typographer
DAVID WAKEFIELD

Agency
BMP DDB NEEDHAM

Marketing Manager
MIKE CORNISH

Client
VAG UK LIMITED

Consumer Magazines
Colour

Art Director
MARK ROALFE

Copywriter
ROBERT CAMPBELL

Typographer
JOE HOZA

Agency
ABBOTT MEAD
VICKERS.BBDO
LIMITED

Car Marketing Manager
OLIVER JOHNSON

Client
VOLVO
CONCESSIONAIRES

Consumer Magazines
Colour

Art Director
ROONEY CARRUTHERS

Copywriter
LARRY BARKER

Photographer
JEAN LOUP SIEFF

Typographer
MATTHEW KEMSLEY

Agency
BARTLE BOGLE
HEGARTY

Marketing Director
SIMON ESBERGER

Client
HAAGEN DAZS UK
LIMITED

Which handbag would you rather drop?

*Consumer Magazines
Colour*

Art Director
JOHN HORTON

Copywriter
RICHARD FOSTER

Photographer
NEIL BARSTOW

Typographer
JOE HOZA

Agency
ABBOTT MEAD
VICKERS.BBDO
LIMITED

Senior Product Manager
JO EDWARDS

Client
SMITH & NEPHEW
CONSUMER
PRODUCTS

Amazing revelation. Women have legs.

To look at most other press-on towels, you would think they were designed by somebody from another planet.

Why else would they be shaped like a brick (and just about as comfortable to wear)?

Shapes press-on towels, by contrast, are shaped like you.

They curve where you curve.

The sides are slightly cut away, so they follow the contours of your legs. This makes them so comfortable to wear, you can hardly feel them at all.

It also makes them much easier to position correctly, and therefore totally reliable.

Shapes are raised in the middle and tapered at the ends. So you get protection, without detection.

(Shapes are completely invisible even under the tightest jeans.)

If you'd like a free sample pack of three Shapes, and a money-off voucher, just clip the coupon below.

And welcome back to the human race. **Shapes**

*Consumer Magazines
Colour*

Art Director
JOHN HORTON

Copywriter
RICHARD FOSTER

Photographer
JOHN PARKER

Typographer
JOE HOZA

Agency
ABBOTT MEAD
VICKERS.BBDO
LIMITED

Marketing Controller
BRYCE RUSSELL

Client
SMITH & NEPHEW
CONSUMER
PRODUCTS

There are feet that will never climb in the Andes. There are feet that will never photograph gorillas in the Congo. There are feet that will never catalog the native lichens of Northern Wales. Dunham. They get the job done.

*Consumer Magazines
Colour*

Art Director
JOHN DOYLE

Copywriter
ERNIE SCHENCK

Photographer
NADAV KANDER

Typographer
JOHN DOYLE

Agency
DOYLE ADVERTISING
& DESIGN GROUP

*Vice President Marketing &
Product*
MICHAEL COOGAN

Client
THE DUNHAM
COMPANY

Wrangler Classic jeans. Ruggedly constructed for rugged chaps.

BE MORE THAN
JUST A NUMBER

*Consumer Magazines
Colour*

Art Directors
MARK DENTON
ANDY MCKAY

Copywriter
CHRIS PALMER

Photographer
JOHN CLARIDGE

Agency
SIMONS PALMER
DENTON CLEMMOW &
JOHNSON LIMITED

Managing Director
FRANK DIMECH

Client
WRANGLER UK
LIMITED

Consumer Magazines
Colour

Art Director
NICK WOOTTON

Copywriter
JONATHAN JOHN

Photographer
JASON HAWKES

Typographer
JOANNE CHEVLIN

Agency
J WALTER THOMPSON

Campaign Manager
DEBORAH COOTE

Client
CENTRAL OFFICE OF
INFORMATION

**TO DISCOVER HOW DULL LIFE COULD BE.
SIMPLY JOIN THE DOTS.**

ROYAL AIR FORCE
— OFFICER —

Consumer Magazines
Colour

Art Director
JOHN DOYLE

Copywriter
ERNIE SCHENCK

Photographer
NADAV KANDER

Typographer
JOHN DOYLE

Agency
DOYLE ADVERTISING
& DESIGN GROUP

*Vice President Marketing &
Product*
MICHAEL COOGAN

Client
THE DUNHAM
COMPANY

AND FOR THE OPPOSITION, WE DO AN EXCELLENT RANGE OF RUNNING SHOES.

They won the Grand Slam. They have a combined weight of a ton and a half. They wear Nike. So, a word of advice to anyone thinking of tackling them. Don't.

Consumer Magazines
Colour

Art Director
KEITH COURTNEY

Copywriter
PAUL DIVER

Photographer
TIM O'SULLIVAN

Agency
SIMONS PALMER
DENTON CLEMMOW &
JOHNSON LIMITED

Marketing Director
JOHNNY TRAINOR

Client
NIKE INC

THE
TASTIEST
FISH
AREN'T
ALWAYS
THE GOOD
LOOKING
ONES.

Just because some fish look a little odd, it doesn't mean they'll taste that way. So why not make a change from the usual?

BAKED POTATO WITH COLEY.
Poach a Coley fillet in lemon juice and sweetcorn for 6-8 minutes (8-10 if frozen). Flake the fish, then fill a baked potato with the mixture. Top with grated cheese and grill.

Beautiful.

Consumer Magazines
Colour

Art Director
JEREMY CARR

Copywriter
JEREMY CRAIGEN

Photographers
MIKE PARSONS
GUS FILGATE

Typographer
DAVID WAKEFIELD

Agency
BMP DDB NEEDHAM

Marketing Director
BOB KENNEDY

Client
SEAFISH AUTHORITY

Consumer Magazines
Colour

Art Director
GARY GOLDSMITH

Copywriter
TY MONTAGUE

Photographer
STEVE HELLERSTEIN

Agency
GOLDSMITH/JEFFREY

Director of Public Relations
RINI ADER

Client
EVERLAST USA

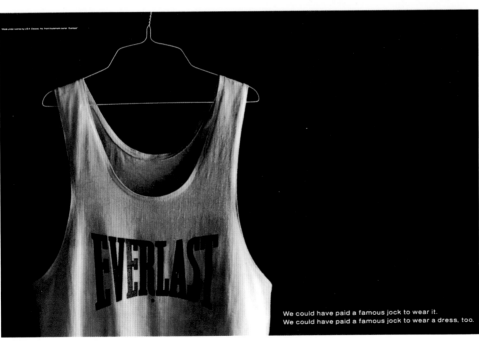

Consumer Magazines
Colour

Art Director
GARY GOLDSMITH

Copywriter
TY MONTAGUE

Photographer
STEVE HELLERSTEIN

Agency
GOLDSMITH/JEFFREY

Director of Public Relations
RINI ADER

Client
EVERLAST USA

Newspapers
Black and White

Art Director
BRIAN FRASER

Copywriter
SIMON LEARMAN

Agency
OGILVY & MATHER

Marketing Director
ROB McNEVIN

Client
GUINNESS BREWING

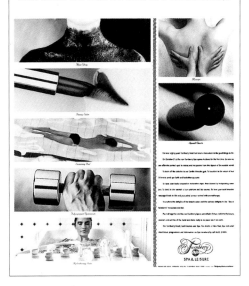

Newspapers
Black and White

Art Director
BRIAN WILLIAMS

Copywriter
WILL ATKINSON

Photographer
GRAHAM WYLIE

Typographer
KATRINA BURNS

Agency
THE BRIDGE/
ALLIANCE

Sales & Marketing Director
KEITH ALLISON

Client
TUNBERRY HOTEL
AYRSHIRE

Newspapers
Black and White

Art Director
ROB OLIVER

Copywriter
DAVID ABBOTT

Photographer
MARTIN ARGLES

Typographer
JOE HOZA

Agency
ABBOTT MEAD
VICKERS.BBDO
LIMITED

*Marketing & Advertising
Director*
ROBIN WHITBREAD

Client
J SAINSBURY PLC

Newspapers
Black and White

Art Director
CHRISTINE JONES

Copywriter
GILES MONTGOMERY

Photographer
JOHN CLARIDGE

Typographer
JEFF LEWIS

Agency
LEAGAS DELANEY

Marketing Manager
DAVID TYE

Client
NATIONWIDE
BUILDING SOCIETY

We believe there's a certain age when all children should become financially independent. Seven.

Nationwide
The Nation's Building Society

Newspapers
Black and White

Art Director
FRANK BUDGEN

Copywriter
FRANK BUDGEN

Typographer
DAVID WAKEFIELD

Agency
BMP DDB NEEDHAM

Marketing Director
MIKE CORNISH

Client
VAG UK LIMITED

Save money on a Vauxhall Nova.

Don't buy one.

Polo

THERE'S SOME PSYCHO WOMAN OUT THERE KILLING GUYS.

A SCENE FROM THE FILM · SEA OF LOVE

YOU'VE READ THE SCRIPT   NOW BUY THE VIDEO

Newspapers
Black and White

Art Director
ALAN FLEMING

Copywriter
PHIL DEARMAN

Agency
LOWE
HOWARD-SPINK

Marketing Manager
KARL OLIVER

Client
CIC VIDEO

AND FOR THE OPPOSITION, WE DO AN EXCELLENT RANGE OF RUNNING SHOES.

They won the Grand Slam. They have a combined weight of a ton and a half. They wear Nike. So a word of advice to anyone thinking of tackling them. Don't.

Newspapers
Black and White

Art Director
KEITH COURTNEY

Copywriter
PAUL DIVER

Photographer
TIM O'SULLIVAN

Typographer
PAUL BEER

Agency
SIMONS PALMER
DENTON CLEMMOW &
JOHNSON LIMITED

Marketing Director
JOHNNY TRAINOR

Client
NIKE INC

Newspapers
Black and White

Art Director
PAUL BRIGINSHAW

Copywriter
MALCOLM DUFFY

Photographer
DON McCULLIN

Typographer
JEFF MERRELLS

Agency
COLLETT DICKENSON
PEARCE & PARTNERS
LIMITED

General Manager
IAN DICKENS

Client
OLYMPUS

The Don McCullin exhibition. Featuring the work of Idi Amin, Pol Pot and Ho Chi Minh.

For over twenty years Don McCullin travelled to the battlefields of the world armed only with a camera.

In Cambodia his pictures bore witness to the work of the Khmer Rouge and their fanatical leader Pol Pot.

In Vietnam he was party to both the horrors of war and the dangers of war coverage. Forty-five journalists and photographers were killed and another eighteen are still missing.

In the Congo he found himself embroiled in a conflict made all the dirtier by the involvement of gun-toting mercenaries.

And he visited places whose names have become synonymous with suffering: Beirut, Biafra and Bangladesh.

But if war and oppression gave us his most powerful pictures then surely peacetime has given us his most appealing ones.

From his travels in the East are photographs of New Guinea tribes, a religious festival on the banks of the Ganges, and scenes from the Sumatra Islands.

From our shores there are dramatic landscapes.

And from his own home there is a series of still lifes.

For this major retrospective includes McCullin photographs that have never been shown before.

McCullin used Olympus cameras for many of these pictures, and Olympus in return are proud to be sponsoring this exhibition.

His work can be viewed at The Royal Photographic Society, Milsom Street, Bath from June 29th to September 1st.

Don McCullin has seen it all. Now so can you. **OLYMPUS**

Newspapers
Black and White

Art Director
GEOFF TURNER

Copywriter
MARK COOPER

Photographer
DAVID BAILEY

Typographer
JEFF MERRELLS

Agency
COLLETT DICKENSON
PEARCE & PARTNERS
LIMITED

General Manager
IAN DICKENS

Client
OLYMPUS

When Helen chose the Olympus she had one thing on her mind. Space.

Newspapers
Black and White

Art Director
PAUL BRIGINSHAW

Copywriter
MALCOLM DUFFY

Typographer
JEFF MERRELLS

Agency
COLLETT DICKENSON
PEARCE & PARTNERS
LIMITED

General Manager
IAN DICKENS

Client
OLYMPUS

Newspapers
Black and White

Art Director
BRIAN FRASER

Copywriter
SIMON LEARMAN

Agency
OGILVY & MATHER

Marketing Director
ROB MCNEVIN

Client
GUINNESS BREWING

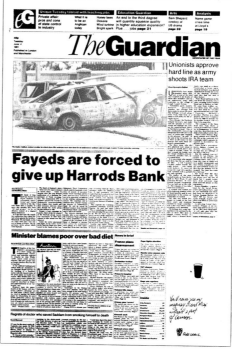

**Would you buy a used car from this man?
(Depends on the car.)**

Happily, with used cars not all guarantees are created equal.

Or to put it another way, a Volkswagen dealer offers a guarantee no other dealer can get close to.

A Volkswagen.

After all, you have to ask yourself what a used car was like when it was an unused car.

Was it given the best possible start in life? To ensure it keeps on starting first time, every time?

Did it have 3 thick coats of paint lavished on it? So gravel and grit get the brush-off?

Were 71⁄4lbs of rust-inhibiting wax pumped into every nook and cranny? Using a process so thorough it was patented?

Was it sealed every which-way with heavy-duty PVC? Signed by 3,199 inspectors? And then, and only then, delivered?

All this could explain why What Car? recently voted our Golf, Golf GTi and old style Passat top used cars in their class.

And why even our Jetta as a runner-up was considered virtually unimpeachable.

One more coat won't hurt it.

Before we paint a Volkswagen, we give it a first protective coat. A zinc phosphate solution.

Then we add a second protective coat. An electrostatic primer.

Then to more vulnerable areas, we add a third protective coat. A tough, plasticised solution.

Then we add a fourth protective coat. A thick uniform filler.

Then, and only then, do we apply a paint coat. Then another paint coat. Then another paint coat.

Then again, we don't just seal with any old PVC. We use only heavy duty.

We don't just bond with standard adhesive. We stick with one that's rust-inhibiting.

We don't just settle for extra bitumen under the front wheel arches. We fit plastic shields.

Of course, we could always skip the odd measure. Chivvy things along a bit.

We could pump through a nice, round 700% of niche-sealing wax instead of 714lb. And we could test our engines at 30° below instead of 40°.

We could. But we won't.

Once you start down that road, things have a habit of snowballing.

*Newspapers
Black and White*

Art Director
MIKE ORR

Copywriter
DAVID DENTON

Photographer
RUSSELL PORCAS

Typographer
MIKE ORR

Agency
BMP DDB NEEDHAM

Marketing Director
MIKE CORNISH

Client
VAG UK LIMITED

*Newspapers
Black and White*

Art Director
MIKE ORR

Copywriter
DAVID DENTON

Photographer
RUSSELL PORCAS

Typographer
KEVIN CLARKE

Agency
BMP DDB NEEDHAM

Marketing Director
MIKE CORNISH

Client
VAG UK LIMITED

Newspapers
Black and White

Art Director
ANTONY EASTON

Copywriter
ADAM KEAN

Photographer
ANDREW
MACPHERSON

Typographer
ROGER KENNEDY

Agency
SAATCHI & SAATCHI

Chairman & Chief Executive
Officer
MICHAEL HARVEY

Head of Marketing
NICK HUTTON

Client
THE HABITAT GROUP

Newspapers
Black and White

Art Director
GREG MARTIN

Copywriter
NICK BELL

Photographer
MIKE RUSSELL

Typographer
GARY TODD

Agency
ABBOTT MEAD
VICKERS.BBDO
LIMITED

Car Marketing Manager
OLIVER JOHNSON

Client
VOLVO
CONCESSIONAIRES

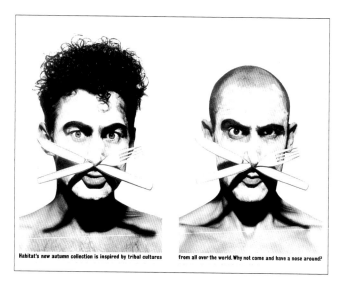

Habitat's new autumn collection is inspired by tribal cultures   from all over the world. Why not come and have a nose around?

DON'T SPOIL YOUR CHILDREN. SPEND £9,990 ON THEM.

£9,990 may seem a lot to spend on your children. But when you invest it in a Volvo 440, you get a lot in return.

As in all Volvos, you get a high strength, solid steel safety cage with impact-absorbing crumple zones at both front and rear.

You get a side-impact protection bar in all four doors.

You get child-proof, anti-burst locks. You get three rear seat belts. And should you require it, you even get a free child seat.

Of course there are plenty of other family cars you could look at. But if you want this much protection for your children, you're not exactly spoilt for choice. **VOLVO 440**

Read the Parker Knoll brochure in the discomfort of your own armchair.

Are you sitting uncomfortably?

Then we'll begin. The Parker Knoll brochure

has 40 full-colour pages of contemporary and

traditional suites, chairs

and sofa-beds. And it's

free.

To reserve your copy

(together with price list

and stockist list) send

the coupon now.

Please send me your colour brochure, stockist
list and price list. To Sue Black, Parker Knoll
Ltd., P.O. Box 22, Frogmoor, High Wycombe,
Bucks HP13 5DJ.

Name_____

Address_____

_____

_____

Parker Knoll

Postcode_____ A CORNWELL PARKER COMPANY

*Newspapers
Black and White*

Art Director
JOHN HORTON

Copywriter
RICHARD FOSTER

Typographer
JOE HOZA

Agency
ABBOTT MEAD
VICKERS.BBDO
LIMITED

Marketing Director
ANTHONY P D
MAYNARD

Client
PARKER KNOLL
LIMITED

*Newspapers
Black and White*

Art Director
JAMES SPINDLER

Copywriter
JAMES SPINDLER

Agency
KIRSHENBAUM &
BOND

Vice President Product Director
JOHN PELLATON

Client
SCHIEFFELIN &
SOMERSET

THE NEW YORK TIMES, FRIDAY, MARCH 1, 1991

PLEASE TEAR THIS PAGE
INTO MANY SMALL PIECES AND TOSS HIGH INTO THE AIR
IN CELEBRATION OF PEACE.

★

Champagne
MOËT & CHANDON

A fish pond in Lincolnshire as seen from a York to Kings Cross train.

Just what top managers need. Time for reflection.

Sometimes the best thing you can do in business is to find a private place, close the door, gaze out of the window. And think. (Oh, and get to important meetings at up to 125 mph.)

INTERCITY

Line of sheep as seen from a Cardiff to Paddington train.

They look rather like the traffic on the M4, don't they?

Who are the better businessmen? Those who race to meetings by train at 100 mph or those who sit nose to tail on the M4? (Clue: ever known a sheep to make it to chairman?)

INTERCITY

A Lake District farmhouse as seen from a Penrith to Euston train.

Well. They always said that senior management should take the wider view.

When looking at the broader perspective, considering the wider implications and taking the big decisions, don't you need more space?

INTERCITY

Newspapers
Black and White

Art Director
ALEXANDRA TAYLOR

Copywriter
JAMES LOWTHER

Photographer
MICHAEL KENNA

Typographer
ROGER KENNEDY

Agency
SAATCHI & SAATCHI

Marketing Director
ROBERT MASON

Client
INTERCITY

Newspapers
Black and White

Art Director
ANDY McKAY

Copywriter
TIM RILEY

Photographer
TIM O'SULLIVAN

Typographer
PAUL BEER

Agency
SIMONS PALMER
DENTON CLEMMOW &
JOHNSON LIMITED

Marketing Director
JOHNNY TRAINOR

Client
NIKE INC

Newspapers
Black and White

Art Director
STEVE DUNN

Copywriter
TIM DELANEY

Typographer
STEVE DUNN

Agency
LEAGAS DELANEY

Marketing Manager
STEPHEN PALMER

Client
THE GUARDIAN

Newspapers
Black and White

Art Director
CHRISTINE JONES

Copywriter
GILES MONTGOMERY

Photographer
JOHN CLARIDGE

Typographer
CHRISTINE JONES

Agency
LEAGAS DELANEY

European Marketing Director
VINCENT DESSAIN

Client
TIMBERLAND

AT 10,000 FEET IT'S ESSENTIAL TO WEAR BREATHING APPARATUS. ON YOUR FEET.

The Gore-Tex linings in Timberland boots contain billions of holes. They're small enough to stop water getting in, big enough to let perspiration out, allowing your feet to breathe in any conditions. As low as -40°F. And as high as 10,000 ft.

Newspapers
Black and White

Art Director
ANDY CHEETHAM

Copywriter
TONY VEAZEY

Typographer
ALAN ROGERS

Agency
BROADBENT
CHEETHAM VEAZEY

Marketing Executive
JULIE PICKERING

Client
LODGE GARAGE

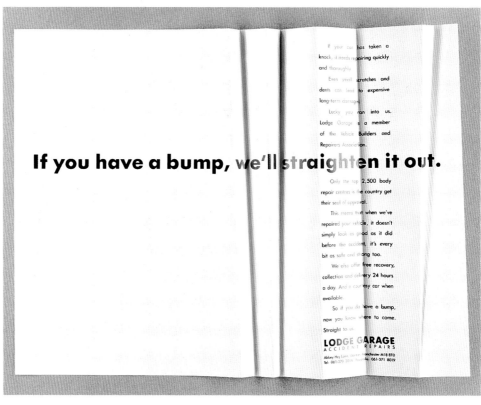

OUR SHOES ARE MADE BY THE MOST ADVANCED EQUIPMENT KNOWN TO MAN. MAN.

These days, it seems almost everything is built by a machine or a robot.

Televisions, hi-fi's, cars. There's hardly a single product that can't be made by some miracle of modern technology.

Except when it comes to making shoes. That's a job for which you need a piece of equipment that is far more advanced. One that has 206 moving parts. An optical system that sees in full colour 3D. And a central computer that thinks intelligently, makes decisions and learns as it works. And has even been known to make a decent cup of coffee.

Yes, we are pleased to say that most of the shoes, boots and clothes made here at Timberland are still hand-sewn by man.

Of course, we could install machinery to do the job in half the time. Probably a lot cheaper too. But could these machines match the craftsmanship of the old boys who toil away in our workshop up in Hampton, New Hampshire? Somehow we doubt it.

Take our boat shoe for example. Just like the best shipwrights, we have to build these shoes with the finest materials to make sure they withstand storms, gales and anything else the ocean wants to dish out.

This rules out using just any old leather. So we trek right across America to the few remaining tanneries who still know how to turn tough, full-grain hides into soft, durable shoe leathers.

After we've shipped the leathers all the way back to Hampton, the first thing we do is soak them in a vat of dye. That way, unlike those landlubbers who merely paint their shoes, ours will never lose their colour, even after

a lifetime at sea. And to keep them supple we also impregnate the leathers with silicone oils.

It's at this stage in the process, when most other manufacturers would be more than happy to let their machines start sewing. But not us.

To stop the leathers cracking we stretch them on geometric lasts, another job that can only be done correctly by man. After all, we have to watch for flaws as the leather stretches.

Then, with the good

name of Timberland in mind, our craftsmen take a single piece of leather and start to sew it deftly into a moccasin. The Red Indians came up with this design hundreds of years ago. We simply recognised its unparalleled comfort and promptly stole it for ourselves.

Mind you, we have had some ideas of our own. Such as using high strength nylon thread to make sure the stitching won't ever come adrift. Sealing the seams with latex, to produce a barrier against the water. And injection moulding our midsoles to the uppers, creating a permanent, watertight bond.

A Timberland boat shoe's outsole is also designed with more thought than some people

give to designing boats. The tread, for instance, features a system of 'scuppers', channels which run the length of the sole, connected to outlet gulleys along the edge.

Without this design, the shoe would hydroplane and, in effect, you'd end up walking on water. And as we hardly need to remind

you, only one person ever managed that.

Last of all, we add (by hand, naturally), rustproof brass eyelets, self-oiling rawhide laces that won't rot and padded collars that provide a snug, watertight fit.

The result? A shoe perfectly suited to life on the ocean wave. (A fact borne out during the last America's Cup, when many of the crews wore Timberlands.)

Needless to say though, the hands of our craftsmen are adept at making other items too. Like our walking shoes which have glove leather linings for comfort, and dual density polyurethane soles for lightness and durability. And our split suede coats which are double stitched and waterproofed.

Fact is, every Timberland is built to be around as long as our customers. Perhaps longer. A claim machine-made products find hard to live up to.

Of course, maybe one day technology will make our way of doing things obsolete. But we reckon it's got quite a lot of catching up to do. After all, our equipment took over four million years to develop.

Timberland ®

Newspapers
Black and White

Art Director
CHRISTINE JONES

Copywriter
GILES MONTGOMERY

Photographer
JOHN CLARIDGE

Typographer
JEFF LEWIS

Agency
LEAGAS DELANEY

European Marketing Director
VINCENT DESSAIN

Client
TIMBERLAND

FIRST WE TAN, DOUBLE STITCH AND WATERPROOF YOUR COAT. THEN YOU LINE OUR POCKETS.

Timberland jackets are made from the finest chrome tanned Weatherbuck leathers, a Gore-Tex waterproof layer and the strongest premium grade nylon thread. No expense is spared. But then, who cares? It's you who's paying.

Timberland ®

Newspapers
Black and White

Art Director
CHRISTINE JONES

Copywriter
GILES MONTGOMERY

Photographer
JOHN CLARIDGE

Typographer
CHRISTINE JONES

Agency
LEAGAS DELANEY

European Marketing Manager
VINCENT DESSAIN

Client
TIMBERLAND

Newspapers
Black and White

Art Director
GARY MARSHALL

Copywriter
PAUL MARSHALL

Typographer
JEFF LEWIS

Agency
LEAGAS DELANEY

Marketing Manager
STEPHEN PALMER

Client
THE GUARDIAN

G

uts, determination and months of hard training aren't always enough to win a gold medal. Yet many pundits believe this year's World Athletics Championships in Tokyo will be the first to be completely drug free. This week in the Guardian Matthew Engel and John Rodda will tell you if they're right and, of course, give you all the latest news views and race results. In fact, we're sure you'll find their coverage quite addictive.

*The***Guardian**

Does the Soviet Union's best chance of a gold medal still lie in the shot?

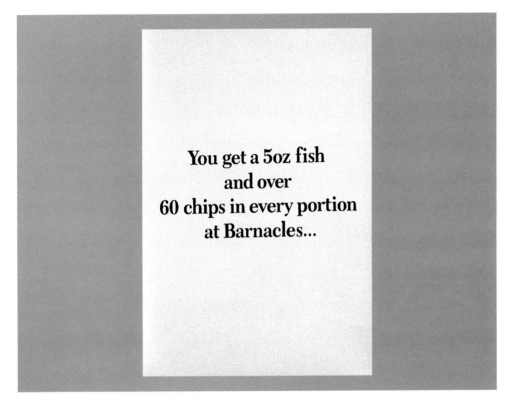

Newspapers
Black and White

Art Director
ANDY CHEETHAM

Copywriter
TONY VEAZEY

Typographer
STEVE JAMES

Agency
BROADBENT
CHEETHAM VEAZEY

Marketing Executive
BRENDA ROBERTS

Client
BARNACLES

Newspapers
Black and White

Art Director
CASEY GRADY

Copywriter
PATRICIA DOHERTY

Photographer
JAMES COTIER

Typographer
ROGER KENNEDY

Agency
SAATCHI & SAATCHI

Operations Director
TERRY SYLVESTER

Client
UNICLIFFE

Supercalafragilistic exit halitosis.

Mouthwashing with TCP spells the end for germs that cause bad breath.

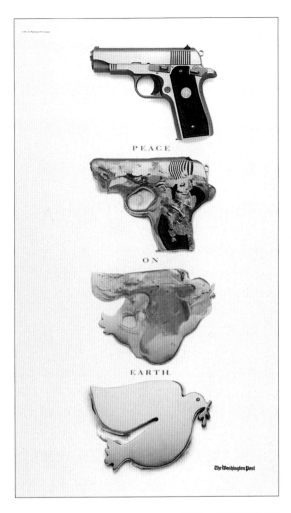

PEACE

ON

EARTH

The Washington Post

Newspapers
Black and White

Art Director
JOHN MORRISON

Copywriter
TOM McELLIGOTT

Photographer
BEN SALTZMAN

Typographer
JIM POOLE

Agency
McELLIGOTT WRIGHT
MORRISON WHITE

Circulation Marketing Director
CANDACE MEDD

Client
THE WASHINGTON
POST

So you've passed your A-levels. Poor you.

LOCAL EDUCATION AUTHORITY

Lloyds Bank

THE THOROUGHBRED BANK.

Newspapers
Black and White

Art Director
SIMON MORRIS

Copywriter
GEOFF SMITH

Photographer
STEVE CAVALIER

Typographer
SIMON WARDEN

Agency
LOWE HOWARD-SPINK

Marketing Communications
Chief Manager
MIKE BULPITT

Client
LLOYDS BANK PLC

*Newspapers
Black and White*

Art Director
ALAN FLEMING

Copywriter
PHIL DEARMAN

Agency
LOWE HOWARD-SPINK

Marketing Manager
KARL OLIVER

Client
CIC VIDEO

*Newspapers
Black and White*

Art Director
GARY MARSHALL

Copywriter
PAUL MARSHALL

Typographer
JEFF LEWIS

Agency
LEAGAS DELANEY

Marketing Manager
STEPHEN PALMER

Client
THE GUARDIAN

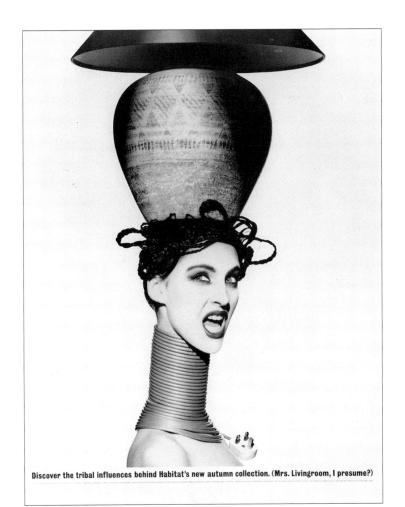

Discover the tribal influences behind Habitat's new autumn collection. (Mrs. Livingroom, I presume?)

*Newspapers
Black and White*

Art Director
ANTONY EASTON

Copywriter
ADAM KEAN

Photographer
ANDREW
MACPHERSON

Typographer
ROGER KENNEDY

Agency
SAATCHI & SAATCHI

*Chairman & Chief Executive
Officer*
MICHAEL HARVEY

Head of Marketing
NICK HUTTON

Client
THE HABITAT GROUP

*Newspapers
Black and White*

Art Director
ANTONY EASTON

Copywriter
ADAM KEAN

Photographer
ANDREW
MACPHERSON

Typographer
ROGER KENNEDY

Agency
SAATCHI & SAATCHI

*Chairman & Chief Executive
Officer*
MICHAEL HARVEY

Head of Marketing
NICK HUTTON

Client
THE HABITAT GROUP

We've travelled all over the world for ideas for Habitat's new tribal collection. Drop by if you haven't got too much on your plate.

Newspapers Colour

Art Director
MITCH LEVY

Copywriter
SEAN TOAL

Photographer
ROLPH GOBITS

Typographer
JEFF MERRELLS

Agency
COLLETT DICKENSON
PEARCE & PARTNERS
LIMITED

Marketing Director
IAN CHUBB

Client
WHYTE & McKAY

Newspapers Colour

Art Director
JONATHAN HALL

Copywriter
ROGER NOKES

Photographer
KELVIN MURRAY

Typographer
ROB WALLIS

Agency
McCANN-ERICKSON

Marketing Director
BILL YOUNG

Client
VAN DEN BERGHS

"Whatever the English think about us Scots they love our whisky.

Whatever we think about the English we love our whisky too."

RODDY GLEN

In 1986 "I Can't Believe It's Not Butter!" was introduced to millions of Americans. It was an instant success.

In fact "I Can't Believe It's Not Butter!" has become one of America's favourite vegetable fat spreads.

Now America is the land of free speech. If you want to say "I Can't Believe It's Not Butter!," you can come right out and say so.

On television. In front of millions of your fellow Americans.

But not in Britain. Over here, some people – including a certain food lobby – say if it isn't butter, you can't put butter in the name.

We could show you our commercial. But only if we change our name. Silly, isn't it? Because all we wanted to tell you is how good "I Can't Believe It's Not Butter!" actually tastes.

You see, we make it with buttermilk.

It has a fresh butter-like taste.

We can tell you it's a vegetable fat spread, high in polyunsaturates, low in saturates and containing virtually no cholesterol.

We can also inform you "I Can't Believe It's Not Butter!" is now available in Britain's shops and supermarkets.

And we know we can rely on you to spread the word.

There are feet that will never climb in the Andes. There are feet that will never photograph gorillas in the Congo. There are feet that will never catalog the native lichens of Northern Wales. Dunham. They get the job done.

Newspapers Colour

Art Director
JOHN DOYLE

Copywriter
ERNIE SCHENCK

Photographer
NADAV KANDER

Typographer
JOHN DOYLE

Agency
DOYLE ADVERTISING
& DESIGN GROUP

*Vice President Marketing &
Product*
MICHAEL COOGAN

Client
THE DUNHAM
COMPANY

Ripe Oregon strawberries are
especially selected as we

feel it

best complements the rich cream
flavour of Häagen-Dazs

Dedicated to Pleasure

Newspapers Colour

Art Director
ROONEY CARRUTHERS

Copywriter
LARRY BARKER

Photographer
JEAN LOUP SIEFF

Typographer
MATTHEW KEMSLEY

Agency
BARTLE BOGLE
HEGARTY

Marketing Director
SIMON ESBERGER

Client
HAAGEN DAZS UK
LIMITED

Thanks to Olympus, he's Mummy's blue-eyed boy again.

Rather than sweeten our fruit purees, we just use sweeter fruit.

BODDINGTONS. THE CREAM OF MANCHESTER.

Boddingtons Draught Bitter. Brewed at the Strangeways Brewery since 1778.

Newspapers Colour

Art Director
MIKE WELLS

Copywriter
TOM HUDSON

Photographer
TIF HUNTER

Typographer
NIGEL DAWSON

Agency
BARTLE BOGLE
HEGARTY

Marketing Director
STEVE PHILPOTT

Client
THE WHITBREAD
BEER COMPANY

PAGE 3-D DELIGHT

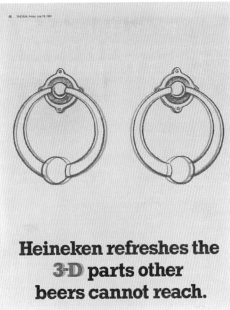

Heineken refreshes the
3-D parts other
beers cannot reach.

Newspapers Colour

Art Director
GRAHAM STOREY

Copywriter
PHIL COCKRELL

Illustrator
MICK BROWNFIELD

Typographer
JASVIR GARCHA

Agency
LOWE HOWARD-SPINK

Marketing Director
STEVE PHILPOTT

Client
THE WHITBREAD
BEER COMPANY

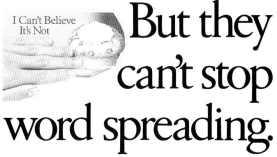

They'd love to stop us using a certain word. But they can't stop word spreading.

Far be it from us to name names. But some people (including a certain food lobby) want us to cut out 'butter' from our name altogether.

Could it be they're afraid of a little healthy competition? After all, "I Can't Believe It's Not Butter!" is high in polyunsaturates, low in saturates and contains virtually no cholesterol.

Or is it simply a question of taste?

You see, our vegetable fat spread is made with buttermilk. It has a fresh, butter-like taste that's proving rather popular.

So popular, indeed, word about it's been spreading like wildfire.

But why take our word for it? Take a pack home, spread it on and tuck in. If it doesn't live up to its name, we'll eat our words.

If you don't believe this flask is unbreakable, order it by post.

We find the fresh eggs
in Haagen-Dazs
provide delicate flavour.

body

and

texture

Häagen-Dazs

Dedicated to Pleasure

Newspapers Colour

Art Director
ROONEY CARRUTHERS

Copywriter
LARRY BARKER

Photographer
JEAN LOUP SIEFF

Typographer
MATTHEW KEMSLEY

Agency
BARTLE BOGLE
HEGARTY

Marketing Director
SIMON ESBERGER

Client
HAAGEN DAZS UK
LIMITED

Newspapers Colour

Art Director
RON BROWN

Copywriter
DAVID ABBOTT

Typographer
JOE HOZA

Agency
ABBOTT MEAD
VICKERS.BBDO
LIMITED

Managing Director
DAVID GORDON

Client
THE ECONOMIST

Do you suffer from sharp, stabbing pains in the back? We may be too late to help you.

The Economist

Newspapers Colour

Art Director
GERARD STAMP

Copywriter
LOZ SIMPSON

Illustrator
ROBIN
HEIGHWAY-BURY

Agency
BSB DORLAND

Marketing Director
LAWRENCE BALFE

Client
H J HEINZ COMPANY
LIMITED

Newspapers Colour

Art Director
GERARD STAMP

Copywriter
LOZ SIMPSON

Illustrator
ROBIN
HEIGHWAY-BURY

Agency
BSB DORLAND

Marketing Director
LAWRENCE BALFE

Client
H J HEINZ COMPANY
LIMITED

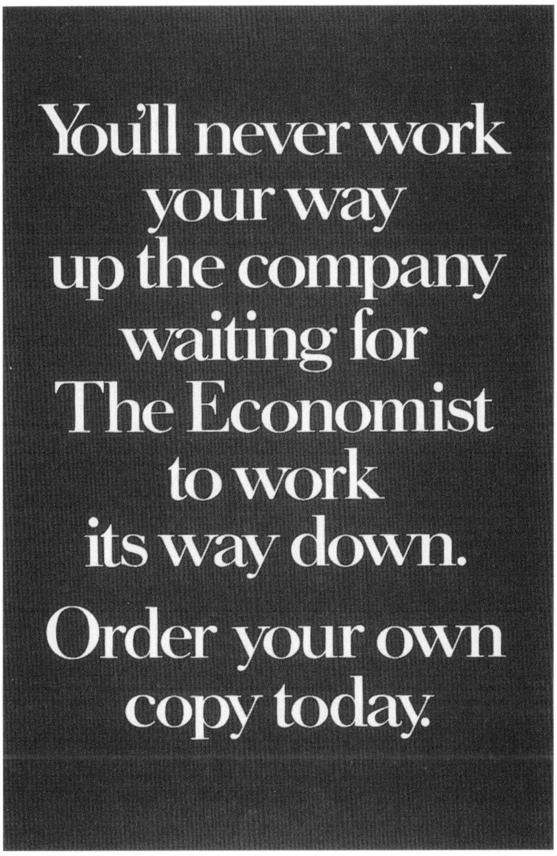

You'll never work your way up the company waiting for The Economist to work its way down. Order your own copy today.

Newspapers Colour

Art Director
RON BROWN

Copywriter
DAVID ABBOTT

Typographer
JOE HOZA

Agency
ABBOTT MEAD
VICKERS.BBDO
LIMITED

Managing Director
DAVID GORDON

Client
THE ECONOMIST

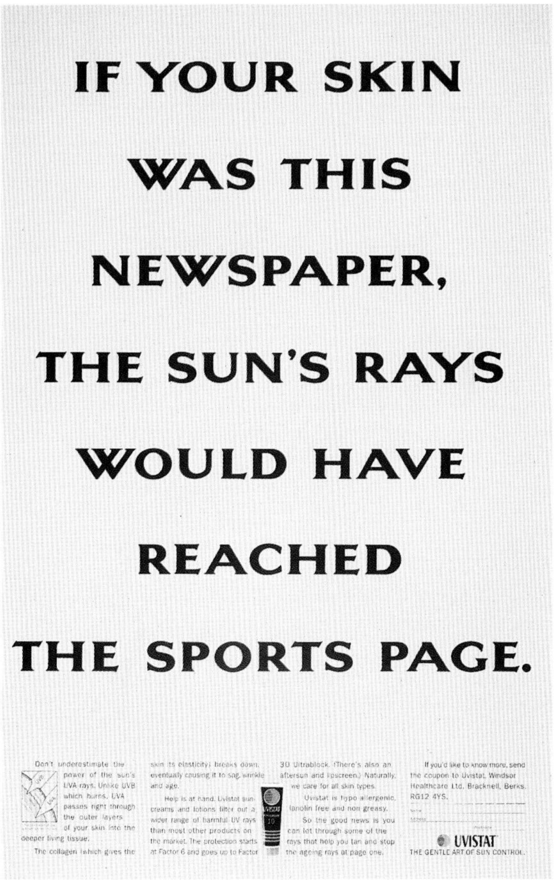

IF YOUR SKIN WAS THIS NEWSPAPER, THE SUN'S RAYS WOULD HAVE REACHED THE SPORTS PAGE.

Newspapers Colour

Art Director
PAUL SHEARER

Copywriter
ROB JACK

Typographer
MIKE RIX

Agency
BUTTERFIELD DAY
DEVITO HOCKNEY

Marketing Manager
ANDREW DIXON

Client
WINDSOR
HEALTHCARE

Newspapers Colour

Art Director
MIKE WELLS

Copywriter
TOM HUDSON

Photographer
TIF HUNTER

Typographer
NIGEL DAWSON

Agency
BARTLE BOGLE
HEGARTY

Marketing Director
STEVE PHILPOTT

Client
THE WHITBREAD
BEER COMPANY

Newspapers Colour

Art Director
JOHN DOYLE

Copywriter
ERNIE SCHENCK

Photographer
NADAV KANDER

Typographer
JOHN DOYLE

Agency
DOYLE ADVERTISING
& DESIGN GROUP

*Vice President Marketing &
Product*
MICHAEL COOGAN

Client
THE DUNHAM
COMPANY

We put people in front of cars.

At Volkswagen, we've always wanted our little heads about even little hands.
We were among the first motor car manufacturers to make all our models capable of running on unleaded fuel.
The first to produce a range of small cars, the Polo with a catalytic converter as standard.
The first to produce the world's cleanest production car, the Umwelt Diesel. And one of the first to replace toxic paints with water based paints.
That said, we can hardly expect you to buy a Volkswagen out of the goodness of your heart.
Nor, heaven forbid, should you buy one simply because we've been named Environmental Manufacturer of the Year.
We were, after all, among the first to introduce a reinforced safety cell with crumple zones front and rear.
The first to include rear seat belts as standard across the range.
And one of the first to make self-stabilising steering a standard feature.
When it comes to protecting your family, it seems, we rarely let anything get in our way.

Newspapers Colour

Art Director
MARK REDDY

Copywriter
TONY COX

Photographer
JAMES STEWART

Typographer
DAVID WAKEFIELD

Agency
BMP DDB NEEDHAM

Marketing Director
MIKE CORNISH

Client
VAG UK LIMITED

From the front, few small cars are as attractive as our new Polo.
From the back, though, we're tempted to say no small car is as attractive as our new Polo.
Because no other small cars come with a catalytic converter as standard.
An advanced 'three-way' catalyst at that.
One capable of reducing by more than 90% the trio of toxic pollutants in exhaust fumes.
It may not be perfect but it's 90% more perfect than no 'cat' at all.
That said, you may be wondering what sort of effect this has on the Polo's performance.
Wonder not. Thanks to the introduction of fuel injection, it's well up to speed.
The brakes are now servo. So stopping suddenly gives you even less of a start.
And not least, the uprated suspension makes for even nimbler handling and an even smoother ride.
All in all, you could say our new Polo leaves the competition behind.
But very little else.
The new catalytic Polo.

Newspapers Colour

Art Director
MIKE ORR

Copywriter
DAVID DENTON

Illustrator
MEL CALMAN

Typographer
DAVID WAKEFIELD

Agency
BMP DDB NEEDHAM

Marketing Director
MIKE CORNISH

Client
VAG UK LIMITED

Consumer Campaigns

Art Director
KATE STANNERS

Copywriter
TIM HEARN

Photographer
JOHN PARKER

Typographer
LEN CHEESEMAN

Agency
GGT

Marketing Director
ANNE FREEL

Client
MD FOODS UK
LIMITED

Consumer Campaigns

Art Director
DAVE JOHNSON

Copywriter
JONATHAN
KNEEBONE

Photographer
ROBERT
SHACKLETON

Typographer
RICHARD
BONNER-MORGAN

Agency
D'ARCY MASIUS
BENTON & BOWLES
LIMITED

Head of Personal Mail
YVETTE TURNER

Client
ROYAL MAIL

Photographer
LEWIS MULATERO

Consumer Campaigns

Art Director
ALEXANDRA TAYLOR

Copywriter
JAMES LOWTHER

Photographer
MICHAEL KENNA

Typographer
ROGER KENNEDY

Agency
SAATCHI & SAATCHI

Marketing Director
ROBERT MASON

Client
INTERCITY

A windmill in Warwickshire, as seen from a Southampton to Birmingham train.

Business is ninety per cent perspiration and ten per cent inspiration. (Here's our ten per cent). You can really get your head down and work on a train. But it could be when you lift it up that you'll really see the light.

INTERCITY

A river in Buckinghamshire, as seen from a Birmingham to Euston train.

With some peace and qui t, you'll ave less rouble concentrating on your ork. If you've a report to write, the extra comfort, privacy and tranquillity you get in First Class is not a luxury. It's a necessity.

INTERCITY

Line of sheep as seen from a Cardiff to Paddington train.

They look rather like the traffic on the M4, don't they? Who are the better businessmen? Those who race to meetings by train at 100mph or those who sit nose to tail on the M4? (Clue: ever known a sheep to make it to chairman?)

INTERCITY

Morning sun as seen from a Liverpool to Euston train.

It's the early bird that catches the full British breakfast. You can now catch a morning Pullman with full steward service to virtually every main business centre in the country. So, who's for a real power breakfast?

INTERCITY

A fish pond in Lincolnshire as seen from a York to Kings Cross train.

Just what top managers need. Time for reflection.

Sometimes the best thing you can do in business is to find a private place, close the door, gaze out of the window. And think. (Oh, and get to important meetings at up to 125 mph.)

INTERCITY

A Cumbrian field as seen from a Carlisle to Euston train.

Health farm for stressed businessmen. (First Class accommodation available daily.)

Let our wide seats and wide views slow the pulse, quicken the brain, exercise the grey matter, tone up the strategies and fight the flabby thinking.

INTERCITY

A view as seen from a Pullman carriage of an Edinburgh to Kings Cross Train.

Announcing the most luxurious way to get to London. (Offer only lasts 3 hours, 59 minutes).

Hot towels, breakfast on white china, attentive stewards. Enjoy every single minute of your Pullman journey; there are so few of them.

INTERCITY

A Lake District farmhouse as seen from a Penrith to Euston train.

Well. They always said that senior management should take the wider view.

When looking at the broader perspective, considering the wider implications and taking the big decisions, don't you need more space?

INTERCITY

Consumer Campaigns

Art Director
BRIAN STEWART

Copywriter
GREG DELANEY

Photographer
PAMELA HANSON

Typographers
BRIAN STEWART
CHRIS DEVONALD

Agency
DELANEY FLETCHER
SLAYMAKER &
BOZELL

Marketing Director
ROGER ADAMS

Client
TRIUMPH
INTERNATIONAL

Makes me feel good. Hugs me. Flatters me. (Shame it's only a bra.)

Triumph
The bra for the way you are.

The bra designed for the woman's movement.

Triumph
The bra for the way you are.

There are times when you can allow the man in your life to choose your bra.

Triumph
The bra for the way you are.

Support. Confidence. Freedom. (Why can't a man give you all that a bra does?)

Triumph
The bra for the way you are.

Mostly I never think about my bra. (I said mostly.)

Triumph
The bra for the way you are.

Consumer Campaigns

Art Directors
JOHN BAYLEY
NICK PARTON

Copywriters
JOHN BAYLEY
NICK PARTON

Photographer
PETER RAUTER

Typographer
STEVE RONCHETTI

Agency
OGILVY & MATHER

Company Advertising Manager
JEREMY STUBBS

Client
LEVER BROTHERS

DON'T ROUGH IT. LIVE LIFE IN COMFORT.

DON'T ROUGH IT. LIVE LIFE IN COMFORT.

DON'T ROUGH IT. LIVE LIFE IN COMFORT.

DON'T ROUGH IT. LIVE LIFE IN COMFORT.

Consumer Campaigns

Art Director
PAUL BRIGINSHAW

Copywriter
MALCOLM DUFFY

Photographer
DON McCULLIN

Typographer
KAREN SPINKS

Agency
COLLETT DICKENSON
PEARCE & PARTNERS
LIMITED

General Manager
IAN DICKENS

Client
OLYMPUS

The Don McCullin exhibition.
Featuring the work of Idi Amin,
Pol Pot and Ho Chi Minh.

For over twenty years Don McCullin travelled to the battlefields of the world armed only with a camera.

In Cambodia his pictures bore witness to the work of the Khmer Rouge and their fanatical leader Pol Pot.

In Vietnam he was party to both the horrors of war and the dangers of war coverage. Forty-five journalists and photographers were killed and another eighteen are still missing.

In the Congo he found himself embroiled in a conflict made all the dirtier by the involvement of gun-toting mercenaries.

And he visited places whose names have become synonymous with suffering: Beirut, Biafra and Bangladesh.

But if war and oppression gave us his most powerful pictures then surely peacetime has given us his most appealing ones.

From his travels in the East are photographs of New Guinea tribes, a religious festival on the banks of the Ganges, and scenes from the Sumatra Islands.

From our shores there are dramatic landscapes.

And from his own home there is a series of still lifes.

For this major retrospective includes McCullin photographs that have never been shown before.

McCullin used Olympus cameras for many of these pictures, and Olympus in return are proud to be sponsoring this exhibition.

His work can be viewed at The Royal Photographic Society, Milsom Street, Bath from June 29th to September 1st.

Don McCullin has seen it all. Now so can you. **OLYMPUS**

Jeffrey Bernard is unwell.

Jeffrey Bernard is fine.

I used to like my photograph being taken. As a baby I couldn't stop smiling and was a willing target for the Box Brownie.

Now that I am a miserable old man who has lost his looks and has discovered that it takes 420 muscles to make you smile, I have gone off it. I don't like saying cheese and the alternative a showgirl once told me is to have a fixed smile all day long. While she kicked her heels up she kept saying money, pronounced moneee.

But recently I discovered Olympus Cameras and looking through the lens of one of them, I found my friends not to be so ugly as I thought them to be. They suddenly became quite beautiful. I nearly did too.

Known for years as the most hoodshot man on earth, Olympus has cleared my eyes, face and reputation. A miracle of modern science. Physics and optics were never my strong suit but all I know is that when the flash fires, slow red-eye has all but vanished. Clever people these Olympus egg heads.

I may be in the title of the play but it "unwell" but I can at last face the birdie. The only trouble is that in my case the birdie is a vulture.

Jeffrey Bernard

OLYMPUS CAMERAS

Art Director
DENNIS WILLISON
Copywriter
GERARD EDMONDSON
Photographer
BRUCE FLEMING

Photographer
CLIVE ARROWSMITH

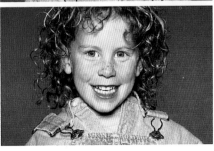

Thanks to Olympus, he's Mummy's blue-eyed boy again.

You remove the worms from his grubby little grasp and the semolina from his hair.

You pop him into a fresh pair of dungarees, distract him with talk of diggers and dinosaurs and check his nose.

Then you get him to sit still for a record breaking fifteen seconds, zoom in at the touch of a button and capture those precious album photos.

You do all this for him and what happens?

The dreaded red-eye.

Your little cherub takes on the appearance of a mad hell hound.

You mustn't blame yourself though, it's not something he picked up at nursery.

It's the flash on your camera. In low light the pupils dilate and when the flash fires, light bounces off the retina causing red-eye.

Happily this nightmarish condition can be eased by using a camera from the Olympus Superzoom range.

There are four Superzoom cameras in all, each one with a list of features as long as a restless night.

If you're shooting in low light, just switch the camera to Auto S mode and zoom in.

The flash will emit a series of soft pulsing pre-flashes causing the pupils to contract.

When the flash fires, the red-eye all but disappears.

Devilishly simple, you might say. But not infernally expensive.

The AZ 210 costs as little as £179.99 and the top of the range AZ 330 no more than £229.99.

If you'd like more information on the Superzoom range, contact your nearest local dealer or fill in the coupon below.

Between us, we can make sure your little ones turn out well.

Olympus Superzoom Direct - Olympus Optical Co (UK) Ltd, 2-8 Honduras St, London EC1Y 0TX. Tel. 071-405 2172.

Name_____

Address_____

_____Postcode____

OLYMPUS SUPERZOOM

Consumer Campaigns

Art Director
MARTIN GALTON

Copywriter
WILL AWDRY

Typographers
MATTHEW KEMSLEY
NIGEL DAWSON

Agency
BARTLE BOGLE
HEGARTY

Marketing Director
JILL PRESTON

Client
CHIVAS &
GLENLIVET GROUP

Consumer Campaigns

Art Director
MITCH LEVY

Copywriter
SEAN TOAL

Photographer
ROLPH GOBITS

Typographer
JEFF MERRELLS

Agency
COLLETT DICKENSON
PEARCE & PARTNERS
LIMITED

Marketing Director
IAN CHUBB

Client
WHYTE & McKAY

"My wife's English. But I blame her parents."

ALASTAIR McILWRAITH

"I support two teams. Scotland, and whoever's playing England."

DONALD CAMERON

"Whatever the English think about us Scots they love our whisky.

Whatever we think about the English we love our whisky too."

RODDY GLEN

Consumer Campaigns

Art Director
WARREN BROWN

Copywriter
JOHN McCABE

Photographer
ELLIOT ERWITT

Typographer
WARREN BROWN

Agency
BARTLE BOGLE
HEGARTY

Marketing Director
ANDREW KNIBBS

Client
LEVI STRAUSS UK
LIMITED

Photographer
GEORGIA BRAUER

Consumer Campaigns

Art Director
ANTON EZER

Copywriter
SIMON
DARWELL-TAYLOR

Photographer
CHRIS CHEETHAM

Typographer
BILL NAYLOR

Agency
BURKITT WEINREICH
BRYANT CLIENTS &
COMPANY

General Manager
DAVID ACHESON

Client
R M WILLIAMS PTY
LIMITED

CLOTHES for
the LAND

Authentic Australian working clothes. Ford. Gammon Ranges, 10am, Wed, March 23rd 1932. 179-181 Regent St, London W1. 15 Kensington Church St, London W8. Tel: 071-434 0961.

Authentic Australian working clothes. Bold. Gammon Ranges, 10am, Wed, March 22nd 1932. 179-181 Regent St, London W1. 15 Kensington Church St, London W8. Tel: 071-434 0961.

Consumer Campaigns

Art Director
ANTONY EASTON

Copywriter
ADAM KEAN

Photographer
ANDREW
MACPHERSON

Typographer
ROGER KENNEDY

Agency
SAATCHI & SAATCHI

*Chairman & Chief Executive
Officer*
MICHAEL HARVEY

Head of Marketing
NICK HUTTON

Client
THE HABITAT GROUP

The end of line sale at Habitat, Cardiff. Up to 50% off to make way for new lines.

Art Director
ANTONY EASTON

Copywriter
ADAM KEAN

Illustrator
PROFESSOR LO

Revolutionary china at Habitat this week. From a mug to a dinner service. Put a reminder in your little red book.

COUP D'HABITAT

1960's   1990's

Come and witness the revolution at Habitat. We're open to the people this Bank Holiday weekend.

Art Director
PAUL ARDEN

Copywriters
JAMES LOWTHER
ADAM KEAN

Photographer
ANDREW
MACPHERSON

HAVE A REVOLTING BANK HOLIDAY

Shoppers of the world unite. Join the revolution at Habitat this Bank Holiday. A Das Kapital idea.

Art Director
PAUL ARDEN

Copywriters
JAMES LOWTHER
ADAM KEAN

Photographer
ANDREW
MACPHERSON

HABITAT IS REVOLTING

This weekend, come along and see how Habitat has changed. You have nothing to lose but your preconceptions.

Art Director
ANTONY EASTON

Copywriter
ADAM KEAN

Photographer
ANDREW
MACPHERSON

Consumer Campaigns

Art Director
ROB OLIVER

Copywriter
PETER RUSSELL

Photographer
GRAHAM
CORNTHWAITE

Typographers
JOE HOZA
GARY TODD

Agency
ABBOTT MEAD
VICKERS.BBDO
LIMITED

Retail Marketing Director
EMMA DINWOODIE

Client
WATERSTONE &
COMPANY

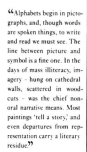

"Alphabets begin in pictographs, and, though words are spoken things, to write and read we must see. The line between picture and symbol is a fine one. In the days of mass illiteracy, imagery – hung on cathedral walls, scattered in woodcuts – was the chief non-oral narrative means. Most paintings 'tell a story,' and even departures from representation carry a literary residue."

From a volume of art appreciation called JUST LOOKING. *From a centre of literary appreciation called* WATERSTONE'S

"It was on a morning of May that Peter Featherstone was buried. In the prosaic neighbourhood of Middlemarch, May was not always warm and sunny, and on this particular morning a chill wind was blowing the blossoms from the surrounding gardens on to the green mounds of Lowick churchyard. Swiftly-moving clouds only now and then allowed a gleam to light up any object, whether ugly or beautiful, that happened to stand within its golden shower."

From the classic novel MIDDLEMARCH. *From the classic bookshop* WATERSTONE'S.

"I wonder if you could settle a few things for me. 'Of course, Bey.' 'I've been a bit extravagant at the tailor. Three or four suits. Four pairs of shoes at Lobb's. And there's the poor old Bentley.' She had to have a new radiator.' 'I'll see what I can do,' I said. I went to the tailor and asked for the Bey's bill. I went to Lobb. I discovered from Jack Barclay the cost of the radiator. The Bey's prices were never excessive; but, in the best Oriental tradition, we always had a haggle at the end. Otherwise, the deal would not be a deal."

From a stimulating collection called WHAT AM I DOING HERE. *From a stimulating bookshop called* WATERSTONE'S.

"This is the city in which the young Dickens worked and lived. There were no restaurants then, but taverns and chop-houses. There were eating houses with fourpenny plates and sixpenny plates, penny bread and penny potatoes. There were no railways and urban sanitation did not exist. Water was expensive to buy, as were clothes and newspapers; there were no 'holidays' for working people but the city had not yet become a prey to that wild and violent energy which now seems so characteristic of the Victorian period."

From a revealing biography of DICKENS *by Peter Ackroyd. From a revealing bookshop called* WATERSTONE'S.

"My favourite customers, welcome!' Madame Koto said, in a voice of such extreme unctuousness that I turned to her, surprised. Her face glistened. She rubbed her palms together. The two men sat. The people outside came in, bringing their thick perfume smells, their crackling lace, their clinking bangles and trinkets and strange jewellery, and the smell of new money. 'More light!' cried one of the men. 'And plenty of your best palm-wine!' said another."

From the Booker judges' choice THE FAMISHED ROAD. *From the book lovers' choice* WATERSTONE'S.

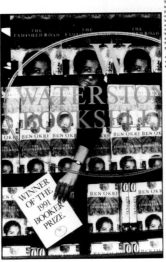

" 'Quick,' said a man, coming to his rescue, 'there's an empty seat up the front.' Before Paddington knew what was happening he found himself being bundled on to the bus while several other willing hands in the crowd took charge of the cardboard box for him and placed it in the gangway behind the driver's compartment. He barely had time to raise his hat in order to thank everyone for their trouble before there was a sudden jerk and the bus set off again on its journey.**"**

From a delightful book called PADDINGTON GOES TO TOWN. *From a delightful bookshop called* WATERSTONE'S.

"Within two or three minutes we have spent £3.00 and have not set bought our parmesan or gruyère for grating on to the delicate little ravioli we have bought from the goat cheese lady. They are tiny, these ravioli, filled with a mixture of parsley and comté, the gruyère-like cheese of Franche Comté. They take *one* minute to cook, warns the lady."

From an entertaining book called AN OMELETTE AND A GLASS OF WINE *From an entertaining bookshop called* WATERSTONE'S

"When Belinda returned we climbed the stands to watch the race and to everyone's blank surprise number eight came in first. The strained crowd received the no-hopers victory in silence, and Belinda stopped Ken's wide grin in its tracks by announcing a shade defiantly that she hadn't put his fiver on eight but on the favourite instead. 'People have been divorced for less,' Ken said, just about managing civility."

From a thrilling novel called COMEBACK *From a thrilling bookshop called* WATERSTONE'S

"With cities, it is as with dreams: everything imaginable can be dreamed, but even the most unexpected dream is a rebus that conceals a desire or, its reverse, a fear. Cities, like dreams, are made of desires and fears, even if the thread of their discourse is secret, their rules are absurd, their perspectives deceitful, and everything conceals something else."

From an extraordinary book by Italo Calvino called INVISIBLE CITIES *From an extraordinary bookshop called* WATERSTONE'S

"They sit without speaking, looking straight ahead.
They've said it all before,
they've seen it all before.
They're content.

They sit without moving:
Ozymandias and Sphinx.

He says something? –
and she answers, smiling,
and taps him flirtatiously
on the arm:
Daphnis and Chloe:
with Edinburgh accents."

From a wonderful new edition of NORMAN MACCAIG COLLECTED POEMS *From a wonderful bookshop called* WATERSTONE'S

Consumer Campaigns

Art Director
JOHN DOYLE

Copywriter
ERNIE SCHENCK

Photographer
NADAV KANDER

Typographer
JOHN DOYLE

Agency
DOYLE ADVERTISING
& DESIGN GROUP

*Vice President Marketing &
Product*
MICHAEL COOGAN

Client
THE DUNHAM
COMPANY

There are feet that have never seen a David Hockney. There are feet that have never walked the streets of Cannes. There are feet accustomed with foliage at midnight. Dunham. They get the job done.

There are feet that have never gotten the corner office. There are feet that have never sat through a shareholder's meeting. There are feet that have never had under the bench. There are feet that have never won the trade at an Italian loafer. Dunham. They get the job done.

Consumer Campaigns

Art Director
JOHN HORTON

Copywriter
RICHARD FOSTER

Photographer
GRAHAM FORD

Typographer
JOE HOZA

Agency
ABBOTT MEAD
VICKERS.BBDO
LIMITED

Car Marketing Manager
OLIVER JOHNSON

Client
VOLVO
CONCESSIONAIRES

THE FERRARI F40 VERSUS THE VOLVO 480 TURBO. (NO, HONESTLY.)

WHO SAYS POWER CORRUPTS?

Art Director
MARK ROALFE

Copywriter
ROBERT CAMPBELL

Photographer
JERRY OKE

HOW TO IMPROVE A GOLF'S TURNING CIRCLE.

INSTEAD OF A COAT OF PAINT, WE GIVE IT A SUIT OF ARMOUR.

If any car can claim to be weatherproof, the Volvo 460 is that car.

It shrugs off rain, hail, sleet or snow.

(To be honest, its clean the line at 6-inch nails – our picture is intended only as a symbol of the car's durability.)

The 460's resistance to the elements is largely due to an element used in its construction.

Zinc. As any metallurgist will tell you, zinc is the last word in rustproofing. That's why over 60% of the 460's body weight is made of zinc-coated steel.

Even then, we spray the entire body shell (including the zinc coated parts) with a further layer of zinc phosphate.

We then immerse it in a bath of primer.

We spray exposed parts of the underbody with p.v.c. to protect them from stone chips.

We inject the inner cavities with a special wax-based fluid.

We close off and seal all welded seams, inside and out.

And then we paint it. And then we paint it again. And then, for metallic finishes, we paint it again.

By the time we've finished with it, the Volvo 460 is cocooned in a multi-layered shell of anti-corrosive material.

It's a car that comes in its own garage.

THE VOLVO 460.

THE NEW 2 LITRE TURBO VOLVO 940 ESTATE. NOT BAD FOR YOUR FIRST CAR.

To be honest, cars used to bore me to tears. Then we got a Volvo. A Volvo 2 litre Turbo 940 Estate to be precise.

155 bhp, according to dad. And below the £19,250 and the 2 litre tax limits. Whatever they are.

Of course, being a Volvo, it's as safe as houses. It's got steel bars reinforcing every door. Crumple zones. And Volvo's legendary rigid steel safety cage.

Being an estate car, it's also got more than enough room for my travel cot, my pushchair and a generous supply of nappies.

And bags of space for all the paraphernalia that mums and dads like to cart about with them.

When the time comes for me to get behind the wheel myself, they say it should still be on the road.

So you never know. My first car might well turn out to be my first car.

VOLVO

Art Director
ROB OLIVER

Copywriter
PETER RUSSELL

Photographer
MARTIN THOMPSON

Consumer Campaigns

Art Director
GERARD STAMP

Copywriter
LOZ SIMPSON

Illustrator
ROBIN
HEIGHWAY-BURY

Agency
BSB DORLAND

Marketing Director
LAWRENCE BALFE

Client
H J HEINZ COMPANY
LIMITED

Consumer Campaigns

Art Director
ALAN FLEMING

Copywriter
PHIL DEARMAN

Agency
LOWE HOWARD-SPINK

Marketing Manager
KARL OLIVER

Client
CIC VIDEO

I'M GOING TO GREECE FOR THE SEX. SEX FOR BREAKFAST. SEX FOR DINNER. AND SEX FOR TEA.

A SCENE FROM THE FILM SHIRLEY VALENTINE

YOU'VE READ THE SCRIPT NOW BUY THE VIDEO.

YOU MADE THE RAIN BLACK. AND YOU SHOVED YOUR VALUES DOWN OUR THROATS.

A SCENE FROM THE FILM BLACK RAIN

YOU'VE READ THE SCRIPT   NOW BUY THE VIDEO.

THERE'S SOME PSYCHO WOMAN OUT THERE KILLING GUYS.

A SCENE FROM THE FILM · SEA OF LOVE

YOU'VE READ THE SCRIPT.   NOW BUY THE VIDEO

AFTER I BLOW A HOLE IN SOMEBODY AND SLIP AROUND ON THEIR GUTS, I LIKE TO MAKE BALLOON ANIMALS.

A SCENE FROM THE FILM PARENTHOOD.

YOU'VE READ THE SCRIPT.   NOW BUY THE VIDEO.

Mixed Media
Campaigns

Director
JOHN LLOYD

Copywriters
TIM HEARN
MARK COLLIS

Art Directors
KATE STANNERS
JOHN CLIFFORD

Creative Director
TIM MELLORS

Producer
CAROLINE WARNER

Agency Producer
DIANE CROLL

Editors
RICHARD LEAROYD
STEVE GANDOLFI

Lighting Cameraman
JOHN STANIER

Production Company
LIMELIGHT
COMMERCIALS

Agency
GGT

Marketing Director
CAROL FISHER

Client
HOLSTEN
DISTRIBUTORS
LIMITED

TRAFFIC LIGHTS

Video:
Open on close-up of traffic lights.

Jeff is sitting in his pick-up truck at the lights, elbow on the window, tapping his fingers impatiently. He keeps looking to see if the traffic lights have changed.

Identical men are mowing the lawn. All the lawns of the houses are beautifully kept, and each house has an identical white picket fence and an identical estate car in each drive.

Every time Jeff starts to move, he is held up by another set of red traffic lights.

He looks to camera.

Jeff:
You know, I could have sworn I saw 2.2 kids back there.

But I haven't seen a Holsten Pils anywhere.

The sooner I get out of here the better.

Video:
He holds a remote control, points it and all the sets of lights change to green.

Cut to the woman. She is stringing a banner across the street. On the banner is written:
STOPS IN HELL.

HOST

Video:

Open on an idyllic lake surrounded by woodland.

We see Jeff walking past a tree.

Jeff:

It's strange you know. Last night I had an out of body experience.

I felt my spirit leave my body and go down to the off-license.

Sometime later it returned.

Video:

He comes into a clearing where camp has been set up. He picks up a bottle of Holsten Pils and opens it. He then takes a glass from a bucket of ice.

Jeff:

I knew it had. I felt a sudden chill and a voice said 'I'm back would you hand me that bottle opener?'

I felt somehow...purified.

Video:

An enigmatic woman watches from a floating platform.

Jeff sips from the glass.

Cut back to the enigmatic woman. Cut to a close-up of ouji board type arrangement of letters. Woman puts last card down to spell: HOST IN SPELL.

Cut to Jeff sipping Pils.

DENTIST

Video:
Open on foot dangling.

Cut to Jeff in black tuxedo walking along a long stretch of sand. He is drinking from a glass of Pils.

Jeff:
I've been out with an old flame, Ulrika, my little German dentist.

Video:
He looks dreamily ahead, obviously nostalgic.

Jeff:
It was five years ago she fixed my crown. I took her out for a drink the same night...

Video:
He sighs reminiscently, slightly sad.

Jeff:
Gee, seeing her again brought back all those old feelings...

Video:
He raises the glass to drink. He slooshes the Pils then spits it out. He realises what he's done and looks shocked.

Jeff:
My gosh!

Video:
He takes another sip.

Jeff:
Mmmm Mmmm.

Video:
Quick cuts to a lifeguard's chair. On it is the woman dressed as a lifeguard. She looks towards us and on the front of her bathing hat is written:
SPLOSH INLET.

CHARITY

Video:
Open on Jeff standing at the door as if seeing the last guests out of his house.

Jeff:
Goodbye. And don't worry about it...I'm just sorry you couldn't stay longer...Auf wiedersehen!

Video:
He closes the door and leans against it. He speaks to the camera.

The entire room is full of flowers. There are vases of them and bunches of them on every available surface.

Jeff:
I like to help the afflicted. Every year right around this time, I like to throw a party in aid of charity.

Video:
He walks to table in the middle of the room which has dozens of unopened bottles of Holsten Pils on it.

Jeff:
This year it was a bring a bottle fundraiser for some delightful folks from Hamburg representing the Association of Hayfever Sufferers...

Video:
Jeff picks up a bottle of Pils from the table and eyes the rest appreciatively.

We see Jeff starting to stack up the bottles in a fridge. the cupboard is divided into sections, each marked with the name of a different month: January, February, etc.

He surveys the flowers with wicked satisfaction and opens the Pils.

Cut to him eyeing the bottles smugly. He pours and sips from his.

We see looking up at the woman.

Cut to the woman placing the final flower into a wall of flowers.

Cut to full view of the wall of flowers. They are arranged to spell the words:
SH...IT'S POLLEN.

Cut back to Jeff sniffing a flower with a wicked grin. He sniggers.

Concept Creator
TIM MELLORS

Copywriters
ROBERT SAVILLE
JULIAN DYER

Agency Producer
JASMINE KIMERA

Directors
ROBERT SAVILLE
JULIAN DYER

Recording Engineer
NICK ANGELL

Agency
GGT

Recording Studio
ANGELL SOUND

Marketing Director
CAROL FISHER

Client
HOLSTEN
DISTRIBUTORS
LIMITED

TITLE: PETS

MVO: (Intense voice)
My goldfish is high in the Malverns
My poodle is sitting there too
My hamster's away in the Chilterns
And the Mendips have claimed my Gnu.

My rabbit's hopped off to the Cotswolds
The Brecon Beacons are home to my cat
But I'm drinking lager in Ludlow
From the bottle with a green foil cap
(and yellow label)

FVO: That was *PETS ON HILL*.There's no
mistaking it. If you have any poems
about domestic animals, we suggest you
burn them.

TITLE: STARE

SFX: Library music.
FVO: Amanda and Leonard embraced passionately
in the glow of the roaring fire. How
they had yearned for this moment.

Amanda leaned out and grasped Leonard's
cool bottle of German lager with a green
foil top and yellow label. Leonard's
hand clasped Amanda's. They sighed, they
gazed, they sighed. It was all too much,
Leonard dropped his robe and stood there
in the full glory of Amanda's red silk
underwear.

But she didn't care, because Amanda
loved *LENS HOT SLIP*.

There was no mistaking it.

```
TITLE:      LATERAL THINKER

MVO:        And now here's today's lateral thinking
            puzzle...

FVO:        A girl called Holl orders a drink from
            a barman Enso.

            PSST ONE HILL she says. Ens hands her
            a green foil topped bottle with a yellow
            label. HOLL TIPS ENS.

            Pouring the pure liquid, Holl stands by
            the window with Steph.

            NO SILL STEPH Holl tells her, savouring
            the original German flavour.

            So why is there no mistaking PHIL'S
            STONE L?

MVO:        Answers on a beer mat please.
```

```
TITLE:      MEDICINE

MVO:        Old fashioned BBC radio voice:
            (and musical accompaniment)

            Problems with ingrowing toe-nails,
            verrucas, corns, bunions or dropped
            arches?

            Put your feet up and take a bottle of
            NHS TOE PILLS.

            Yes, with its yellow label there's no
            mistaking, NHS TOE PILLS.

            Brewed in Hamburg and not available on
            prescription.

            NHS TOE PILLS.
            Absolutely no good for your feet at all.
            Cheery bye.
```

```
TITLE:      LILLIAN

SFX:        Supermarket atmos.

FVO 1:      Shall we get some lagers Lillian?

FVO 2:      Yes Lillian. Shall we split a case with
            Lillian?

FVO 3:      Good idea Lillian. What d'you reckon,
            Lillian?

FVO 4:      My favourite's this yellow can with the
            shiny green top Lillian.

FVO 5:      Apparently it's imported from Hamburg
            Lillian.

FVO 6:      You don't say Lillian?

FVO 7:      It's brewed purely from hops, yeast,
            malt and water Lillian.

FVO 8:      And all the sugar turns to you know
            what Lillian.
```

```
FVO 9:      That's right Lillian. Now where's
            Lillian got to with that shopping
trolley?    Lillian?

Unison:     Lillian!

SFX:        Approaching shopping trolley.

FVO 10:     (Out of breath)
            Sorry Lillian, Lillian, Lillian,
            Lillian, Lillian, Lillian, Lillian,
            Lillian, Lillian and Lillian, I thought
            you were calling Gillian.

MVO:        There's no mistaking TEN LILS SHOP. At
            a supermarket near you.
```

Art Directors
GRAHAM FINK
JOHN CLIFFORD
Copywriters
TIM MELLORS
MARK COLLIS
Illustrator
DAVID JUNIPER
Typographers
LEN CHEESEMAN
GAVIN FERGUSON

ARE YOU TUNED IN?

People move in rhythm but no music is heard, just the whirr of the projector.

SFX:

Suddenly, shouts are heard. A unique quadrophonic track gives the impression that the shouts are coming from the audience.

A title now appears: If you want the sound for this commercial tell the projectionist.

Inspired by this and the shouts, the audience joins in.

The commercial is visually rewound. It restarts with the music (Salt 'n' Pepa's 'Let's Talk About Sex'), but not quite at full volume.

A voice asks the projectionist to 'turn it up'.

The crowd becomes more rowdy and finally the music is heard at full blast.

Title:
KISS 100 FM

Mixed Media Campaigns

Director
PATRICIA MURPHY

Copywriter
TOM CARTY

Art Director
WALTER CAMPBELL

Creative Director
DAVID ABBOTT

Producer
JENNY SELBY

Set Designer
JENNY SELDEN

Agency Producer
FRANCINE LINSEY

Editor
RICK RUSSELL

Lighting Cameraman
ANTONY STANIER

Music Composer/Arranger
SALT 'N' PEPA

Production Company
TONY KAYE FILMS
LIMITED

Agency
ABBOTT MEAD
VICKERS.BBDO
LIMITED

Head of Marketing
MALCOLM COX

Client
KISS 100 FM

Art Director
WALTER CAMPBELL

Copywriter
TOM CARTY

Typographer
GARY TODD

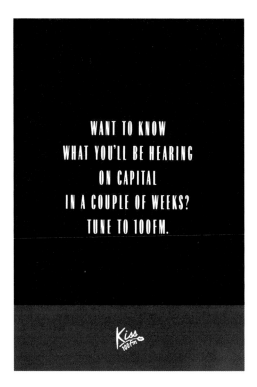

TUBECARD: SLEEP

*A group of young
people were hired to sit
underneath these
tubecards and fall
asleep listening to one
of Kiss's competitors.*

Mixed Media Campaigns

Art Director
WARREN BROWN

Copywriter
JOHN McCABE

Photographers
ELLIOT ERWITT
GEORGIA BRAUER
(Baby)

Typographer
WARREN BROWN

Agency
BARTLE BOGLE
HEGARTY

Marketing Director
ANDREW KNIBBS

Client
LEVI STRAUSS UK
LIMITED

Director
CHRIS HARTWILL

Copywriter
JOHN MᶜCABE

Art Director
WARREN BROWN

Creative Director
JOHN HEGARTY

Producer
PAULINE HURST

Set Designer
NICK SWINGLER

Agency Producer
KATE O'MULLOY

Editor
BRIAN DYKE

Lighting Cameraman
PHIL MEHEUX

Music Composer/Arranger
MARC BOLAN

Production Company
RSA FILMS LIMITED

Agency
BARTLE BOGLE
HEGARTY

Senior Marketing Manager
LARRY RUFF

CAMERA
Soundtrack:
T-Rex "20th Century Boy".

Video:
An innocent young man is released from a South American jail, all his possessions bar a battered 35 mm camera having been stolen by the prison guards.

A watching guard grins as the young man is left standing in the desert in just his boxer shorts and T-shirt, dwarfed by the prison building.

Suddenly, a classic convertible pulls up. His beautiful girlfriend steps out, throwing a pair of well-worn 501s over to him.

After pulling on his Levi's, the young man walks over to greet his girlfriend, as the prison guard looks on, jealously. Finally, our hero takes some shots of his girlfriend and throws the camera to the guard before driving off into the sunset.

Super:
Originals stand the test of time.

Levi's (logo).

THE SWIMMER
Soundtrack:
Dinah Washington 'Mad about the boy'

A boy from the wrong side of the tracks swims across several swimming pools to get to his girlfriend, who is celebrating her 18th birthday. He whisks her off and they dive into the great wide ⁓yonder. Proving along the way, that...

Super:

The more you wash them the better they get.

Levi's (logo).

Concept Creator
MARTIN GALTON

Copywriter
WILL AWDRY

Agency Producer
LUCY MARSDEN

Recording Engineer
RICHIE BECKER

Producer
JOY GOLDEN

Agency
BARTLE BOGLE
HEGARTY

Production Company
JOY RADIO INC

Marketing Director
ANDREW KNIBBS

```
TITLE:        SAX

SFX:          Music

Sax Player:   This horn here, this horn is broke in
              already, I mean, but if it was new it would
              take a little getting used to. New pads, new
              springs, you gotta work at it....

SFX:          Music, plucking sound

Sax Player:   more air, one needs less. Takes working
              at, you know, it could sound hard, like
              this...

SFX:          Music

Sax Player:   I mean, you got to check it out. You know,
              make sure it's nice and groovy all across
              the whole range. And then you play it a
              little while. It's like a part of you.
              Sounds like this...

SFX:          Music

VO:           Levis original 501s. They take a lot of
              getting used to.
```

```
TITLE:        STRAT

Guitarist:    (Plays) You know, I don't care what anybody
              says, the original Strats are different.

SFX:          Music

Guitarist:    The ones made before '65, they go for big
              money nowadays. So when Leo Fender sold the
              company, I mean, you can get the Stratocaster
              copies, but the originals, I don't know...

SFX:          Music

Guitarist:    I guess most of the guys play 'em 'cos
              you can make your own sound with them,
              they're individual, they've got these
              pick-ups...

SFX:          Music

Guitarist:    Mmm... there's even a couple of players I
              know that knock holes in 'em for a different
              sound. This one here, this is, this is good,
              it's loosened up.

SFX:          Music

Guitarist:    It's got that resonance to it. But it cuts,
              you know, it's got that Strat bite

VO:           Levis original 501s. Every pair you'll ever
              have is different.
```

Trade and Professional Magazines Singles

Art Director
ANTONY EASTON

Copywriters
JAMES LOWTHER
ADAM KEAN

Photographer
PETER LAVERY

Typographer
ROGER KENNEDY

Agency
SAATCHI & SAATCHI

Marketing Manager
PAUL WIELGUS

Client
ALLIED BREWERIES
BRANDS MARKETING

Trade and Professional Magazines Singles

Art Directors
NIK STUDZINSKI
ALEXANDRA TAYLOR

Copywriter
JASON FRETWELL

Photographer
MARTIN THOMPSON

Typographer
ROGER KENNEDY

Agency
SAATCHI & SAATCHI

Marketing Manager
PAUL WIELGUS

Client
ALLIED BREWERIES
BRANDS MARKETING

Trade and Professional Magazines Singles

Art Director
NIK STUDZINSKI

Copywriter
JASON FRETWELL

Photographer
PETER LAVERY

Retoucher
DAN TIERNY

Typographer
ANDY DYMOCK

Agency
SAATCHI & SAATCHI

Marketing Manager
PAUL WIELGUS

Client
ALLIED BREWERIES
BRANDS MARKETING

*Trade and
Professional
Magazines Singles*

Art Director
CHRISTOPHER
GREGORY

Copywriter
CHRISTIAN
MARÉCHAL

Photographer
JACK BANKHEAD

Typographer
ADRIAN GREENAWAY

Agency
GREENAWAY
BURDETT MARTYN

Advertising Manager
CHRIS COTTON

Client
SHELL UK LIMITED

THE LATEST LABOUR SAVING GADGET.
A WASHING MACHINE.

YOU CAN TELL WHEN IT'S SHELL.

SHELL UNLEADED.
FAVOURITE WITH YOUR SUNDAY DRIVER.

YOU CAN TELL WHEN IT'S SHELL.

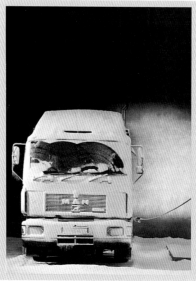

THE LOW TEMPERATURE WASH
FOR PERFECT RESULTS EVERY TIME.

PORSCHE APPROVE OUR WASHING LIQUID FOR THEIR FRONT LOADER.

YOU CAN TELL WHEN IT'S SHELL.

FOR THE BODY, WAX POLISH APPLIED BY HAND. FOR THE ENGINE, DETERGENT APPLIED BY THE RIGHT FOOT.

YOU CAN TELL WHEN IT'S SHELL.

Trade and Professional Magazines Singles

Art Director
CHRISTOPHER GREGORY

Copywriter
CHRISTIAN MARÉCHAL

Photographer
JACK BANKHEAD

Typographer
ADRIAN GREENAWAY

Agency
GREENAWAY BURDETT MARTYN

Advertising Manager
CHRIS COTTON

Client
SHELL UK LIMITED

Trade and
Professional
Magazines Singles

Art Director
ANTONY EASTON

Copywriter
ADAM KEAN

Typographer
ANDY DYMOCK

Agency
SAATCHI & SAATCHI

Marketing Manager
PAUL WIELGUS

Client
ALLIED BREWERIES
BRANDS MARKETING

Trade and
Professional
Magazines Singles

Art Director
DAVE DYE

Copywriter
KEIRON SIMPSON

Photographer
JERRY OKE

Modelmaker
GAVIN LINDSAY

Typographer
ANDY DYMOCK

Agency
EDWARDS MARTIN
THORNTON LIMITED

Senior Brand Manager
FRANCES GREGORY

Client
BASS BREWERIES
LIMITED

*Trade and
Professional
Magazines Singles*

Art Director
CARL LE BLOND

Copywriter
TONY STRONG

Photographer
PETER RAUTER

Illustrator
IVAN ALLEN

Typographers
STEVE RONCHETTI
CHRIS HYDE

Agency
OGILVY & MATHER

Chairman
MIKE WALSH

Client
OGILVY & MATHER

Does your advertising
pass this simple test?

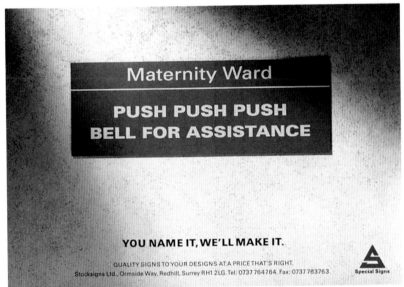

Trade and Professional Magazines Singles

Art Director
CLARE HOWELLS

Copywriter
CAROL HAIG

Photographer
KELVIN MURRAY

Typographers
STEPHEN KETTELL
ALISON GREENWAY

Agency
GGK LONDON LIMITED

Client Marketing Executive
KAREN JIGGENS

Client
STOCKSIGNS

Trade and
Professional
Magazines Campaigns

Art Directors
ANTONY STILEMAN
PAUL CATMUR

Copywriters
STUART BLAKE
MIKE O'SULLIVAN

Photographers
COLIN ELSEY
ANDREW COWIE

Illustrator
HARVEY CARMICHAEL

Typographer
RICHARD LAWSON

Agency
YOUNG & RUBICAM

Marketing Executive
MIKE SARGENT

Client
H J HEINZ COMPANY
LIMITED

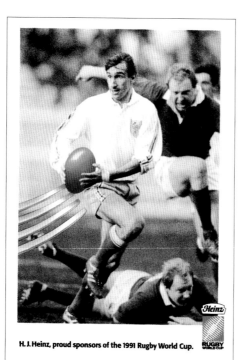

H. J. Heinz, proud sponsors of the 1991 Rugby World Cup.

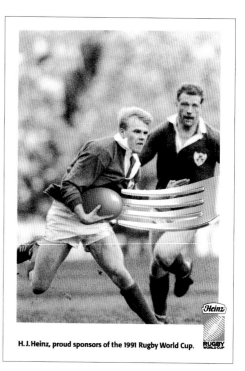

H. J. Heinz, proud sponsors of the 1991 Rugby World Cup.

H. J. Heinz, proud sponsors of the 1991 Rugby World Cup.

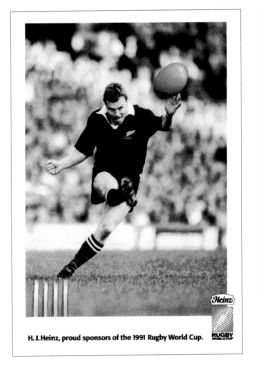

H. J. Heinz, proud sponsors of the 1991 Rugby World Cup.

H. J. Heinz, proud sponsors of the 1991 Rugby World Cup.

H. J. Heinz, proud sponsors of the 1991 Rugby World Cup.

Trade and
Professional
Magazines Campaigns

Art Director
JOHN DOYLE

Copywriter
ERNIE SCHENCK

Photographer
NADAV KANDER

Typographer
JOHN DOYLE

Agency
DOYLE ADVERTISING
& DESIGN GROUP

Vice President Marketing &
Product
MICHAEL COOGAN

Client
THE DUNHAM
COMPANY

There are feet that have never seen a David Hockney. There are feet that have never walked the streets of Cannes. There are feet unfamiliar with beluga at midnight. Dunham. They get the job done.

There are feet that have never pressed the corner office. There are feet that have never sat through a shareholder's meeting. There are feet that have never had sushi for lunch. There are feet that have never seen the inside of an Indian loafer. Dunham. They get the job done.

*Trade and
Professional
Magazines Campaigns*

Art Director
DAVID GODFREE

Copywriter
NICK HASTINGS

Photographer
RUSSELL PORCAS

Typographer
JEFF MERRELLS

Agency
COLLETT DICKENSON
PEARCE & PARTNERS
LIMITED

Managing Director
BERT HARDY

Client
NEWSPAPER
PUBLISHERS
ASSOCIATION

You were happy to spend a fortune advertising on TV. Then you had to go and read this.

NO-ONE can deny that television advertising is expensive. The reason advertisers are willing to pay up is because they've been told time and time again - and have had no reason to doubt - that television is a good investment.

Given the huge audiences and the 'intrusive' nature of the medium, for those who can afford it there is no real alternative.

We may think of this as the accepted wisdom. In fact it's the accepted folly.

The figures that make the case for television advertising are based on a method of research which records the times at which viewers turn their sets on, change channels and switch off.

There is also a 'people meter' that records who is in the room, provided they remember to press the button.

This method asks us to make a rather important assumption.

That when people are in a room with the TV set switched on, they are actually watching.

Everyday experience, common sense and a little elementary sleuthing will show us that this assumption can't be entirely accurate.

Just how wildly inaccurate has recently been demonstrated by research psychologist Dr. Peter Collett, who used the unassailable method of videoing people watching commercials by loading a camera in their TV sets.

His findings make uncomfortable reading for anyone who spends large sums on television advertising. Let's assume that you 'invest' £10 million. Dr. Collett saw (literally) that 20% of commercials played to empty rooms. Bang goes £2 million.

The videotapes also revealed that advertising breaks were the cue for people to escape the commercials.

Some people left the room. Others used their remote-control 'zappers' to sample the action on other channels.

As a result, another 10% of commercials (and £1million of your budget) were lost.

Only 70% of commercials had any audience at all. But the tapes show people talking, reading, sleeping. Some, who evidently forgot they were being filmed, even got down to some serious canoodling.

Half the time, no-one was actually watching the TV set.

In effect, only one third of all commercials had the viewers' attention. £7 million of your £10 million was totally wasted.

Whichever way you look at it, television advertising is less than half as effective as you thought it was. Or more than twice as expensive.

In publishing this newspaper advertisement, we do not wish to imply that your television advertising budget is wasted. Just two thirds of it.

Of course we're not suggesting that you stop using television, only that you stop to think about what other, powerful options are available. Newspapers, for example.

You cannot read a newspaper whilst behaving as if it isn't there.

If you put down your cup of tea, the ads will still be there when you come back. (It is probably impossible to canoodle while reading a newspaper, but if Dr. Collett's research teaches us anything, it is not to be dogmatic.)

Some of the most famous campaigns in advertising history have been conducted in newspapers. We've already featured several of them on these pages. This advertisement contains two more examples.

Newspaper advertisements can be intrusive, powerful and compelling.

You've spent three minutes on this ad already and read every word so far. How much would it cost you to hold someone's attention on TV for three minutes? (Don't forget that TV is more than twice as expensive as you thought it was.)

If you'd like more information, please telephone 071-433 1500.

PEOPLE READ NEWS-PAPERS

This advertisement was placed by the Newspaper Publishers Association.

Some people are being conned by TV commercials. The people who pay for them.

YOU ARE all too aware of the high costs of advertising on television. When you receive the bill, however, you will no doubt be comforted by the knowledge that television commands a huge audience and gives your brand status because of its impact and intrusiveness.

At least, in common with hundreds of people in your position, this is what you have been told it does.

But just how intrusive is it? A revealing new piece of research confirms that television has far less impact than most advertisers are being told.

By putting a hidden camera into their television sets, a research psychologist called Dr. Peter Collett was able to video people 'watching' the commercials.

Let's assume that your television budget is £10 million. How much of that money is actually doing you any good?

Dr. Collett saw (literally) that 20% of the commercials played to an empty room.

That's £2 million of your money spent communicating with inanimate objects.

Another 10% of the commercials were missed as people used the breaks to flick through other channels. Curiosity accounts for a further £1 million of your money.

Of the remaining 70% of the commercials that could have been seen, half were missed whilst the audience behaved as if the television wasn't there. (Some didn't behave at all, they just canoodled.)

Which means that only one third of the commercials got the benefit of the viewers' attention.

Around £7 million of your £10 million was totally wasted.

Now you know that television is less than half as effective as you thought it was. Or put another way, more than twice as expensive.

In the advertising world, however, this will not be a bolt out of the blue.

For years the advertising industry has known that millions of people do not watch the commercial breaks.

It is well-known, for instance, that during the break after Coronation Street, the power and water industries experience massive 'surges' of demand.

What could this be but millions of ITV viewers abandoning their sets to put the kettle on?

In fact a long line of research studies beginning as long ago as 1956, has cast doubt on how much attention viewers pay to commercials.

The problem is that if you hadn't read about Dr. Collett's research here, most advertising agencies wouldn't have fallen over themselves in a rush to bring it to your attention.

Naturally the television companies cannot wish to highlight these facts.

But why should some people in the advertising industry join in a conspiracy of silence?

The explanation is probably as simple as this: Most senior agency management ('creative' people, and even some clients, think that going on television will make them more famous, more plausible and, ultimately, make them richer than advertising in the press.

An idea that is, if nothing else, rich in irony.

For Dr. Collett observed that some people who stop watching television during the commercials pick up a newspaper.

The point of this advertisement is not to imply that television is a complete waste of money.

Nor is it to suggest that you demand of your agency that television never again appear on your media schedule.

It is to ask why they have not kept you in touch with the real story about how people watch television (or don't watch it).

And why they have not written you a press campaign as powerful as the one featured here for VW and Timberland.

If you'd like more information, please call 071-433 1500.

PEOPLE READ NEWS-PAPERS

This advertisement was placed by the Newspaper Publishers Association.

The chairs love your commercial. The table isn't so sure.

THERE'S ONE PROBLEM with the theory that television advertising is highly intrusive: avoiding commercials is easy.

Now the less we are assured that they reach a huge and attentive audience.

For support we are given figures based on a method of research which records the time at which viewers switch their sets on, change channels, and switch off.

A method which asks us to assume that when the commercials are on, there's someone watching.

Questionable unless you are armed with the knowledge that the demand for electricity and water rises and falls like a curtain's heartbeat with each commercial break.

It is safe enough to deduce that this is the result of people putting the kettle on, or visiting the loo. (Doesn't common sense tell us that viewers are far more likely to leave the room in a commercial break, than during their favourite programmes?)

Indeed, a number of research studies confirmed once the point thirty years later suggested that millions of people, whose attention you are paying for, are not watching when the commercials come. And now, a new and revealing report has confirmed this.

A research psychologist called Dr. Peter Collett videoed people watching commercials by putting a hidden camera into their television sets.

He saw (literally) that 20% of the commercials ran to empty rooms.

To put it bluntly, you are spending 20% of your budget communicating with tables and chairs. (If only they had high disposable incomes.)

The videotapes also revealed that advertising breaks were the cue to escape the commercials.

Some people left the room. Others used their remote-control 'zappers' to find out what was on the other channels. That's another 10% of the commercials missed.

That leaves 70% of the commercials with a potential audience. But the tapes show people talking, reading, sleeping. Some, who evidently forgot they were being filmed, used the ad's for activities normally reserved for the bedroom.

Half of the time no one was watching the TV set.

These insights into domestic reality show that only a third of all commercials were blessed with the viewers' attention.

The fact is that television advertising is less than half as effective as you thought it was. Or put another way, twice as expensive.

An opposite moment to bring your attention to newspaper advertising.

You cannot read a newspaper whilst behaving as if it isn't there.

If you put your newspaper down to make a cup of tea, the ads will still be there when you come back.

You will have seen a series of famous newspaper advertisements, featured as part of this campaign. Reminders of the compelling and powerful nature of the written word.

And a timely incentive for agencies to think twice before herding advertisers towards television.

They might find it beyond even their powers of persuasion to convince you that talking to furniture is going to help you shift your product.

And rather easier to sell you on the idea of advertising in the newspapers. The effectiveness of which, for the last thirty minutes, you have been busy proving.

If you'd like more information, please call 071-433 1500.

PEOPLE READ NEWS-PAPERS

This advertisement was placed by the Newspaper Publishers Association.

You shouldn't have to wait 18 years to get an accurate paternity test.

You can wait a few years for an accurate paternity test. Or you can consult Memorial Blood Center of Minneapolis.

Memorial Blood Center is the most experienced testing facility in the Midwest. And experience is vital because paternity test results are not simply "yes or no." They're complicated, and require skillful interpretation.

That's why all of our laboratory personnel have paternity testing experience, along with degrees in medical technology or a related science.

So the next time you have a paternity case, don't wait.

Consult the experts at Memorial Blood Center. Call (612) 871-3300, ext. 239 for more information today. **Memorial Blood Center**

Trade and Professional Magazines Campaigns

Art Director
JOHN MORRISON

Copywriter
TOM McELLIGOTT

Photographer
STEVE UMLAND

Typographer
JIM POOLE

Agency
McELLIGOTT WRIGHT
MORRISON WHITE

Chief Executive Officer
JERRY HAARMANN

Client
MEMORIAL BLOOD
CENTER

How to raise the odds of winning your next paternity case.

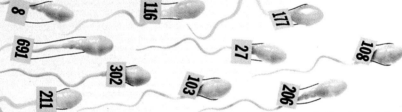

Paternity testing is, by nature, a complicated process requiring skill in interpretation. And no testing facility is more skilled or experienced than Memorial Blood Center.

At Memorial Blood Center of Minneapolis all paternity testing is performed by experienced, certified laboratory personnel with degrees in medical technology or related science. And all test results include a review and letter of explanation from

H. F. Polesky, M.D., world-renowned for his work in perfecting paternity blood-testing methodologies—and an experienced, highly credible expert witness.

So the next time you have a paternity case, talk to the people who have more blood testing experience over more years than any laboratory in the Midwest. Call (612) 871-3300, ext. 239 for more information today. **Memorial Blood Center**

How to avoid spending $236,000 to raise the milkman's son.

These days, it can cost over $200,000 to raise a child to adulthood. Which makes the stakes in paternity testing rather high.

That's why you should choose the most experienced facility in the Midwest. Memorial Blood Center of Minneapolis. We've been conducting paternity tests for over 40 years. And all paternity

testing is performed by certified laboratory personnel with experience in paternity testing and degrees in medical technology or a related science.

Think about it. When the question is as serious as the father of a child, shouldn't you consult Memorial Blood Center? Call (612) 871-3300, extension 239 for more information today. **Memorial Blood Center**

pu
blic serv
ice and

3

ch

arities

What's it like to be raped as a 3 year old? A victim explains.

I FIRST remember being sexually abused by my father when I was about 3. It may have happened before, I don't know.

I can see it now, me lying in bed, with that big face coming towards me. He'd kiss me goodnight, but he didn't stop at kissing.

He used to tell me it was our secret. And if I ever told anyone about it I'd be sent away.

But even as a child I knew something wasn't right. It was those words, "I'll protect you". How could he be protecting me? He was bloody hurting me.

It's strange really, he was my enemy, but at the same time my only friend in the world. He made me depend on him. He controlled me. My body was his toy for more than 9 years.

At school I found it hard to mix. I felt different. I'd never let anyone get close to me. In the changing rooms after P.E. I hated people seeing my naked body. I was so ashamed, thought they might be able to tell what had been happening to me and call me a poofter.

Even when I managed to find a girlfriend I still wasn't sure if I was heterosexual. I was terribly rough with her. I suppose I wanted to be in control of someone, like my father was with me.

Sex terrified me. Having an orgasm just made me think of what my father did inside of me. And that big smiling face.

I met someone else eventually. We got married. After 2 years she left me. She said I was cold and didn't understand her.

But that's how I was. I just wasn't aware of causing or feeling mental or physical pain. Something inside me had been switched off long ago. There were times when I could actually cut myself with a knife and not feel a thing.

After the divorce, I turned to drink. It was a way of escaping. But I still suffered deep depressions.

Last year, my father finally died. I think that's what made me contact the NSPCC. I was 53 years old, and it was the first time I'd ever told anyone about my childhood.

Once a week for 6 months a Child Protection Officer worked with me. He got me to tell him everything about my experience. Talking about it was very painful. For over 40 years I guess I'd been trying not to think about it.

Eventually though, it started to work. He made me realise that what happened wasn't my fault.

For the first time I can ever remember I actually began to feel good about myself. It was just like being let out of a dark and lonely cell.

I'll never forget what happened to me. But at least I can start to live my life.

For further information on the work of the NSPCC, or to make a donation, please write to: NSPCC, 67 Saffron Hill, London, EC1N 8RS or call 071 242 1626.

To report a suspected case of child abuse, call the NSPCC Child Protection Helpline on 0800 800 500.

NSPCC
Act Now For Children.

NO RED NOSE

Adrian Edmonson tries to make his nose go red.

All shots are slapstick cartoon style

He tries hitting his nose with a mallet, a rake, a boxing glove, a cricket bat, a baseball bat, a suction arrow.

He sticks his nose in a vice, a washing mangle, a beehive, a mousetrap, under a garden roller, into a ceiling fan.

He slams it in a door and then into a huge book.

He sprays it with a yellow paint (by mistake).

He tries a toilet plunger. Tries catching a cold. Falls flat on his face.

As a last resort dynamite!

Nothing works.

VO:
There's a simpler way to get a red nose.

Video:
A red nose pops into Adrian's face followed by other size noses. He complains bitterly about the price.

VO:
Buy one for 60p.

Also available in car and truck nose size.

Title:

Red Nose Day 5th March.

15th Comic Relief.

SILVER AWARD
*for the most outstanding
Film in Public Service and
Charity*

Director
PAUL WEILAND

Copywriter
PAUL WEILAND

Producer
MARY FRANCIS

Set Designer
MIKE HALL

Editor
IAN WEIL

Lighting Cameraman
ROGER PRATT

Production Company
PAUL WEILAND FILM
COMPANY

Agency
CHARITY PROJECTS

Client
CHARITY PROJECTS

SILVER AWARD
NOMINATION
for the most oustanding
Advertisement in Public
Service and Charity

Art Director
PAUL GAY

Copywriter
STEVE REEVES

Photographer
ALAN McPHAIL

Typographer
KEVIN CLARKE

Agency
BMP DDB NEEDHAM

Advertising Manager
KATE POCOCK

Client
HEALTH EDUCATION
AUTHORITY

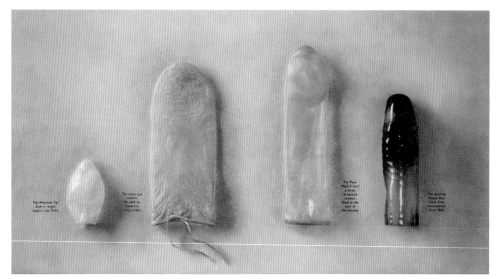

SEX HASN'T CHANGED MUCH OVER THE YEARS. FORTUNATELY CONDOMS HAVE.

SILVER AWARD
NOMINATION
*for the most outstanding
Film in Public Service and
Charity*

Directors
BOB HERON
JACK MELVILLE

Copywriter
BOB HERON

Art Director
JACK MELVILLE

Creative Directors
BOB HERON
JACK MELVILLE

Producer
PAUL ENDACOTT

Agency Producer
JUSTINE PETERS

Editor
PAUL ENDACOTT

Photographer
GARY OWENS

Rostrum Cameraman
PETER JONES

Music Composer/Arranger
CHRIS REA

Production Company
JIM BAMBRICK &
ASSOCIATES LIMITED

Agency
THE JOHNSON
AGENCY

Publicity Manager
DENNIS KINGSHOT

Client
NSPCC

EXCUSES

Soundtrack:
*'Tell Me There's a Heaven' by
Chris Rea plays throughout.*

Super:
phen broke his arm falling off his
bike.

Fade to black.

Fade up to:
*ys revealed seven other unreported
fractures.*

Fade to black.

Fade up to:
*t of small girl cuddling her Teddy
Bear.*

Super:
*ah tripped over her Teddy and fell
down the stairs.*

Fade to black.

Fade up to:
*t didn't explain the weal marks on
her back.*

Fade to black.

Fade up to:
hot of a boy wrapped in a towel.

Super:
*bin jumped into the bath before I
could stop him.*

Fade to black.

Fade up:
*t explained the scalding, but why
id he have cigarette burns on his
arms?*

Fade to black.

Fade up to:
icture of a girl playing on a swing

Super:
ust turned my back for a minute...

Fade to black.

Fade up to:
*e coroner's report showed multiple
ruises, internal bleeding, fractured
bs, malnutrition, and dehydration
nsistent <u>only</u> with long term abuse.*

Fade to black.

Fade up to:
There's <u>no</u> excuses for ignoring it.

Fade to black.

Fade up end frame.

NSPCC (logo).

We <u>don't</u> accept excuses.

NSPCC CHRISTMAS

BREATHING NEW LIFE INTO THE OLDEST IDEAS CAN BE THE TEACHER'S MOST DEMANDING ROLE.

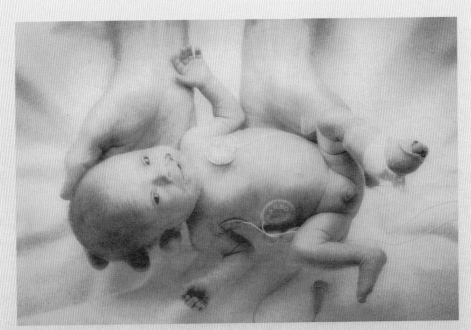

With your help we can now put him back in the womb.

Baby Hollingsworth was so keen to start this life he arrived three months early.

Weighing in at only twenty-four ounces.

A few years ago he'd have died within the hour.

But nowadays modern technology gives him a very good chance of living a full and healthy life.

For the next twelve weeks his home will be an intensive care unit fitted out with lifelines.

As near to a man-made womb as science and the love of nurses and doctors can get.

Ventilators will help him breathe until his lungs are big enough.

Computers will feed him drip by drip until he's strong enough to suck.

Other devices will monitor his pulse, his temperature, his heartbeat, his brain.

The air around him will be kept at precisely 95°F.

Alas (and this is where we need you to push) it all costs money. More money than any health service in the world can afford.

Every hospital we know could do with another baby life support system.

Or two. Or three.

Without them they sometimes have to make the agonising choice of which of two premature babies lives (and even, can you bear it, which twin).

No doctor should have to make such decisions. No parents should suffer such pain. This is why we started BLISS.

We're a charity which gathers donations to buy baby life support systems.

Would you or your company sponsor one or part of one, anything from just under £500 for a respiration monitor to £60,000 for the complete system?

You can specify the item. Even the hospital you want to benefit.

Please send a donation with the coupon. Or organise payroll giving at work. Or simply fax us your business card and we'll get in touch with you.

One last point:

We are not a rich charity. This ad will probably be the only one you'll see from us for a long while.

There's a saying in advertising that if the customer turns the page you're dead.

In our case it's only too true. Please act now.

To BLISS, 17/21 Emerald Street, London WC1N 3QL. Tel: 071-831 9393. Fax: 071-404 0676.
I want to help, please send me your brochure and covenant forms. Meanwhile here is a donation for £_____

NAME
COMPANY
ADDRESS
POSTCODE
PHONE NO.

BLISS
BABY LIFE SUPPORT SYSTEMS   REG. CHARITY NO. 802872

Press Advertising

Art Director
CATHY HENG

Copywriter
TONY BRIGNULL

Photographer
BARNEY EDWARDS

Retoucher
DAN TIERNEY

Typographer
ED CHURCH

Agency
D'ARCY MASIUS
BENTON & BOWLES
LIMITED

Director
JUDY KAY

Client
BLISS (BABY LIFE
SUPPORT SYSTEMS)

*Press Advertising
Campaigns*

Art Director
DAVE BEVERLEY

Copywriter
ROB BURLEIGH

Photographer
PAUL WINDSOR

Typographer
ANDY PALMER

Agency
EURO RSCG

Section Head (Fundraising)
FIONA HESSELDEN

Client
SHELTER

Photographer
STUART BAKER

He was willing to give his life for the same country that wouldn't give him a council house.

After 4 years serving on the streets of Northern Ireland John found himself homeless on the streets of England.

John had joined the Royal Irish Rangers straight from school.

He decided to leave the services when his wife became pregnant for the second time.

They moved back to her home town in the South West.

That's when they nearly ended up sleeping on the streets. They couldn't find anywhere they could afford to live.

They were left with no choice but to move in with his wife's parents while they applied to the council for accommodation.

The local authority, however, had recently taken a tough line on army families and refused to give them a house.

The council even tried to persuade John to go back to Northern Ireland.

The only people more at risk than soldiers in Northern Ireland are ex-soldiers so John was understandably reluctant to return.

John came to Shelter in desperate need of help.

His relationship with his wife was fast deteriorating because of the stress of having to live with her parents.

We took up John's case with the local housing authority and showed them that they were wrong to turn John and his family away.

After numerous phone calls we finally convinced them that John should be treated as a priority case and he was given temporary accommodation.

Within a month of coming to us the council offered John a permanent new home.

He had sorted out the problems with his wife and was looking forward to moving in.

John is just one of the thousands of people who come to us for help every year.

They are made homeless by a variety of circumstances. Redundancy, repossession or even divorce.

We never turn away anyone who comes to Shelter for help. But to keep this policy we need your help.

Each hour of advice costs us £42. We rely greatly on your donations.

The more you give the more people we'll be able to fight for.

Shelter

When Emma told us she'd been abused, we put her into a special home. Her own.

It began when her mum started working nights and Emma and her father were left alone in the house. The sexual abuse went on for eight years.

Emma was too terrified to tell anyone about it. Then one day, when she couldn't take any more, she came to Shelter. She was extremely upset and distressed.

Over a cup of tea and in confidential surroundings she revealed to one of our caseworkers what had been happening.

We put her in touch with specialists who could offer her counselling

and advice. With their help she decided that she needed somewhere quiet to stay. A place where she could get herself back on her feet and plan for the future.

(Sometimes it can be just as important to get someone out of a home as it is to get them in.)

We were able to offer her several housing options.

In the end Emma decided that the Women's Refuge would be the best and safest place to stay for the time being.

We arranged a place for her and helped her settle in.

Then we contacted the local housing authority and arranged a permanent home for her when she was ready to leave the refuge.

Emma has now moved into her own home and is much happier.

She has a good job and feels that she wouldn't be where she is today if it wasn't for our help.

Emma is just one of the thousands of women who come to us for help every year. They are made homeless by a variety of circumstances. Abuse is just one.

At Shelter we work closely with local authorities, using hostels and refuges to find them new homes.

As in Emma's case, we can even help them find a home of their own if that's what they want.

The cost of running a housing aid centre isn't cheap, however.

Every hour of advice costs us £42.

So we really do rely on your donations.

Without them people like Emma would be forced to live on the streets or worse still, at home.

Shelter

55 Old Street, London EC1V 9HL. Tel: 071 253 0202.

Photographer
TOM JENKINS

Her husband meant the world to her. Unfortunately he also meant the house.

When Mr Sanderson left his wife he didn't leave her on her own.

He left her with two children and a substantial mortgage.

Jane and Bill Sanderson had been happily married for nearly 20 years.

Mrs Sanderson thought they still were, until one day last November Bill vanished.

Mrs Sanderson had been a housewife and so totally dependent on her husband's income.

Because she was still married and couldn't prove that her husband had left (she couldn't contact him) she was refused benefit.

It wasn't long before the mortgage arrears built up, not to mention the overdraft at the bank.

The building societies informed her that they were taking her to court in order to repossess her home.

Because of all her problems she had been unable to make a payment for 6 months.

Mrs Sanderson was at her wits' end.

She feared that she and her children would end up on the streets.

She came to Shelter just six days before the court hearing.

We carefully examined her financial situation and at the end of the interview we came to the reluctant conclusion that there was little chance of Mrs Sanderson keeping her house.

We contacted the building society and arranged for the interest on her mortgage to be frozen.

Unfortunately nothing could

prevent the property from being repossessed.

However, we managed to delay the date of the bailiff's warrant until the council had arranged a permanent new home for Jane Sanderson and her children.

They now feel they have a safe and secure base in which they can plan for the future.

Homelessness is something that can happen to anyone at any time of their lives, including you and us.

Without Shelter, 40,000 people would have found themselves either homeless or in severe housing difficulty last year.

This year we expect to be needed even more.

We rely greatly on donations. So please give as much as you can afford.

However much it is, it'll mean a lot to people like Mrs Sanderson.

Shelter

88 Old Street, London EC1V 9HU. Tel: 071 253 0202

Photographer
JETHRO BURTON

It's hard leaving home at 18. It's even harder at 47.

The first time Marie left home was when Alan proposed to her.

The second time was when he raped her.

Marie married Alan in 1962.

Three years later she had two young children.

They grew up and eventually left home themselves.

And that's when Marie's problems began.

After all the years of looking after the kids she realised she and her husband had little left in common.

Their relationship deteriorated and in the end Marie's husband attacked her.

Marie had no choice but to leave home.

She applied to the local authority for housing but was refused because she couldn't prove that she was homeless.

(She still jointly owned a house with her husband.)

They also refused to consider her a priority case, as she wasn't pregnant, had no young children and wasn't physically or mentally disabled.

Marie didn't know where to turn to for help.

She was too embarrassed and frightened to tell her children.

When she came to Shelter, her only accommodation was a friend's sofa.

Her friend had a large family in an already overcrowded house.

Because of the strain this was putting on everyone, Marie desperately needed to move out into a place of her own.

The first thing we did was to put her in touch with the Rape Crisis Centre.

Then we contacted her local housing authority as we thought they had made the wrong decision.

We pointed out that the law clearly states that even if a person has accommodation they can still be considered homeless.

(If it is 'unreasonable' for them to remain in that accommodation or if continued occupation would put them at risk.)

The local authority reconsidered their decision and agreed to offer Marie accommodation.

Marie now has a permanent new home and is very optimistic about the future.

She feels that without our help she would probably still be sleeping on her friend's sofa.

Last year Shelter helped many women like Marie.

And with more and more marriages ending in separation nowadays, we expect we'll be needed to help even more next year.

However, we rely greatly on your generosity.

We couldn't survive without your donations and neither could the women we help.

So please put a donation in the post next time you leave home.

Shelter

88 Old Street, London EC1V 9HU. Tel: 071 253 0202

Press Advertising

Art Director
PAUL BRAZIER

Copywriter
PETER SOUTER

Photographer
MIKE PARSONS

Typographer
JOE HOZA

Agency
ABBOTT MEAD
VICKERS.BBDO
LIMITED

Director of Campaigns and PR
GAVIN GRANT

Client
RSPCA

When it was a puppy they couldn't put it down. When it became a dog they did.

People don't tie unwanted dolls in sacks and throw them into rivers.

They don't abandon toy train sets in remote lay-bys.

And they don't hurl skateboards out into the street on Boxing Day.

But there's something about the gift of a living animal that brings out the worst in people.

For the RSPCA the season of goodwill is the busiest and perhaps most depressing time of year.

We rescue hundreds of animals from a variety of unpleasant situations.

Within weeks many of our kennels overflow.

Then, if it's impossible to find them homes, we have to put them down.

The killing is a strange activity for a society that was founded to prevent cruelty to animals.

We hate it.

And we want you to help us stop it.

Don't give animals as presents.

They aren't just a gift they're a responsibility.

The average cat will eat its way through over £2000 worth of food in its lifetime.

A dog will need to be walked somewhere around 15,000 miles.

Christmas too, with all its chaotic comings and goings, loud noises and crowded rooms, is the very worst time to introduce a pet into a new home.

Even a loving one.

So even if you know a child who's dying for a puppy, try to resist.

Or one day the puppy might die for the child.

If you give a damn, don't give a pet. RSPCA

Press Advertising

Art Director
STUART BUCKLEY

Copywriter
PAUL BURKE

Photographer
ROGER CHARITY

Typographer
KEVIN CLARKE

Agency
BMP DDB NEEDHAM

Advertising Manager
KATE POCOCK

Client
HEALTH EDUCATION
AUTHORITY

IF YOUR SEX LIFE IS UNPROTECTED, SO TOO IS YOUR RELATIONSHIP.

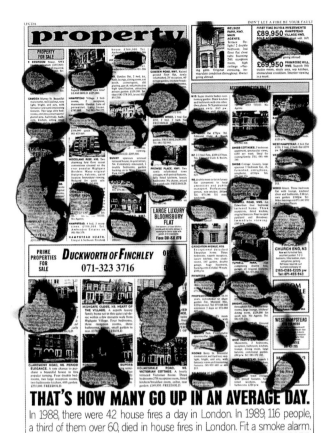

THAT'S HOW MANY GO UP IN AN AVERAGE DAY.
In 1988, there were 42 house fires a day in London. In 1989, 116 people,
a third of them over 60, died in house fires in London. Fit a smoke alarm.
It's not just an early warning – it's the only warning. LONDON FIRE BRIGADE

Read this page.
Then you'll know as much
about drugs as the
average twelve year old.

Partnership for a
Drug-Free America

Nowadays, smoking is socially unacceptable.

In 1914, they shot you for it.

One crack rang out.

Across the area we called No Man's. A strip of clagged clay no more than 60 feet wide.

Potted with holes. Stuffed with bodies. Rank with fear.

Just a few hours before, at twilight, our entire battalion had rushed madly over that field of doom.

Rabid mongrels we were. Frothing, snarling and sloshing through bog up to our knees.

Lemmings we were. Recklessly leaping up from a trench. And into a barrage of bullets.

Taking cover behind a soldier, who had been dead for at least two weeks, I witnessed what had become a normal, everyday occurance.

Two thousand men in overalls the weight of anvils. Cement boots. Burdensome uniforms. Rifles in hand. Clumsy bloody soldiers.

Easy targets.

We had advanced all of thirty feet. Tomorrow, the Hun would retaliate.

And another small town's population will be slaughtered. Just to recapture that ever-so-vital, strategic, thirty feet of foul-smelling mire.

Soldiers, with families, died face down in mud. No ceremony. No salute. No tears.

I had spent two years in this land of the damned.

Dodging dysentery and gangrene. Dodging human remains, horses carcasses and excrement.

Dodging hunger and reality.

A cigarette with friends and a fading memory of a normal life was all we could cling to. It was all we could ever look forward to. It wasn't much.

And now it was night.

We couldn't see any shapes. No trees. No flowers. No birds looping by. Not even the moon.

A chance to sleep? Hardly. Sleep is always broken by thunder.

Not from rain-clouds. But shells. Pounding the Front Line.

Fire sets the horizon aglow.

And as you lean against a trench wall dripping of blood, urine and clay, you can feel the vibration of shockwave after shockwave rippling past you.

Or you hide in terror as a Fokker Albatross comes in low, following the line of trenches, scraping us with a spitting Sten gun.

As it dives, the wire struts between its wings wail at you.

Or you catch the occasional faint whiff of mustard gas wafting from miles away.

Sometimes your eyes would water. Sometimes they would sting for hours.

Like mine were now.

No, it was not the gas. I was crying.

There in my wasted arms lay my friend Edward. My friend for the last two weeks. My lifetime friend.

Gripping his uniform, I shook his sinewy body. Violently.

I heard a shrill scream echo over No Man's. Just as the single shot had done only moments before.

That scream was mine. That scream beheld all the senselessness I'd seen since I was forced to live as an animal in a furrow.

That scream, in a second, saw the futility of being prepared to pass up my life for a strip of dirt devoid of any.

And that scream mocked me. It grabbed me and it twisted me and it spat at me.

That scream knew. I had killed Edward with my own hands.

But only a minute ago we had been talking. And laughing in the gloom.

I'd offered my battered tin of Woodbine cigarettes to Ed and Billy.

I lit mine and dragged long.

An alert Hun, spotting the flame, grappled for his gun.

Billy was next. Puff. Puff.

The Jerry Soldier had taken aim.

And Edward. Edward the third. The flame to his face.

He was extinguished by a solitary bullet.

TO THIS DAY, MANY PEOPLE CONSIDER IT CRUCIAL TO LIGHT A THIRD CIGARETTE BY THE SAME MATCH.

A SILLY SUPERSTITION PERHAPS. BUT A WORLD WAR AND EVERY CARELESS THIRD SOLDIER IN THE TRENCHES AT NIGHT SHOULD GIVE THIS ANY OPTION.

NOTHING MUCH HAS CHANGED.

IN 1991, ONE IN THREE SMOKERS STILL DIE BEFORE THEIR TIME.

He spits at his teachers, beats up other children and drinks. What he needs is a damned good cuddle.

YOU'D PROBABLY feel sorry for Simon's parents. He looks like a right little handful.

But a good hiding is the last thing children like Simon need.

Every day they already suffer a worse punishment. It's called emotional abuse. Their parents make them feel completely worthless by relentlessly attacking them with insults and put-downs.

To a growing boy or girl the damage can be irreparable.

Imagine what it must feel like. You're 11 years old, and you can't remember ever having any love or affection.

At school you simply don't know how to mix. So you take out your anger and frustration by bullying other children.

You're always in trouble. It's the only way you know of getting some attention.

For once though, you've done some good work. You take it home to show your parents but they laugh at you and call you "thicko" and "ugly". Then they tell you to "---- off" out of their sight.

You go down to the park and sit under that same tree you always do. You've pinched a half-full bottle of scotch from your dad. It helps to numb the pain.

Children like Simon don't want

pity. They want help. Maybe you know a child who you suspect is being emotionally abused. Please don't leave the child at risk by just hoping for the best.

And don't be put off because you're worried about splitting up

the family. This only happens in very extreme cases.

When a case is reported to us, an NSPCC Child Protection Officer or Local Authority social worker may visit the child's home.

After this, we then make a careful assessment of the family to identify why the parents have been mistreating their child. In numerous cases, they don't even realise they've been doing wrong. A period of counselling may then follow which can involve helping the parents learn how to love and understand their children.

Of course, reporting a case isn't the only way you can help.

We're always crying out for more donations. 80% of our funding relies on the public's generosity.

But, above all, please keep a look out for children like Simon. They may not look abused. But looks can be cruelly deceiving.

For further information on the work of the NSPCC, or to make a donation, write to: NSPCC, 67 Saffron Hill, London, EC1N 8RS or call 071-242 1626.

To report a suspected case of child abuse, call the NSPCC, Child Protection Helpline on 0800 800 500.

NSPCC
Act Now For Children.

Press Advertising

Art Director
CARL LE BLOND

Copywriter
TONY STRONG

Photographer
DAVID
STEWART-SMITH

Typographers
STEVE RONCHETTI
CHRIS HYDE

Agency
OGILVY & MATHER

Chief Executive
DON McCREADY

Client
THE ROMANIAN
ORPHANAGE TRUST

If you kept hearing the child next door screaming, is this how you'd stop it?

IT'S THAT NOISE again. The same one that you heard last night, and two nights ago.

It sounds like a child screaming, but you'd rather not think about it. So you turn the TV up, or do the hoovering. Anything to blot it out.

No matter what you do though, it doesn't stop you thinking. Countless thoughts race through your mind.

You try to persuade yourself it's something else. A hungry cat for instance. Or a whistling kettle.

And even if it is the child, he's probably a right little handful, and deserves to be taught a lesson.

Though he doesn't seem like a naughty kid. Maybe he is being ill-treated. But it's nothing to do with you what people get up to in their own houses, is it?

The fact of the matter is, it is your business. You could be the child's only chance of being saved from the horrors of physical abuse. Ignoring the screams can't stop the child's suffering. Calling the NSPCC Child Protection Helpline can.

We realise reporting a neighbour is a difficult decision to make. But don't be put off by thinking that you'll split up the family. Children only get taken into care in very few cases.

When a case is reported to us, first we listen closely to what is said and then decide on the best course of action. An NSPCC Child Protection Officer or Local Authority social worker may then visit the child's home.

After this, we then make a careful assessment of the family to identify why the parents have been mistreating their child. In a lot of cases, they don't even realise they've been doing wrong. A period of counselling may then follow which can often involve helping the parents learn how to love and understand their children.

We always prefer it if you give your name, but the most important thing to us is to stop a child being at further risk from abuse.

Maybe you think it can't be going on next door to you. But unfortunately, that's what most people think.

Reporting a case isn't the only way you can help, however. We're always crying out for donations. 80% of our funding relies on the generosity of the public.

And please remember, if you keep hearing a child scream, picking up the TV remote control can't stop it. Picking up the phone can.

For further information on the work of the NSPCC, or to make a donation, write to: NSPCC, 67 Saffron Hill, London, EC1N 8RS or call 071-242 1626.

To report a suspected case of abuse, call the NSPCC Child Protection Helpline on 0800 800 500.

NSPCC
Act Now For Children.

Press Advertising

Art Director
JERRY HOLLENS

Copywriter
MIKE BOLES

Photographer
JERRY HOLLENS

Typographer
ANDY DYMOCK

Agency
SAATCHI & SAATCHI

Heaed of Media & Publicity
DENNIS KINGSHOT

Client
NSPCC

Press Advertising

Art Director
NEIL GODFREY

Copywriter
INDRA SINHA

Typographer
JEFF MERRELLS

Agency
COLLETT DICKENSON
PEARCE & PARTNERS
LIMITED

Promotions Officer
DIANE ALLARD

Client
AMNESTY
INTERNATIONAL

Should we give up?

The pictures on the other page are upsetting.

Normally, we wouldn't publish them. Our advertisements purposely stay away from violent and horrific pictures.

When we publicised the murders of street urchins by Brazilian and Guatemalan police, we spared you the sight of children with their tongues ripped out and eyes burned from their sockets.

When we wrote about Iraq's use of chemical weapons against Kurdish civilians, we deliberately did not use the photographs that made our volunteers cry.

We at Amnesty have no choice but to look at these pictures. And hear the stories that go with them.

The story of Agostinho Neto.

The African doctor's waiting room was full of people when the Portuguese secret police arrived.

They dragged him out of his surgery, past his terrified patients. Ignoring the screams of his wife, they began methodically to flog him in front of her and his young children.

Later, he was flung in jail. There were no charges. There would never be a trial.

The case of Dr Agostinho Neto was one of six which, in 1961, prompted a British lawyer, Peter Benenson to write an article in the Observer.

'Open your newspaper any day of the week and you will find a report from somewhere in the world of someone being imprisoned, tortured or executed because his opinions or religion are unacceptable to his government. There are several million such people in prison – and their numbers are growing. The newspaper reader feels a sickening sense of impotence. Yet if those feelings of disgust all over the world could be united into common action, something effective could be done.'

With these words, he founded Amnesty.

A passion for human rights.

Amnesty began as a small group of lawyers, writers and publishers who shared a passionate commitment to human rights.

From a small office in London, they started gathering information about people who were in prison for their political or religious beliefs.

They wrote letters of support and comfort to prisoners, and of protest to their jailers.

Out of this early work grew the Amnesty reports, the letter-writing groups and the urgent action network, which can muster thousands of protest telegrams within hours of a prisoner's arrest.

For three decades Amnesty has campaigned against the terrible things to which the pictures opposite bear witness.

We've tried to show that turning a blind eye to a government's human rights crimes is both immoral and foolish. (It took the Gulf War to demonstrate this – but we'd been issuing warnings about Saddam Hussein every year since 1980.)

During the last thirty years, we have examined the human rights record of every nation on earth and, regrettably, have had cause to criticise most.

(Each end of the political spectrum thinks we're biased towards the other. In fact we're non-partisan. We speak out for the rights of individuals, whatever their views, and against those who abuse them, whatever theirs.)

In the last thirty years, we have been able to close the files of more than 97% of the cases we had taken up.

No-one can deny that it's an outstanding achievement for a small, chronically underfunded, organisation.

Except that it's not enough.

A million failures.

Among the files we closed was that of Agostinho Neto, the Angolan doctor who was one of Amnesty's first 'prisoners of conscience.'

In 1975, when Angola won its independence from Portugal, Dr Neto became his country's first president.

Sadly, during his Presidency, his government was accused of imprisoning without trial, torturing and unlawfully killing many of its political opponents. How could such things happen under the rule of someone who had himself suffered so much?

Were we naive to imagine we could make a difference? In the last thirty years, things have not got better, but worse.

In 1961 we believed, didn't we, that the world would never tolerate another genocide? Since then we've had Suharto, Pol Pot, Idi Amin and Saddam Hussein.

We've had Emperor Bokassa who stocked his fridge with human heads.

For every prisoner freed, thousands are still in prison. For every person plucked from the torturers, thousands suffer agonies beyond our imagining. For every life saved, hundreds of thousands have been lost.

Between them, Suharto, Pol Pot, Idi Amin and Saddam Hussein have executed and tortured to death more than a million people.

For Amnesty that's a million failures.

All we've done in the last thirty years is bale a few buckets from a sea of human misery.

Should we give up?

So we come to the crucial question. Should we give up?

Please think carefully before you answer. While you make up your mind, here's a poem by Agostinho Neto.

Next door
someone groans
his fingers edged with blood streaming
from nails broken by the palamatoria

He is thinking of victory
and no sleep comes to his prison days
or dreams to fill his solitude

There are minutes when the world
is summed up in the torture chamber
Oh! Who will sleep
when he hears his best friend go mad
there in the next cell
his spirit is killed by torture?

"Who will sleep?" asks Neto. Dare any of us?

Left to themselves, governments will go on imprisoning, torturing and killing, and other governments will go on turning a blind eye.

Until they start respecting human rights there can be little hope of any real political, social or environmental progress.

How can we persuade certain Latin American governments to stop the killing of trees in the rainforest if we can't persuade them to stop the killing of their own street children?

Name a single nation that took positive action when Saddam Hussein gassed 5,000 Kurdish civilians with chemical weapons *three years before* the Gulf War.

War and famine are still, in 1991, devastating the Horn of Africa where, in the past two decades, millions of people have become refugees or have died because of repressive regimes with scant regard for human rights.

So long as such regimes are allowed to rule unchallenged, there will be poverty and disease and famine and war.

Only one power can stop it.

Only one power is strong enough to say to the world's governments 'I will no longer allow this to happen.'

That power brought democracy to Eastern Europe.

That power won women the vote.

Western governments did not lift a finger to save the Kurdish people from slaughter until that power forced them to intervene.

That power is public opinion.

'Pressure of opinion a hundred years ago brought about the emancipation of the slaves. It is now for man to insist upon the same freedom for his mind as he has won for his body.'
(Peter Benenson, The Observer 28th May 1961.)

Think twice before saying to us 'No, don't give up.' You cannot ask us to continue, yet do nothing yourself to help.

The strongest voice on earth belongs to you. Use it. Join us.

Press Advertising

Art Director
MARK ROALFE

Copywriter
ROBERT CAMPBELL

Typographer
JOE HOZA

Agency
ABBOTT MEAD
VICKERS.BBDO
LIMITED

Director of Campaings & PR
GAVIN GRANT

Client
RSPCA

It's not our advertising that should be banned. It's this.

Last November the RSPCA began campaigning for an eight hour limit on the long distance transport of live animals for slaughter.

Long distance animal transport is cruel.

Long distance animal transport is unnecessary.

Yet after 1992, Britain will be forced to comply with European laws that will make the problems of animal transport worse, not better.

You may remember the advertisements we ran as part of the campaign.

One of them featured a pony hanging from a butcher's hook. A symbol of the fate that awaits British ponies after a needlessly cruel journey across Europe.

We were forced to withdraw the advertisement.

We were criticised for being sensationalist.

And this in spite of the fact that in a recent survey* 95% of people asked supported our campaign.

(To date, over 1,000,000 of you have signed our petition demanding an eight hour limit on the transportation of live animals for slaughter.)

We're sorry if a minority found our advertising offensive.

But the conditions in which animals are transported across Europe are far more offensive.

If our critics witnessed what RSPCA inspectors have witnessed, we think they'd agree.

Animals shut in transporters for the entire length of their journey across Europe. That can be for up to 36 hours.

Often they get no food. No water. No rest. No sleep.

By the time they reach the slaughterhouse, many are battered, bruised and bleeding.

Some have broken limbs. Some of them are collapsing from exhaustion. Some of them are dead.

If it were dogs or cats that were suffering such cruelty, there'd be a massive public outcry.

Farm animals feel pain too.

An eight hour limit on the transport of live animals for slaughter would help stop this cruelty.

It would mean animals would not have to suffer these intolerably long journeys.

It would mean that animals would have to be slaughtered much closer to the point of their production.

A far more humane solution.

On the opposite page are pictures taken from a video made by undercover RSPCA inspectors in four separate Spanish slaughterhouses.

The video is now in the hands of the European Commission and forms part of an official complaint.

It shows animals being stabbed repeatedly in the spine until they are paralysed.

The slaughtermen could not be bothered to use humane stunning methods.

It shows electrodes designed to stun painlessly being carelessly applied to a pig.

First the current paralyses the pig, then it causes a series of agonising heart palpitations.

It shows fully conscious horses', cows', pigs', and goats' throats being slit.

Our inspectors said they'd never seen cruelty like it.

At present the British refuse to transport animals to Spanish slaughterhouses like these.

After 1992, European law will oblige us to.

Obviously, we are campaigning to stamp out the illegal practices that our inspectors witnessed in these slaughterhouses.

But until we do so, the eight hour limit will help.

(If animals are prevented from being transported to these distant slaughterhouses, they won't suffer these atrocities when they get there.)

Please, we need your support.

Decisions are about to be made in Europe which will be irreversible.

We must present our case for the eight hour limit now.

If you care about animals phone 0800 400 478, and we'll tell you how you can help.

The long distance transport of live animals for slaughter is cruel and unnecessary.

It, and all the cruelty that is associated with it, should be banned.

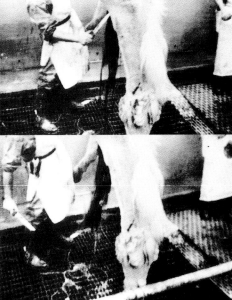

A fully conscious horse's throat is slit at a Spanish slaughterhouse.

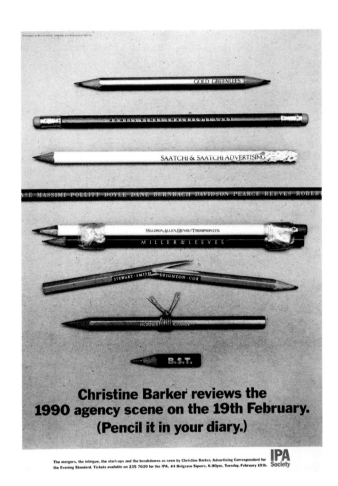

Posters

Art Director
DAVE DYE

Copywriter
MIKE McKENNA

Photographer
MALCOLM VENVILLE

Modelmaker
DAVE DYE

Retoucher
ROGER KENNEDY

Typographer
ANDY DYMOCK

Agency
PUBLICIS

Marketing Director
CHRIS THOMAS

Client
IPA SOCIETY

Posters

Art Director
STEVE CHETHAM

Copywriter
TREVOR BEATTIE

Typographer
RICHARD O'MEARA

Agency
TBWA/HOLMES
KNIGHT RITCHIE

Director of Marketing
JOHN WILKINSON

Client
WORLDWIDE FUND
FOR NATURE

Posters

Art Director
NEIL GODFREY

Copywriter
INDRA SINHA

Photographer
DON McCULLIN

Typographer
JEFF MERRELLS

Agency
COLLETT DICKENSON
PEARCE & PARTNERS
LIMITED

Head of Publicity
JULIAN BRADLEY

Client
METROPOLITAN
POLICE

THEY'VE SAVED OVER THREE HUNDRED WOMEN FROM ABUSE, BEATINGS, HUMILIATION, RAPE AND MURDER.

Could you comfort a teenager who is crying because her husband has kicked her during her eighth month of pregnancy? Or a man whose wife attacked him with a hammer? Police officers Zinnia Shah and Kate Parker and their colleagues in the Met's Domestic Violence Units do it every day.

0800 300 313

MENTAL.

HELP STOP THE INSANITY. CALL WWF'S RAINFOREST HOTLINE, FREE ON 0800 30 40 40.

Film

Directors
STEVE REEVES
PAUL GAY

Copywriter
STEVE REEVES

Art Director
PAUL GAY

Creative Director
TONY COX

Producer
SIMON DIVINE

Editor
ROGER CHERRILL

Lighting Cameramen
PAUL GAY
STEVE REEVES

Production Company
C.O.I.

Agency
BMP DDB NEEDHAM

Marketing Director
KATE POCOCK

Client
HEALTH EDUCATION
AUTHORITY

MRS DAWSON

Mrs Dawson:

Of course, working here we're the first to notice the change in people's behaviour.

We're making more of these things than ever before.

Obviously it's down to AIDS and HIV.

Young people can't afford to take chances these days.

It seems they've got their head screwed on though.

After all I've never been so busy.

GERONIMO

Mr Campbell:

*I just don't know why young
people complain about having to
wear condoms against HIV virus
and AIDS. Look what we had to
put up with.*

I called it Geronimo - my friend.

*Compared with the condoms of
today it was like wearing the inner
tube of a cycle.*

*It wasn't disposable like the
modern condoms. It was designed
to be used again and again.*

*When the action was finished I
used to have to wash it, dry it and
powder it with French chalk, and
put it by for a future lucky day.*

*It was like having a bath with
your socks on.*

But it never stopped me in no way.

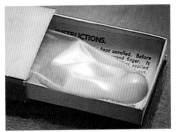

Film

Directors
STEVE REEVES
PAUL GAY

Copywriter
STEVE REEVES

Art Director
PAUL GAY

Creative Director
TONY COX

Producer
ANDREW JONES

Editor
CATHY ALFORD

Lighting Cameraman
RICK STRATTON

Production Company
C.O.I.

Agency
BMP DDB NEEDHAM

Head of Advertising
CHARLES GALLICHAN

Client
HEALTH EDUCATION
AUTHORITY

Film

Directors
ROB SCHAPIRO
TY HARPER

Copywriter
ROB SCHAPIRO

Art Director
TY HARPER

Producer
ROBIN SHERMAN

Editor
DAVID CORMAN

Agency
EARLE PALMER
BROWN/RICHMOND

Marketing Director
SALLY BAKER

Client
NOAH'S FRIENDS

THIS MESSAGE

Music:
Jungle drums (by In Your ear).

SFX:
*Each scene is punctuated with a
primal scream.*

Video:
*Open on a snowshoe rabbit
running in snow.*

*Quick shots of an ermine, a weasel,
a wolf running free and then being
caught in traps, intercut with type:*

*This Message is NOT Brought To
You By The Fur Industry.*

Fade to black screen.

Camera card:
Noah's Friends.

SMOKING BABY

VO:

*Lead, cadmium, cyanide and
carbon monoxide.*

*The blood a pregnant smoker
shares with her baby contains these
plus 2,995 other toxic compounds.*

*So next time you light up,
remember it's not only you who's
smoking.*

For help call the Quitline.
071 487 3000

Film

Director
IAN GILES

Copywriter
MURRAY BLACKET

Art Director
RUTH YEE

Creative Directors
MURRAY BLACKET
RUTH YEE

Producer
FRED ROBINSON

Agency Producer
VICTORIA GARDNER

Editor
JOHN OSBORNE

Lighting Cameraman
IAN GILES

Production Company
ANNEXE FILMS

Communications Director
KARIN
WENTWORTH-PING

Client
QUIT

Film

Director
JEFF BEDNARZ

Copywriter
DAVID MORRING

Art Director
KEVIN FOREMAN

Creative Director
STAN RICHARDS

Producer
DIANE GREENE

Agency Producer
LISA HEARNDON

Editor
MICHAEL
VAN DE KAMMER

Lighting Cameraman
LARRY ROBERTSON

Production Company
BEDNARZ FILM

Agency
THE RICHARDS
GROUP

Information Specialist
DOUG McBRIDE

Client
TEXAS DEPARTMENT
OF HEALTH

DOWNTOWN –
WHAT

Soundtrack:
Rhythmic drums.

Interviewer:
*Excuse me, see that man
over there ?*

Woman:
Yeah.

Interviewer:
You've had sex with him ?

Woman:
What ?

Interviewer:
*Well see, he used to go out
with this girl, Paula.*

Woman:
So.

Interviewer:
*Then Paula moved in with
Brent. Brent started seeing
Cindy. And Cindy later
dated Eric. Eric dated
Shauna. Shauna dated
Vinnie. Vinnie dated
Jeanna. Jeanna dated Greg.
Greg dated Risa. Risa
dated Allen. Allen dated
Debbie. Then Debbie
dated Troy...Troy walker.*

Woman:
You mean, my Troy ?

Announcer:
*Someone you've never even
met could give you the
virus that causes AIDS.*

ANTARTICA

*A group of powerful
international industrialists
play a board game. What
happens in the game
parallels the destruction of
the World's natural
resources.*

*In the end only one
continent remains
untouched - Antartica.*

Super:
*Only one continent on
Earth remains untouched
by man...*

Help us to keep it that way.

*Greenpeace International
trust (logo).*

Film

Director
TONY KAYE

Copywriter
CHRIS PALMER

Art Director
MARK DENTON

Creative Directors
CHRIS PALMER
MARK DENTON

Producer
EUGENIA KAYE

Agency Producer
PAUL FENTON

Editors
PATRICK MOORE
JOHN MALLERMAN

Lighting Cameraman
TONY KAYE

Music Composer/Arranger
JEREMY HEALY

Production Company
TONY KAYE FILMS
LIMITED

Agency
SIMONS PALMER
DENTON CLEMMOW &
JOHNSON LIMITED

Marketing Director
NICK GALLIE

Client
GREENPEACE

Film

Director
BRIAN SMITH

Copywriter
CHRISTOPHER
WILSON

Art Director
SALLY WAGNER

Creative Director
LYLE WEDEMEYER

Producer
ANNE SWARTS

Agency Producer
ANNE SWARTS

Editor
TOM GILMAN

Music Composer/Arranger
TOM LECHER

Production Company
NORTHWEST
TELEPRODUCTIONS

Agency
MARTIN/WILLIAMS
INC

Client
AMERICAN HUMANE
ASSOCIATION

JESSE JAMES

SFX:
From Movie Soundtrack.

Video:
*Open on a slow-motion sequence
from 'Jesse James' movie. Supers
appear over footage as horse
gallops over cliff.*

Super:
*This is from the 1939 western
'Jesse James'.*

The cliff is 70 feet high.

The stunt man lost his hat.

The horse lost his life.

*Nobody's going to pull a stunt like
this again.*

*AMERICAN HUMANE
ASSOCIATION.*

ONLY SON

Close up of a young boy who is lip syncing to an old man's voice.

Young Boy:
When you've been through wars and see your mates falling by your side, it's terrible and a lot of people accuse us at Anzac time of 'oh they're just getting ready for a beer and a get together', but that's nothing to do with when we go to a parade on Anzac Day, our thoughts are with those that are still over there, that didn't come back and having lost a son, only son in the last war, I know what it means to me.

Young Announcer:
Whoever says the R.S.L. is just a group of old soldiers, should think again. Today, more than ever, we're helping victims and their families from all wars. so please, change the way you think about the R.S.L.

And think about supporting us.

End graphic:
THE R.S.L.
WE'RE NOT DEAD YET.

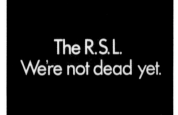 

Film

Director
TERRY BUNTON

Copywriter
SCOTT WHYBIN

Art Director
GRAHAME SMITH

Creative Director
SCOTT WHYBIN

Producer
ANNIE SCHUTT

Agency Producer
AMANDA BERRY

Editor
KRISTINE HURLEY

Lighting Cameraman
GARRY WAPSHOTT

Production Company
BUNTON FILMS

Agency
THE CAMPAIGN
PALACE

Client
R.S.L.

Film

Director
DAVID GARFATH

Copywriter
JOHN DEAN

Art Director
SIMON GREEN

Creative Director
DAVE HORRY

Producer
PAUL ROTHWELL

Agency Producer
JOAN ARNOTT

Editor
SIMON WILLCOX

Lighting Cameraman
ROGER PRATT

Music Composer/Arranger
HOWARD BLAKE

Production Company
PAUL WEILAND FILM
COMPANY

Agency
STILL PRICE COURT
TWIVY
D'SOUZA:LINTAS

Chairman (BPA)
DR ADRIAN WHITESON

Client
BRITISH PARALYMPIC
ASSOCIATION

AGAINST ALL ODDS

Soundtrack:
Rousing and emotional choral piece.

MVO:
Three years ago in Seoul, Great-Britain broke eighteen world records and brought home 182 medals.

This year in Barcelona, we're going to prove once more that our disabilities don't get in the way of our abilities.

BRITISH PARALYMPIC ASSOCIATION

DONATIONS CAN BE MADE
AT YOUR POST OFFICE.

ROYAL MAIL · OFFICIAL SPONSORS TO THE BRITISH PARALYMPIC TEAM.   Barcelona-Madrid 92

adv
-tising cra
30

er

ts

SILVER AWARD
for the most outstanding
Use of Photography
Campaigns

Photographer
NADAV KANDER

Art Director
JOHN DOYLE

Copywriter
ERNIE SCHENCK

Agency
DOYLE ADVERTISING
& DESIGN GROUP

Vice President, Marketing &
Product
MICHAEL COOGAN

Client
THE DUNHAM
COMPANY

There are feet that will never meet the gas pedal of a Range Rover.
There are feet that will never see a condo in Aspen. There are feet that will
never winter in Palm Springs or Palm Beach or Palm anywhere.
Dunham. They get the job done.

There are feet that don't care what a Bentley Turbo is going for these days.
There are feet that could care less what the Nasdaq is doing. There are feet that
wouldn't know an espresso machine if they tripped over one.
Dunham. They get the job done.

There are feet that have never gotten the corner office. There are feet that have never sat through a shareholder's meeting. There are feet that have never had sushi for lunch. There are feet that have never seen the inside of an Italian loafer. Dunham. They get the job done.

SILVER AWARD
for the most outstanding
Copy
Individual

Copywriter
GERARD EDMONDSON

Art Director
DENNIS WILLISON

Photographer
BRUCE FLEMING

Typographer
JEFF MERRELLS

Agency
COLLETT DICKENSON
PEARCE & PARTNERS
LIMITED

General Manager
IAN DICKENS

Client
OLYMPUS

Jeffrey Bernard is unwell.

Jeffrey Bernard is fine.

I used to like my photograph being taken. As a baby I couldn't stop smiling and was a willing target for the Box Brownie.

Now that I am a miserable old man who has lost his looks and has discovered that it takes 120 muscles to make you smile, I have gone off it. I don't like saying cheese and the alternative a showgirl once told me is to have a fixed smile all day long. While she kicked her heels up she kept saying money, pronounced moneee.

But recently I discovered Olympus Cameras and looking through the lens of one of them, I found my friends not to be so ugly as I thought them to be. They suddenly became quite beautiful. I nearly did too.

Known for years as the most bloodshot man on earth, Olympus has cleared my eyes, face and reputation. A miracle of modern science. Physics and optics were never my strong suit but all I know is that when the flash fires, then red-eye has all but vanished. Clever people these Olympic egg heads.

I may be as the title of the play has it "unwell" but I can at last face the birdie. The only trouble is that in my case the birdie is a vulture.

Jeffrey Bernard

OLYMPUS CAMERAS

SILVER AWARD
for the most outstanding
Use of Illustration
Individual

Illustrator
ROBIN
HEIGHWAY-BURY

Art Director
GERARD STAMP

Copywriter
LOZ SIMPSON

Agency
BSB DORLAND

Marketing Director
LAWRENCE BALFE

Client
H J HEINZ COMPANY
LIMITED

SILVER AWARD
for the most outstanding
Use of Illustration
Campaigns

Illustrator
ROBIN
HEIGHWAY-BURY

Art Director
GERARD STAMP

Copywriter
LOZ SIMPSON

Agency
BSB DORLAND

Marketing
LAWRENCE BALFE

Client
H J HEINZ COMPANY
LIMITED

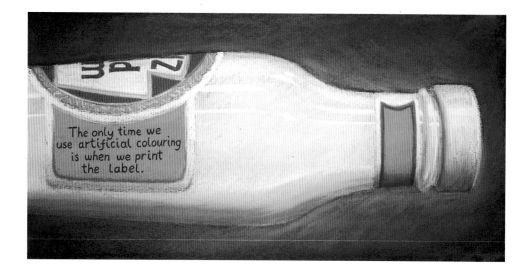

SILVER AWARD
NOMINATION
for the most outstanding
Use of Photography
Campaigns

Photographer
ANDREW
MACPHERSON

Art Director
ANTONY EASTON

Copywriter
ADAM KEAN

Typographer
ROGER KENNEDY

Agency
SAATCHI & SAATCHI

Chairman & Chief Executive
Officer
MICHAEL HARVEY

Head of Marketing
NICK HUTTON

Client
THE HABITAT GROUP

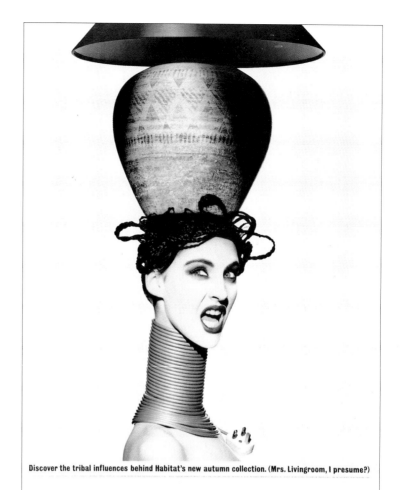

Discover the tribal influences behind Habitat's new autumn collection. (Mrs. Livingroom, I presume?)

We've travelled all over the world for ideas for Habitat's new tribal collection. Drop by if you haven't got too much on your plate.

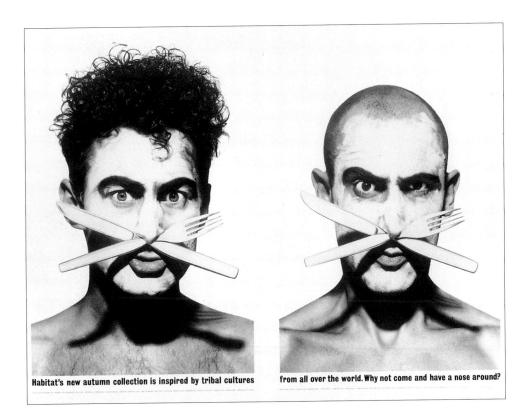

Habitat's new autumn collection is inspired by tribal cultures from all over the world. Why not come and have a nose around?

Best use of
Typography
Individual

Typographer
STEPHEN
WOLSTENHOLME

Design Director
PETER SAVILLE

Designers
PETER SAVILLE
STEPHEN
WOLSTENHOLME

Design Group
PENTAGRAM DESIGN

Head of Public Relations
Tokyo
MADELEINE
FUKAHARA

Head of Public Relations Paris
NATALIE BOURS

Client
YOHJI YAMAMOTO

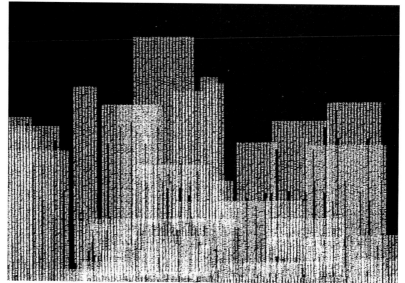

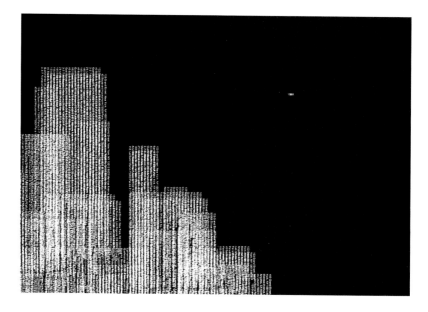

IF YOU'RE
NOT LISTENING
TO KISS FM
YOU OBVIOUSLY
NEED YOUR
EARS
TESTED

Best use of
Typography
Individual

Typographer
GARY TODD

Art Director
WALTER CAMPBELL

Copywriter
TOM CARTY

Agency
ABBOTT MEAD
VICKERS.BBDO
LIMITED

Head of Marketing
MALCOLM COX

Client
KISS 100 FM

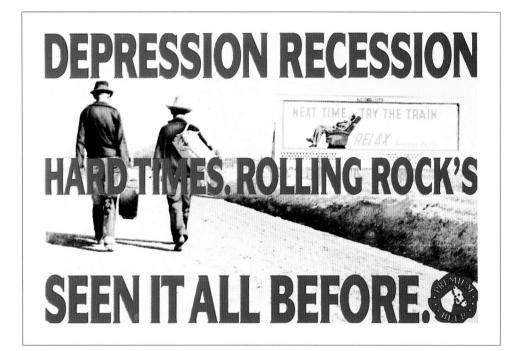

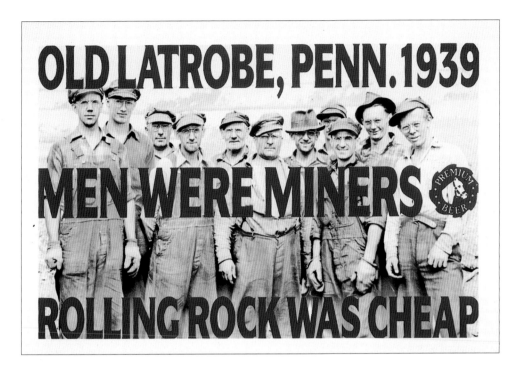

Best use of
Typography
Individual

Typographer
GARY TODD

Art Director
MARK ROALFE

Copywriter
ROBERT CAMPBELL

Agency
ABBOTT MEAD
VICKERS.BBDO
LIMITED

Marketing Director
PHILIP PARKER

Client
LABATT BREWING
UK LIMITED

Best use of
Typography
Individual

Typographer
GARY TODD

Art Director
MARK ROALFE

Copywriter
ROBERT CAMPBELL

Agency
ABBOTT MEAD
VICKERS.BBDO
LIMITED

Marketing Director
PHILIP PARKER

Client
LABATT BREWING
UK LIMITED

Best use of
Typography
Individual

Typographer
ROGER KENNEDY

Art Director
ALEXANDRA TAYLOR

Copywriter
JAMES LOWTHER

Photographer
MICHAEL KENNA

Agency
SAATCHI & SAATCHI

Marketing Director
ROBERT MASON

Client
INTERCITY

It's the early bird that catches the full British breakfast. You can now catch a morning Pullman with full steward service to virtually every main business centre in the country. So, who's for a real power breakfast?

Best use of
Typography
Individual

Typographer
ROGER KENNEDY

Art Director
ALEXANDRA TAYLOR

Copywriter
JAMES LOWTHER

Photographer
MICHAEL KENNA

Agency
SAATCHI & SAATCHI

Marketing Director
ROBERT MASON

Client
INTERCITY

Well. They always said that senior management should take the wider view. When looking at the broader perspective, considering the wider implications and taking the big decisions, don't you need more space?

A fish pond in Lincolnshire as seen from a York to Kings Cross train.

Just what top managers need. Time for reflection.

Sometimes the best thing you can do in business is to find a private place, close the door, gaze out of the window. And think. (Oh, and get to important meetings at up to 125 mph.)

INTERCITY

Best use of
Typography
Individual

Typographer
ROGER KENNEDY

Art Director
ALEXANDRA TAYLOR

Copywriter
JAMES LOWTHER

Photographer
MICHAEL KENNA

Agency
SAATCHI & SAATCHI

Marketing Director
ROBERT MASON

Client
INTERCITY

Flatoutontheoutside.

London 2.55pm you've got to get to Edinburgh in a hurry so you board the new InterCity 225 at Kings Cross and Britain's fastest train races out of the station and the grey of North London becomes the green of Hertfordshire and surely this can't be Peterborough already but yes it is or rather yes it was because you're off again and this is your driver speaking we are now flying at a height of 6 feet above the ground at speeds up to 125 mph and countryside rushes past a blur of green and gold fast forward to York don't blink or you'll miss the historic Minster all aboard and once again you're going flat-out across Yorkshire's hills and dales with no roadworks radar-traps or flashing blue lights to stop you and the cars in the fast lane on a motorway race past you backwards coming soon to a window near you Newcastle phew its a wonder you don't need seat belts on this train and the Northumberland coast is clear and you sprint along beside the sea to picturesque Berwick and one day you decide you'd like to stay here longer but not today and you're in Scotland now don't take the high road or the low road take the railway and you'll be there before anyone because time waits for no man except you travelling on the InterCity 225 it's now three hours fifty nine minutes since you left today this must be a record welcome to Edinburgh.

Laid back on the inside.

London, 2.55pm.

You have to get to Edinburgh, but you want to enjoy travelling there as much as arriving there.

So you board the new InterCity 225 at Kings Cross.

The whistle goes and Britain's most comfortable train glides effortlessly out of the station.

You sink slowly back into your seat (ahh, bliss) and look around.

Outside, the world rushes past at up to 125mph.

Inside, on the other hand, it seems unusually tranquil.

The effect of the soft lighting, muted colours and tinted glass.

Even the electronic doors at either end slide to and fro with a soothing shhhhhh.

What was it you were worrying about just a few minutes ago?

Funny, you can't remember.

Time to wander along to the buffet, perhaps.

Relax, the buffet comes to you, courtesy of a steward with a trolley.

Coffee? Tea? Orange Juice?

Sandwiches? Friendly repartee?

A sense of well-being now begins to fill you and you start to unwind, as if you were starting a holiday.

Cocooned in the comfort of the InterCity 225, you have plenty of something that normally you have precious little of.

Time to yourself and peace and quiet in which to enjoy it.

Here, life seems wonderful indeed.

Peterborough, York, Newcastle and Berwick must have passed by at some point.

Because you arrive at your destination, three hours fifty nine minutes after you left Kings Cross.

For too soon.

Oh, if only you were travelling further than Edinburgh. *INTERCITY*

Best use of
Typography
Individual

Typographer
ROGER KENNEDY

Art Director
MATT RYAN

Copywriter
JOHN PALLANT

Photographer
JIMMY WORMSER

Agency
SAATCHI & SAATCHI

Marketing Director
ROBERT MASON

Client
INTERCITY

Best use of
Typography
Individual

Typographer
LEN CHEESEMAN

Art Director
GRAHAM FINK

Copywriter
TIM MELLORS

Photographer
MONICA CURTIN

Agency
GGT

Managing Director
KEN PIGGOTT

Client
CHILDREN'S WORLD
LIMITED

Best use of
Typography
Individual

Typographer
JOE HOZA

Art Director
JOHN HORTON

Copywriter
RICHARD FOSTER

Agency
ABBOTT MEAD
VICKERS.BBDO
LIMITED

Managing Director
DAVID GORDON

Client
THE ECONOMIST

Warning.
This product can cause
blisters, aching
and shortness of breath.

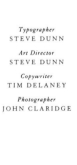

Ordnance Survey.
The most detailed maps in the land.

*Best use of
Typography
Campaigns*

Typographer
STEVE DUNN

Art Director
STEVE DUNN

Copywriter
MIKE LESCARBEAU

Photographer
JOHN CLARIDGE

Agency
LEAGAS DELANEY

Manager of Information
CHARLIE PAYNE

Client
ORDNANCE SURVEY

Typographer
STEVE DUNN

Art Director
STEVE DUNN

Copywriter
TIM DELANEY

Photographer
JOHN CLARIDGE

*Best use of
Typography
Campaigns*

Typographer
LEN CHEESEMAN

Art Director
KATE STANNERS

Copywriter
TIM HEARN

Photographer
JOHN PARKER

Agency
GGT

Marketing Director
ANNE FREEL

Client
M D FOODS UK
LIMITED

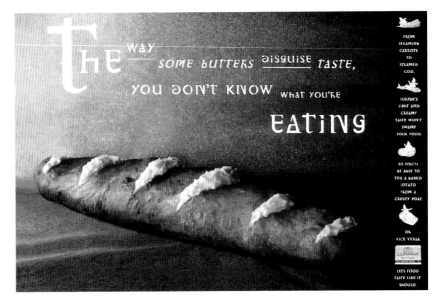

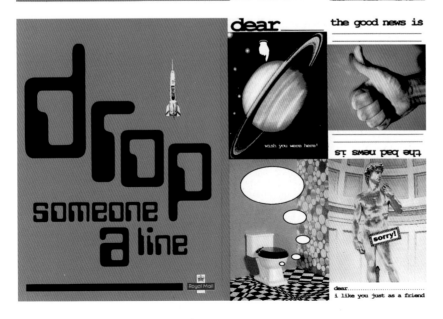

*Best use of
Typography
Campaigns*

Typographer
RICHARD
BONNER-MORGAN

Art Director
DAVE JOHNSON

Copywriter
JONATHAN
KNEEBONE

Photographer
ROBERT
SHACKLETON

Agency
D'ARCY MASIUS
BENTON & BOWLES
LIMITED

Head of Personal Mail
YVETTE TURNER

Client
ROYAL MAIL

Photographer
LEWIS MULATERO

Best use of
Typography
Campaigns

Typographers
KENNETH HODGSON
CAROLE GREGORY

Art Director
KENNETH HODGSON

Copywriters
CHRISTOPHER
HARRALD
KENNETH HODGSON
PAUL HEINEY

Agency
ARC ADVERTISING

Promotions Director
ANDREW KITCHING

Client
NEWS
INTERNATIONAL

Oooh-arrr!

Paul Heiney. Every Saturday in the Weekend Times.

THE TIMES
KEEP OUR WITS ABOUT YOU

Typographers
KENNETH HODGSON
CAROLE GREGORY

Copywriters
CHRISTOPHER
HARRALD
KENNETH HODGSON
LYNNE TRUSS

Zap!

Lynne Truss. Every Saturday.

THE TIMES
KEEP OUR WITS ABOUT YOU

Typographers
KENNETH HODGSON
CAROLE GREGORY

Copywriters
CHRISTOPHER
HARRALD
KENNETH HODGSON
JONATHAN MEADES

Gulp!

Jonathan Meades. Every Saturday.

THE TIMES
KEEP OUR WITS ABOUT YOU

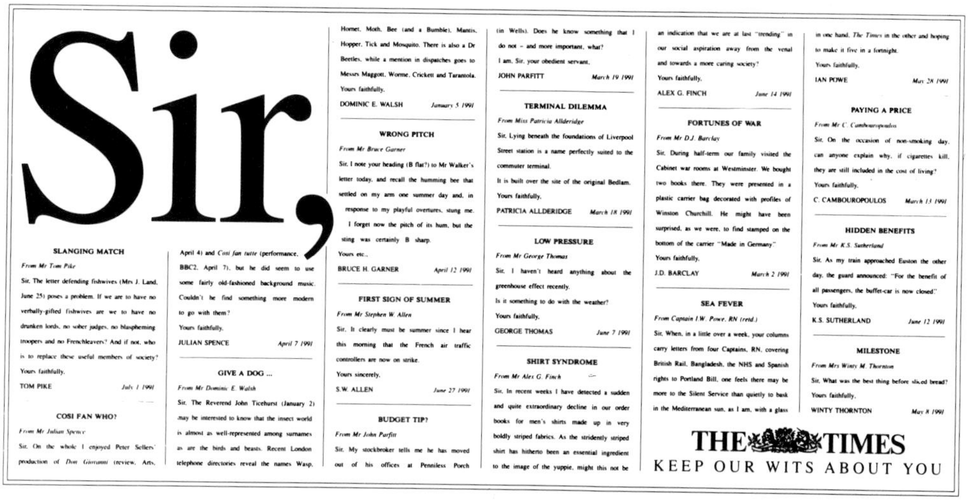

Sir,

THE TIMES

KEEP OUR WITS ABOUT YOU

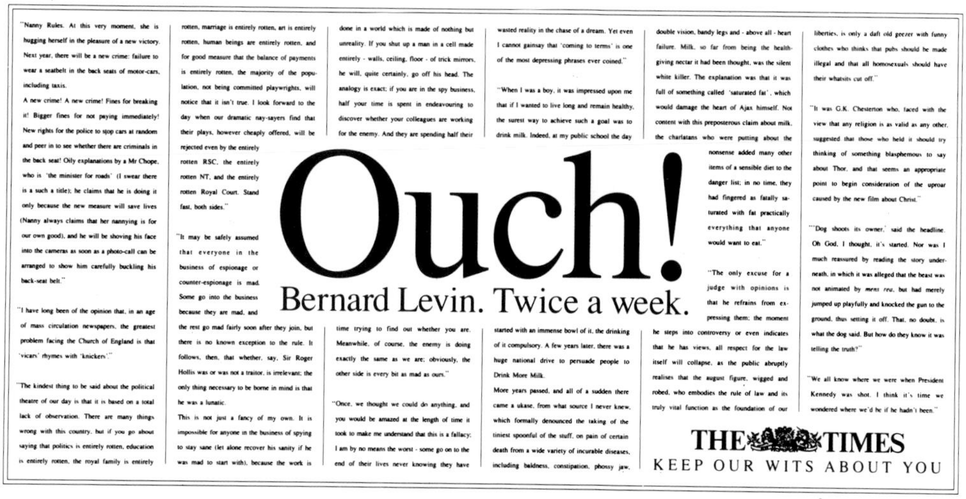

Ouch!

Bernard Levin. Twice a week.

THE TIMES

KEEP OUR WITS ABOUT YOU

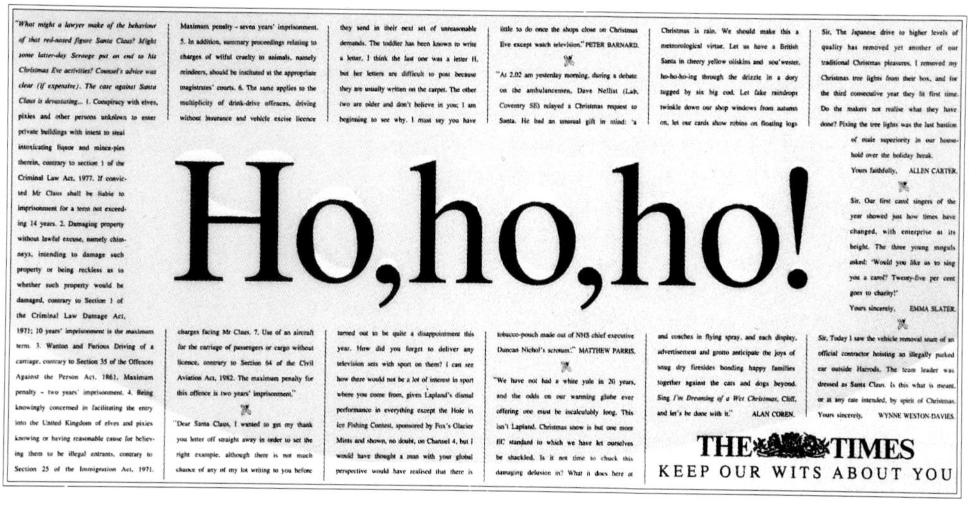

Ho, ho, ho!

THE TIMES

KEEP OUR WITS ABOUT YOU

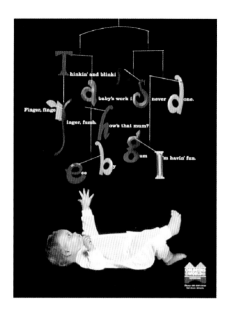

Best use of
Typography
Campaigns

Typographer
LEN CHEESEMAN

Art Director
GRAHAM FINK

Copywriter
TIM MELLORS

Photographer
MONICA CURTIN

Agency
G G T

Managing Director
KEN PIGGOTT

Client
CHILDREN'S WORLD
LIMITED

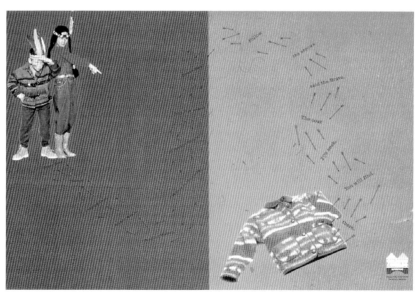

*Best use of
Typography
Campaigns*

Typographer
MATTHEW
KEMSLEY

Art Director
ROONEY CARRUTHERS

Copywriter
LARRY BAKER

Photographer
JEAN LOUP SIEFF

Agency
BARTLE BOGLE
HEGARTY

Marketing Director
SIMON ESBERGER

Client
HAAGEN DAZS UK
LIMITED

It is the

intense

flavour of
the finest ingredients
combined with

fresh

cream that is
essentially Häagen-Dazs.

Dedicated to Pleasure

Ripe Oregon strawberries are
especially selected as we

feel
it

best complements the rich cream
flavour of Häagen-Dazs.

Dedicated to Pleasure

*Best use of
Typography
Campaigns*

Typographer
GARY TODD

Art Director
MARK ROALFE

Copywriter
ROBERT CAMPBELL

Agency
ABBOTT MEAD
VICKERS.BBDO
LIMITED

Marketing Director
PHILIP PARKER

Client
LABATT BREWING
UK LIMITED

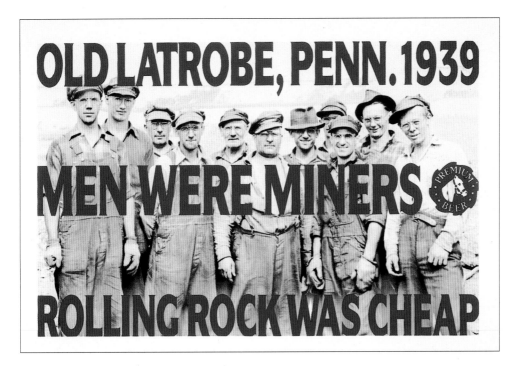

Best use of
Typography
Campaigns

Typographer
ROGER KENNEDY

Art Director
ALEXANDRA TAYLOR

Copywriter
JAMES LOWTHER

Photographer
MICHAEL KENNA

Agency
SAATCHI & SAATCHI

Marketing Director
ROBERT MASON

Client
INTERCITY

A windmill in Warwickshire, as seen from a Southampton to Birmingham train.

Business is ninety per cent perspiration and ten per cent inspiration. (Here's our ten per cent). You can really get your head down and work on a train. But it could be when you lift it up that you'll really see the light.

INTERCITY

A river in Buckinghamshire, as seen from a Birmingham to Euston train.

With some peace and qui t, you'll ave less rouble concentrating on your ork. If you've a report to write, the extra comfort, privacy and tranquillity you get in First Class is not a luxury. It's a necessity.

INTERCITY

Line of sheep as seen from a Cardiff to Paddington train.

They look rather like the traffic on the M4, don't they? Who are the better businessmen? Those who race to meetings by train at 100 mph or those who sit nose to tail on the M4? (Clue: ever known a sheep to make it to chairman?)

INTERCITY

Morning sun as seen from a Liverpool to Euston train.

It's the early bird that catches the full British breakfast. You can now catch a morning Pullman with full steward service to virtually every main business centre in the country. So, who's for a real power breakfast?

INTERCITY

A fish pond in Lincolnshire as seen from a York to Kings Cross train.

Just what top managers need. Time for reflection. Sometimes the best thing you can do in business is to find a private place, close the door, gaze out of the window. And think. (Oh, and get to important meetings at up to 125 mph.)

INTERCITY

A Cumbrian field as seen from a Carlisle to Euston train.

Health farm for stressed businessmen. (First Class accommodation available daily.) Let our wide seats and wide views slow the pulse, quicken the brain, exercise the grey matter, tone up the strategies and fight the flabby thinking.

INTERCITY

A view as seen from a Pullman carriage of an Edinburgh to Kings Cross train.

Announcing the most luxurious way to get to London. (Offer only lasts 3 hours, 59 minutes). Hot towels, breakfast on white china, attentive stewards. Enjoy every single minute of your Pullman journey; there are so few of them.

INTERCITY

A Lake District farmhouse as seen from a Penrith to Euston train.

Well. They always said that senior management should take the wider view. When looking at the broader perspective, considering the wider implications and taking the big decisions, don't you need more space?

INTERCITY

Discover the tribal influences behind Habitat's new autumn collection. (Mrs. Livingroom, I presume?)

John Cleese: Cardmember since 1971

Membership Has Its Privileges
Call (800) *66-*** to apply

There are feet that will never meet the gas pedal of a Range Rover. There are feet that will never see a condo in Aspen. There are feet that will never winter in Palm Springs or Palm Beach or Palm anywhere. Dunham. They get the job done.

Best use of Photography Individual

Photographer
NADAV KANDER

Art Director
JOHN DOYLE

Copywriter
ERNIE SCHENCK

Agency
DOYLE ADVERTISING & DESIGN GROUP

Vice President, Marketing & Product
MICHAEL COOGAN

Client
THE DUNHAM COMPANY

It's surprising what you can see when you look through the right camera.

THE NEW NIKON F-401x.
BECAUSE IT'S TIME YOU TOOK
PHOTOGRAPHS SERIOUSLY.

Nikon

Best use of Photography Individual

Photographer
LEE TREWITT

Art Director
BRIAN STEWART

Copywriter
GREG DELANEY

Typographers
BRIAN STEWART
CHRIS DEVONALD

Agency
DELANEY FLETCHER
SLAYMAKER
DELANEY & BOZELL

Marketing Director
SIMON COLEMAN

Client
NIKON UK LIMITED

Best use of
Photography
Individual

Photographer
TIM O'SULLIVAN

Art Director
ANDY McKAY

Copywriter
TIM RILEY

Typographer
PAUL BEER

Agency
SIMONS PALMER
DENTON CLEMMOW &
JOHNSON LIMITED

Marketing Director
JOHNNY TRAINOR

Client
NIKE INC

Best use of
Photography
Individual

Photographer
PETER LAVERY

Art Directors
ALEXANDRA TAYLOR
NIK STUDZINSKI

Copywriter
JASON FRETWELL

Typographer
ANDY DYMOCK

Agency
SAATCHI & SAATCHI

Marketing Director
PAUL WIELGUS

Client
ALLIED BREWERIES
BRANDS MARKETING

Best use of
Photography
Individual

Photographer
MICHAEL KENNA

Art Director
ALEXANDRA TAYLOR

Copywriter
JAMES LOWTHER

Typographer
ROGER KENNEDY

Agency
SAATCHI & SAATCHI

Marketing Director
ROBERT MASON

Client
INTERCITY

Best use of
Photography
Individual

Photographer
NADAV KANDER

Art Director
NIGEL ROSE

Agency
COLLETT DICKENSON
PEARCE & PARTNERS
LIMITED

Marketing Manager
DEREK STOTHARD

Client
GALLAHER LIMITED

Best use of
Photography
Individual

Photographer
MALCOLM VENVILLE

Art Directors
MARK DENTON
ANDY McKAY

Copywriter
CHRIS PALMER

Agency
SIMONS PALMER
DENTON CLEMMOW &
JOHNSON LIMITED

Managing Director
FRANK DIMECH

Client
WRANGLER UK
LIMITED

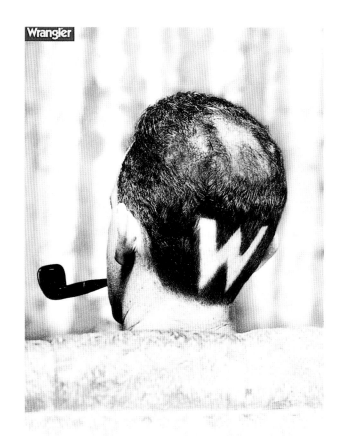

Best use of
Photography
Individual

Photographer
JOHN CLARIDGE

Art Director
DAVID MAY

Copywriter
JASPER SHELBORNE

Typographer
JOANNE CHEVLIN

Agency
J WALTER
THOMPSON

Marketing Director
NIALL O'KEEFFE

Client
GALLAHER LIMITED

*Best use of
Photography
Individual*

Photographer
ELLIOT ERWITT

Art Director
WARREN BROWN

Copywriter
JOHN McCABE

Typographer
WARREN BROWN

Agency
BARTLE BOGLE
HEGARTY

Marketing Director
ANDREW KNIBBS

Client
LEVI STRAUSS UK
LIMITED

*Best use of
Photography
Individual*

Photographer
ELLIOT ERWITT

Art Director
WARREN BROWN

Copywriter
JOHN McCABE

Typographer
WARREN BROWN

Agency
BARTLE BOGLE
HEGARTY

Marketing Director
ANDREW KNIBBS

Client
LEVI STRAUSS UK
LIMITED

Best use of
Photography
Individual

Photographer
BRUCE WEBER

Photographer Pack Shot
GRAHAM FORD

Art Directors
ROGER PEARCE
BILL GALLACHER

Copywriters
RICHARD MYERS
MICK PETHERICK

Typographer
ANDY DYMOCK

Agency
SAATCHI & SAATCHI

General Manager
ROBERT WILSON

Client
SEIKO EUROPE
LIMITED

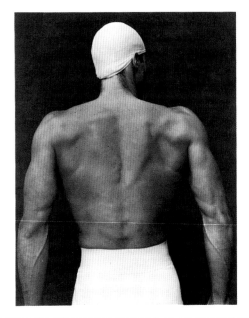

He's spent 21 years 3 months
and 2 days getting here.

But all that matters is the next
48.62 seconds.

SEIKO

Best use of
Photography
Individual

Photographer
JEAN LOUP SIEFF

Art Director
ROONEY CARRUTHERS

Copywriter
LARRY BARKER

Typographer
MATTHEW KEMSLEY

Agency
BARTLE BOGLE
HEGARTY

Marketing Director
SIMON ESBERGER

Client
HAAGEN DAZS UK
LIMITED

It is the

intense

flavour of
the finest ingredients
combined with

fresh

cream that is
essentially Haagen-Dazs

Häagen-Dazs

Dedicated to Pleasure

"Within two or three minutes we have spent £7.00 and have not yet bought our parmesan or gruyère for grating on to the delicate little *ravioles* we have bought from the goat cheese lady. They are tiny, these *ravioles*, filled with a mixture of parsley and comté, the gruyère-like cheese of Franche Comté. They take *one minute* to cook, warns the lady."

From an interesting book called AN OMELETTE AND A GLASS OF WINE. From an interesting bookshop called WATERSTONE'S.

INSTEAD OF A COAT OF PAINT, WE GIVE IT A SUIT OF ARMOUR.

THE VOLVO 440.

It's the early bird that catches the full British breakfast. You can now catch a morning Pullman with full steward service to virtually every main business centre in the country. So, who's for a real power breakfast?

Best use of
Photography
Individual

Photographer
SEBASTIAO SALGADO

Art Director
ANTONY EASTON

Copywriter
ADAM KEAN

Typographer
ANDY DYMOCK

Agency
SAATCHI & SAATCHI

Managing Director
STEPHEN MARFLEET

Client
LE CREUSET
KITCHENWARE
MERCHANTS
LIMITED

Best use of
Photography
Individual

Photographer
NADAV KANDER

Art Director
JOHN DOYLE

Copywriter
ERNIE SCHENCK

Agency
DOYLE ADVERTISING
& DESIGN GROUP

Vice President, Marketing &
Product
MICHAEL COOGAN

Client
THE DUNHAM
COMPANY

Best use of
Photography
Individual

Photographer
DANIEL JOUANNEAU

Art Director
STEVE DUNN

Copywriter
TIM DELANEY

Typographer
STEVE DUNN

Agency
LEAGAS DELANEY

Advertising & Marketing
Manager
ANDREW WILES

Client
HARRODS LIMITED

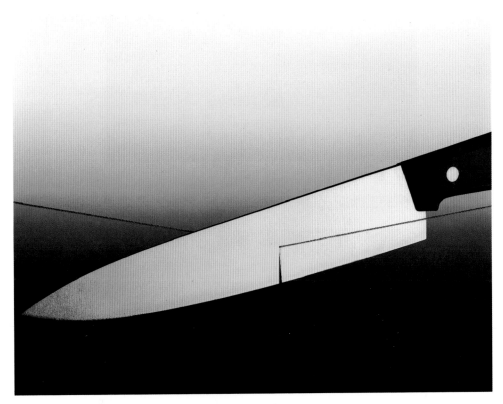

Best use of
Photography
Individual

Photographer
MIKE PARSONS

Art Director
COLIN JONES

Copywriter
NEIL PAVITT

Modelmaker
GAVIN LINDSAY

Agency
SAATCHI & SAATCHI

Marketing Manager
IAN CALLOW

Client
GALLAHER LIMITED

Best use of
Photography
Individual

Photographer
NADAV KANDER

Art Director
JOHN DOYLE

Copywriter
ERNIE SCHENCK

Agency
DOYLE ADVERTISING
& DESIGN GROUP

Vice President, Marketing &
Product
MICHAEL COOGAN

Client
THE DUNHAM
COMPANY

Best use of
Photography
Campaigns

Photographer
DENIS WAUGH

Art Director
JOHN CONNOLLY

Copywriter
SIMON RODWAY

Agency
MACALISTER &
COMPANY

Client
SHELL
INTERNATIONAL
CHEMICAL COMPANY
LIMITED

*Best use of
Photography
Campaigns*

Photographer
DAVID TACK

Art Director
GUY MOORE

Copywriter
TONY MALCOLM

Typographer
MARK OSBORNE

Agency
STILL PRICE COURT
TWIVY
D'SOUZA:LINTAS

Editor
JOHN BIRD

Client
THE BIG ISSUE

Best use of
Photography
Campaigns

Photographer
BRUCE WEBER

Photographer Pack Shot
GRAHAM FORD

Art Directors
BILL GALLACHER
ROGER PEARCE

Copywriters
RICHARD MYERS
MICK PETHERICK

Typographer
ANDY DYMOCK

Agency
SAATCHI & SAATCHI

General Manager
ROBERT WILSON

Client
SEIKO EUROPE
LIMITED

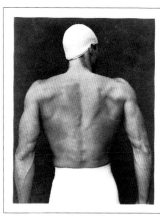

He's spent 21 years 3 months
and 2 days getting here.

But all that matters is the next
48.62 seconds.

1.05 seconds faster,
and he's back in the team.

Anything less,
and he's back on the bench.

3 minutes 46.7 seconds will
break the record.

3 minutes 47.1 seconds will
break his heart.

You have
exactly 5 minutes to win.

Or a lifetime
to forget if you don't.

*Best use of
Photography
Campaigns*

Photographer
KEN GRIFFITHS

Art Directors
RUPERT STUBBS
FERGUS FLEMING

Copywriter
TOM WNEK

Typographer
OLAF LUINBERG

Agency
SAATCHI & SAATCHI

General Manager
PATRICK BOWDEN

Client
VISA
INTERNATIONAL

Best use of
Photography
Campaigns

Photographer
MICHAEL KENNA

Art Director
ALEXANDRA TAYLOR

Copywriter
JAMES LOWTHER

Typographer
ROGER KENNEDY

Agency
SAATCHI & SAATCHI

Marketing Director
ROBERT MASON

Client
INTERCITY

A windmill in Warwickshire, as seen from a Southampton to Birmingham train.

Business is ninety per cent perspiration and ten per cent inspiration. (Here's our ten per cent). You can really get your head down and work on a train. But it could be when you lift it up that you'll really see the light.

INTERCITY

A river in Buckinghamshire, as seen from a Birmingham to Euston train.

With some peace and qui t, you'll ave less rouble concentrating on your ork. If you've a report to write, the extra comfort, privacy and tranquillity you get in First Class is not a luxury. It's a necessity.

INTERCITY

Line of sheep as seen from a Cardiff to Paddington train.

They look rather like the traffic on the M4, don't they? Who are the better businessmen? Those who race to meetings by train at 100 mph or those who sit nose to tail on the M4? (Clue: ever known a sheep to make it to chairman?)

INTERCITY

Morning sun as seen from a Liverpool to Euston train.

It's the early bird that catches the full British breakfast. You can now catch a morning Pullman with full steward service to virtually every main business centre in the country. So, who's for a real power breakfast?

INTERCITY

A fish pond in Lincolnshire as seen from a York to Kings Cross train.

Just what top managers need. Time for reflection.

Sometimes the best thing you can do in business is to find a private place, close the door, gaze out of the window. And think. (Oh, and get to important meetings at up to 125 mph.)

INTERCITY

A Cumbrian field as seen from a Carlisle to Euston train.

Health farm for stressed businessmen. (First Class accommodation available daily.)

Let our wide seats and wide views slow the pulse, quicken the brain, exercise the grey matter, tone up the strategies and fight the flabby thinking.

INTERCITY

A view as seen from a Pullman carriage of an Edinburgh to Kings Cross train.

Announcing the most luxurious way to get to London. (Offer only lasts 3 hours, 59 minutes).

Hot towels, breakfast on white china, attentive stewards. Enjoy every single minute of your Pullman journey; there are so few of them.

INTERCITY

A Lake District farmhouse as seen from a Penrith to Euston train.

Well. They always said that senior management should take the wider view.

When looking at the broader perspective, considering the wider implications and taking the big decisions, don't you need more space?

INTERCITY

*Best use of
Photography
Campaigns*

Photographer
ELLIOT ERWITT

Art Director
WARREN BROWN

Copywriter
JOHN McCABE

Typographer
WARREN BROWN

Agency
BARTLE BOGLE
HEGARTY

Marketing Director
ANDREW KNIBBS

Client
LEVI STRAUSS UK
LIMITED

Photographer
GEORGIA BRAUER

Best use of
Photography
Campaigns

Photographer
PETER LAVERY

Art Directors (Tree)
ALEXANDRA TAYLOR
NIK STUDZINSKI

Art Directors (Croc)
PETER GIBB
ZELDA MALAN

Copywriter (Tree)
JASON FRETWELL

Copywriter (Croc)
PETER BARRY

Typographer
ANDY DYMOCK

Agency
SAATCHI & SAATCHI

Marketing Manager
PAUL WIELGUS

Client
ALLIED BREWERIES
BRANDS MARKETING

Photographer
PETER LAVERY

Art Director
ALEXANDRA TAYLOR

Copywriters
ALAN THOMPSON
RACHEL
HEATHERFIELD

Typographer
ANDY DYMOCK

Best use of
Photography
Campaigns

Photographer
GRAHAM
CORNTHWAITE

Art Director
ROB OLIVER

Copywriter
PETER RUSSELL

Typographers
JOE HOZA
GARY TODD

Agency
ABBOTT MEAD
VICKERS.BBDO
LIMITED

Retail Marketing Manager
EMMA DINWOODIE

Client
WATERSTONE &
COMPANY

“Alphabets begin in pictographs, and, though words are spoken things, to write and read we must see. The line between picture and symbol is a fine one. In the days of mass illiteracy, imagery – hung on cathedral walls, scattered in woodcuts – was the chief non-oral narrative means. Most paintings 'tell a story,' and even departures from representation carry a literary residue.”

From a volume of art appreciation called JUST LOOKING. *From a centre of literary appreciation called* WATERSTONE'S.

"Within two or three minutes we have spent £7.00 and have not yet bought our parmesan or gruyere for grating on to the delicate little *raviolis* we have bought from the goat cheese lady. They are tiny, cheese *raviolis*, filled with a mixture of parsley and cumin, the gruyere-like cheese of Franche Comté. They take *one* minute to cook, warns the lady."

From an entertaining book called AN OMELETTE AND A GLASS OF WINE. From an entertaining bookshop called WATERSTONE'S

"When Belinda returned we climbed the stands to watch the race and to everyone's blank surprise number eight came in first. The stunned crowd received the no-hopers victory in silence, and Belinda stopped Ken's wide grin in its tracks by announcing a shade defiantly that she hadn't put his fiver on eight but on the favourite instead. People have been divorced for less. Ken said, just about managing civility."

From a similar book called COMPLEX. From a thrilling bookshop called WATERSTONE'S

"With cities, it is as with dreams: everything imaginable can be dreamed, but even the most unexpected dream is a rebus that conceals a desire or, its reverse, a fear. Cities, like dreams, are made of desires and fears, even if the thread of their discourse is secret, their rules are absurd, their perspectives deceitful, and everything conceals something else."

From an extraordinary book by Italo Calvino called INVISIBLE CITIES. From an extraordinary bookshop called WATERSTONE'S

"They sit without speaking, looking straight ahead. They've said it all before, they've seen it all before. They're content.

They sit without moving: Ozymandias and Sphinx.

He says something! - and she answers, smiling, and taps him flirtatiously on the arm: Daphnis and Chloe: with Edinburgh accents."

From a wonderful new edition of SOMETHING WONDERFUL. From a wonderful bookshop called WATERSTONE'S

"It was on a morning of May that Peter Featherstone was buried. In the prosaic neighbourhood of Middlemarch, May was not always warm and sunny, and on this particular morning a chill wind was blowing the blossoms from the surrounding gardens on to the green mounds of Lowick churchyard. Swiftly-moving clouds only now and then allowed a gleam to light up any object, whether ugly or beautiful, that happened to stand within its golden shower.**"**

"I wonder if you could settle a few things for me.' 'Of course, Bey.' 'I've been a bit extravagant at the tailor. Three or four suits. Four pairs of shoes at Lobb's. And there's the poor old Bentley! She had to have a new radiator.' 'I'll see what I can do,' I said. I went to the tailor and asked for the Bey's bill. I went to Lobb. I discovered from Jack Barclay the cost of the radiator. The Bey's prices were never extortionate; but, in the best Oriental tradition, we always had a haggle at the end. Otherwise, the deal would not be a deal.**"**

"This is the city in which the young Dickens worked and lived. There were no restaurants then, but taverns and chop-houses. There were eating houses with beefsteak plates and eggs-and-bacon plates, penny bread and penny potatoes. There were no railways and urban sanitation did not exist. Water was expensive to buy, as were clothes and newspapers; there were no holidays for working people; but the city had not yet become a prey to that wild and violent energy which now seems so characteristic of the Victorian period.**"**

"My favourite customers, welcome!' Madame Koto said, in a voice of such extreme unctuousness that I turned to her, surprised. Her face glistened. She rubbed her palms together. The two men sat. The people outside came in, bringing their thick perfume smells, their crackling lace, their clinking bangles and trinkets and strange jewellery, and the smell of new money. 'More light!' cried one of the men. 'And plenty of your best palm-wine!' said another.**"**

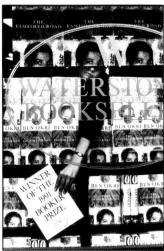

When the bill arrives, it's advisable to have a nurse on hand.

Is there a doctor in the public house?

For those who unwittingly order large rounds of Stella Artois, such first aid may well be required.

In case you needed reminding, brewing our lager is a somewhat expensive affair.

If you knew what we spend on barley alone, you'd turn pale at the thought.

The money we lavish on Czech female hops (the costlier of the species) is enough to bring on feelings of faintness.

While the sheer extravagance of allowing our lager to mature for weeks on end could give one a seizure.

Fortunately, any symptoms will subside as soon as the clothing around the neck is loosened and the Stella is administered to the throat area.

However, if thirst persists, it may be necessary to consult a specialist: your accountant.

Reassuringly expensive.

Best Copy
Individual

Copywriter
PAUL HODGKINSON

Art Director
KEVIN JONES

Photographer
JOHN PARKER

Typographer
SIMON WARDEN

Agency
LOWE HOWARD-SPINK

Marketing Director
STEVE PHILPOTT

Client
THE WHITBREAD
BEER COMPANY

A spirited testimonial for Gore-Tex® fabric.
From a man who came back from the dead.

"I am alive! I am alive!" yelled the ghostlike figure rising to its feet.

Moments later, Keizo Funatsu of Osaka, Japan was safely back in the arms of his tearful colleagues.

Just 16 miles from the finish, the 1990 International Trans-Antarctic Expedition had nearly ended in disaster.

At 4.30pm the previous afternoon (13½ hours earlier), Keizo had walked out in a blinding snowstorm to check on his dogs.

Losing his way between ski markers, he was disorientated in the raging whiteout.

A skilled survivor, Keizo knew instinctively that there was only one way to stay alive. He must bury himself.

Scraping a shallow trench with pliers, the only tool he had, he curled up in it like a sled dog allowing the swirling snow to cover him and act as a insulating blanket.

At 6pm, they knew he was gone. Clenching a rope tied to a sled to help them find their way, the men circled slowly, shouting his name into the blizzard "Keizo! - Keizo! - Keizo!"

Hampered by darkness, storm and a temperature of -29°C, the team with understandable reluctance, postponed its search at 10.30pm.

Seven and a half hours would pass before Keizo, without hurt or frostbite, could rejoin the land of the living.

His own words tell it best. "Finally, I heard the voice outside the ditch and I knew they were close to me...I was very happy to see my friends...everybody had watering eyes, crying and wet. I cried, yes I cried too."

A happy ending. But the hole which he had frantically dug to survive could so easily have been his frozen tomb.

He owes his life to his team-mates. To the fact that he kept his head and waisted.

And to the fact that he, like the others, was protected head to toe from aching cold in GORE-TEX fabric.

In temperatures of 54° below and winds of 90mph.

'All well and good,' you may say. 'But what has a lost Antarctic explorer got to do with me?'

Simple. The same miraculous fabric will protect you outdoors in Britain.

Waterproof and windproof, yet breathable at the same time, it keeps you dry from the elements and dry when you perspire.

Thanks to billions of pores per square inch that prevent water getting through while allowing your body's moisture to escape.

Faced with 6 million ski strides, GORE-TEX fabric wasn't only the first choice in Antarctica, it was the only choice.

It's available in the best leisure and sportswear by such famous and respected names as Berghaus, Mulberry, Musto, The North Face, John Partridge, Phoenix, Pringle, Pro Quip, Sprayway, Sunderland and Timberland. Durable garments which, in most cases, can also easily be washed. (A miracle in itself.)

And the guarantee is as remarkable as the fabric.

All GORE-TEX fabric garments are 'Guaranteed To Keep You Dry' for 3 years. (In the UK or Antarctica.)

So look for the 'Guaranteed To Keep You Dry' diamond when you shop. It's your promise that the complete garment - and not just the fabric - is 100% waterproof.

Ring free on 0800 838527 and we will send you a colour brochure featuring a wide range of clothing made with waterproof, windproof and breathable GORE-TEX fabric.

But inevitably, the final word must surely go to Keizo Funatsu, living proof that it works like we say.

Who simply said with gusto "GORE-TEX fabric saved my life?"

GORE-TEX fabrics
Guaranteed to keep you dry.

Best Copy
Individual

Copywriter
DAVID HARRISON

Art Directors
IAN BANNER
STEPHEN JOHNSON

Photographer
ROBERT WALKER

Typographer
AMANDA BANNER

Agency
BARRINGTON
JOHNSON LORAINS &
PARTNERS LIMITED

Marketing Director
MIKE GRAY

Client
W L GORE &
ASSOCIATES

Best Copy
Individual

Copywriter
SCOTT SHEINBERG

Art Director
BART CLEVELAND

Agency
HENDERSON
ADVERTISING

Senior Director of Marketing
KEVIN MILLER

Client
CHARTER MEDICAL
CORPORATION

It's in here. And it's no smaller than a tumor that's found in a real breast. The difference is, while searching for it in this ad could almost be considered fun and games, discovering the real thing could be a matter of life and death. Breast cancer is one of the most common forms of cancer to strike women. And, if detected at an early enough stage, it's also one of the most curable. That's why the American Cancer Society recommends that women over forty have a mammogram at least every other year, and women under forty have a baseline mammogram between the ages of 35 to 39. You see, a mammogram can discover a tumor or a cyst up to three years before you'd ever feel a lump. In fact, it can detect a tumor or a cyst no bigger than a pinhead. Which, incidentally, is about the size of what you are searching for on this page. At Charter Regional in Cleveland, you can have a mammogram performed for just $101. Your mammogram will be conducted in private, and your results will be held in complete confidence and sent directly to your doctor. After your mammogram, a trained radiology technician will meet with you individually and show you how to perform a breast self-examination at home. And, we'll provide you with a free sensor pad, a new exam tool that can amplify the feeling of anything underneath your breast. Something even as small as a grain of salt. If you would like to schedule a mammogram, just call Charter's Call for Health at 593-1210 or 1-800-537-8184. Oh, and by the way, if you haven't found the lump by now, chances are, you're not going to. It was in the 17th line. The period at the end of the sentence was slightly larger than the others. So think about it, if you couldn't find it with your eyes, imagine how hard it would be to find it with your hands.

CAN YOU FIND THE LUMP IN THIS BREAST?

CHARTER REGIONAL MEDICAL CENTER

CALL FOR HEALTH

5 9 3 • 1 2 1 0

Ouch!

Bernard Levin. Twice a week.

THE TIMES

KEEP OUR WITS ABOUT YOU

Best Copy
Individual

Copywriters
BERNARD LEVIN
CHRISTOPHER
HARRALD
KENNETH HODGSON

Art Director
KENNETH HODGSON

Typographers
KENNETH HODGSON
ALISON BERNARDINI

Agency
ARC ADVERTISING

Promotions Director
ANDREW KITCHING

Client
NEWS
INTERNATIONAL

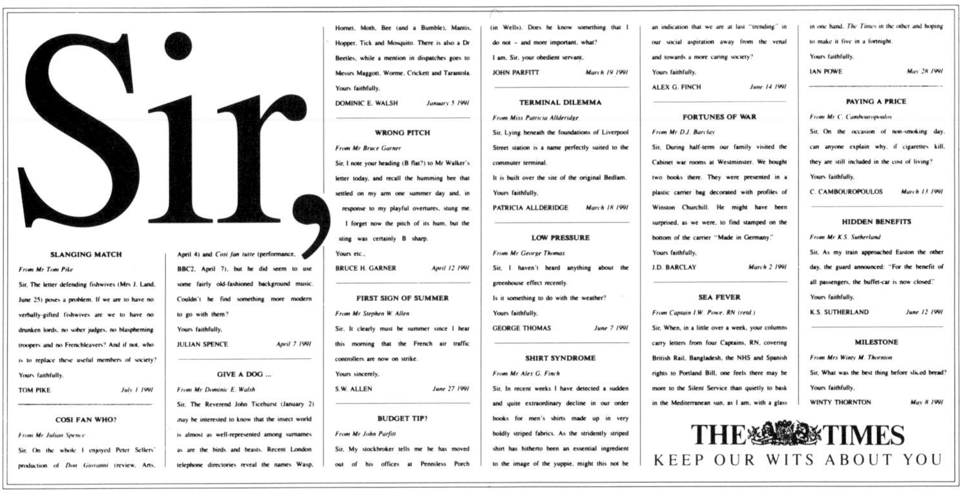

Sir,

THE TIMES

KEEP OUR WITS ABOUT YOU

Best Copy
Individual

Copywriters
CHRISTOPHER
HARRALD
KENNETH HODGSON
TOM PIKE
JULIAN SPENCE
DOMINIC WALSH
BRUCE GARNER
S W ALLEN
JOHN PARFITT
PATRICIA
ALLDERIDGE
GEORGE THOMAS
ALEX FINCH
J D BARCLAY
IAN POWE
C CAMBOUR OPOULOS
K S SUTHERLAND
WINTY THORNTON

Art Director
KENNETH HODGSON

Typographer
KENNETH HODGSON

Agency
ARC ADVERTISING

Promotions Director
ANDREW KITCHING

Client
NEWS
INTERNATIONAL

Best Copy
Individual

Copywriter
TIM DELANEY

Art Director
STEVE DUNN

Photographer
JOHN CLARIDGE

Typographer
JEFF LEWIS

Agency
LEAGAS DELANEY

European Marketing Director
VINCENT DESSAIN

Client
TIMBERLAND

THE LESSONS OF KOREA, VIETNAM AND CAMBODIA HAVE FINALLY COME HOME TO AMERICA.

When American foot soldiers returned home from the wars in South East Asia, they probably had more on their minds than the performance of the boots on their feet.

Yet, putting moral issues aside, there were some important questions that needed to be answered regarding their footwear.

How did the standard issue army boot stand up in the field? Did the leather crack under the pressure of constant wear and tear? Were the boots just plain any good?

And just who exactly wants to know?

A small boot and shoe manufacturer up in Hampton, New Hampshire that goes by the name of Timberland that's who.

How can the regulation US Army boot be of interest to the maker of traditional walking, trekking and climbing boots? Very easily.

In fact, the bright boys in our technical department have learned a good deal from their counterparts in the Pentagon.

To the point that we've had a machine installed in our workshops that tests leathers to the highest standards demanded by the US Military. Known as MaserFlex, the machine puts leathers through the kind of initiation test only the marines could think up.

Each hide has to withstand a minimum of 15,000 flexes to test just how long it remains waterproof in extreme conditions.

Only if they pass the examination with flying colours are the hides certified as being tough and supple enough to receive an AOK from the top brass at Timberland.

We have also learned another important lesson from the US Army, namely, that a boot can never be too waterproof.

So we subject our boots to a programme of weatherproofing that takes in every part of the boot. From top to toe.

It starts with the hides we use.

Every month or so, we go on a mission to find tanneries that are prepared to meet our maddeningly high standards.

When we happen on one, we usually buy up every hide in the place.

(This is not the cheapest way to buy boot leather but we figure if the Pentagon can get away with paying $700 for ashtrays or $3,000 for a coffee pot, who are we to complain?)

We look for premium, full grain leathers

that are well known for their durability. Or a rare oxhide called Norwegian krymp.

Our next task is to impregnate the leather with silicone oil to prevent it absorbing water, and to stop the hides from stiffening.

There's another thing we've picked up in our dealings with the Military: an obsession with effectiveness.

'It ain't pretty but it works' could be the slogan for our boots. So it won't surprise you to learn that we still put all of our faith in good old fashioned craftsmanship rather than new fangled machines when it comes to the all important job of putting the uppers together.

Is there modern technology out there that can mould leather on a geometric last as cleverly as a pair of gnarled, experienced hands? Not that we know of.

Will a pair of sharp eyes and a dextrous set of fingers ever be replaced by a computerised robot? Not in our workshops. In fact, the best protection you can have is the concern we show for our own reputation.

It's the reason we sew all our important seams with four rows of nylon stitching. It's why we tape seal the seams with not one coat of latex but two just to be sure that water won't sneak in on you.

It's also why we don't cheat you in the areas you can't see.

For example, inside our boots the toes are protected from sub-zero temperatures by Ensolite. While the shaft, tongue and quarter

are insulated with 3M's B-400 Thinsulate. To keep your feet snug, the linings and cushioned insoles are even made from soft glove leather.

And in some of our boots we often pop in another boot, or rather a bootie made from Gore-Tex. This remarkable fabric ensures that no water can get in while at the same time billions of tiny pores allow the feet to breathe.

Have the boys in khaki managed to teach us anything else? Yes, sir.

We know that just like any other piece of equipment, every part of the boot counts.

So we only employ solid brass eyelets. Our laces are made of premium grade nylon for extra strength. (Can you imagine stopping in the field of battle to tie a broken boot lace? No, neither can we.)

The soles are dual-density polyurethane because it's tough yet lightweight. Even the self-cleaning treads are designed to stop ice or frozen mud getting trapped and conducting cold through to the feet.

At the end of all our endeavours, our boots are probably second to none. Which may not be much to come out of three wars with. But if Mankind can't learn from its wars, even if it's only how to make better boots, one day there won't be any Mankind to make boots for.

Timberland

"I'll never forget Gleneagles. That's where my wife left me."

I felt a little guilty taking Sarah to Gleneagles. (Which, in the light of subsequent events, is pretty rich!)

Sarah's not a golfer and I'm something of a fanatic. I've dreamed of a week at Gleneagles ever since I went there for a conference and first played on those immaculate courses.

This year I pulled out all the stops to persuade Sarah she would enjoy this golfer's paradise every bit as much as I.

You should have heard me waxing lyrical about the rooms, the heady Highland air, the service, the scenery. I did a pretty good job, too. For, little by little, Sarah succumbed.

I did feel a twinge of conscience, however, as I pulled into the hotel grounds and caught my first glimpse of those wonderful closing holes in the late sun of a warm summer evening.

How tempting they looked.

It all started well enough, though. Tell me, are the Scots really more friendly or is it just the effect Gleneagles has on everyone?

Certainly by the time we'd been ushered into our very pretty room overlooking the croquet lawn Sarah was looking very relaxed.

And what did she see on the hotel video while I was lolling in the generous bath which put such a smile on her face?

And it didn't end there.

The candlelit dinner in the Conservatory as dusk fell on the Ochil Hills was a revelation – even to me.

Since my last visit Gleneagles had managed to entice Alan Hill to join them. Alan was recently voted the best chef in Scotland.

And it showed.

Quite a coup for the hotel, and quite a boon for its guests. Twenty-seven different breads baked daily, rod-caught salmon fresh from the Tay, Aberdeen Angus beef in magical sauces, and puddings – oh those puds!

But I digress.

The upshot was that I teed off next morning with lots of wifely goodwill to draw on, and it was very nearly 6pm when I returned to our room.

Sarah was singing in the bath!

And later in the champagne bar she was positively bubbling. It transpired that she'd met some 'charming' people in the hotel Country Club and was playing tennis with them the next day.

I was delighted, of course. I would be able to play the Queen's all day with a clear conscience. And so I did.

On the third morning I was feeling a little stiff and so I decided, rather generously I thought, to stay with my wife.

"Lovely" she said, "perhaps we could meet up for lunch." Someone called Richard, apparently, had invited her to go riding.

"Come too" she said. But horses and I do not mix and I declined the invitation somewhat huffily and booked myself a session of aromatherapy at the hotel's Champneys Health Spa.

I must say it was most agreeable, and a light lunch and rather good Rioja quickly restored my spirits. I later spent an hour in the gym before flopping by the pool with a good book.

By the time Sarah returned I felt most expansive. So did she, it seemed.

"You must go and see the indoor riding school," she enthused. "It's actually big enough to hold championships ... my pony was so sweet ... Mark Phillips is involved you know ... tomorrow morning we're riding to the hills."

"You and Mark Phillips?"

"No, silly. Me and Richard."

"Hold your horses!" I replied rather wittily. "What about me?"

"You could come, I suppose." But she sounded doubtful and I bristled slightly.

"No, no. I'll have another crack at the King's course tomorrow. You know if I can just keep my wrists cocked, and slow the club in the backswing I might..."

I didn't have her undivided attention.

"Did you know that Jackie Stewart has a shooting range at Gleneagles?" She asked suddenly.

"Yes, it's very good."

"Only Richard has asked me to go there on Thursday with him." She sounded a mite too pleased about that for my liking.

"Has he indeed. Well that sounds fun. Maybe I'll join you." Yes, I thought. Shooting would make a pleasant change. Gleneagles really does have a lot to offer, I mused.

But I digress.

"Wouldn't you rather play golf?" She said.

WRITE OR RING FOR A BROCHURE OR RESERVATIONS. THE GLENEAGLES HOTEL, AUCHTERARDER, PERTHSHIRE PH3 1NF TELEPHONE: 0764 62231. FAX: 0764 62234.

INSTEAD OF A COAT OF PAINT, WE GIVE IT A SUIT OF ARMOUR.

Best Copy
Individual

Copywriter
STUART D'ROZARIO

Art Director
TAN SHEN GUAN

Typographer
TAN SHEN GUAN

Agency
THE BALL
PARTNERSHIP

. *Client*
THE BALL
PARTNERSHIP

HOW TO DOUBLE YOUR SALARY.

There's one old trick in advertising which Ogilvy, Hopkins and Rosser Reeves forgot to mention.

A fundamental, as critical as making money for your clients: The fine art of making money for yourself.

Allow us to explain.

The technique we are about to describe has often been called The Creative Leap. In all it takes about three weeks.

The first step is to spot a vacancy at one of the better agencies in town. (Incidentally, there's one for an art director at The Ball Partnership.)

Next you send in your resume and get an interview.

(To protect yourself against the ignominy of public rejection, the first two steps must be carried out in absolute secrecy.)

If you get past steps one and two and are offered the job, you proceed to step three.

Here's where it starts getting tricky. Because what appears to be routine is actually quite a delicate process.

You must, in a display of supreme indecision, resign, and withdraw your resignation, at least three times in the space of ten days. Without actually accepting the job at the new place.

By now your agency should have offered you at least 33 ⅓% more to stay.

But don't relent.

Take a Media journalist out to tea and let the news slip out. This will become the subject matter for the next two issues.

At this juncture, things start heating up. A few more rags phone you for comments. The two agencies start competing publicly. (Let's face it, for a person neither of them wanted all that badly in the first place.)

And the stakes go up.

Now comes the time to see the light. All of a sudden you realise how foolish you were even to consider leaving.

And like the prodigal son, you are welcomed home at twice the salary.

It's all quite simple, really.

So if you're a smart art director, one more interested in a bank balance than a book, take full advantage of the present vacancy at Ball, and the free advice above.

Of course, if you're one of those fools concerned only with creating great ads, do exactly the same.

At best you could work for Ball.

At worst you'll double your salary.

Best Copy
Individual

Copywriter
GERARD EDMONDSON

Art Director
DENNIS WILLISON

Photographer
CLIVE ARROWSMITH

Typographer
JEFF MERRELLS

Agency
COLLETT DICKENSON
PEARCE & PARTNERS
LIMITED

General Manager
IAN DICKENS

Client
OLYMPUS

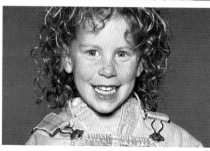

Thanks to Olympus, he's Mummy's blue-eyed boy again.

You remove the worms from his grubby little grasp and the semolina from his hair.

You pop him into a fresh pair of dungarees, distract him with talk of diggers and dinosaurs and check his nose.

Then you get him to sit still for a record breaking fifteen seconds, zoom in at the touch of a button and capture those precious album photos.

You do all this for him and what happens?

The dreaded red-eye.

Your little cherub takes on the appearance of a mad hell hound.

You mustn't blame yourself though, it's not something he picked up at nursery.

It's the flash on your camera.

It how light the pupils dilate and when the flash fires, light bounces off the retina causing red-eye.

Happily this nightmarish redness can be solved by using a camera from the Olympus Superzoom range.

There are four Superzoom cameras in all, each one with a list of features as long as a restless night.

If you're shooting in low light, just switch the camera to Auto S mode and zoom in.

The flash will emit a series of soft pulsing preflashes causing the pupils to contract.

When the flash fires, the red-eye all but disappears.

Decidedly simple, you might say. But not infernally expensive.

The AZ 210 costs as little as £159.99 and the top of the range AZ 330 no more than £229.99.

If you'd like more information on the Superzoom range, contact your nearest local dealer or fill in the coupon below.

Between us, we can make sure your little ones turn out well.

Olympus Superzoom Dept, Olympus Optical Co (UK) Ltd, 2a Honduras St, London EC1Y 0TX. Tel: 071 490 7373.

Name ....

Address ....

.... Postcode ....

OLYMPUS SUPERZOOM

Gulp!

Jonathan Meades. Every Saturday.

THE TIMES
KEEP OUR WITS ABOUT YOU

*Best Copy
Individual*

Copywriters
JONATHAN MEADES
CHRISTOPHER
HARRALD
KENNETH HODGSON

Art Director
KENNETH HODGSON

Typographers
KENNETH HODGSON
CAROLE GREGORY

Agency
ARC ADVERTISING

Promotions Director
ANDREW KITCHING

Client
NEWS
INTERNATIONAL

Zap!

Lynne Truss. Every Saturday.

THE TIMES
KEEP OUR WITS ABOUT YOU

*Best Copy
Individual*

Copywriters
LYNNE TRUSS
CHRISTOPHER
HARRALD
KENNETH HODGSON

Art Director
KENNETH HODGSON

Typographers
KENNETH HODGSON
CAROLE GREGORY

Agency
ARC ADVERTISING

Promotions Director
ANDREW KITCHING

Client
NEWS
INTERNATIONAL

*Best Copy
Campaigns*

Copywriter
ERNIE SCHENCK

Art Director
JOHN DOYLE

Photographer
NADAV KANDER

Typographer
JOHN DOYLE

Agency
DOYLE ADVERTISING
& DESIGN GROUP

*Vice President, Marketing &
Product*
MICHAEL COOGAN

Client
THE DUNHAM
COMPANY

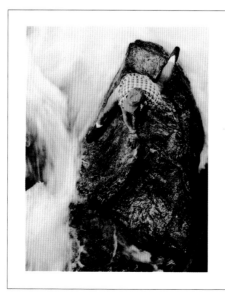

**Warning.
This product can cause
blisters, aching
and shortness of breath.**

Ordnance Survey.
The most detailed maps in the land.

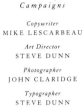

*Best Copy
Campaigns*

Copywriter
MIKE LESCARBEAU

Art Director
STEVE DUNN

Photographer
JOHN CLARIDGE

Typographer
STEVE DUNN

Agency
LEAGAS DELANEY

*Manager of Information
& Public Relations*
CHARLIE PAYNE

Client
ORDNANCE SURVEY

**Ever heard of Cuff-peppers
Dish, Toemen Puddle,
Throop, or Yearlings Bottom?
No? Good.**

Ordnance Survey.
The most detailed maps in the land.

**Whose countryside
would you rather see?
Thomas Hardy's?
Or John McAdam's?**

Ordnance Survey.
The most detailed maps in the land.

Copywriters
TIM DELANEY
MIKE LESCARBEAU

Best Copy Campaigns

Copywriters
KENNETH HODGSON
CHRISTOPHER
HARRALD
BERNARD LEVIN

Art Director
KENNETH HODGSON

Typographers
KENNETH HODGSON
ALISON BERNARDINI

Agency
ARC ADVERTISING

Promotions Director
ANDREW KITCHING

Client
NEWS
INTERNATIONAL

Ouch!
Bernard Levin. Twice a week.

THE TIMES
KEEP OUR WITS ABOUT YOU

Copywriters
KENNETH HODGSON
CHRISTOPHER
HARRALD
TOM PIKE
JULIAN SPENCE
DOMINIC WALSH
BRUCE GARNER
S W ALLEN
JOHN PARFITT
PATRICIA
ALLDERIDGE
GEORGE THOMAS
ALEX FINCH
J D BARCLAY
IAN POWE
C CAMBOUROPOULOSK
S.SUTHERLAND
WINTY THORNTON

Typographer
PETER PEDERSON

Sir,

THE TIMES
KEEP OUR WITS ABOUT YOU

Copywriters
KENNETH HODGSON
CHRISTOPHER
HARRALD
PETER BARNARD
MATTHEW PARRIS
ALAN COREN
ALLEN CARTER
EMMA SLATER
WYNNE
WESTON-DAVIES

Typographer
KENNETH HODGSON

Ho,ho,ho!

THE TIMES
KEEP OUR WITS ABOUT YOU

Zap!

Lynne Truss. Every Saturday.

THE TIMES

KEEP OUR WITS ABOUT YOU

Gulp!

Jonathan Meades. Every Saturday.

THE TIMES

KEEP OUR WITS ABOUT YOU

Oooh-arrr!

Paul Heiney. Every Saturday in the Weekend Times.

THE TIMES

KEEP OUR WITS ABOUT YOU

Best Copy Campaigns

Copywriters
KENNETH HODGSON
CHRISTOPHER HARRALD
LYNNE TRUSS

Typographers
KENNETH HODGSON
CAROLE GREGORY

Copywriters
KENNETH HODGSON
CHRISTOPHER HARRALD
JONATHAN MEADES

Typographers
KENNETH HODGSON
CAROLE GREGORY

Copywriters
KENNETH HODGSON
CHRISTOPHER HARRALD
PAUL HEINEY

Typographers
KENNETH HODGSON
CAROLE GREGORY

Best Copy Campaigns

Copywriters
TIM DELANEY
GILES MONTGOMERY
MIKE LESCARBEAU

Art Directors
STEVE DUNN
CHRISTINE JONES

Photographer
JOHN CLARIDGE

Typographer
JEFF LEWIS

Agency
LEAGAS DELANEY

European Marketing Manager
VINCENT DESSAIN

Client
TIMBERLAND

NOT SINCE THE DAYS OF AL CAPONE HAS ANYONE DEMANDED SO MUCH MONEY FOR PROTECTION.

THE APACHES TAUGHT US HOW TO MAKE SHOES. IT WAS OUR IDEA TO SCALP PEOPLE.

FAREWELL, ALASKA. IT'S WHERE A LOT OF PEOPLE SAY GOODBYE TO THEIR FEET.

IF ONLY THE PEOPLE WHO BOUGHT IMITATION TIMBERLAND BOOTS SUFFERED IMITATION FROSTBITE.

THE LESSONS OF KOREA, VIETNAM AND CAMBODIA HAVE FINALLY COME HOME TO AMERICA.

OUR SHOES ARE MADE BY THE MOST ADVANCED EQUIPMENT KNOWN TO MAN. MAN.

Best Copy
Campaigns

Copywriter
RICHARD FOSTER

Art Director
JOHN HORTON

Photographer
GRAHAM FORD

Typographer
JOE HOZA

Agency
ABBOTT MEAD
VICKERS.BBDO
LIMITED

Marketing Manager
OLIVER JOHNSON

Client
VOLVO
CONCESSIONAIRES

THE FERRARI F40 VERSUS THE VOLVO 480 TURBO. (NO, HONESTLY.)

You might think the Volvo is somewhat out of its class in such exalted company.

And on the race-track, you'd be right. But on the road?

The Ferrari may reach 60 mph about four seconds faster than the Volvo, but what are you going to do with the four seconds?

(Sorry, your time's up.)

The Ferrari's top speed may be 78 mph higher than the Volvo's, but where will those 78 mph take you? (To jail, most likely.)

The truth is, the Volvo 480 Turbo is quite fast enough for most drivers.

(It's certainly faster than the Audi 80 Quattro,

the BMW 518i and the Saab 900 Turbo.)

And unlike the Ferrari, the Volvo comes with rear seats and a boot, to boot.

Not to mention a welded box-steel safety cage and side-impact protection bars.

What's more, of the two cars it's the Volvo that impresses the ladies.

So much so, several thousand of them have actually bought one.

Admittedly, our car is the more affordable of the two.

Only £16,985 as opposed to £192,502. The Ferrari F40 versus the Volvo 480 Turbo?

No contest. **THE VOLVO 480 TURBO.**

WHO SAYS POWER CORRUPTS?

What Lord Acton actually said was "power tends to corrupt."

Not that he was talking about the new 2 Litre Turbo Volvo 940 SE, of course.

A powerful car, certainly. More powerful than BMW 520i 24V in fact.

But still every inch a Volvo.

Under the bonnet its 155 bhp turbocharged engine accelerates from 50-70 in 8.1 seconds.

While behind it lies Volvo's legendary rigid steel safety cage.

Falling below both the £19,250 and the 2 litre

tax limits, the 940 Turbo also offers protection from the Inland Revenue.

And protection to the environment by way of its Lambda Sond. (A simple attachment which gives a more efficient catalytic conversion of exhaust gases.)

To arrange a test drive, contact your local Volvo dealer.

But beware.

Power, as Henry Kissinger put it, "is the ultimate aphrodisiac."

THE NEW 2·0 TURBO VOLVO 940 SE.

Copywriter
ROBERT CAMPBELL

Art Director
MARK ROALFE

Photographer
JERRY OKE

HOW TO IMPROVE A GOLF'S TURNING CIRCLE.

"I can't drive a great big car like a Volvo estate around town," we hear you say.

Actually, you can. The Volvo 940's power steering, excellent all round visibility, and surprisingly

light clutch make battling with city traffic a pleasure.

Well, almost a pleasure.

And when it comes to tight corners (and tight parking spaces) the Volvo has been specially designed

to out-manoeuvre much smaller cars.

In fact at 32.5 feet, its turning circle is tighter than a Volkswagen Golf's.

Then there's Volvo's familiar front and rear

crumple zones, the steel bars reinforcing its doors, and, of course, its rigid steel safety cage.

It all stacks up, doesn't it?

THE NEW VOLVO 940 ESTATE.

INSTEAD OF A COAT OF PAINT, WE GIVE IT A SUIT OF ARMOUR.

If any car can claim to be weatherproof, the Volvo 460 is that car.

It shines come rain, hail, sleet or snow.

(To be honest, we chose the line at which nails – our picture is intended only as a symbol of the car's durability.)

The 460's resistance to the elements is largely due to an element used in its construction.

Zinc. As any metallurgist will tell you, zinc is the last word in rustproofing. That's why over 60% of the 460's bodyweight is made of zinc-coated steel.

Even then, we spray the entire body shell (including the zinc coated parts) with a further layer of zinc phosphate.

We then immerse it in a bath of primer.

We spray exposed parts of the underbody with p.v.c. to protect them from stone chips.

We inject the inner cavities with a special wax-based fluid.

We close off and seal all welded seams, inside and out.

And then we paint it. And then we paint it again.

And then, for metallic finishes, we paint it again.

By the time we've finished with it, the Volvo 460 is cocooned in a multi-layered shell of anti-corrosive material.

It's a car that comes in its own garage.

THE VOLVO 460.

Copywriter
PETER RUSSELL

Art Director
ROB OLIVER

Photographer
MARTIN THOMPSON

Typographer
JOE HOZA

THE NEW 2 LITRE TURBO VOLVO 940 ESTATE. NOT BAD FOR YOUR FIRST CAR.

To be honest, cars used to bore me to tears. Then we got a Volvo. A Volvo 2 litre Turbo 940 Estate to be precise.

155 bhp, according to dad. And below the £19,250 and the 2 litre tax limits. Whatever they are.

Of course, being a Volvo, it's as safe as houses. It's got steel bars reinforcing every door. Crumple zones. And Volvo's legendary rigid steel safety cage.

Being an estate car, it's also got more than enough room for my travel cot, my pushchair and a generous supply of nappies.

And bags of space for all the paraphernalia that mums and dads like to cart about with them.

When the time comes for me to get behind the wheel myself, they say it should still be on the road.

So you never know. My first car might well turn out to be my first car.

VOLVO

Best use of
Illustration
Individual

Illustrator
MEL CALMAN

Art Director
MIKE ORR

Copywriter
DAVID DENTON

Typographer
DAVID WAKEFIELD

Agency
BMP DDB NEEDHAM

Marketing Director
MIKE CORNISH

Client
VAG UK LIMITED

Best use of
Illustration
Individual

Illustrator
DAVID JUNIPER

Art Director
GRAHAM FINK

Copywriter
TIM MELLORS

Typographer
LEN CHEESEMAN

Agency
GGT

Marketing Director
CAROL FISHER

Client
HOLSTEN
DISTRIBUTORS
LIMITED

Best use of
Illustration
Individual

Illustrator
BARRY CRADDOCK

Art Director
JOHN GORSE

Copywriter
NICK WORTHINGTON

Typographers
JOHN GORSE
NIGEL DAWSON

Agency
BARTLE BOGLE
HEGARTY

Retail Advertising Manager
CHRIS COTTON

Client
SHELL UK LIMITED

Best use of
Illustration
Individual

Illustrator
GEOFFREY
APPLETON

Art Director
JOHN GORSE

Copywriter
NICK WORTHINGTON

Typographers
JOHN GORSE
NIGEL DAWSON

Agency
BARTLE BOGLE
HEGARTY

Retail Advertising Manager
CHRIS COTTON

Client
SHELL UK LIMITED

*Best use of
Illustration
Individual*

Illustrator
ANDY McKAY

Art Directors
MARK DENTON
ANDY McKAY

Copywriter
CHRIS PALMER

Agency
SIMONS PALMER
DENTON CLEMMOW &
JOHNSON LIMITED

Marketing Director
FRANK DIMECH

Client
WRANGLER UK
LIMITED

Best use of
Illustration
Campaigns

Illustrator
RONALD SEARLE

Art Director
KATE STANNERS

Copywriter
TIM HEARN

Typographer
KATE STANNERS

Agency
G G T

Marketing Director
PAT WALL

Client
CADBURY LIMITED

Best use of
Illustration
Campaigns

Illustrators
MARVIN MATTELSON

Art Directors
MARK DENTON
ANDY McKAY

Copywriter
CHRIS PALMER

Agency
SIMONS PALMER
DENTON CLEMMOW &
JOHNSON LIMITED

Marketing Director
KAREN BRAY

Client
BOTTOMS UP

Illustrators
PAUL SLATER
(*Lautrec*)
MARK HESS
(*Mona Lisa*)

Illustrators
JAMES MARSH
(*Carmen*)
C F PAYNE
(*Prost*)

*Best use of
Illustration
Campaigns*

Illustrator
OLIVIA BEASLEY

Art Director
BRIAN STEWART

Copywriters
GREG DELANEY
MARTIN LORAINE

Typographers
BRIAN STEWART
CHRIS DEVONALD

Agency
DELANEY FLETCHER
SLAYMAKER
DELANEY & BOZELL

Marketing Manager
CHIP LLOYD

Client
CPC UK LIMITED

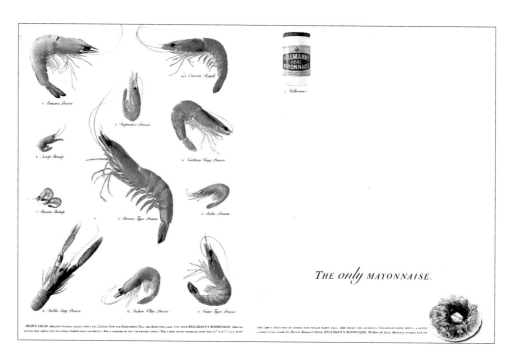

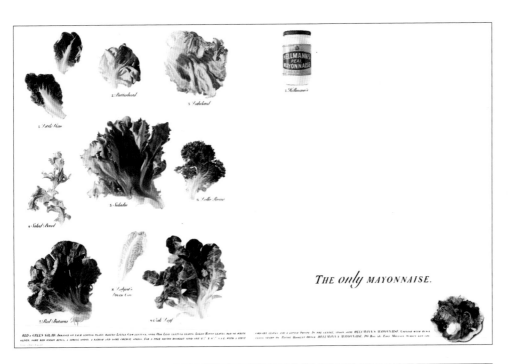

THE *only* MAYONNAISE.

THE *only* MAYONNAISE.

Best use of
Illustration
Campaigns

Illustrator
BRAD HOLLAND

Art Director
GUY MARINO

Agency
DOREMUS & CO

Client
BANKERS TRUST & CO

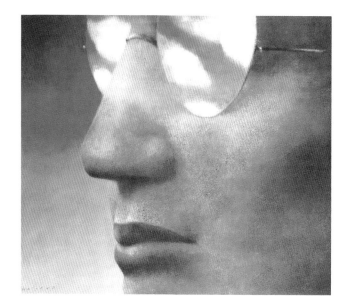

p

oste
rs₃₀

SILVER AWARD
for the most outstanding
Poster Campaign

Art Director
GERARD STAMP

Copywriter
LOZ SIMPSON

Illustrator
ROBIN
HEIGHWAY-BURY

Agency
BSB DORLAND

General Manager Marketing
LAWRENCE BALFE

Client
H J HEINZ COMPANY
LIMITED

SILVER AWARD
for the most outstanding
48 & 96 Sheet Poster

Art Director
JOHN HORTON

Copywriter
RICHARD FOSTER

Typographer
JOE HOZA

Agency
ABBOTT MEAD
VICKERS.BBDO
LIMITED

Managing Director
DAVID GORDON

Client
THE ECONOMIST

**AUSTRALIANS WOULDN'T GIVE A XXXX
FOR ANYTHING ELSE.**

SILVER AWARD
NOMINATION
*for the most outstanding
48 & 96 Sheet Poster*

Art Directors
ZELDA MALAN
PETER GIBB

Copywriter
PETER BARRY

Photographer
PETER LAVERY

Typographer
ROGER KENNEDY

Agency
SAATCHI & SAATCHI

Marketing Manager
PAUL WIELGUS

Client
ALLIED BREWERIES
BRANDS MARKETING

SILVER AWARD
NOMINATION
*for the most outstanding
Campaign*

Art Director
ALEXANDRA TAYLOR

Copywriters
ALAN THOMPSON
RACHEL
HEATHERFIELD

Photographer
PETER LAVERY

Typographer
ANDY DYMOCK

Agency
SAATCHI & SAATCHI

Marketing Manager
PAUL WIELGUS

Client
ALLIED BREWERIES
BRANDS MARKETING

Art Directors
ALEXANDRA TAYLOR
NIK STUDZINSKI

Copywriter
JASON FRETWELL

Art Directors
PETER GIBB
ZELDA MALAN
Copywriter
PETER BARRY

Art Director
ALEXANDRA TAYLOR
Copywriter
JAMES LOWTHER

SILVER AWARD
NOMINATION
*for the most outstanding
Poster Campaign*

Art Director
GREG MARTIN

Copywriter
NICK BELL

Typographer
JOE HOZA

Agency
ABBOTT MEAD
VICKERS.BBDO
LIMITED

Managing Director
DAVID GORDON

Client
THE ECONOMIST

Art Director
JOHN HORTON

Copywriter
RICHARD FOSTER

Art Director
RON BROWN

Copywriter
DAVID ABBOTT

The Economist

Art Director
JOHN HORTON
Copywriter
RICHARD FOSTER
Photographer
GEOFF SENIOR

Top desk publishing.

The Economist

Art Director
RON BROWN
Copywriter
DAVID ABBOTT

Meat on Fridays.

The Economist

Art Director
RON BROWN
Copywriter
DAVID ABBOTT

Keep your ear to the ground.

The Economist

Art Director
JOHN HORTON
Copywriter
RICHARD FOSTER

Art Director
RON BROWN

Copywriter
DAVID ABBOTT

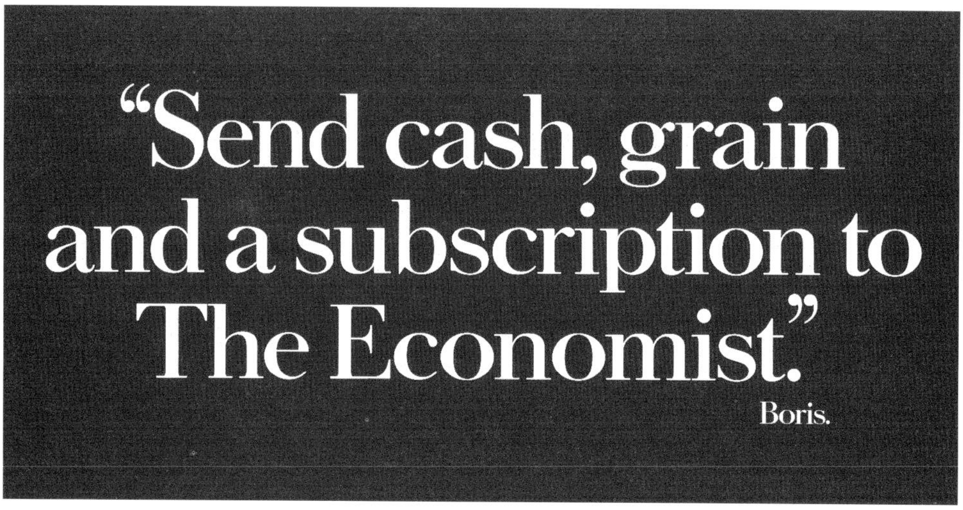

"Send cash, grain and a subscription to The Economist."

Boris.

Art Director
GREG MARTIN

Copywriter
NICK BELL

Read

The Economist

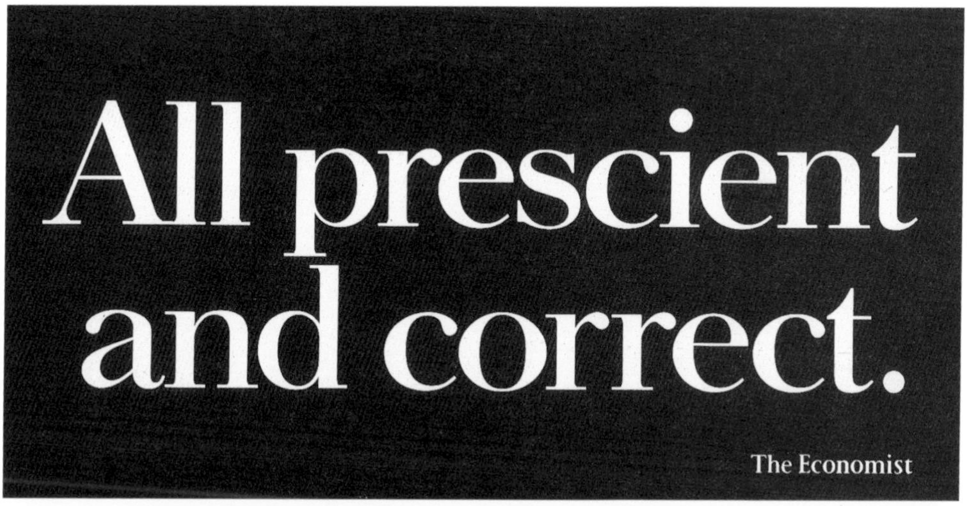

All prescient and correct.

The Economist

Art Director
RON BROWN
Copywriter
DAVID ABBOTT

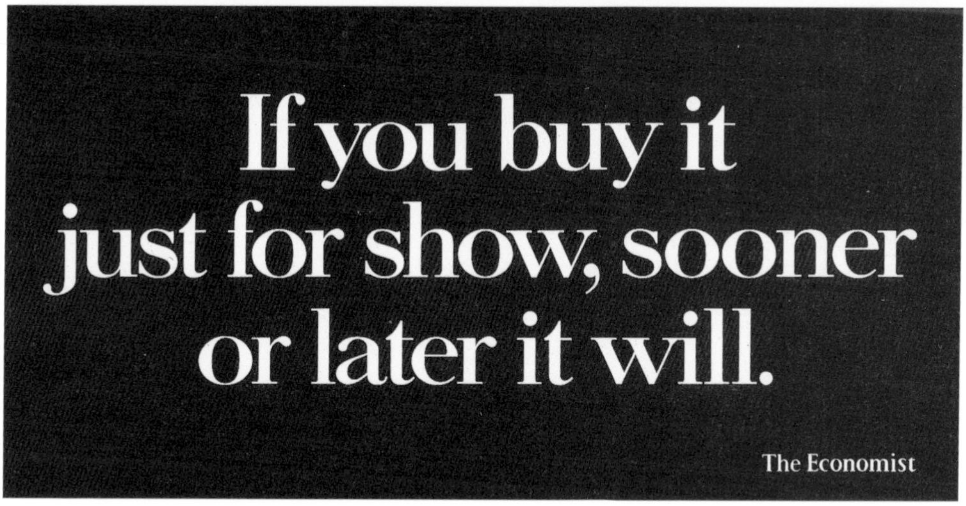

If you buy it just for show, sooner or later it will.

The Economist

Art Director
RON BROWN
Copywriter
DAVID ABBOTT

Up to 4 Sheet

Art Director
NIGEL ROSE

Photographer
NADAV KANDER

Agency
COLLETT
DICKENSON PEARCE
& PARTNERS LIMITED

Marketing Manager
DEREK STOTHARD

Client
GALLAHER LIMITED

MIDDLE TAR As defined by H.M.Government
Warning: SMOKING CAN CAUSE LUNG CANCER,
BRONCHITIS AND OTHER CHEST DISEASES
Health Departments' Chief Medical Officers

If your offspring have too much surplus energy, why not donate them to the Science Museum for the day? We have lots of colourful, noisy, exhausting interactive experiments, specially designed to appeal to enquiring young minds. The Science Museum, South Kensington. Open Monday – Saturday 10.00 – 18.00. Sunday 11.00 – 18.00. Nearest tube, South Kensington.

Up to 4 Sheet

Art Director
STEVE DEPUT

Copywriter
PHIL BIRD

Agency
SIMONS PALMER
DENTON CLEMMOW &
JOHNSON LIMITED

Marketing Director
MARK PEMBERTON

Client
THE SCIENCE
MUSEUM

Up to 4 Sheet

Art Directors
MARK DENTON
ANDY McKAY

Copywriter
CHRIS PALMER

Photographer
MALCOLM VENVILLE

Agency
SIMONS PALMER
DENTON CLEMMOW &
JOHNSON LIMITED

Managing Director
FRANK DIMECH

Client
WRANGLER UK
LIMITED

Up to 4 Sheet

Art Director
JELLY HELM

Copywriter
RAYMOND McKINNEY

Photographer
JIM ERICKSON

Typographer
KATHERINE BLEVINS

Agency
THE MARTIN
AGENCY

Marketing Director
DAVID HELM

Client
BERNIE'S
TATTOOING

Up to 4 Sheet

Art Director
JAY POND-JONES

Copywriter
MARK WAITES

Photographer
CHARLES LIDDELL

Agency
EMERSON
POND-JONES
LIMITED

Chief Executive
HARRY DRNEC

Client
MAISON CAURETTE
LIMITED

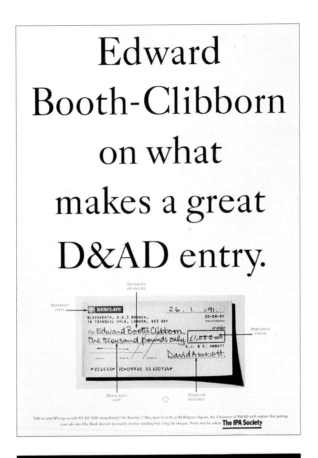

Edward Booth-Clibborn on what makes a great D&AD entry.

Up to 4 Sheet

Art Director
ANDY LAWSON

Copywriter
LAURENCE BLUME

Typographer
ANDY LAWSON

Agency
BURKITT WEINREICH
BRYANT CLIENTS &
COMPANY LIMITED

IPA Committee Member
PETER KNOWLAND

Client
THE IPA SOCIETY

Up to 4 Sheet

Art Director
JEREMY CARR

Copywriter
JEREMY CRAIGEN

Photographer
MIKE PARSONS

Typographer
DAVID WAKEFIELD

Agency
BMP DDB NEEDHAM

Marketing Director
BOB KENNEDY

Client
SEAFISH AUTHORITY

48 and 96 Sheet

Art Director
JOHN CLIFFORD

Copywriter
MARK COLLIS

Illustrator
DAVID JUNIPER

Typographer
GAVIN FERGUSON

Agency
GGT

Marketing Director
CAROL FISHER

Client
HOLSTEN
DISTRIBUTORS
LIMITED

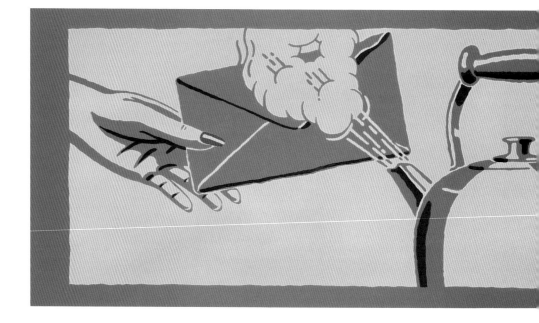

48 and 96 Sheet

Art Director
GRAHAM FINK

Copywriter
TIM MELLORS

Illustrator
DAVID JUNIPER

Typographer
LEN CHEESEMAN

Agency
GGT

Marketing Director
CAROL FISHER

Client
HOLSTEN
DISTRIBUTORS
LIMITED

48 and 96 Sheet

Art Director
JOHN CLIFFORD

Copywriter
MARK COLLIS

Illustrator
DAVID JUNIPER

Typographer
GAVIN FERGUSON

Agency
GGT

Marketing Director
CAROL FISHER

Client
HOLSTEN
DISTRIBUTORS
LIMITED

48 and 96 Sheet

Art Director
MATT MURRAY

Copywriter
GILES HARGREAVES

Photographer
TERRY O'NEILL

Agency
LEAGAS SHAFRON
DAVIS CHICK

Marketing Manager
PAUL WIELGUS

Client
ALLIED BREWERIES
BRANDS MARKETING

48 and 96 Sheet

Art Directors
GRAHAM CAPPI
MATT MURRAY

Copywriter
TONY BARRY

Photographer
DAVID MONTGOMERY

Agency
LEAGAS SHAFRON
DAVIS CHICK

Marketing Manager
PAUL WIELGUS

Client
ALLIED BREWERIES
BRANDS MARKETING

48 and 96 Sheet

Art Director
CHRISTINE JONES

Copywriter
GILES MONTGOMERY

Typographer
STEVE DUNN

Agency
LEAGAS DELANEY

Head of Sales & Marketing
KATY TURNER

Client
JAZZ FM

48 and 96 Sheet

Art Director
STEVE DUNN

Copywriter
TIM DELANEY

Typographer
STEVE DUNN

Agency
LEAGAS DELANEY

Head of Sales & Marketing
KATY TURNER

Client
JAZZ FM

48 and 96 Sheet

Art Director
GARY MARSHALL

Copywriter
PAUL MARSHALL

Typographer
STEVE DUNN

Agency
LEAGAS DELANEY

Head of Sales & Marketing
KATY TURNER

Client
JAZZ FM

48 and 96 Sheet

Art Director
GERARD STAMP

Copywriter
LOZ SIMPSON

Illustrator
ROBIN
HEIGHWAY-BURY

Agency
BSB DORLAND

General Manager Marketing
LAWRENCE BALFE

Client
H J HEINZ COMPANY
LIMITED

48 and 96 Sheet

Art Director
GERARD STAMP

Copywriter
LOZ SIMPSON

Illustrator
ROBIN
HEIGHWAY-BURY

Agency
BSB DORLAND

General Manager Marketing
LAWRENCE BALFE

Client
H J HEINZ COMPANY
LIMITED

48 and 96 Sheet

Art Director
GERARD STAMP

Copywriter
LOZ SIMPSON

Illustrator
ROBIN
HEIGHWAY-BURY

Agency
BSB DORLAND

General Manager Marketing
LAWRENCE BALFE

Client
H J HEINZ COMPANY
LIMITED

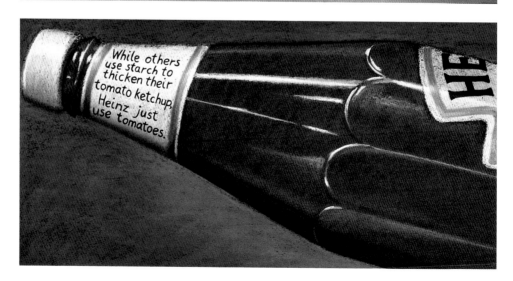

48 and 96 Sheet

Art Director
GERARD STAMP

Copywriter
LOZ SIMPSON

Illustrator
ROBIN
HEIGHWAY-BURY

Agency
BSB DORLAND

General Manager Marketing
LAWRENCE BALFE

Client
H J HEINZ COMPANY
LIMITED

48 and 96 Sheet

Art Director
GERARD STAMP

Copywriter
LOZ SIMPSON

Illustrator
ROBIN
HEIGHWAY-BURY

Agency
BSB DORLAND

General Manager Marketing
LAWRENCE BALFE

Client
H J HEINZ COMPANY
LIMITED

48 and 96 Sheet

Art Directors
PETER GAUSIS
STEVE DUNN

Copywriter
TIM DELANEY

Typographer
PETER GAUSIS

Agency
LEAGAS DELANEY

Manager New Media Services
EDDIE CHENG

Client
YELLOW PAGES

Fancy Dress? Call Talking Pages

48 and 96 Sheet

Art Directors
PETER GAUSIS
STEVE DUNN

Copywriter
TIM DELANEY

Typographer
PETER GAUSIS

Agency
LEAGAS DELANEY

Manager New Media Services
EDDIE CHENG

Client
YELLOW PAGES

Garden Centres? Call Talking Pages and we'll do the searching for you. 071-600 9000.

e searching for you. 071-600 9000.

Riding Schools? Call Talking Pages and we'll do the searching for you. 071-600 9000.

48 and 96 Sheet

Art Directors
PETER GAUSIS
STEVE DUNN

Copywriter
TIM DELANEY

Typographer
PETER GAUSIS

Agency
LEAGAS DELANEY

Manager New Media Services
EDDIE CHENG

Client
YELLOW PAGES

48 and 96 Sheet

Art Director
GEOFF TURNER

Photographer
NADAV KANDER

Illustrator
BEN CASEY

Agency
COLLETT DICKENSON
PEARCE & PARTNERS
LIMITED

Marketing Manager
DEREK STOTHARD

Client
GALLAHER LIMITED

MIDDLE TAR As defined by H.M. Government
Warning: SMOKING CAN CAUSE LUNG CANCER, BRONCHITIS AND OTHER CHEST DISEASES
Health Departments' Chief Medical Officers

48 and 96 Sheet

Art Director
NIGEL ROSE

Photographer
NADAV KANDER

Agency
COLLETT DICKENSON
PEARCE & PARTNERS
LIMITED

Marketing Manager
DEREK STOTHARD

Client
GALLAHER LIMITED

AUSTRALIANS WOULDN'T GIVE A XXXX FOR ANYTHING ELSE.

PHEW!

48 and 96 Sheet

Art Directors
ALEXANDRA TAYLOR
NIK STUDZINSKI

Copywriter
JASON FRETWELL

Photographer
PETER LAVERY

Typographer
ANDY DYMOCK

Agency
SAATCHI & SAATCHI

Marketing
PAUL WIELGUS

Client
ALLIED BREWERIES
BRANDS MARKETING

48 and 96 Sheet

Art Director
JOHN HORTON

Copywriter
RICHARD FOSTER

Typographer
JOE HOZA

Agency
ABBOTT MEAD
VICKERS.BBDO
LIMITED

Managing Director
DAVID GORDON

Client
THE ECONOMIST

48 and 96 Sheet

Art Director
RON BROWN

Copywriter
DAVID ABBOTT

Top desk publishing.

The Economist

48 and 96 Sheet

Art Director
JOHN HORTON

Copywriter
RICHARD FOSTER

Keep your ear to the ground.

The Economist

The Economist

Meat on Fridays.

The Economist

48 and 96 Sheet

Art Director
RON BROWN
Copywriter
DAVID ABBOTT

48 and 96 Sheet

Art Director
GREG MARTIN
Copywriter
NICK BELL

Read

The Economist

48 and 96 Sheet

Art Director
PAUL BRIGINSHAW

Copywriter
MALCOLM DUFFY

Photographer
BARRY LATEGAN

Agency
COLLETT DICKENSON
PEARCE & PARTNERS
LIMITED

Marketing Manager
DEREK STOTHARD

Client
GALLAHER LIMITED

48 and 96 Sheet

Art Directors
NIGEL ROSE
ALAN CURSON

Photographer
NADAV KANDER

Agency
COLLETT DICKENSON
PEARCE & PARTNERS
LIMITED

Marketing Manager
DEREK STOTHARD

Client
GALLAHER LIMITED

48 and 96 Sheet

Art Director
ALEXANDRA TAYLOR

Copywriters
ALAN THOMPSON
RACHEL
HEATHERFIELD

Photographer
PETER LAVERY

Typographer
ANDY DYMOCK

Agency
SAATCHI & SAATCHI

Marketing Manager
PAUL WIELGUS

Client
ALLIED BREWERIES
BRANDS MARKETING

48 and 96 Sheet

Art Director
MARK ROALFE

Copywriter
ROBERT CAMPBELL

Typographer
JOE HOZA

Agency
ABBOTT MEAD
VICKERS.BBDO
LIMITED

Car Marketing Manager
OLIVER JOHNSON

Client
VOLVO
CONCESSIONAIRES

All new Polos come with a catalytic converter as standard.

48 and 96 Sheet

Art Director
MIKE ORR

Copywriter
DAVID DENTON

Illustrator
MEL CALMAN

Typographer
DAVID WAKEFIELD

Agency
BMP DDB NEEDHAM

Marketing Director
MIKE CORNISH

Client
VAG UK LIMITED

48 and 96 Sheet

Art Director
PAUL GAY

Copywriter
STEVE REEVES

Typographer
KEVIN CLARKE

Agency
BMP DDB NEEDHAM

Director of Marketing
R MASON

Client
INTERCITY

We've made the Times Crossword
even harder to finish.

London to Bristol 1 hour 9 minutes.

Fastest journey time from 8th July 1991.

INTERCITY

48 and 96 Sheet

Art Director
PAUL SIMBLETT

Copywriter
JOHN BEDFORD

Illustrator
LOUISE BRIERLY

Typographer
RICHARD BATEMAN

Agency
BMP DDB NEEDHAM

Marketing Director
ROBERT ORME

Client
BRITISH RAIL
(SCOTRAIL)

Glasgow to Edinburgh 38 trains a day.

SCOTRAIL

48 and 96 Sheet

Art Director
PAUL GAY

Copywriter
STEVE REEVES

Typographer
KEVIN CLARKE

Agency
BMP DDB NEEDHAM

Director of Marketing
R MASON

Client
INTERCITY

If you're a train spotter,
bring a pencil sharpener.

London to Birmingham every half-hour.

Weekday daytime service

INTERCITY

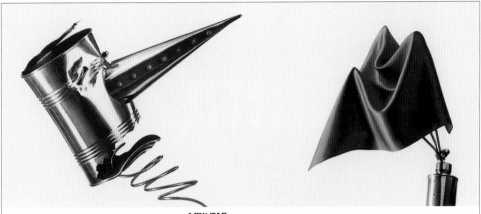

LOW TAR As defined by H.M. Government
Warning: SMOKING CAN CAUSE LUNG CANCER, BRONCHITIS AND OTHER CHEST DISEASES
Health Departments' Chief Medical Officers

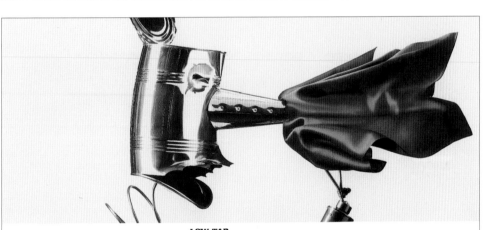

LOW TAR As defined by H.M. Government
Warning: SMOKING CAN CAUSE LUNG CANCER, BRONCHITIS AND OTHER CHEST DISEASES
Health Departments' Chief Medical Officers

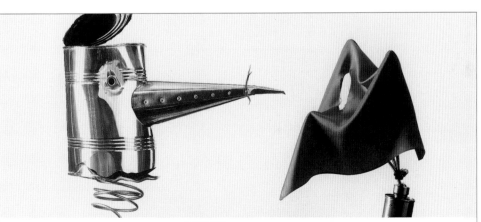

LOW TAR As defined by H.M. Government
Warning: SMOKING CAN CAUSE LUNG CANCER, BRONCHITIS AND OTHER CHEST DISEASES
Health Departments' Chief Medical Officers

Campaigns

Art Director
GIDEON TODES

Copywriter
GIDEON TODES

Photographer
GRAHAM FORD

Agency
SAATCHI & SAATCHI

Marketing Manager
IAN CALLOW

Client
GALLAHER LIMITED

Art Director
PAUL AKINS
Copywriter
JOHN MESSUM
Photographer
GRAHAM FORD

Art Director
BILL GALLACHER
Copywriter
JEREMY CLARKE
Photographer
EDWARD MAXEY

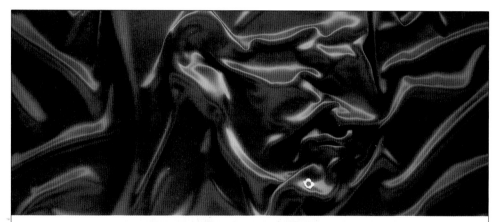

LOW TAR As defined by H.M. Government
Warning: MORE THAN 30,000 PEOPLE DIE EACH YEAR IN THE UK FROM LUNG CANCER
Health Departments' Chief Medical Officers

Art Director
ALEXANDRA TAYLOR

Copywriter
JAY WINTER

Photographer
JAN GROOVER

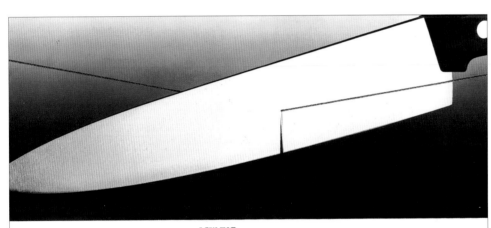

LOW TAR As defined by H.M. Government
Warning: SMOKING CAN CAUSE LUNG CANCER, BRONCHITIS AND OTHER CHEST DISEASES
Health Departments' Chief Medical Officers

Art Director
COLIN JONES

Copywriter
NEIL PAVITT

Photographer
MIKE PARSONS

Campaigns

Art Director
WALTER CAMPBELL

Copywriter
TOM CARTY

Typographer
RETLAW MOTT

Agency
ABBOTT MEAD
VICKERS.BBDO
LIMITED

Managing Director
MIKE HARDWICK

Client
TIME OUT

A friend of mine was saying that he believed in reincarnation. He told me that he liked the idea of coming back as a different person. Apparently a lot of famous people can remember their previous lives. I told him he didn't have to wait for reincarnation. It's possible to live another life now. I do every week with a little help from my Time Out. Every Tuesday for £1.20 it introduces you to a whole new world. A martial arts display at the Finsbury Leisure Centre, a fringe play at the Carib Theatre or Wim Wenders' new movie at the Lumière. And now it's got a complete TV guide, it can radically change your viewing habits. From French fine art films to a series on whippet training. So I said to my friend what's the use of putting off what you could do in this life and waiting for the next? After all, you could come back as a goldfish.

Art Director
WALTER CAMPBELL

Copywriter
ALFREDO
MARCANTONIO

Amsterdam. Barcelona. New York. You always buy the guide books don't you? You want to know the places to go, the places to eat, the places to see. When it's time to return home, you kick yourself because you haven't done everything you wanted to do. It's your last day and you realise you are going to miss a great show because your flight leaves at 2.30 in the afternoon instead of 12.30 at night. You even think about changing your flight, but it's too much hassle. You're being met by someone at the airport and it's all arranged. Why don't you have the same attitude back home? There are adventures to be had here too. You don't have to pack a suitcase or change your currency. And Time Out is the only guide book you need. For £1.20 you've got a magazine that's jam-packed with things to do. Including the weird and the wonderful. A jazzy New Zealand saxophonist here, a Guatemalan crafts festival there. I kid you not, London has as much to offer as New York. It's all out there. Just outside the doors of this tube station. Why do you think so many tourists come here? It isn't to get a suntan.

There was this bloke who went to the doctor and the doctor told him he only had a week to live. But he had a great attitude this bloke, and instead of feeling down, he went out and spent £1.20 on a copy of Time Out and called all his mates. From then on it was a whirlwind of clubs, concerts, restaurants, art galleries, plays, pubs. This guy lived life twenty four hours a day for the week (he nearly killed himself). At the end of the week, however, he was broke and he thought it was only fair to go in to the doctor and tell him he couldn't pay his bill. The doctor gave him another couple of weeks.

Art Director
WALTER CAMPBELL

Copywriter
TOM CARTY

Art Director
WALTER CAMPBELL

Copywriter
TOM CARTY

Is it my imagination or has spontaneity gone out of fashion? I mean, what did you do last night? Go to see a jazz band at Ronnie Scott's? No. An exhibition at The Riverside or Watermans Gallery? No. A late film at The Scala perhaps? No. A quiet night in? Oh. And where are you going now? The same place you were going this time yesterday? I admit I'm not the most spontaneous type myself, but I try. Since I've been reading Time Out there have been one or two departures from the routine. £1.20 every Tuesday and London's your oyster. A little bit of Schubert here and a touch of alternative theatre there. The TV guide's even got me tuning into some rather unusual programmes for those impulsive evenings in. Maybe you should pick up a copy of Time Out. I mean, you don't want to be standing there reading this again tomorrow night.

Art Director
WALTER CAMPBELL

Copywriter
TOM CARTY

Isn't it strange that many of the words we use don't actually relate to what we mean? Phrases like 'I'm catching the train' conjure up very strange images. My mother always used to say to me: 'Watch yourself when you go out.' And my grandmother often used to tell me to shut my mouth and eat my dinner (that's not easy). But I've always had respect for things that mean what they say and say what they mean. Time Out magazine for example, how wonderfully simple. No further explanation needed. £1.20 every Tuesday and you've got yourself a magazine which tells you everything you can do if you fancy going out. But wait a cotton picking minute (there's another one), I've just discovered Time Out is now carrying a complete TV guide, satellite and all. I suppose they'll just have to change their name. 'Time In And Out' perhaps? Or 'Time Out And In'? But then there's also a lot of articles in it these days. I know, maybe it should be 'Time Out And In And Something To Read If There's Nothing Worth Watching On Telly.' Knockout.

Campaigns

Art Directors
JOHN BAYLEY
NICK PARTON

Copywriters
JOHN BAYLEY
NICK PARTON

Photographer
PETER RAUTER

Typographer
STEVE RONCHETTI

Agency
OGILVY & MATHER

Company Advertising Manager
JEREMY STUBBS

Client
LEVER BROTHERS

DON'T ROUGH IT.   LIVE LIFE IN COMFORT.

DON'T ROUGH IT.   LIVE LIFE IN COMFORT.

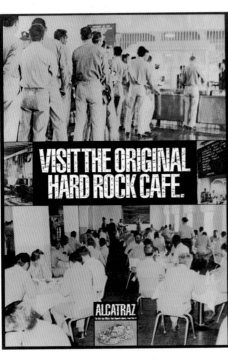

Campaigns

Art Director
JIM NOBLE

Copywriter
MICHAEL WILDE

Illustrator
MICHAEL WILDE

Typographer
MARK A WALSH

Agency
GOLDBERG MOSER
O'NEILL

Marketing Manager
TERRY F KOENIG

Client
THE RED & WHITE
FLEET

Campaigns

Art Directors
GRAHAM CAPPI
MATT MURRAY

Copywriters
MICK GREER
GILES HARGREAVES

Photographer
TERRY O'NEILL

Agency
LEAGAS SHAFRON
DAVIS CHICK

Marketing Manager
PAUL WIELGUS

Client
ALLIED BREWERIES
BRANDS MARKETING

Art Director
MATT MURRAY

Copywriter
GILES HARGREAVES

Photographer
PAUL BEVITT

Art Director
MATT MURRAY
Copywriter
GILES HARGREAVES
Photographer
TERRY O'NEILL

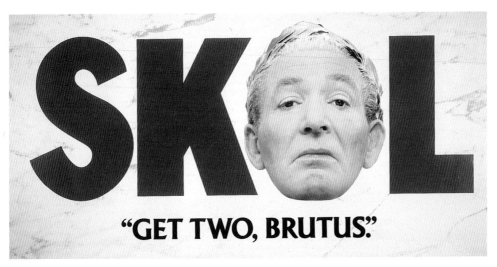

Art Directors
MATT MURRAY
GRAHAM CAPPI
Copywriter
TONY BARRY
Photographer
DAVID MONTGOMERY

Campaigns

Art Director
CHRIS HODGKISS

Copywriter
PIP BISHOP

Photographer
MIKE PARSONS

Modelmaker
MATTHEW WURR

Typographer
CHRIS HODGKISS

Agency
COGENT

Commercial Director
BOB HILL

Client
MILTON KEYNES
DEVELOPMENT
CORPORATION

SORRY. THIS CITY IS FULL

Move to Milton Keynes.

WE APOLOGISE FOR THE LONG DELAYS. THIS IS DUE TO NORMAL TRAFFIC FLOW.

Move to Milton Keynes.

No road works in London.

They do in Milton Keynes.

Campaigns

Art Director
CABELL HARRIS

Copywriter
DION HUGHES

Photographer
RICK DUBLIN

Agency
CHIAT/DAY/MOJO-NY

Director of Marketing
BERNARD
BLOOMFIELD

Client
NYNEX
INFORMATION
RESOURCES

Campaigns

Art Director
CABELL HARRIS

Copywriter
DION HUGHES

Photographer
RICK DUBLIN

Agency
CHIAT/DAY/MOJO-NY

Director of Marketing
BERNARD
BLOOMFIELD

Client
NYNEX
INFORMATION
RESOURCES

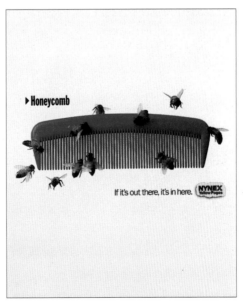

Campaigns

Art Director
ALAN SIMPSON

Copywriter
MARIA PRCHLIK

Photographer
PAUL JONES

Typographer
ALAN SIMPSON

Agency
THE COMPANY WITH
NO NAME

Managing Director
AVRIL PRCHLIK

Client
GOOD GRIEF

BELTS BY GOOD GRIEF.

ACCESSORIES TO ORDER 0484 647586.

DICKIE-BOWS BY GOOD GRIEF.

ACCESSORIES TO ORDER 0484 647586.

TIES BY GOOD GRIEF.

ACCESSORIES TO ORDER 0484 647586.

Any Other

Art Director
WALTER CAMPBELL

Copywriter
TOM CARTY

Typographer
RETLAW MOTT

Agency
ABBOTT MEAD
VICKERS.BBDO
LIMITED

Marketing Director
MIKE HARDWICK

Client
TIME OUT

Is it my imagination or has spontaneity gone out of fashion? I mean,

what did you do last night? Go to see a jazz band at Ronnie Scott's?

No. An exhibition at The Riverside or Watermans Gallery? No. A late

film at The Scala perhaps? No. A quiet night in? Oh. And where are

you going now? The same place you were going this time yesterday?

I admit I'm not the most spontaneous type myself, but I try. Since I've

been reading Time Out there have been one or two departures from

the routine. £1.20 every Tuesday and London's your oyster. A little

bit of Schubert here and a touch of alternative theatre there. The TV

guide's even got me tuning into some rather unusual programmes

for those impulsive evenings in. Maybe you should pick up a copy

of Time Out. I mean, you don't want to be standing there reading

this again tomorrow night.

NOW WITH 8 DAY TV GUIDE.

Any Other

Art Director
RICHARD SMITH

Copywriter
ROLAND DAVIES

Photographer
PAUL BEVITT

Typographer
STEVE RONCHETTI

Agency
OGILVY & MATHER

Advertising Manager
JEREMY STUBBS

Client
LEVER BROTHERS

Any Other

Art Director
KEVIN BRATLEY

Copywriter
JOHN TOWNSHEND

Photographer
ROBERT DOWLING

Typographer
KEVIN BRATLEY

Agency
YELLOWHAMMER

Marketing Director
WILSON MARSHALL

Client
W M TEACHER & SON

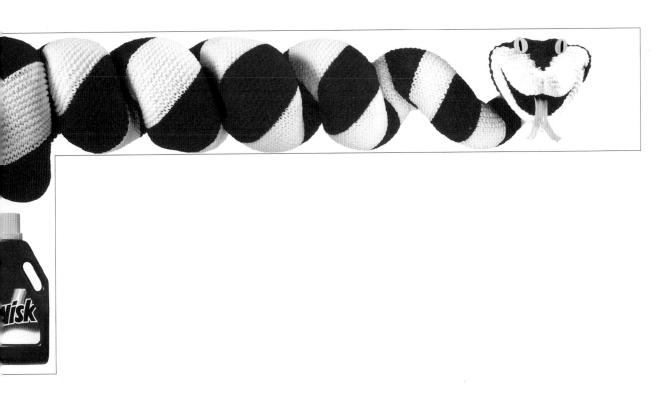

IT OUT OF THE ORDINARY

Any Other

Art Director
MICHAEL WILDE

Copywriter
JIM NOBLE

Illustrator
MICHAEL WILDE

Typographer
MARK A WALSH

Agency
GOLDBERG MOSER
O'NEILL

Marketing Manager
TERRY F KOENIG

Client
THE RED & WHITE
FLEET

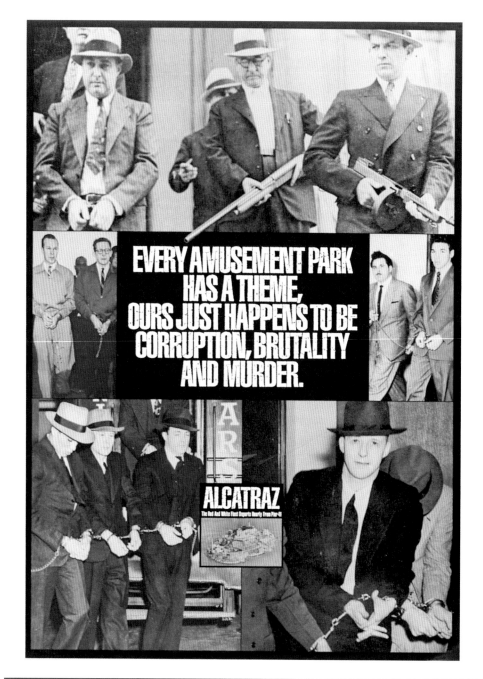

Any Other
Art Director
WALTER CAMPBELL

Copywriter
TOM CARTY

Typographer
GARY TODD

Agency
ABBOTT MEAD
VICKERS.BBDO
LIMITED

Head of Marketing
MALCOLM COX

Client
KISS 100 FM

Any Other

Art Director
MICHAEL
O'SULLIVAN

Copywriter
PAUL CATMUR

Illustrator
H G VASEY

Typographer
RICHARD LAWSON

Agency
YOUNG & RUBICAM

Brand Manager
ROBIN TYLER

Client
COURAGE LIMITED

Any Other

Art Director
WALTER CAMPBELL

Copywriter
TOM CARTY

Typographer
GARY TODD

Agency
ABBOTT MEAD
VICKERS.BBDO
LIMITED

Head of Marketing
MALCOLM COX

Client
KISS 100 FM

Any Other

Art Director
PETER GAUSIS

Copywriter
DAVID ROSSITER

Typographer
JOE HOZA

Agency
ABBOTT MEAD
VICKERS.BBDO
LIMITED

Managing Director
DAVID GORDON

Client
THE ECONOMIST

Any Other

Art Director
GREG MARTIN

Copywriter
NICK BELL

Typographer
JOE HOZA

Agency
ABBOTT MEAD
VICKERS.BBDO
LIMITED

Managing Director
DAVID GORDON

Client
THE ECONOMIST

Any Other

Art Director
JOHN HORTON

Copywriter
RICHARD FOSTER

Photographer
GEOFF SENIOR

Typographer
JOE HOZA

Agency
ABBOTT MEAD
VICKERS.BBDO
LIMITED

Managing Director
DAVID GORDON

Client
THE ECONOMIST

Any Other

Art Director
LYNN KENDRICK

Copywriter
DAVID SHANE

Illustrator
LYNN KENDRICK

Agency
CHIAT/DAY INC

Managing Director
ROBIN BINES

Client
FULL MOON

Any Other

Art Director
CABELL HARRIS

Copywriter
DION HUGHES

Photographer
RICK DUBLIN

Agency
CHIAT/DAY/MOJO-NY

Director of Marketing
BERNARD
BLOOMFIELD

Client
NYNEX
INFORMATION
RESOURCES

di-

m$_{30}$

rect
ail

Business to Business
Individual Items

Art Director
ALAN SIMPSON

Copywriter
MARIA PRCHLIK

Typographer
ALAN SIMPSON

Agency
WHITAKER'S

Client
WHITAKER'S

ABSOLUTE PROOF THAT WHITAKER'S UNDERSTAND YOUR ADVERTISING PROBLEMS.

Right now, you're being inundated with literature from advertising agencies.

And yes, we admit, we're adding to the pile. But we think our message is a valid one and, therefore, worthy of consideration.

That message is, we understand your marketplace.

And with our experience and expertise, we can help you strengthen your position within it.

Which is why, when you receive this mailer, we hope the only thing you'll put in the bin is the liner.

For agency mailers.

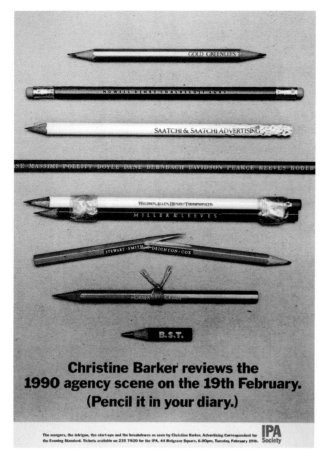

**Christine Barker reviews the
1990 agency scene on the 19th February.
(Pencil it in your diary.)**

The mergers, the intrigue, the start-ups and the breakdowns as seen by Christine Barker, Advertising Correspondent for the Evening Standard. Tickets available on 235 7020 for the IPA, 44 Belgrave Square, 6.00pm, Tuesday, February 19th.

IPA Society

*Business to Business
Individual Items*

Creative Director
BARRY SMITH

Art Director
DAVE DYE

Copywriter
MIKE McKENNA

Typographer
ANDY DYMOCK

Modelmaker
DAVE DYE

Photographer
MALCOLM VENVILLE

Retoucher
ROGER KENNEDY

Agency
PUBLICIS

Marketing Director
CHRIS THOMAS

Client
THE IPA SOCIETY

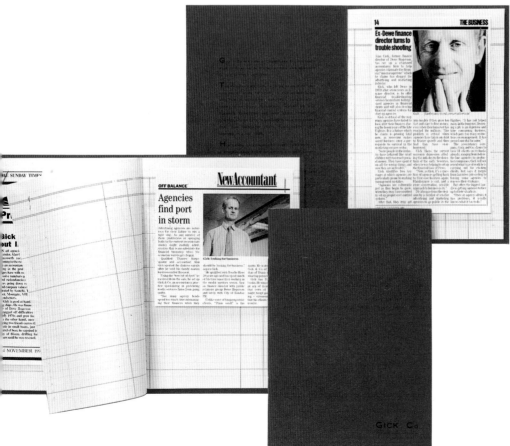

*Business to Business
Individual Items*

Design Directors
BRIGID McMULLEN
MARTIN DEVLIN

Designers
BRIGID McMULLEN
MARTIN DEVLIN

Copywriter
ALAN GICK

Typographer
BRIGID McMULLEN

Design Group
THE WORKROOM

Director
ALAN GICK

Client
GICK & CO

Business to Business
Individual Items

Art Director
TONY MURANKA

Copywriter
KEN MULLEN

Typographers
TONY MURANKA
SIMON GRIMWOOD

Agency
THE CREATIVE
DEPARTMENT

Managing Director
JEREMY LEATHERS

Client
STOCKSIGNS

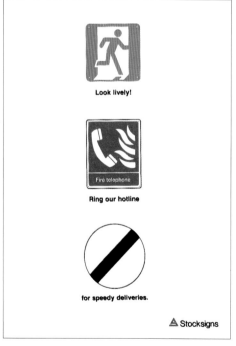

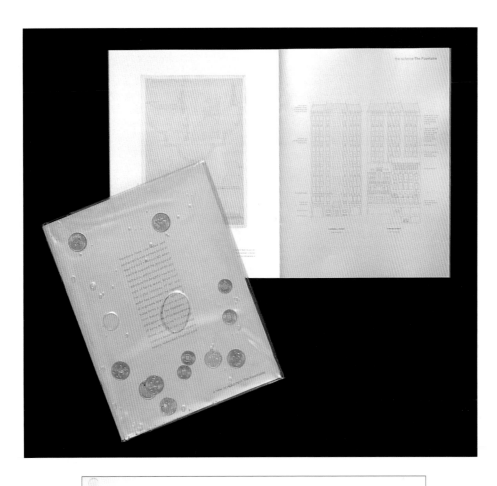

*Business to Business
Individual Items*

Design Director
STEPHEN GIBBONS

Designer
MARTIN
McLOUGHLIN

Copywriter
SIMON RODWAY

Typographers
MARTIN
McLOUGHLIN
DAVID KIMPTON

Design Group
THE PARTNERS

Managing Director
JOHN WATKINS

Client
FIVE OAKS
INVESTMENTS

PERPETUA LIGHT TITLING 480

SYNOPSIS IN 14 POINT

ABCDEFGHIJKLMNOPQRSTUVWXYZ&ÆŒ
£1234567890 .,:!?"-([†8$*—

HAPPYCH RISTMAS FROM THE COMPOSI NGROOM 430·0861

For further information apply to The Composing Room Limited, 18 Leather Lane, London EC1N 7SU.

*Business to Business
Individual Items*

Designer
GRAHAM POWELL

Typographer
GRAHAM POWELL

Design Group
THE COMPOSING
ROOM

Sales Director
JOHN BALDWIN

Client
THE COMPOSING
ROOM

Business to Business
Individual Items

Design Directors
SIMON PEMBERTON
ADRIAN
WHITEFOORD

Designer
SIMON PEMBERTON

Copywriter
LIZ PIPER

Typographers
SIMON PEMBERTON
BEVERLY STEVENS

Illustrator
JOHN HOLDER

Design Group
PEMBERTON &
WHITEFOORD

National Marketing Manager
ALISON VICKERY

Client
TESCO STORES
LIMITED

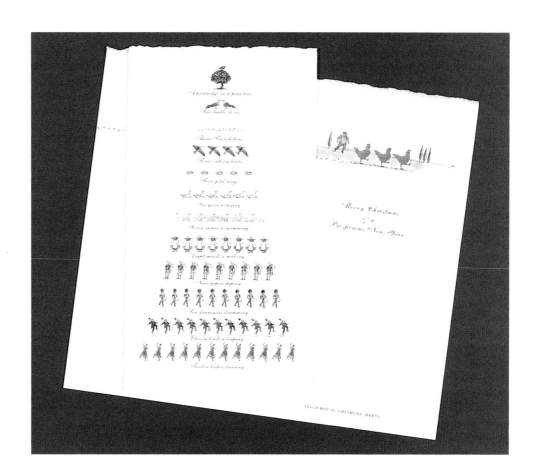

LOOK
FORWARD TO
THE END OF
THE
RECESSION

THE
LIGHT AT
THE END OF
THE TUNNEL
PARTY

Business to Business
Individual Items

Design Director
DAVID TURNER

Designer
DAVID TURNER

Copywriters
HOLLY DAY
JIM KANE

Typographers
JEFFREY STEVENTON

Design Group
TURNER STUDIO
LIMITED

Client
TURNER STUDIO
LIMITED

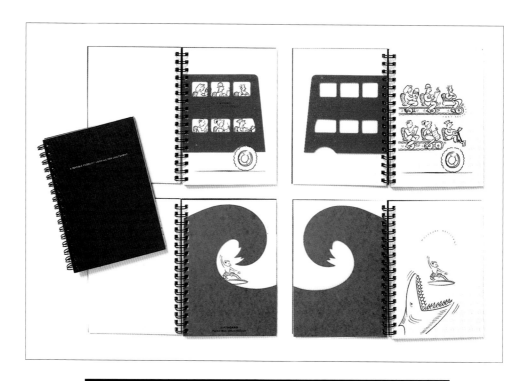

*Business to Business
Individual Items*

Design Director
AZIZ CAMI

Designer
MARITA LASHKO

Copywriter
BERYL McALHONE

Typographers
MARITA LASHKO
GREG QUINTON

Illustrator
MALCOLM ENGLISH

Design Group
THE PARTNERS

Managing Director
MARNIX ZETTELER

Client
ISTD FINE PAPERS
LIMITED

*Business to Business
Individual Items*

Design Director
NANCY WILLIAMS

Designer
DAVID BAIRD

Design Group
WILLIAMS AND PHOA

Marketing Director
LUCY LUCAS

Client
NORWICH UNION
INSURANCE GROUP

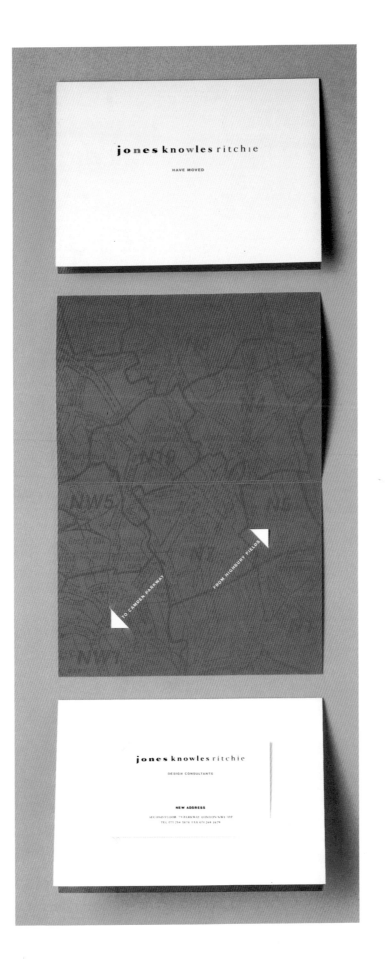

*Business to Business
Individual Items*

Design Director
IAN RITCHIE

Designers
SILAS AMOS
JO BROCK

Typographer
SILAS AMOS

Design Group
JONES KNOWLES
RITCHIE

Client
JONES KNOWLES
RITCHIE

Business to Business
Individual Items

Designer
JERRY KETEL

Copywriter
CARL LOEB

Typographer
JERRY KETEL

Design Group
BANG BANG BANG

Client
ART DIRECTORS
AGAINST FUTURA
EXTRA BOLD
CONDENSED

IMAGINE IF SADDAM HUSSEIN WERE A TYPEFACE:

HE WOULD BE BIG.

HE WOULD BE BOLD.

HE WOULD BE LOUD.

HE'D BE ANNOYING.

HE WOULD BE FAT AND WEAR A MUSTACHE.

HE WOULD HAVE TO BE ELIMINATED.

FUTURA EXTRA BOLD CONDENSED: THE MOTHER OF ALL TYPEFACES.

It's time for Art Directors the world over to boycott the use of Futura Extra Bold Condensed—the most over-used typeface in advertising history. Destroy the Great Satan of clichés and the Little Satan of naked convenience, and rally to the cause of better type selection.

Please fill out the enclosed petition and mail it to our headquarters. It will be used to sway the opinion-makers of our industry toward our just and worthy cause. Together, we can whip this mother.

ART DIRECTORS AGAINST FUTURA EXTRA BOLD CONDENSED.

*Business to Business
Individual Items*

Designer
NEIL DAWSON

Copywriter
NEIL DAWSON

Typographer
MIKE BRANT

Agency
LEO BURNETT
ADVERTISING

Account Director
STEPHEN CALCRAFT

Client
LEO BURNETT
ADVERTISING

*Business to Business
Individual Items*

Design Directors
AZIZ CAMI
DAVID STUART

Designers
JAMES BEVERIDGE
SHAUN DEW
STEPHEN GIBBONS
GREG QUINTON

Copywriter
DAVID GIBBS

Typographer
GREG QUINTON

Photographer
JOHN EDWARDS

Retouching
HILL HEADLAND

Modelmaker
MICHAEL MOORE

Design Group
THE PARTNERS

Client
THE PARTNERS

*Business to
Consumer Individual
Items*

Designers
NICKY REGAN
COLIN GRAY

Photographer
COLIN GRAY

Design Group
BLUE PEACH DESIGN
CONSULTANTS

Client
COLIN GRAY

*Business to
Consumer Individual
Items*

Designer
TONY EVANS

Typographer
TONY EVANS

Photographer
TONY EVANS

Client
PENBRYN PRESS

p

ing

30

ack

ag

SILVER AWARD
for the most outstanding
Range of Packaging

Design Director
JOHN BLACKBURN

Designer
BELINDA DUGGAN

Copywriter
BELINDA DUGGAN

Typographer
BELINDA DUGGAN

Illustrator
GRAY JOLIFFE

Design Group
BLACKBURN'S
LIMITED

Marketing Director
JEAN CONWAY

Client
CLARA CANDY
LIMITED

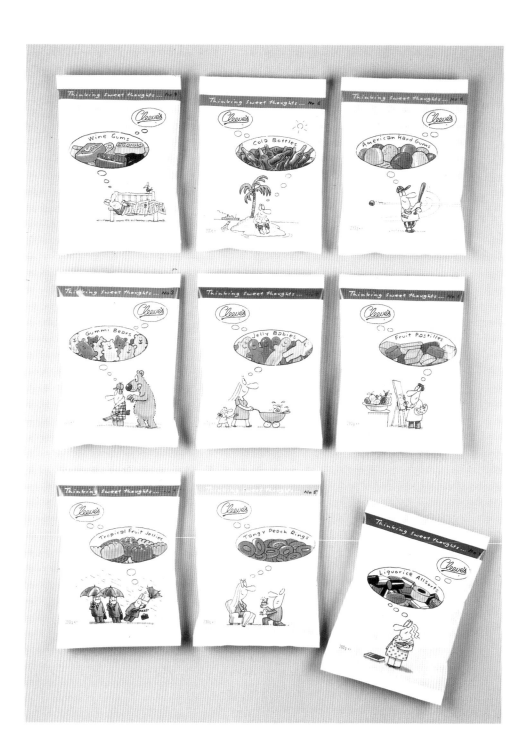

Individual Pack

Design Director
JOHN BLACKBURN

Designer
BELINDA DUGGAN

Copywriter
BELINDA DUGGAN

Typographer
BELINDA DUGGAN

Illustrator
GRAY JOLIFFE

Design Group
BLACKBURN'S
LIMITED

Marketing Director
JEAN CONWAY

Client
CLARA CANDY
LIMITED

Individual Pack

Design Director
GLENN TUTSSEL

Designers
GARRICK HAMM
GLENN TUTSSEL
MICHAEL PATON

Typographer
GARRICK HAMM

Design Group
MICHAEL PETERS
LIMITED

Client
BP

Individual Pack

Design Director
MARY LEWIS

Designer
JIMMY YANG

Copywriters
MARY LEWIS
CHRISTINE LALUMIA

Typographer
JIMMY YANG

Illustrator
JIMMY YANG

Design Group
LEWIS MOBERLY

Director
DAVID DEWING

Keeper of Museum Services
CHRISTINE LALUMIA

Client
GEFFRYE MUSEUM

Individual Pack

Design Director
MARY LEWIS

Designer
MARGARET NOLAN

Typographer
MARGARET NOLAN

Photographer
NICK KNIGHT

Design Group
LEWIS MOBERLY

Marketing Manager of SMA
STEFANO FABRUCCI

Client
LA RINASCENTE

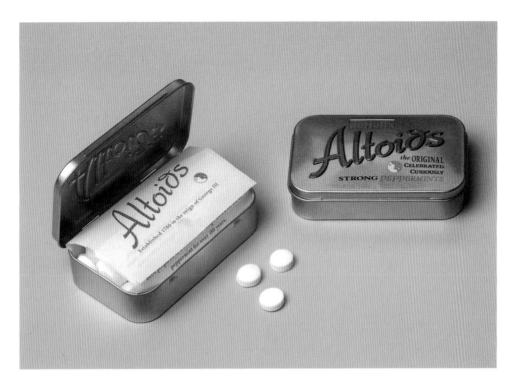

Individual Pack

Design Director
SIMON JOHN

Designers
SIMON JOHN
TIM PERKINS
ANDY JOHNSON

Typographers
TIM PERKINS
ANDREW JOHNSON
JOHN BEECH

Illustrator
WESLEY TRUMBLE

Design Group
COLEY PORTER AND
BELL LIMITED

Marketing Controller
MANDY FERGUSON

Client
TERRYS GROUP

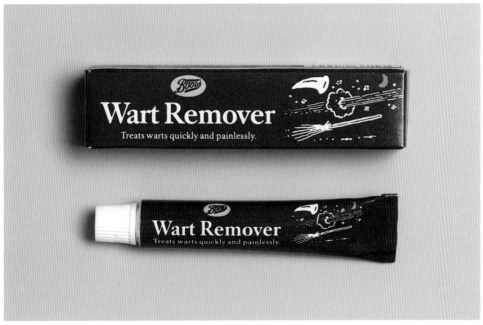

Individual Pack

Design Director
HARRY PEARCE

Designers
HARRY PEARCE
DOMENIC LIPPA

Typographer
HARRY PEARCE

Illustrator
IAN DICKS

Design Group
LIPPA PEARCE
DESIGN LIMITED

Group Buyer
VALERIE TUTCHER

Client
THE BOOTS
COMPANY PLC

Individual Pack

Design Director
STEVE DAVIES

Designer
STEVE DAVIES

Typographer
STEVE DAVIES

Illustrator
TIM LESLIE-SMITH

Design Group
DAVIES HALL
LIMITED

Design Controller
PETER DAY

Client
J SAINSBURY PLC

Range of Packaging

Design Director
SIGI MAYER

Designer
SIGI MAYER

Copywriter
PATSY HASLINGER

Typographer
SIGI MAYER

Design Group
PROJEKTAGENTUR
SIGI MAYER

Client
SARTORI &
RUCHSWURM GESMBH

Range of Packaging

Designer
RICHARD LEALAN

Typographer
RICHARD LEALAN

Photographer
MARTIN BARRAUD

Design Group
SMITH & MILTON

Client
GEOFF MAGEE

Range of Packaging

Design Directors
MICHAEL CHEUNG
MAN
CHUNG CHAN

Designer
MICHAEL CHEUNG
MAN
CHUNG CHAN

Copywriter
SOO WAH POON

Typographers
MICHAEL CHEUNG
MAN
CHUNG CHAN

Illustrator
WAI KEUNG LOO

Design Group
CHAU WAI HANG
WONG WAI SHING

Manager
CAN WONG

Client
JAP BUHT LUN
COMPANY

Range of Packaging

Design Director
MARY LEWIS

Designer
DAVID PIKE

Typographer
DAVID PIKE

Illustrator
GEOFFREY APPLETON

Photographer
PAUL KEMP

Design Group
LEWIS MOBERLY

Marketing Manager of SMA
STEFANO FABRUCCI

Client
LA RINASCENTE

Range of Packaging

Design Director
JIM DOLLERY

Designer
MARIA PIATKOWSKA

Design Group
DOLLERY RUDMAN
DESIGN ASSOCIATES
INC

Product Manager
ANDY MACCULLOCH

Client
H J HEINZ COMPANY
LIMITED

Range of Packaging

Design Director
MARY LEWIS

Designer
BRUCE DUCKWORTH

Typographers
BRUCE DUCKWORTH
NICKY PERKINS

Illustrator
GEOFFREY
APPLETON

Design Group
LEWIS MOBERLY

Marketing Manager of SMA
STEFANO FABRUCCI

Client
LA RINASCENTE

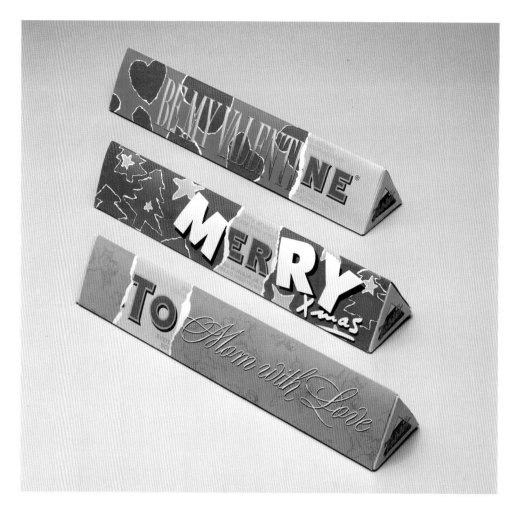

Range of Packaging

Design Director
MARK POSNETT

Designer
MARK POSNETT

Typographer
MARK POSNETT

Design Group
PENTAGRAPH
DESIGN

National Sales Manager
ROB SUTTLE

Client
TOBLERONE
CHOCOLATES
JACOBY & COMPANY
PTY LIMITED

Range of Packaging

Design Director
MARY LEWIS

Designers
KARIN DUNBAR
MARY LEWIS
ANN MARSHALL
JOANNE SMITH

Typographers
KARIN DUNBAR
JOANNE SMITH

Illustrators
KARIN DUNBAR
JOANNE SMITH

Design Group
LEWIS MOBERLY

Director of Buying
PETER FALCONER

Design Co ordinations Manager
DOUGLAS COOPER

Client
WAITROSE LIMITED

Range of Packaging

Design Director
JOHN BLACKBURN

Designer
KATHY MILLER

Typographer
KATHY MILLER

Design Group
BLACKBURN'S
LIMITED

Marketing Director
MAGGIE LEWIS

Client
WAITROSE/
JOHN LEWIS
PARTNERSHIP

SILVER AWARD
for the most outstanding
Self Promotional Item

Design Directors
HANS BOCKTING
WILL DE L'ECLUSE

Designers
HANS BOCKTING
WILL DE L'ECLUSE
VERO CRICKX

Typographer
WILL DE L'ECLUSE

Copywriter
GOVERT SCHILLING

Cartography
DIRK FORTUIN

Design Group
UNA AMSTERDAM

Client
ANDO/BLOEM/UNA
AMSTERDAM

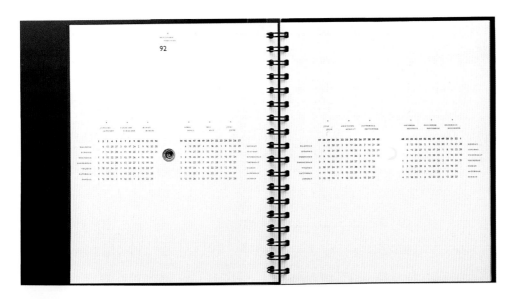

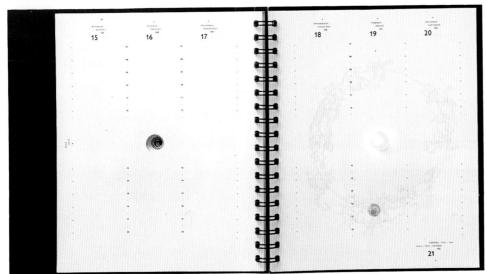

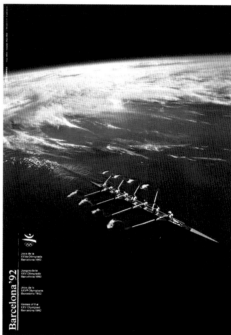

SILVER AWARD
for the most outstanding
Poster Campaign

Design Director
BRENT
OPPENHEIMER

Designers
MADELEINE
BENNETT
BRENT
OPPENHEIMER

Typographer
MADELEINE
BENNETT

Retoucher
JONES BLOOM

Design Group
ADDISON DESIGN
CONSULTANTS

Director
JAUME MASFERRER

Client
C.O.O.B.'92 SA

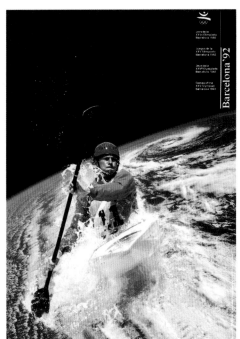

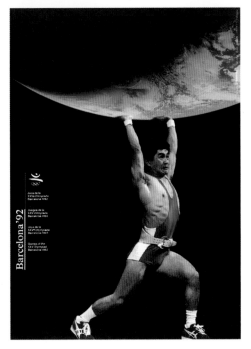

SILVER AWARD
for the most outstanding
Applied Graphic Design

Design Director
STEPHEN GIBBONS

Designer
JANICE DAVISON

Copywriter
JOHNNY BRUCE

Typographer
JANICE DAVISON

Design Group
THE PARTNERS

Manager
ERIK PAGANO

Client
SC PROPERTIES

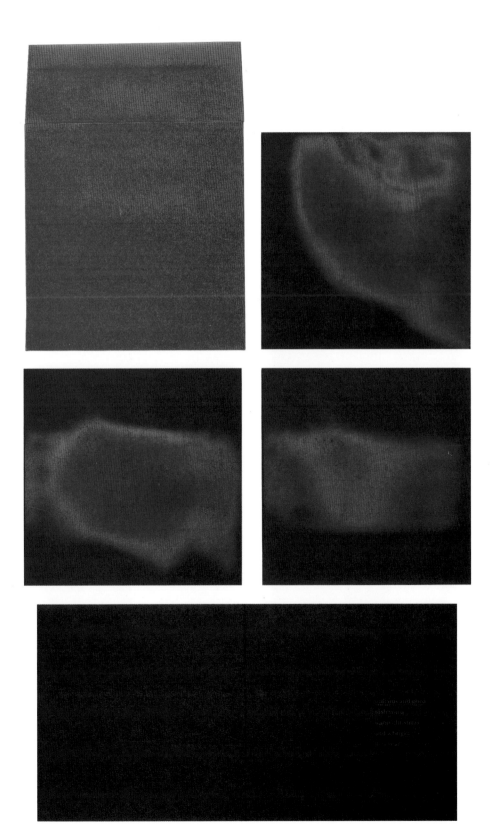

SILVER AWARD
NOMINATION
for the most outstanding
Self Promotional item

Design Director
NANCY WILLIAMS

Designers
SARAH JANE
McKENZIE
NEIL BALFOUR

Design Group
WILLIAMS AND PHOA

Client
WIILIAMS AND PHOA

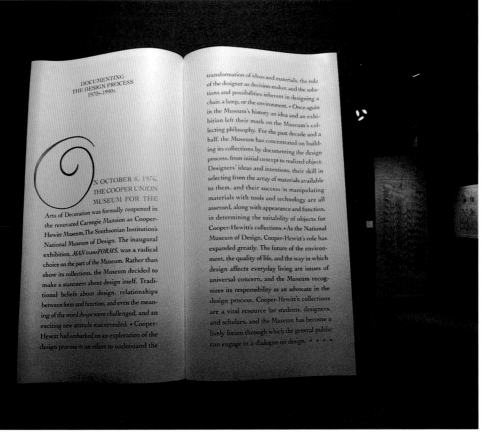

Technical Literature

Designers
LYNN TRICKETT
BRIAN WEBB
SUZANNE EVANS

Copywriter
NEIL MATTINGLEY

Design Group
TRICKETT & WEBB

Marketing Director
BOB LATHAM

Client
SVECIA ANTIQUA

Technical Literature

Design Director
AZIZ CAMI

Designers
MARITA LASHKO
GREG QUINTON

Copywriter
BERYL McALHONE

Typographers
MARITA LASHKO
GREG QUINTON

Illustrator
MALCOLM ENGLISH

Design Group
THE PARTNERS

Managing Director
MARNIX ZETTELER

Client
ISTD FINE PAPERS
LIMITED

Technical Literature

Design Director
DAVID STUART

Designers
NINA JENKINS
ROMAN HUSZAK
SIMON CARTER

Copywriter
DAVID GIBBS

Typographers
NINA JENKINS
ROMAN HUSZAK
SIMON CARTER

Photographers
MARK HALL
JENNY MAY
IAN McKINNELL
SAM McCONNELL

Design Group
THE PARTNERS

Chariman
JOHN WOOD

Client
WOOD & WOOD
INTERNATIONAL
SIGNS LIMITED

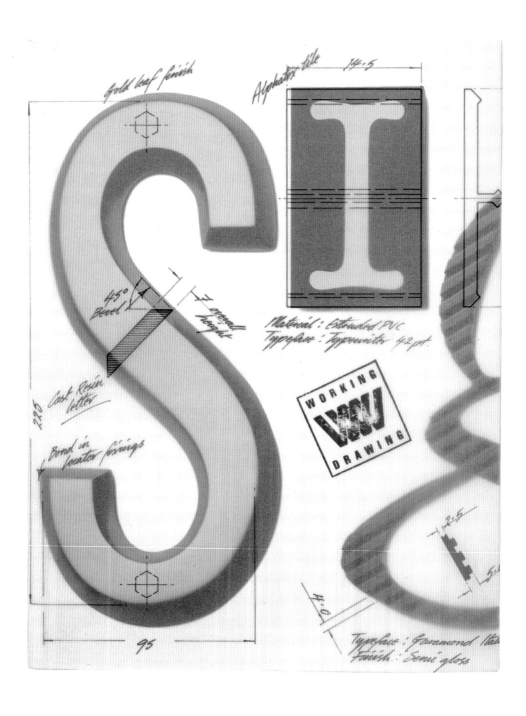

EAGLE STAR
Insurance Company

A TRICKY BLEND of art, artifice, modern technology and traditional craft were key to the development and manufacture of the Eagle Star emblem.

EAGLE STAR

Romney Room
Adelphi Room
Drawing Room
Folkestone Room
Great Room
Library
Shipley Room
Benjamin Franklin Room
Tavern Room
Durham Street Auditorium
Sulhers Court
Vaults

Gentlemens Toilets
Ladies Toilets
Disabled Toilet
Cloakroom

RSA
Society for Arts

THE RSA, or to give it its full title the Royal Society for the Encouragement of Arts, Manufactures and Commerce, has long championed the designer's cause.

RSA

LEICA
Optical Equipment

LEICA IS ONE of the most venerable names in optical instruments and cameras. This old Swiss company's reputation for constant innovation and the precision of its engineering has been growing since it introduced the world's first 35 mm camera in 1913.

Leica

Technical Literature

Design Director
TIMOTHY EATON

Designer
MICHAEL SKJEI

Copywriters
PHIL SANDAHL
MEG McCORMICK
LAURA SHORE

Photographer
LEO KIM

Design Group
EATON &
ASSOCIATES

Manager, Communications &
Promotional Services
LAURA SHORE

Client
MOHAWK PAPER
MILLS INC

Technical Literature

Design Director
GLENN TUTSSEL

Designer
PAUL WILLS

Typographer
PAUL WILLS

Design Group
MICHAEL PETERS
LIMITED

Marketing Director
ANNA SCOTTI

Client
PIRELLI
CO ORDINAMENTO
PNEUMATICI SPA

Brochures

Design Director
TOM KAMINSKY

Designers
TOM KAMINSKY
ALICIA ZAMPITELLA
BOB MANLEY

Copywriter
CRAIG WALKER

Design Group
KAMINSKY DESIGN

Marketing Director
MARGARET CARLISE

Client
SPRINGHILL BY
INTERNATIONAL
PAPER COMPANY

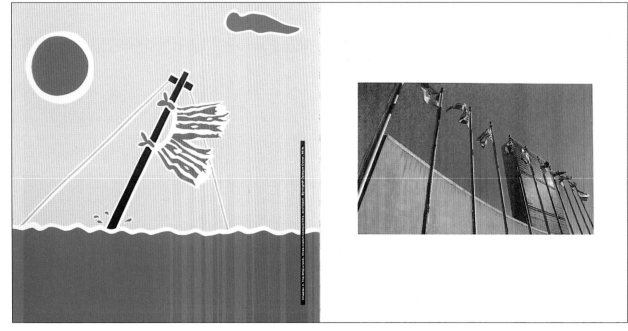

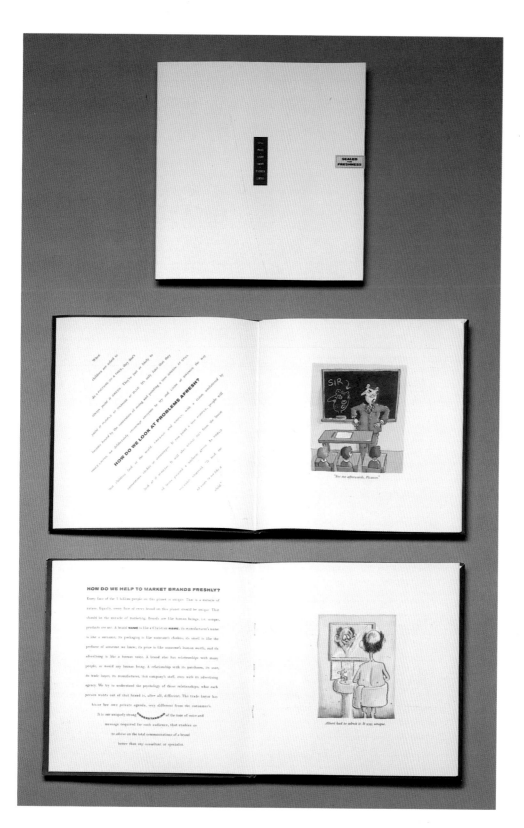

Brochures

Designer
ROB KITCHEN

Copywriter
PAUL TWIVY

Typographer
MARK OSBORNE

Illustrator
NICK SCHON

Agency
STILL PRICE COURT
TWIVY
D'SOUZA:LINTAS

Chairman
CHRIS STILL

Client
STILL PRICE COURT
TWIVY
D'SOUZA:LINTAS

Brochures

Design Director
AZIZ CAMI

Designer
MARITA LASHKO

Copywriter
DAVID GIBBS

Typographer
MARITA LASHKO

Illustrator
NICK BELL

Photographers
SNOWDON
ZAFER BARAN
PETER MARLOW
LOUIS MUTALERO
JOHN EDWARDS

Design Group
THE PARTNERS

Director of Corporate Affairs
DAVD LIVERMORE

Client
IBM UK LIMITED

Brochures

Design Director
MICHAEL DENNY

Designers
MICHAEL DENNY
SARAH PERRY
DARREN
RICHARDSON

Typographer
DARREN
RICHARDSON

Photographer
DAVID TEDMAN

Design Group
ROUNDEL DESIGN
GROUP

Strategic Planning Manager
ROD GRAY

Client
RAIL EXPRESS
SYSTEMS
BRITISH RAILWAYS
BOARD

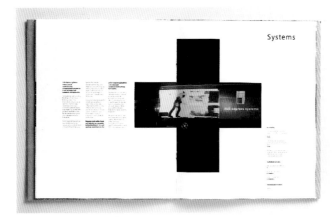

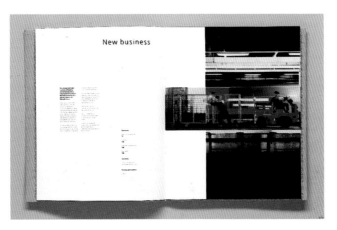

Brochures

Design Director
DAVID STUART

Designers
PETER CARROW
JIM SUTHERLAND

Copywriter
STEPHANIE
COCHRANE

Typographers
PETER CARROW
JIM SUTHERLAND

Photographer
MATTHEW WEINREB

Design Group
THE PARTNERS

Marketing Directors
TIM GRIGGS
ROY TAYLOR
LISA
MOUNTSTEPHEN

Client
BUTLERS WHARF
LIMITED

The Butlers Wharf Building

Clove Building

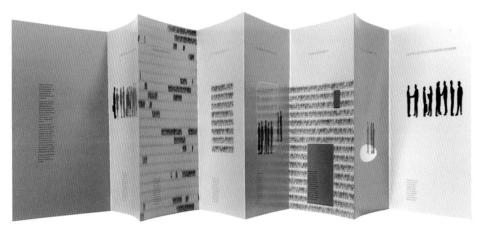

Brochures

Design Director
PHOA KIA BOON

Designers
SARAH JANE
McKENZIE
ROBERT MYTTON
TIM WEBB-JENKINS

Copywriter
GRAHAM JONES

Photographer
DONALD CHRISTIE

Design Group
WILLIAMS AND PHOA

Group Publishing Director
TANYA GOODIN

Client
BLENHEIM GROUP
PLC

Brochures

Designer
SIOBHAN KEANEY

Copywriters
ROBIN SHENFIELD
MARTIN NEWMAN

Typographer
SIOBHAN KEANEY

Illustrators
AMELIA DAVIES
SIOBHAN KEANEY

Photographer
ROBERT
SHACKLETON

Facilities Director
ROBIN SHENFIELD

Client
THE MILL

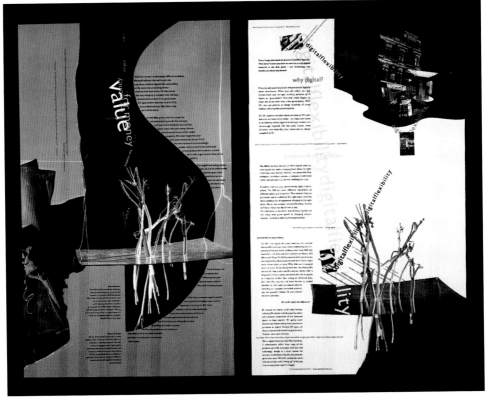

Brochures

Designers
PAUL JENKINS
JANE ALEXANDER
MORAG MYERSCOUGH

Typographers
PAUL JENKINS
JANE ALEXANDER
MORAG MYERSCOUGH

Illustrators
PAUL JENKINS
JANE ALEXANDER
MORAG MYERSCOUGH
LIAM LONGMAN
DAVID LEWIS
RENE EYRE

Photographer
LIAM LONGMAN

Design Group
RANCH ASSOCIATES

Marketing Directors
JAMES MACKAY
DAVID LEWIS

Client
BASILISK LIMITED

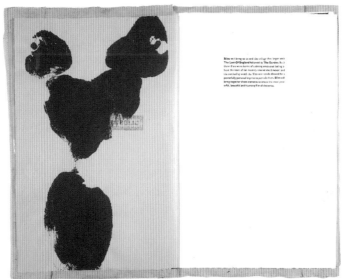

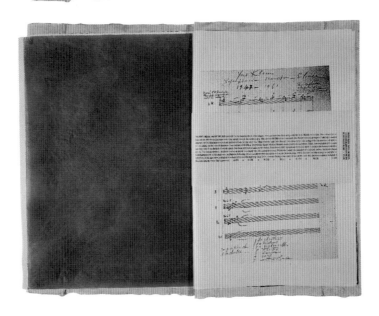

Brochures

Design Director
PHOA KIA BOON

Designer
SARAH JANE
McKENZIE

Copywriter
DAVID CRAWFORD

Black & White Photography
JIM ARNOULD

Design Group
WILLIAMS AND PHOA

Client
CECIL DENNY
HIGHTON

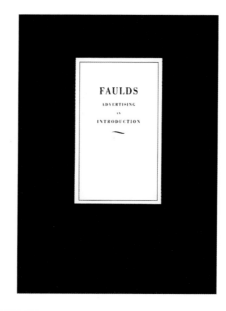

Brochures

Design Director
IAN McILROY

Designers
IAN McILROY
GRAHAM SCOTT
ALAN AINSLEY

Copywriters
SIMON SCOTT
ANDREW LINDSAY

Typographer
GRAHAM SCOTT

Illustrators
AIRD McKINSTRIE
ANDREW BAILEY

Design Group
McILROY COATES
LIMITED

Managing Director
JIM FAULDS

Client
FAULDS
ADVERTISING
LIMITED

Brochures

Design Directors
AZIZ CAMI
JAMES BEVERIDGE
SHAUN DEW
STEPHEN GIBBONS
DAVID STUART

Designer
GREG QUINTON

Copywriter
DAVID GIBBS

Typographer
GREG QUINTON

Photographer
JOHN EDWARDS

Retouching
HILL HEADLAND

Models
MICHAEL MOORE

Design Group
THE PARTNERS

Client
THE PARTNERS

Brochures

Design Director
MARTIN J SIMPSON

Designer
CARL BEBBINGTON

Typographer
CARL BEBBINGTON

Photographer
MIKE INCH

Design Group
HURLSTON DESIGN
LIMITED

Client
HURLSTON DESIGN
LIMITED

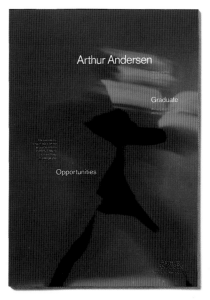

Brochures

Design Director
NICHOLAS THIRKELL

Designer
TOM CREW

Copywriter
SARAH GALL

Typographer
TOM CREW

Photographer
RICHARD J
BURBRIDGE

Design Group
CARROLL DEMPSEY &
THIRKELL

UK Director of Personnel
FAITH JENNER

Client
ARTHUR ANDERSEN &
COMPANY

Brochures

Design Directors
MARK FARROW
NEIL TENNANT
CHRIS LOWE

Designers
MARK FARROW
ROB PETRIE
SIAN CLEAVER

Copywriter
CHRIS HEATH

Typographers
MARK FARROW
ROB PETRIE
SIAN CLEAVER

Photographers
PAUL RIDER
ERIC WATSON
PENNIE SMITH
LAWRENCE WATSON

Design Group
FARROW

Client
PET SHOP BOYS
PARTNERSHIP
LIMITED

Product

Performances

Brochures

Design Director
FRANCES NEWELL

Designers
SIMON WRIGHT
LIN WONG

Copywriter
JOHN SIMMONS

Typographers
SIMON WRIGHT
LIN WONG

Illustrators
BILL SANDERSON
CAROLYN GOWDY
SIMON WRIGHT
LIN WONG
NICOLA SARGENT
PAUL GRIST
QUENTIN BLAKE
GLEN BAXTER
DOUG JAMES
LIONEL KOECHLIN

Photographers
BRUCE WILLS
FELICITY NOCK

Design Group
NEWELL AND
SORRELL

Marketing Director
GEMMA BLENCOWE

Client
ROYAL MAIL

Brochures

Design Director
ROBERT VALENTINE

Designer
ROBERT VALENTINE

Copywriter
CHUCK CARLSON

Photographer
CRAIG PERMAN

Design Group
ROBERT VALENTINE
INC

*Manager Marketing Strategy &
Communication*
SU McLOUGHLIN

Client
GILBERT PAPER

Brochures

Design Director
GABOR PALOTAI

Designer
GABOR PALOTAI

Art Director
JÖRGEN WALDÉN

Illustrator
GABOR PALOTAI

Photographer
DENISE GRÜNSTEIN

Design Group
GABOR PALOTAI
DESIGN
OBSERVERA/GREY

Marketing Director
CHRISTER MALM

Client
POSTGIRO

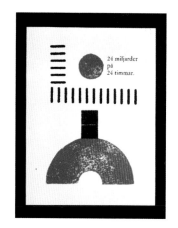

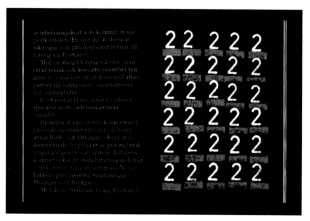

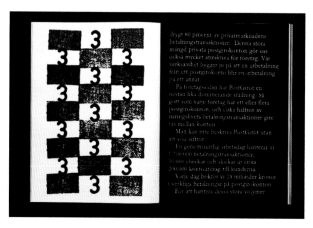

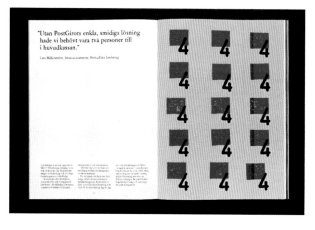

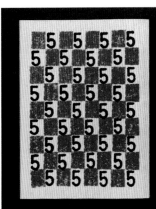

räcker det inte med att ha en av Sveriges största datacentraler, högt driven automatik med bland annat optisk läsning och bildfångst. Det måste också till erfaret folk som kan jobbet, klarar stressen och har ögonen på skaft.

På PostGirot arbetar cirka 4.000 personer med att se till att betalningarna hamnar hos rätt personer och företag varje dag.

Om du lägger ett fullpackat, portofritt brunt kuvert på lådan någonstans i Sverige en tisdag, behandlar vi dina transaktioner på onsdagen. På torsdag har du den fullständiga redovisningen av alla in- och utbetalningar med posten. Allt detta på ett mycket kostnadseffektivt sätt, där priset bestäms av företagets totala engagemang i postgirosystemet.

PostGirots grundprincip är att behandla och redovisa betalningsuppdrag inom Sverige på 24 timmar. Alla transaktioner görs över eget kontosystem, ej via bank

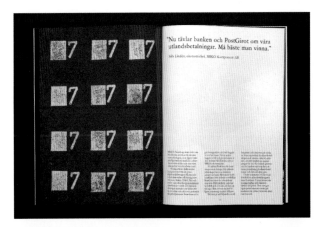

"Nu tävlar banken och PostGirot om våra utlandsbetalningar. Må bäste man vinna."

Nils Lindén, eko-tenniskel, MIKO Komponent AB

för dina utlandsaffärer. Framtiden kommer att tillhöra den betalningsförmedlare som inte bryr sig om avstånder. Det ska vara lika lätt och okomplicerat att förmedla betalningar till Tokyo som till Tomelilla.

Redan idag går en tredjedel av alla utlandstransaktioner som görs i Sverige via PostGirot. Med den utveckling på informationsområdet vi nu påbörjat kommer vi att snabbt öka vår marknadsandel. Kunderna finns, behovet finns. Vi har resurserna och kunnandet.

Nu vet du att PostGirot är mer än bruna kuvert. Ett offensivt, utvecklings inriktat företag som arbetar i konkurrens och lever på att våra kostnadseffektivare än andra aktörer på betalningsmarknaden.

Då inser du också att du kan ha mer nytta av ditt postgirokonto än enbart för att betala moms, skatt och arbetsgivaravgifter.

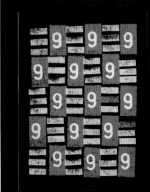

24 miljarder på 24 timmar.

Brochures

Design Director
JOHN VAN DYKE

Designer
JOHN VAN DYKE

Copywriter
JON BELL

Calligrapher
SACHA
BELOSLUDTSEV

Photographer
RICK ENGLISH

Design Group
VAN DYKE COMPANY

Advertising Manager
SHAWN PALMER

Client
MEAD CORPORATION

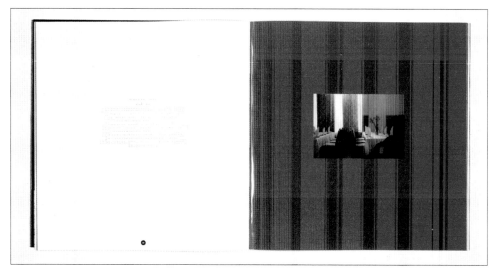

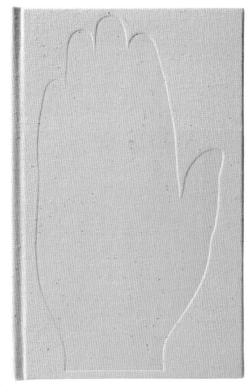

Brochures

Design Director
JACK PEARCE

Designers
HARVEY LYON
ANDREW ROSS

Copywriter
NEIL MATTINGLEY

Typographers
HARVEY LYON
JACK PEARCE

Illustrator
ROBIN DEAN

Photographers
JOHN ELLARD
PETER SILK

Design Group
SILK PEARCE

Marketing Director
ANDREW HIPWELL

Client
HIPWELL
BOOKBINDERS

Brochures

Design Director
MICHAEL DENNY

Designers
JOHN BATESON
RACHAEL DINNIS
MARION HARE

Copywriter
CHARLOTTE LAWRIE

Typographers
RACHAEL DINNIS
MARION HARE

Photographer
MICHAEL BANKS

Design Group
ROUNDEL DESIGN
GROUP

Project Manager
JOHN HAWTHORNE

Client
RAILFREIGHT
DISTRIBUTION
BRITISH RAILWAYS
BOARD

Brochures

Designer
STEPHEN MALE

Photographer
DONALD CHRISTIE

Design Group
NICE

Client
LEVI STRAUSS UK
LIMITED

Brochures

Design Director
AZIZ CAMI

Designer
MARITA LASHKO

Copywriter
DAVID GIBBS

Typographer
MARITA LASHKO

Photographers
TIM MOTION
NADAV KANDER
CÉDRIC TARNAUD
MARC DENEYER

Design Group
THE PARTNERS

Director
IVOR OWEN

Client
THE DESIGN
COUNCIL

Brochures

Designers
PAUL JENKINS
JANE ALEXANDER

Copywriter
JULIA THRIFT

Typographers
PAUL JENKINS
JANE ALEXANDER

Illustrators
PAUL JENKINS
JANE ALEXANDER
ROBERT
SHACKLETON

Photographer
ROBERT
SHACKLETON

Design Group
RANCH ASSOCIATES

Marketing Manager
MANDY
DIAMANT DAVIES

Client
TAPE ONE STUDIOS

Catalogues

Design Director
BEN CASEY

Designer
LISE WARBURTON

Typographer
LISE WARBURTON

Design Group
THE CHASE
CREATIVE
CONSULTANTS
LIMITED

Marketing Director
FIONA CANDY

Client
LANCASHIRE
POLYTECHNIC

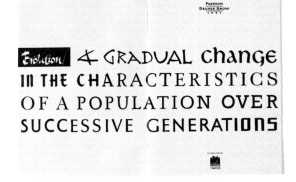

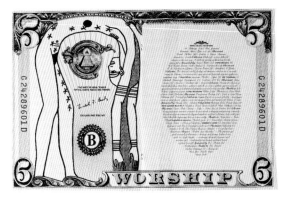

Catalogues

Designer
MICHEL DE BOER

Typographer
MICHEL DE BOER

Photographers
LEX VAN PIETERSON
MAARTEN LAUPMAN
PAUL MARTENS

Design Group
STUDIO DUMBAR

Marketing Director
WILLEM VAN
VELDHUIZEN

Client
DRUKKERIJ
PLANTIJN BV

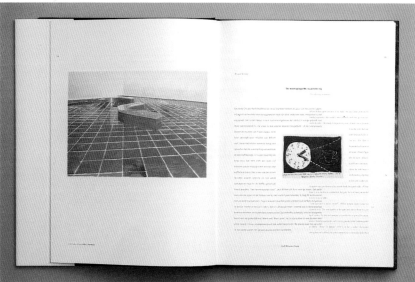

Catalogues

Designers
RICHARD
BONNER-MORGAN
STEPHEN MALE
NEIL EDWARDS

Photographer indoors
GARETH McCARTHY

Photographer outdoors
STEFAN RUIZ

Design Group
NICE

Client
LEVI STRAUSS UK
LIMITED

product description guide autumn/winter 1992

blue
full season · june/nov

all american tops
full season · june/nov

517

518

60507

70507

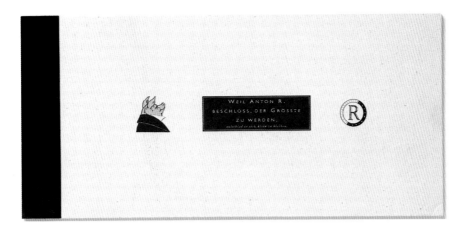

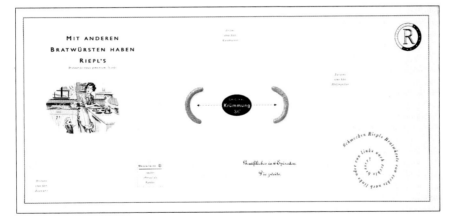

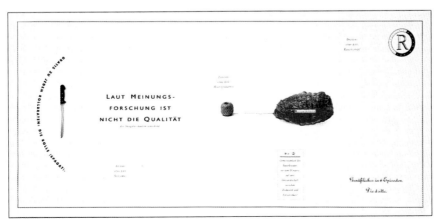

Catalogues

Design Director
SIGI MAYER

Designers
THOMAS
SCHERNHUBER
SIGI MAYER

Copywriter
THOMAS
SCHERNHUBER

Typographer
SIGI MAYER

Illustrator
MANFRED KIRCHMAYR

Photographer
GERHARD MERZEDER

Design Group
PROJEKTAGENTUR
SIGI MAYER

Marketing Director
ANTON RIEPL

Client
A RIEPL
FLEISCHMANUFAKTUR

Catalogues

Design Director
SIGI MAYER

Designer
SIGI MAYER

Copywriter
MR ILK

Typographer
SIGI MAYER

Photographer
MARIO KATZMAIER

Design Group
PROJEKTAGENTUR
SIGI MAYER

Client
ILK & ILK

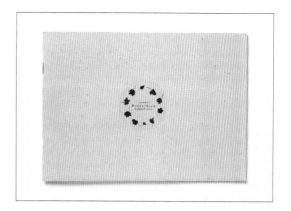

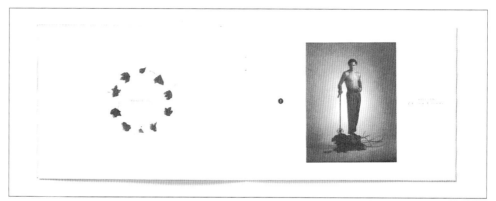

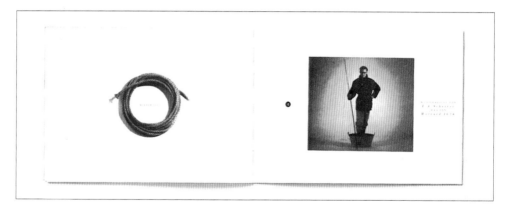

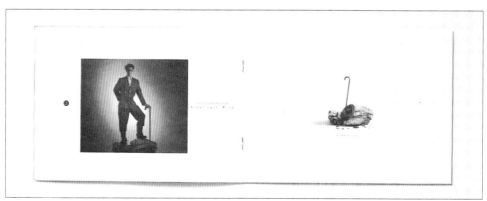

Catalogues

Designer
MICHAEL JOHNSON

Copywriter
MICHAEL JOHNSON

Typographer
MICHAEL JOHNSON

Photographers
EVAN HURD
MARTIN BARRAUD
MICHAEL HARDING

Design Group
SMITH & MILTON

Marketing Director
HRH THE PRINCE OF
HANOVER

Client
THE WATCH
GALLERY

Annual Reports

Designer
KATE STEPHENS

Artist
ANDY
GOLDSWORTHY

Client
ABSA

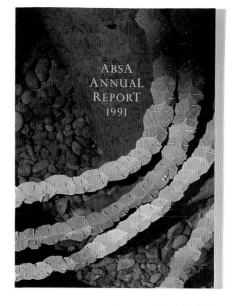

THE
CHAIRMAN'S
FOREWORD

SIR SIMON HORNBY

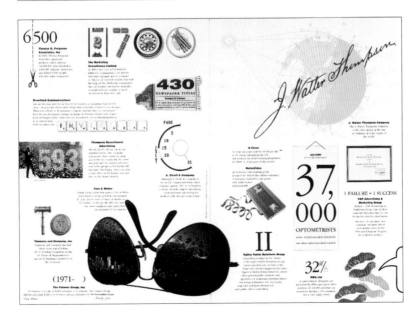

Annual Reports

Designers
JON HENRY
SHAUN WESTGATE

Copywriter
MARTIN SORRELL

Typographers
JON HENRY
SHAUN WESTGATE

Creative Director
DAVID FREEMAN

Illustrators
ROY KNIPE
PAUL SLATER
BILL BUTCHER
KIRA JOSEY
DESMOND LYNCH
JULIE SMITH
ANDY HUNT
DAVID FREEMAN
SHAUN WESTGATE

Photographer
MARTIN LANGFIELD

Design Group
SAMPSON TYRRELL
LIMITED

Group Chief Executive, WPP Group plc
MARTIN SORRELL

Client
WPP GROUP PLC

Annual Reports

Design Director
WILL DE L'ECLUSE

Designers
WILL DE L'ECLUSE
INGEBORG BLOEM

Typographer
WILL DE L'ECLUSE

Photographer
LEX VAN PIETERSON

Design Group
UNA AMSTERDAM

Client Marketing Executive
J. P. E. BARBAS

Client
VRG GROUP

What we said we'd do

What we did

And where we're going...

Addison in 1996

We said we'd return to operating profit of £1,050,000. We achieved a profit of £1,053,000. We said we'd improve net dividend to...

We resolved to be
more creative

We undertook to
be profitable...

Annual Reports

Design Director
GRAHAM TAYLOR

Designers
MIKE TURNER
GRAHAM TAYLOR

Copywriters
STEVE SMITH
ROBIN DOW

Typographers
MIKE TURNER
GRAHAM TAYLOR

Photographer
CHRIS MOYSE

Design Group
ADDISON

Chairman
STEVE SMITH

Client
ADDISON
WORLDWIDE
LIMITED

Annual Reports

Design Director
MIKE DEMPSEY

Designer
BARBRO OHLSON

Typographer
BARBRO OHLSON

Photographer
RICK CORDELL

Design Group
CARROLL DEMPSEY &
THIRKELL

Marketing Executive
JOHN BURKE

Client
BP CHEMICALS

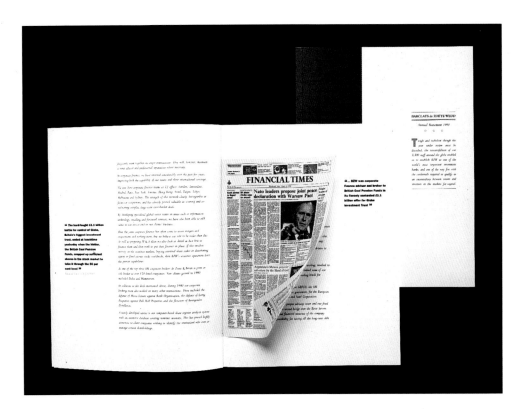

Annual Reports

Design Director
DAVID STUART

Designer
PETER CARROW

Copywriters
ALAN PAGE
HARARI PAGE

Typographer
PETER CARROW

Photographers
ANDREW MORANI
NIGEL PARRY

Design Group
THE PARTNERS

*Assistant Director Corporate
Communications*
LOUISE POOLE

Client
BARCLAYS DE ZOETE
WEDD

Leaflets

Design Director
MARY LEWIS

Designer
JIMMY YANG

Copywriters
MARY LEWIS
CHRISTINE LALUMIA

Typographer
JIMMY YANG

Illustrator
JIMMY YANG

Design Group
LEWIS MOBERLY

Director
DAVID DEWING

Keeper of Museum Services
CHRISTINE LALUMIA

Client
GEFFRYE MUSEUM

The Geffrye Museum is set in elegant 18th century almshouses with pleasant gardens in Shoreditch, East London, once the heart of London's furniture industry. The Geffrye presents the changing style of typical English domestic interiors from 1600 to the present day. Exhibitions, activities and events all year round make the Geffrye one of London's most friendly and enjoyable museums. Kingsland Road, London E2 8EA. Telephone 071 739 9893.

Leaflets

Design Director
NANCY WILLIAMS

Designer
LAURA HEARD

Photographer
TREVOR KEY

Design Group
WILLIAMS AND PHOA

Marketing Director
RUSS DAVENPORT

Client
LEEDS CITY
COUNCIL

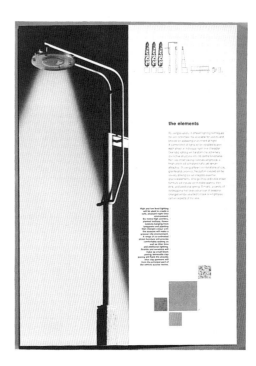

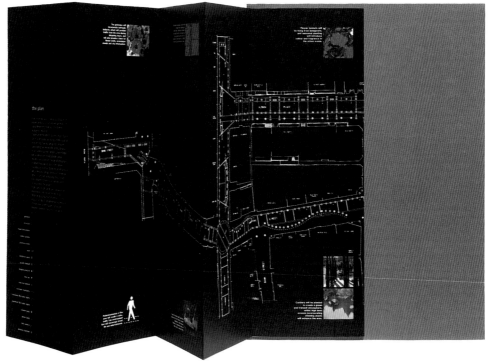

Leaflets

Design Director
PHOA KIA BOON

Designers
SARAH JANE
McKENZIE
JO SHACKLETON

Copywriter
GORDON FIELDING

Design Group
WILLIAMS AND PHOA

Creative Director
ROD JEFFS

Client
THE PARK COMPANY

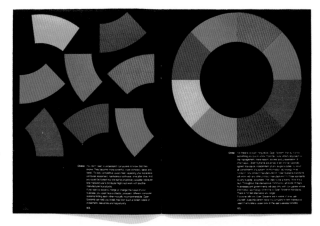

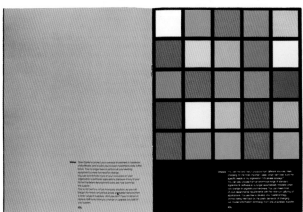

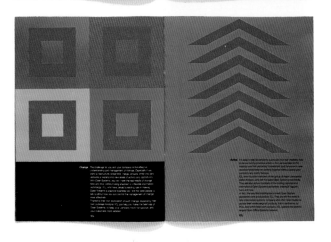

Calendars

Designers
JACQUES
KOEWEIDEN
PAUL POSTMA

Typographers
JACQUES
KOEWEIDEN
PAUL POSTMA

Photographer
YANI

Design Group
KOEWEIDEN/POSTMA

Marketing Director
JANET HAZELAAR

Client
MINISTRY OF
ECONOMIC AFFAIRS

Calendars

Design Director
JOHN BATESON

Designers
MICHAEL DENNY
CHRIS BRADLEY
MARION HARE
RACHAEL DINNIS
JOHN BATESON

Copywriter
NEIL MATTINGLEY

Typographer
MARION HARE

Photographer
STUART REDLER

Design Group
ROUNDEL DESIGN
GROUP

Account Manager
STEVE PRICE

Design Manager
PAUL STEPHENSON

Client
TRAINLOAD FREIGHT
BRITISH RAILWAYS
BOARD

Stamps

Designer
JEAN MICHEL FOLON

Illustrator
JEAN MICHEL FOLON

Design Director
BARRY ROBINSON

Client
ROYAL MAIL

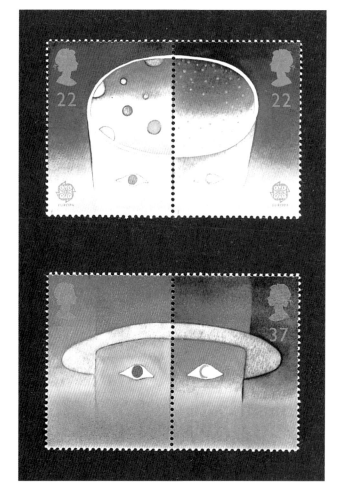

Stamps

Designer
HOWARD BROWN

Typographer
HOWARD BROWN

Design Director
BARRY ROBINSON

Client
ROYAL MAIL

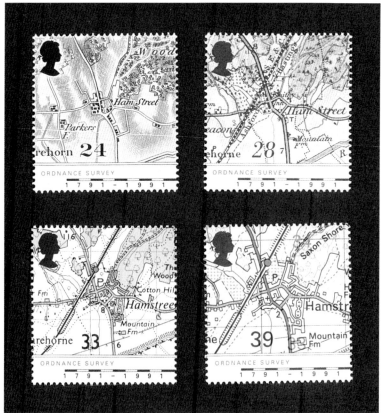

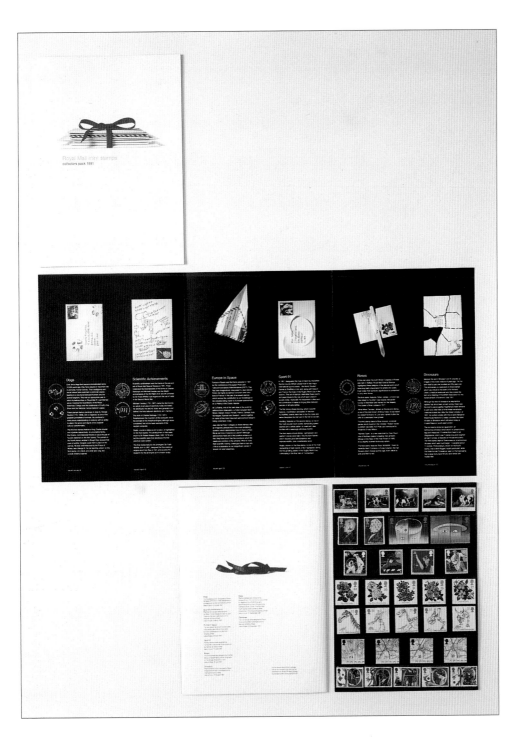

Any Other

Design Director
NANCY WILLIAMS

Designers
RICHARD SCHOLEY
ROBERT MYTTON

Illustrators
RICHARD SCHOLEY
ROBERT MYTTON

Photographer
JOHN STONE

Design Group
WILLIAMS AND PHOA

Marketing Director
ANGELA REEVES

Client
ROYAL MAIL

Any Other

Design Director
ALBERT KUEH

Designer
ALBERT KUEH

Typographer
ALBERT KUEH

Design Group
ALBERT KUEH

Client
KATE SPENCE

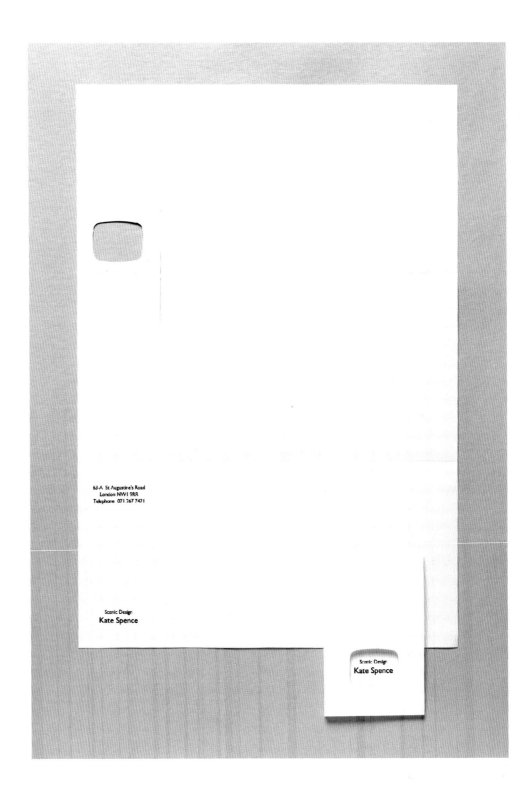

63-A St Augustine's Road
London NW1 9RR
Telephone 071 767 7471

Scenic Design
Kate Spence

Scenic Design
Kate Spence

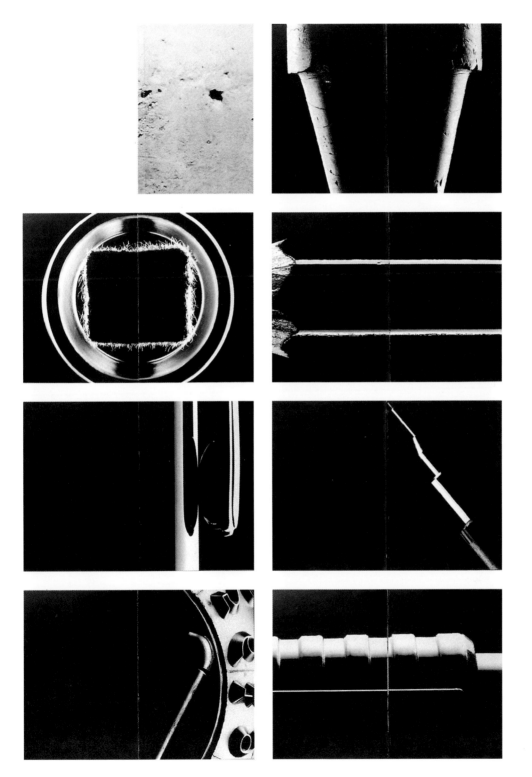

Any Other

Design Director
JOHN RUSHWORTH

Designers
JOHN RUSHWORTH
PETER WOOD

Photographer
PETER WOOD

Design Group
PENTAGRAM DESIGN

Any Other

Designers
BARBRO OHLSON
MARIANN WISSA

Typographers
BARBRO OHLSON
MARIANN WISSA

Photographer
ANDREW OLNEY

Design Group
PERSONA

Managing Director
NICHOLAS
DESCHAMPS

Client
PRECISE LITHO
LIMITED

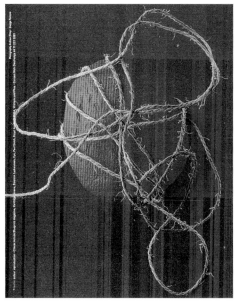

Any Other

Design Director
TONY VEAZEY

Designer
ANDY CHEETHAM

Copywriter
TONY VEAZEY

Typographer
ANDY CHEETHAM

Photographer
CHRIS CHEETHAM

Design Group
BROADBENT
CHEETHAM VEAZEY

Marketing Director
DAVID AUERBACH

Client
DAVID AUERBACH

Any Other

Design Director
IVAN DODD

Designer
IAN SMITH

Copywriter
IVAN DODD

Typographer
LEZ BRANSCOMBE

Illustrator
MARIANNE BEHM

Design Group
IVAN DODD
DESIGNERS

Client
IVAN DODD
DESIGNERS

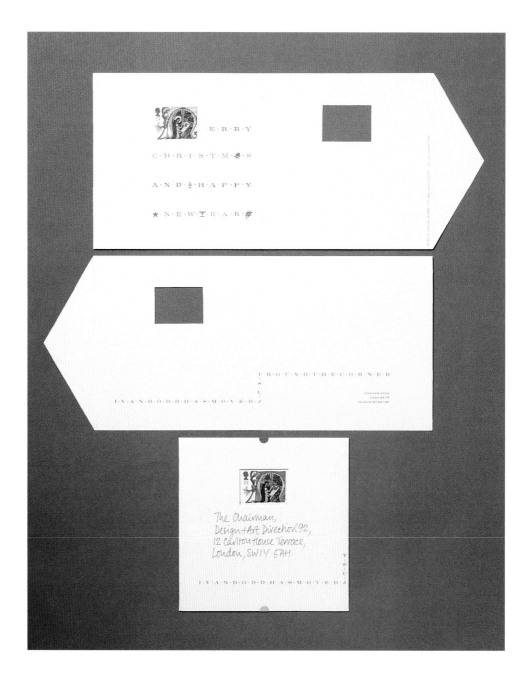

Listen, I don't wanna be a whiner but nobody here really appreciates me or has the slightest idea how creative I could be if they'd just keep their blundering meathooks to themselves and stop trashing my stuff and now I've got this *1991 Addy Call for Entries* in front of me and all I can think is how good it would feel to win but let's face it, 1991 was a sorry year and frankly a big dud for me since I don't have any decent work to show, even though the cleaning lady seemed to like that piece I did a while back and maybe I should stop being so modest and seriously think about entering it and maybe a few more pieces, too, I mean they might be better than I'm giving myself credit for, they might actually win and jeez, if I won, it would be complete vindication, NAH-nah-nah-NAH-nah nirvana, it would be just like in my dreams, people would leap up to give me a standing ovation and crowd around me to pump my hand, they'd fight to woo me away, everybody would be smarmy and coveting, and all that would be just fine, it would be terrific, if I won all my clients would personally thank me for working on their accounts, all my co-workers would throw me a gala victory party, all my ex-lovers would rue the day they left me and it's a sure bet if I won I would get more respect, more recognition, more money, yeah maybe a bonus, and maybe even a bonus on top of a salary raise, maybe even a huge Christmas bonus on top of that because nobody's more talented than me me me me

Any Other

Design Directors
JUDY SMITH
PETER SHIKANY

Designers
JUDY SMITH
PETER SHIKANY
MARGARET BEATTY

Copywriter
JOANNE BELL-SMITH

Design Group
PS STUDIOS

Client
PHOENIX
ADVERTISING CLUB

Any Other

Design Director
ROBIN HUNNAM

Copywriter
CONRAD BIRD

Typographer
ROBIN HUNNAM

Illustrator
FRANCESCA
PELIZZOLI

Design Group
HUNNAM BIRD
LIMITED

President
PER BRICK

Marketing Director
YLVA KLINGVAL

Client
ABID KORT

THERE WAS ONCE a King and Queen whose only wish in life was to have a daughter. As the years passed, their sadness grew and it seemed they would never laugh again.

The greatest physicians from the four corners of the kingdom were called to the castle, but no cure could be found.

"Their hearts are breaking," they finally declared, "and there is no remedy for that affliction."

One day an old beggar appeared at the castle gate. His clothes were in rags and he was so weak with hunger that he could barely stand.

On the morning of Freya's tenth birthday, the beggar returned to the castle and demanded to see the King.

"My travels are over," he said. "I must now return with the Golden Rose to my own land."

But by now, the King had forgotten about the Rose and his promise, for his thoughts had only been with Freya.

"You must help," pleaded the King. "Our daughter will not awake and we fear for her life. You are the only person who can return her to us. Do this and you shall have a thousand roses and gold beyond measure."

The beggar did not answer. Instead he pushed past the King and there, in a far corner of the garden, he saw the Rose neglected and dying.

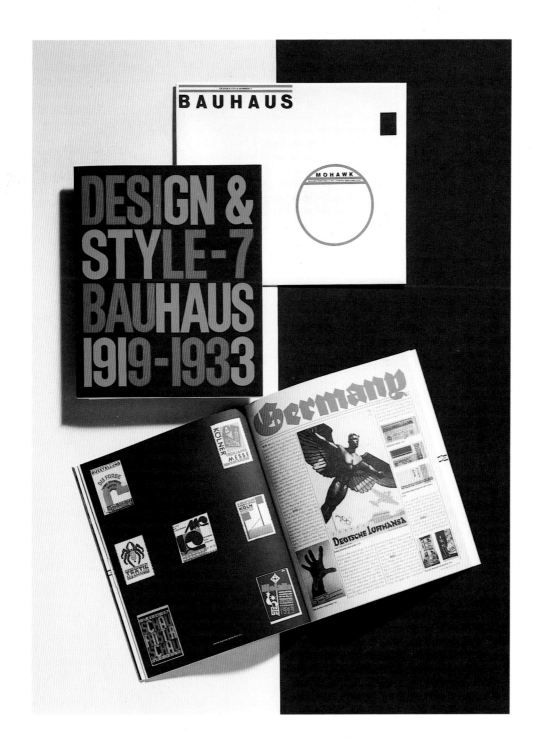

Any Other

Design Director
SEYMOUR CHWAST

Designers
SEYMOUR CHWAST
ROXANNE SLIMAK

Copywriter
STEVEN HELLER

Design Group
THE PUSHPIN GROUP

Manager, Communications &
Promotional Services
LAURA SHORE

Client
MOHAWK PAPER
MILLS INC

Any Other

Designer
MICHAEL JOHNSON

Copywriter
MICHAEL JOHNSON

Typographer
MICHAEL JOHNSON

Photographers
EVAN HURD
MARTIN BARRAUD
MICHAEL HARDING

Design Group
SMITH & MILTON

Marketing Director
HRH THE PRINCE OF
HANOVER

Client
THE WATCH
GALLERY

Any Other

Design Director
JIM NORTHOVER

Designer
JO CLARKE

Copywriter
JIM BODOH

Design Group
LLOYD NORTHOVER

Marketing Director
SARAH HOHN

Client
REUTERS

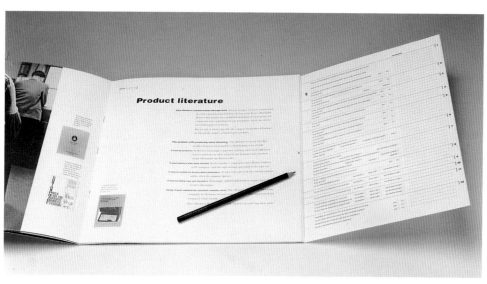

GEFFRYE MUSEUM

ENGLISH DOMESTIC INTERIORS FROM THE 17TH CENTURY

KINGSLAND ROAD, LONDON E2 8EA   TEL 071 739 9893   **FREE** ADMISSION   **OPEN** TUESDAY - SATURDAY 10AM - 5PM
SUNDAY 2PM - 5PM   **CLOSED** MONDAYS   **NEAREST TUBES** LIVERPOOL STREET, OLD STREET (EXIT 2)

TUTTO SUL PACKAGING DESIGN, 23 OTTOBRE 1991, MILANO

Posters Individual

Designer
MARCELLO MINALE

Copywriter
MARCELLO MINALE

Typographer
LIZ KNIGHT

Illustrator
LIZ KNIGHT

Photographer
NICK DALE

Design Group
MINALE
TATTERSFIELD &
PARTNERS

Marketing Director
IDA MORAZZONI

Client
PACKAGING
CONFERENCE

Posters Individual

Design Director
ERWIN PIPLITS

Illustrator
BRAD HOLLAND

Client
ODEON/SERAPIONS
THEATRE

Posters Individual

Designer
JANICE
KIRKPATRICK

Typographer
JANICE
KIRKPATRICK

Design Group
GRAVEN IMAGES

Director
NEIL WALLACE

Client
TRAMWAY

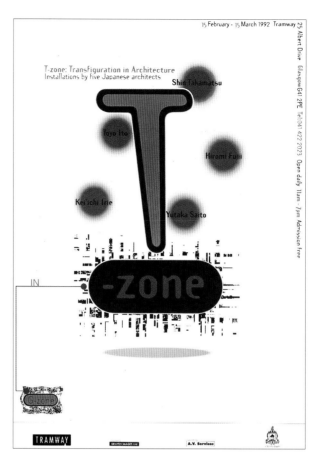

Posters Individual

Design Director
BRUCE DUCKWORTH

Designers
BRUCE DUCKWORTH
PAUL BROWTON

Typographer
BRUCE DUCKWORTH

Illustrator
MARK RYLANDS

Design Group
LEWIS MOBERLY

Marketing Director
MIKE DUCKWORTH

Client
THE ROTARY CLUB
OF CAMBERLEY

Posters Individual

Design Director
GERT DUMBAR

Designer
ROBERT NAKATA

Typographer
ROBERT NAKATA

Photographer
LEX VAN PIETERSON

Design Group
STUDIO DUMBAR

Marketing Director
LEONIE TEN DUIS

Client
ZEEBELT THEATER

Posters Individual

Design Director
JOHN RUSHWORTH

Designers
JOHN RUSHWORTH
MARIE CHRISTINE
ECKLIN

Illustrator
MARIE CHRISTINE
ECKLIN

Design Group
PENTAGRAM DESIGN

Client
WALTER SCHWAIGER
SCHWAIGER
WINSCHERMANN

Posters Individual

Design Director
MARK DENTON

Designers
MARK DENTON
ANDY McKAY

Copywriter
CHRIS PALMER

Photographer
MALCOLM VENVILLE

Design Group
SIMONS PALMER
DENTON CLEMMOW &
JOHNSON LIMITED

Managing Director
FRANK DIMECH

Client
WRANGLER UK
LIMITED

Posters Individual

Designer
MARK DENTON

Copywriter
CHRIS PALMER

Illustrator
HUNT EMERSON

Design Group
SIMONS PALMER
DENTON CLEMMOW &
JOHNSON LIMITED

Managing Director
FRANK DIMECH

Client
WRANGLER UK
LIMITED

Rossini. Donizetti. Arias. Ramon Vargas, Tenor. English Chamber Orchestra. Marcello Viotti, Conductor.

Compact Disc or
Record Sleeves
Individual

Designers
STEPHANIE NASH
ANTHONY MICHAEL

Typographer
ANTHONY MICHAEL

Photographer
TOBY GLANVILLE

Design Group
MICHAEL NASH
ASSOCIATES

Corporate Communications
Manager
SEAN MURRAY

Client
PHILIP MORRIS
CORPORATE
SERVICES INC

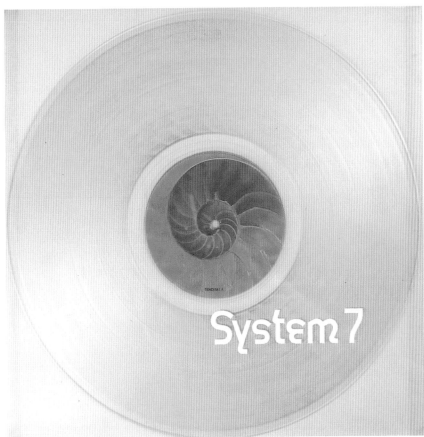

System 7

Compact Disc or
Record Sleeves
Individual

Design Director
DAVID JAMES

Designers
DAVID JAMES
GARETH HAGUE

Typographers
DAVID JAMES
GARETH HAGUE

Photographer
LEWIS MULATERO

Design Group
DAVID JAMES
ASSOCIATES

Head of Marketing
DAVID STEEL

Client
CIRCA RECORDS

*Compact Disc or
Record Sleeve
Campaigns*

Design Director
MARK FARROW

Designers
MARK FARROW
SIAN CLEAVER
ROB PETRIE
PHIL SIMS

Typographers
MARK FARROW
SIAN CLEAVER

Design Group
FARROW

Marketing Director
PETER HADFIELD

Client
DECONSTRUCTION
RECORDS/
PARLOPHONE

*Applied Graphic
Design*

Design Director
STEPHEN GIBBONS

Designers
JANICE DAVISON
DAVID KIMPTON
MARTIN
McLOUGHLIN

Typographers
DAVID KIMPTON
JANICE DAVISON

Artist
CHRIS PERRY

Technical Sign Designer
RICHARD CONN

Design Group
THE PARTNERS

Marketing Director
JAN PESTER

Client
CDP NEXUS

entity

SILVER AWARD
for the most outstanding
Corporate Identity
Programme

Design Director
MIKE DEMPSEY

Designers
STEVEN CARTER
IAN CHILVERS
MIKE DEMPSEY
FERNANDO
GUTIÉRREZ
BARBRO OHLSON

Typographers
STEVEN CARTER
IAN CHILVERS
MIKE DEMPSEY
FERNANDO
GUTIÉRREZ
BARBRO OHLSON

Illustrator
LIZ PYLE

Photographers
MICHAEL BANKS
RICHARD BURBRIDGE
MIKE LAYE
LEWIS MULATERO

Design Group
CARROLL DEMPSEY &
THIRKELL

Marketing Director
KEITH COOPER

Client
ENGLISH NATIONAL
OPERA

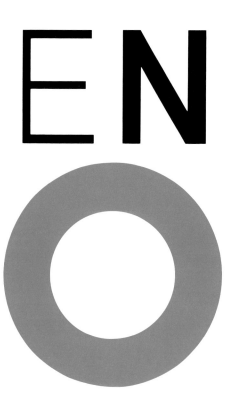

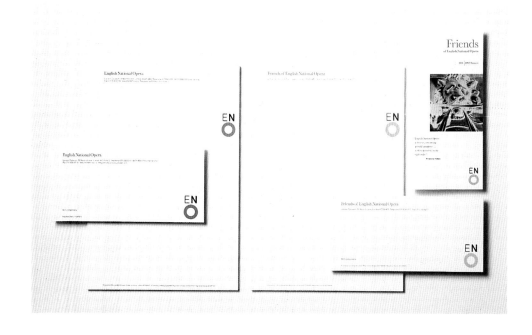

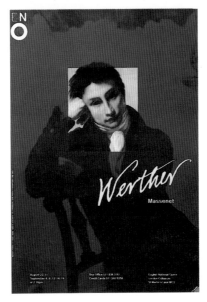

SILVER AWARD
for the most outstanding
Logotype

Design Director
MIKE DEMPSEY

Designer
MIKE DEMPSEY

Typographer
MIKE DEMPSEY

Design Group
CARROLL DEMPSEY &
THIRKELL

Marketing Director
KEITH COOPER

Client
ENGLISH NATIONAL
OPERA

ENO

*Corporate Identity
Programmes*

Design Director
JOHN RUSHWORTH

Designers
JOHN RUSHWORTH
VINCE FROST

Typographer
VINCE FROST

Photographer
STEVE REES

Design Group
PENTAGRAM DESIGN

Head of Public Realtions
JONATHON LORRIE

Client
CRAFTS COUNCIL

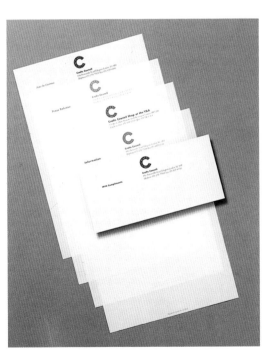

*Corporate Identity
Programmes*

Design Directors
JOHN McCONNELL
JUSTUS OEHLER

Designers
JUSTUS OEHLER
KATE EMAMOODEN

Typographer
JUSTUS OEHLER

Design Group
PENTAGRAM DESIGN

Head of Public Relations
TIM BEAUMENT

Client
THE NATIONAL GRID
COMPANY PLC

Stationery Ranges

Design Director
GLENN TUTSSEL

Designer
GLENN TUTSSEL

Typographer
GLENN TUTSSEL

Illustrator
ANTON MORRIS

Design Group
MICHAEL PETERS
LIMITED

Client
MICHAEL PETERS
LIMITED

Stationery Ranges

Design Director
MIKE DEMPSEY

Designer
FERNANDO
GUTIÉRREZ

Typographer
FERNANDO
GUTIÉRREZ

Photographer
MICHAEL BANKS

Design Group
CARROLL DEMPSEY &
THIRKELL

Marketing Director
PETER ROWE

Client
HILO OFFSET
COLOUR
REPRODUCTION

Symbols and
Logotypes

Design Director
MARY LEWIS

Designer
MARY LEWIS

Design Group
LEWIS MOBERLY

Managing Director
COLIN PILGRIM

Client
HEAL'S

HEAL'S

Stationery Ranges

Design Director
PIERRE VERMEIR

Designer
SIMON DRYLAND

Photographer
ANDREW YATES

Design Group
HALPIN GREY
VERMEIR

Client
ANNI TOWNEND

Stationery Ranges

Design Director
PAUL RODGER

Designer
PAUL RODGER

Typographer
LOL GRINTER

Illustrator
JOZ COOK

Photographer
ALLAN JONES

Design Group
BULL RODGER
LIMITED

Client
ALLAN JONES

Stationery Ranges

Designer
RON VAN DER VLUGT

Illustrator
RON VAN DER VLUGT

Client
MARCEL
VAN DER VLUGT
PHOTOGRAPHY

22 x 11
envelope

21 x 29.7
letter

10 x 21
compliments
card

6 x 10
business
card

Steve Yarnell Sports Photographer
7 Knutsford View, Hale Barns, Cheshire WA15 8SU
061 980 4476

*Individual
Letterheads*

Design Director
TONY VEAZEY

Designer
ANDY CHEETHAM

Copywriter
TONY VEAZEY

Typographer
SIMON BROADBENT

Modelmaker
ROWENA KIDD

Photographer
ROBERT WALKER

Design Group
BROADBENT
CHEETHAM VEAZEY

Marketing Director
STEVE YARNELL

Client
STEVE YARNELL

*Individual
Letterheads*

Design Director
TIM WALKER

Designer
TIM WALKER

Typographer
PAUL IZARD

Design Group
WALKER IZARD

Marketing Director
DR JOHN BROWN

Client
DR JOHN BROWN

ed

itoria

30

anc

books

Book Covers

Design Director
STEPHEN GIBBONS

Designer
MARTIN McLOUGHLIN

Copywriter
SIMON RODWAY

Typographers
MARTIN McLOUGHLIN
DAVID KIMPTON

Design Group
THE PARTNERS

Managing Director
JOHN WATKINS

Client
FIVE OAKS
INVESTMENTS

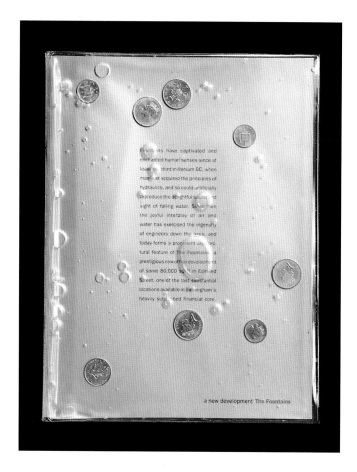

Book Covers

Design Director
DAVID STUART

Designers
NINA JENKINS
ROMAN HUSZAK
SIMON CARTER

Copywriter
DAVID GIBBS

Typographers
NINA JENKINS
ROMAN HUSZAK
SIMON CARTER

Illustrator
RICHARD CONN

Photographer
IAN McKINNELL

Design Group
THE PARTNERS

Chairman
JOHN WOOD

Client
WOOD & WOOD
INTERNATIONAL
SIGNS LIMITED

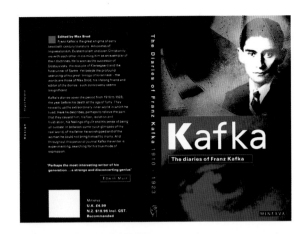

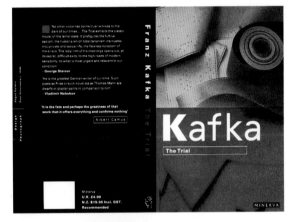

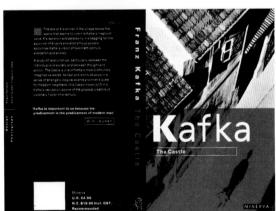

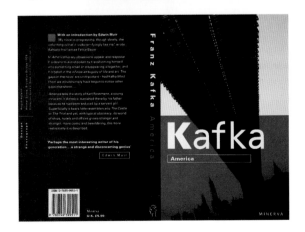

Book Covers

Designer
ANGUS HYLAND

Author
FRANZ KAFKA

Typographer
ANGUS HYLAND

Photographers
WALKER EVANS
JOSEF SUDEK
PAUL SCHUITEMA

Design Group
HYLAND/CANTRILL

Client
OCTOPUS
PUBLISHING

Book Covers

Design Director
NICHOLAS THIRKELL

Designers
IAIN CROCKART
NICHOLAS THIRKELL

Typographers
IAIN CROCKART
NICHOLAS THIRKELL

Illustrators
KIM MARSLAND
BENOIT JACQUES
PETER TILL
JANET WOOLLEY
FRANCES TEE
DAVID HOLMES
DEBBIE LUSH
IRENE VON TRESKOW
ANDREW KULMAN
RICHARD PARENT
LEO DUFF
ELIZABETH HARBOUR
IAN POLLOCK
ANDREW MOCKETT
LIZ PYLE
JEFF FISHER
ANDREW DAVIDSON
DENNIS LEIGH
JANE HUMAN
CHRISTOPHER BROWN
PAUL LEITH
PUI YEE LAU
BRIAN CAIRNS
KAREN LUDLOW
KATIE LESTER
ZAFER BARAN
CHRIS CORR
CLIFFORD HARPER
ROSEMARY WOODS
CHLOE CHEESE
TOBY MORRISON
JEAN-CHRISTIAN
KNAFF
DAN FERN
CAROLYN GOWDY
DOVRAT BEN-NAHUM
LOUISE BRIERLY
ANDRZEJ DUDZINSKI
GRISELDA
HOLDERNESS
MARION DEUCHARS
ASHLEY POTTER

Design Group
CARROLL DEMPSEY &
THIRKELL

Editor
KATHY ROONEY

Client
BLOOMSBURY
PUBLISHING

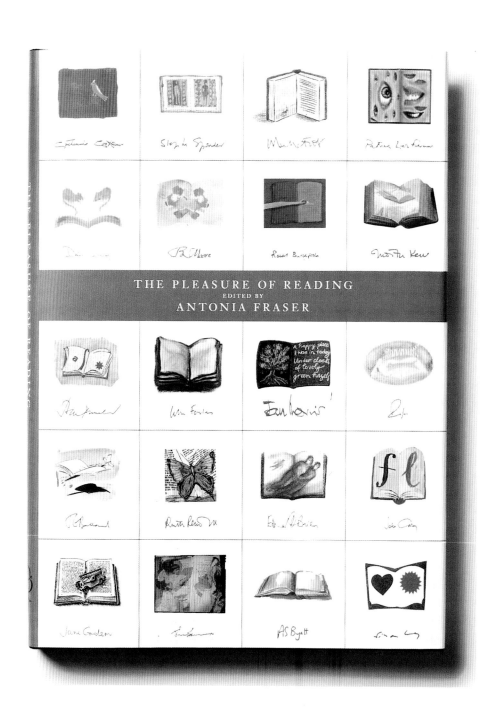

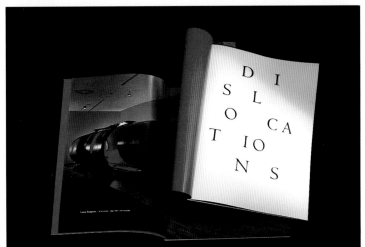

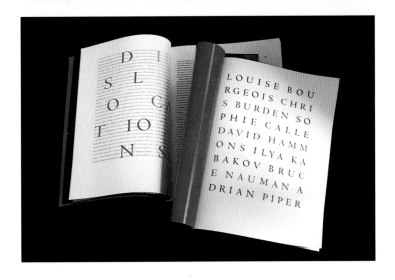

Complete Books

Designers
ANDREW GRAY
STEPHEN DOYLE

Typographer
ANDREW GRAY

Design Group
DRENTTEL DOYLE
PARTNERS

Design Director
MICHAEL HENTGES

Client
THE MUSEUM OF
MODERN ART

Complete Books

Design Director
DAVID HILLMAN

Designers
DAVID HILLMAN
JULIE FITZPATRICK

Copywriter
ARABELLA BOXER

Typographers
DAVID HILLMAN
JULIE FITZPATRICK

Photographer
TESSA TRAEGAR

Design Group
PENTAGRAM DESIGN

Marketing Director
TESSA TRAEGAR

Client
RANDOM CENTURY
LIMITED

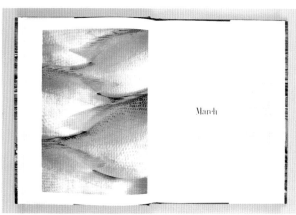

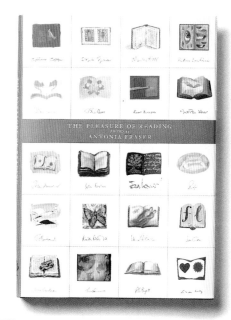

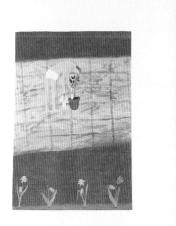

Complete Books

Design Director
NICHOLAS THIRKELL

Designers
IAIN CROCKART
NICHOLAS THIRKELL

Typographers
IAIN CROCKART
NICHOLAS THIRKELL

Illustrators
KIM MARSLAND
BENOIT JACQUES
PETER TILL
JANET WOOLLEY
FRANCES TEE
DAVID HOLMES
DEBBIE LUSH
IRENE VON TRESKOW
ANDREW KULMAN
RICHARD PARENT
LEO DUFF
ELIZABETH HARBOUR
IAN POLLOCK
ANDREW MOCKETT
LIZ PYLE
JEFF FISHER
ANDREW DAVIDSON
DENNIS LEIGH
JANE HUMAN
CHRISTOPHER BROWN
PAUL LEITH
PUI YEE LAU
BRIAN CAIRNS
KAREN LUDLOW
KATIE LESTER
ZAFER BARAN
CHRIS CORR
CLIFFORD HARPER
ROSEMARY WOODS
CHLOE CHEESE
TOBY MORRISON
JEAN-CHRISTIAN
KNAFF
DAN FERN
CAROLYN GOWDY
DOVRAT BEN-NAHUM
LOUISE BRIERLY
ANDRZEJ DUDZINSKI
GRISELDA
HOLDERNESS
MARION DEUCHARS
ASHLEY POTTER

Design Group
CARROLL DEMPSEY &
THIRKELL

Editor
KATHY ROONEY

Client
BLOOMSBURY
PUBLISHING

Complete Books

Art Editors
MARTIN JAQUES
STUART RUSSELL

Designers
MARTIN JAQUES
STUART RUSSELL

Copywriter
JAKE MICHIE

Design Group
GARNER RUSSELL
LIMITED

Marketing Director
TOM SHAW

Publisher
GARNER RUSSELL
LIMITED

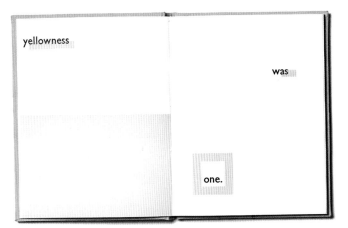

Quasar Flight to strengthen the resolve. **I leaped** into the darkness,

slipped a foot down on the Conran Boost
counter and angled through the pulsing maze
to my beloved machine. 'I hate you,' I thought,
'nothing gets out of here alive,' and feeding
some extra quarters aged chasing things, I
grabbed the joystick and zeroed into the swirling motions of the fiendish Zeradon. An hour
later I was still hunched over the glass glare,
my burning forehead pressed against the screen,

---

the last of my enemies spiralling hopelessly into an imploding galaxy. Orrlriiite! I swivelled on my heels, furiously punching the air, and was immediately caught in a shower of embers. A mumbled 'sorry' emanated from a small rubbery figure retreating across the carpet. I looked at my hand.

There was a *livid burn appearing on my wrist, only an inch or so from my...* 'Sorry? You're sorry!' I shouted, throwing *the mangled cigarette at him, 'D'you know how much this suit cost? Do you? This suit cost more than your house.' A* hundred eyes *bent in my direction.* 'More than all your houses, shit-heads!

Flashing almost imperceptibly,
she fingered the cuff of my jacket. 'I read...I mean

I thought you never left the **States**

What are you doing *here!*
'I...'
'I'm sorry, this is silly, but we don't often get the opportunity to...'
'Hey Isabella, don't worry about it. Really. To tell the truth I'm kinda flattered you recognised me. As you said I, uh, keep sort of a low profile these days.'
'Well, I couldn't miss the suit, could I? They're a bit of a trademark, you must admit.'
'I guess so.'
'I loved the one you wore for the *Newsweek* spread.'
'I got paint on that one.' She laughed again.
'Look, I've kept you long enough, but if you've got the time, drop into the gallery...Well, goodbye for now.'
'Isabella, it's been a pleasure, and really, if I've got a free moment you'll be the first to know.'
We shook hands, her fingers trailing down my palm as she moved away, and with a swish of the hair she was gone. Wow. I had pulled it off, I had been *him*. In fact, for a couple of minutes I was still him. Hey, look at that guy in the green polyester shirt. Face buried in a bag of chips. Get out of my way, scumbag. Ha! I strode past the George (Frank would never drink *there*) and headed for the Cafe des Intellectuels.

Slicing through the pastel hordes, my pockets heavy with imaginary credit cards, I became gripped by a vision of Isabella. I could really... Perhaps I'll pop into see her later. We could have dinner and maybe afterwards we...Yeah right, I was going to bluff my way through a whole evening–'Am I moving towards a more figurative approach?' Ah, well yes, er no, I mean essentially...' I came down hard. Okay, a nice girl thought I was someone else. Big deal. It wasn't me. It's got to be me. Me and my suit. A lone cloud drifted in front of the sun. Perhaps I should just go back to work. Face facts. What facts exactly? That I was, for example, doomed to a life of smiling mediocrity? I had to keep moving. How about that drink?
I couldn't have been more than a hundred yards from the bar when I heard an uncertain voice call out my name. Who the hell...no, it can't be...
God, it is, it's...
'Andrew, remember me?'

'Andrew, of course. Christ, I haven't seen you for years. How are you?'
'I'm fine. Really well, actually. You?'
'Oh, I'm all right. Floating along. What've you been up to?'
'I've been in Liverpool since we left film school. It's a long story, but anyway I'm living in London now. I've just started working at Blue Room Video.'
His eyes fell upon my suit. 'I'm only a runner at the moment but you've got to start somewhere, I suppose.'
'You're a runner at Blue Room? That's amazing because I'm a...I'm also...I work in advertising as well.'
'Yeah? What d'you do?'
'I direct TV commercials.'
Two minutes later I was telling a wide eyed Andrew how difficult it was getting to raise the million or two I required to 'make the kind of ads that I was used to making.'

Complete Books

Designer
KATE STEPHENS

Lettering Artist
MIKE PRATLEY

Photographer
JOHN RIDDY

Client
PRESTEL AND
JOHN TAYLOR
BOOK VENTURES

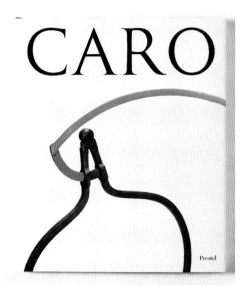

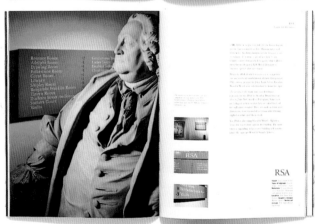

Complete Books

Art Editor
DAVID STUART

Designers
NINA JENKINS
ROMAN HUSZAK
SIMON CARTER

Copywriter
DAVID GIBBS

Typographers
NINA JENKINS
ROMAN HUSZAK
SIMON CARTER

Photographers
MARK HALL
JENNY MAY
IAN McKINNELL
SAM McCONNELL

Design Group
THE PARTNERS

Chairman
JOHN WOOD

Client
WOOD & WOOD
INTERNATIONAL
SIGNS LIMITED

Individual Pages

Art Editor
JOHN McCONNELL

Designer
SARAH MENON

Author
GENE KEMP

Typographer
SARAH MENON

Illustrator
ANDREW DAVIDSON

Client
FABER & FABER

THE INTERNATIONAL REVIEW OF GRAPHIC DESIGN **5|91** DIE INTERNATIONALE FACHZEITSCHRIFT FÜR GRAFIK-DESIGN

eye

Magazine Covers

Art Director
STEPHEN COATES

Editor
RICK POYNOR

Typographer
STEPHEN COATES

Photographer
GEOF KERN

Design Group
WORDSEARCH
PUBLISHING

Advertisement Director
RICHARD LEEKS

Publisher
WORDSEARCH
PUBLISHING

Complete Magazines

Design Director
JOHN RUSHWORTH

Designers
JOHN RUSHWORTH
VINCE FROST

Copywriter
PETER LESTER

Typographer
VINCE FROST

Design Group
PENTAGRAM DESIGN

Editor
RENATO BROGLIA

Client
POLAROID UK

Complete Magazines

Art Editor
DOMENIC LIPPA

Designers
DOMENIC LIPPA
HARRY PEARCE
KAREN WILKS
JEREMY LESLIE
RODNEY MYLIUS
MO COYNE
PAUL PRIESTMAN

Editor
MIKE DAINES

Co Editors
CHRIS GRAY
DOMENIC LIPPA

Authors
MIKE DAINES
MARGOT COATTS
JULIA THRIFT
MERLIN JAMES
HANS-RUDOLPH
LUTZ

Typographers
DOMENIC LIPPA
HARRY PEARCE
KAREN WILKS
JEREMY LESLIE
RODNEY MYLIUS
MO COYNE
PAUL PRIESTMAN

Design Group
LIPPA PEARCE
DESIGN LIMITED

Marketing Manager
CHRIS GRAY

Client
ESSELTE LETRASET
LIMITED

aphic des

crafts 30

gr-

gn

graphic design crafts

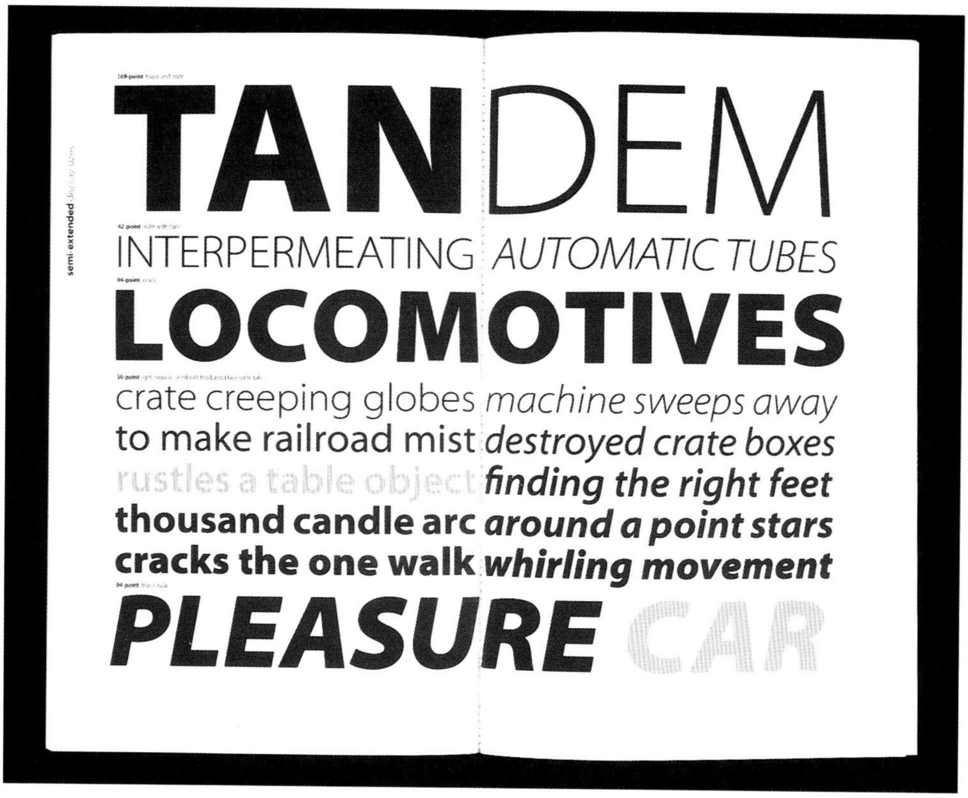
TANDEM
INTERPERMEATING AUTOMATIC TUBES
LOCOMOTIVES
crate creeping globes machine sweeps away
to make railroad mist destroyed crate boxes
rustles a table object finding the right feet
thousand candle arc around a point stars
cracks the one walk whirling movement
PLEASURE CAR
semi extended

Best use of Typography

Typographers
LAURIE SZUJEWSKA
JAMES YOUNG

Design Director
LAURIE SZUJEWSKA

Designers
LAURIE SZUJEWSKA
JAMES YOUNG

Copywriter
E M GINGER

Design Group
ADOBE SYSTEMS

Client
ADOBE SYSTEMS INC

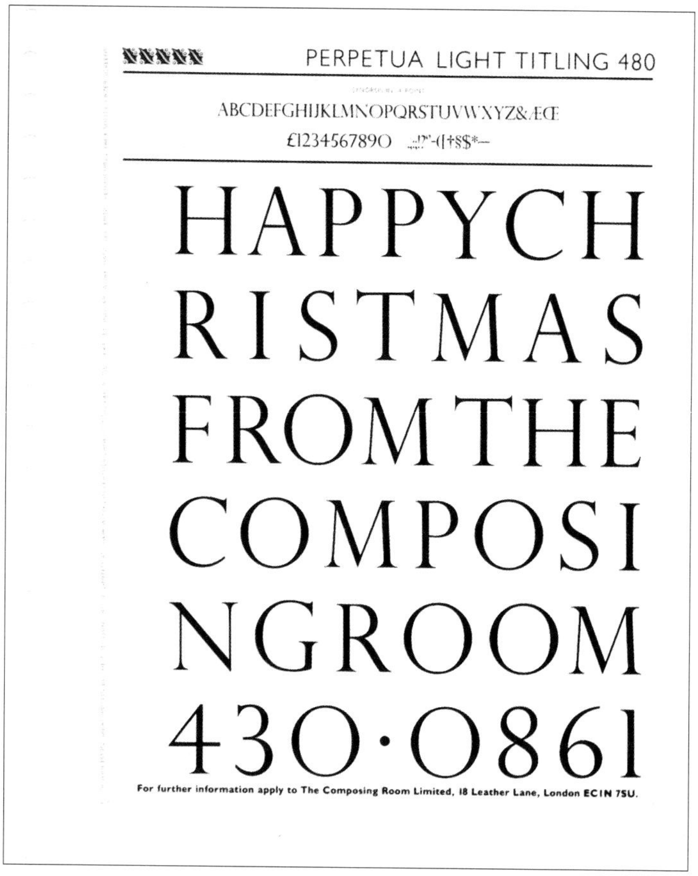
PERPETUA LIGHT TITLING 480
ABCDEFGHIJKLMNOPQRSTUVWXYZ&ÆŒ
£1234567890
HAPPYCH
RISTMAS
FROMTHE
COMPOSI
NGROOM
430·0861
For further information apply to The Composing Room Limited, 18 Leather Lane, London EC1N 7SU.

Best use of Typography

Designer
GRAHAM POWELL

Typographer
GRAHAM POWELL

Design Group
THE COMPOSING ROOM

Sales Director
JOHN BALDWIN

Client
THE COMPOSING ROOM

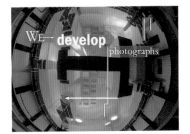

Best use of
Typography

Typographer
JONATHAN
BARNBROOK

Director
TONY KAYE

Art Director
DAVE MAY

Copywriter
JASPER SHELBORNE

Animator
DAVID LODGE

Lighting Cameraman
TONY KAYE

Production Company
TONY KAYE FILMS
LIMITED

Agency
J WALTER
THOMPSON

Marketing Director
HARRY MACAUSLAN

Client
NUCLEAR ELECTRIC

Best use of
Typography

Typographer
PHIL BAINES

Director
TONY KAYE

Art Director
KEVIN BRATLEY

Copywriter
JOHN TOWNSHEND

Animator
DAVID LODGE

Lighting Cameraman
TONY KAYE

Production Company
TONY KAYE FILMS
LIMITED

Agency
YELLOWHAMMER

Marketing Director
RICHARD
HARTLEY-SHARPE

Client
BARCLAYS BANK PLC

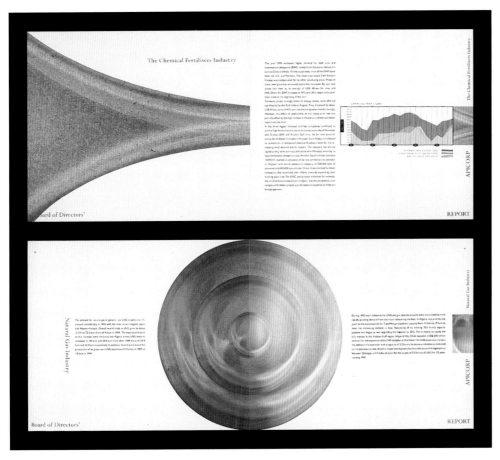

Best use of
Photography

Photographer
ZAFER BARAN

Designer
KAREN WILKS

Copywriter
KEN OWEN

Typographer
KAREN WILKS

Marketing Director
RICHARD THOBURN

Client
APICORP

Best use of
Photography

Photographer
YANI

Designers
JACQUES KOEWEIDEN
PAUL POSTMA

Typographers
JACQUES KOEWEIDEN
PAUL POSTMA

Design Group
KOEWEIDEN/POSTMA

Marketing Director
JANET HAZELAAR

Client
MINISTRY OF
ECONOMIC AFFAIRS

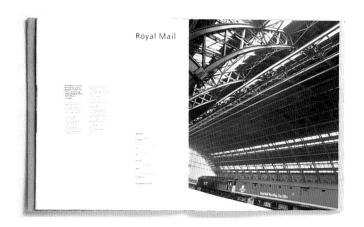

Best use of
Photography

Photographer
DAVID TEDMAN

Design Director
MICHAEL DENNY

Designers
MICHAEL DENNY
DARREN RICHARDSON
SARAH PERRY

Typographer
DARREN RICHARDSON

Design Group
ROUNDEL DESIGN
GROUP

Strategic Planning Manager
ROD GRAY

Client
RAIL EXPRESS
SYSTEMS
BRITISH RAILWAYS
BOARD

Best use of
Photography

Photographers
ZAFER BARAN
BARBARA BARAN

Designer
KAREN WILKS

Typographer
KAREN WILKS

Client
ZAFER AND BARBARA
BARAN

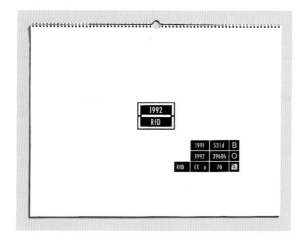

*Best use of
Photography*

Photographer
MICHAEL BANKS

Design Director
MICHAEL DENNY

Designers
MICHAEL DENNY
HAROLD BATTEN
JOHN BATESON
SARAH PERRY

Typographers
HAROLD BATTEN
SARAH PERRY

Design Group
ROUNDEL DESIGN
GROUP

Director Communications
MIKE PARKER

Client
RAILFREIGHT
DISTRIBUTION
BRITISH RAILWAYS
BOARD

*Best use of
Photography*

Photographer
STUART REDLER

Design Director
JOHN BATESON

Designers
MICHAEL DENNY
JOHN BATESON
CHRIS BRADLEY
MARION HARE
RACHAEL DINNIS

Copywriter
NEIL MATTINGLEY

Typographer
MARION HARE

Design Group
ROUNDEL DESIGN
GROUP

Design Manager
PAUL STEPHENSON

Account Manager
STEVE PRICE

Client
TRAINLOAD FREIGHT
BRITISH RAILWAYS
BOARD

Best use of
Photography

Photographer
MARKÉTA
LUSKAČOVÁ

Design Director
NICHOLAS THIRKELL

Designer
CLIFFORD HISCOCK

Typographer
CLIFFORD HISCOCK

Design Group
CARROLL DEMPSEY &
THIRKELL

Director Corporate Affairs
DR KEVIN HAWKINS

Client
W H SMITH PLC

Best use of
Photography

Photographer
RICK CORDELL

Design Director
MIKE DEMPSEY

Designer
BARBRO OHLSON

Typographer
BARBRO OHLSON

Design Group
CARROLL DEMPSEY &
THIRKELL

Marketing Executive
JOHN BURKE

Client
BP CHEMICALS

Best use of
Photography

Photographer
ROBIN BROADBENT

Design Director
MARY LEWIS

Designers
JIMMY YANG
MARY LEWIS

Typographer
JIMMY YANG

Design Group
LEWIS MOBERLY

National Account Manager
RUSSELL ATKINSON

Marketing Director
ANDREW CHATER

Business Development Manager
ANDREW EDYVEAN

Client
SCHOLL CONSUMER
PRODUCTS

Best use of
Illustration

Illustrators
KARIN DUNBAR
JOANNE SMITH

Design Director
MARY LEWIS

Designers
KARIN DUNBAR
MARY LEWIS
ANN MARSHALL
JOANNE SMITH

Typographers
KARIN DUNBAR
JOANNE SMITH

Design Group
LEWIS MOBERLY

Director of Buying Waitrose
Limited
PETER FALCONER

Design Co ordinations Manager
John Lewis Partnership
DOUGLAS COOPER

Client
WAITROSE LIMITED

Best use of
Illustration

Illustrators
LAWRENCE ZEEGEN
JEFF FISHER
MICHAEL BARTALOS
DAN FERN
PHILIPE WEISBECKER
TOBY MORRISON
MARION DEUCHARS
GEORGE HARDIE
PETER BLAKE
ISABELLE DERVAUX
ANDREW KULMAN
IAN BECK

Designers
LYNN TRICKETT
BRIAN WEBB
STEVE EDWARDS

Copywriter
NEIL MATTINGLEY

Design Group
TRICKETT & WEBB
LIMITED

Director
LASCELLE BARROW

Clients
AUGUSTUS MARTIN
LIMITED
TRICKETT & WEBB
LIMITED

Photography Andrew Olney · Design Persona

Precise colour reproduction · Clients include Blueprint magazine, Cartledge Levene, Eszenine Lockerstone, Eye, Paul Smith, Royal Academy, RIBA, Williams and Phoa · Contact Nick Deschamps 071 253 5895

Best use of
Photography

Photographer
ANDREW OLNEY

Designers
BARBRO OHLSON
MARIANN WISSA

Typographers
BARBRO OHLSON
MARIANN WISSA

Design Group
PERSONA

Managing Director
NICHOLAS
DESCHAMPS

Client
PRECISE LITHO
LIMITED

Best use of
Illustration

Illustrators
BRIAN CRAKER
ROY CASTLE

Design Director
MIKE DEMPSEY

Designer
IAN CHILVERS

Copywriter
TIM SHACKLETON

Typographer
IAN CHILVERS

Design Group
CARROLL DEMPSEY &
THIRKELL

Client
THE BRITISH LAND
COMPANY PLC

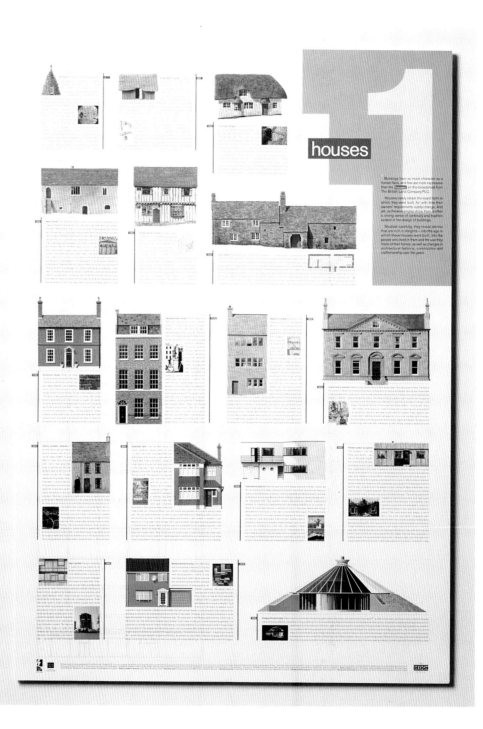

*Best use of
Illustration*

Illustrator
ANDREW DAVIDSON

Designer
SARAH MENON

Author
GENE KEMP

Typographer
SARAH MENON

Client
FABER & FABER

Best use of
Illustration

Illustrators
KIM MARSLAND
BENOIT JACQUES
PETER TILL
JANET WOOLLEY
FRANCES TEE
DAVID HOLMES
DEBBIE LUSH
IRENE
VON TRESKOW
ANDREW KULMAN
RICHARD PARENT
LEO DUFF
ELIZABETH HARBOUR
IAN POLLOCK
ANDREW MOCKETT
LIZ PYLE
JEFF FISHER
ANDREW DAVIDSON
DENNIS LEIGH
JANE HUMAN
CHRISTOPHER BROWN
PAUL LEITH
PUI YEE LAU
BRIAN CAIRNS
KAREN LUDLOW
KATIE LESTER
ZAFER BARAN
CHRIS CORR
CLIFFORD HARPER
ROSEMARY WOODS
CHLOE CHEESE
TOBY MORRISON
JEAN-CHRISTIAN
KNAFF
DAN FERN
CAROLYN GOWDY
DOVRAT BEN-NAHUM
LOUISE BRIERLY
ANDRZEJ DUDZINSKI
GRISELDA
HOLDERNESS
MARION DEUCHARS
ASHLEY POTTER

Design Director
NICHOLAS THIRKELL

Designers
IAIN CROCKART
NICHOLAS THIRKELL

Typographers
IAIN CROCKART
NICHOLAS THIRKELL

Design Group
CARROLL DEMPSEY &
THIRKELL

Editor
KATHY ROONEY

Client
BLOOMSBURY
PUBLISHING

*Best use of
Illustration*

Illustrators
JAKE ABRAMS
MARK ADAMS
RICHARD ADAMS
WILLIAM ALLEN
NANCY ANDERSON
DEBI ANI
DAVID BEZ
EDWARD BRIANT
ANDY BUNDAY
BRIAN CAIRNS
YVONNE CHAMBERS
MARTIN CHATTERTON
CHLOE CHEESE
ROBIN CHEVALIER
MARK CLOUGH
GRAHAM CROWLEY
MELVYN EVANS
STEPHEN FARTHING
DIANNE FISHER
JOHNATHAN GIBBS
ANDY GLENDENNING
JOHN GORHAM
ROBERT GREEN
BRIAN GRIMWOOD
GEORGE HARDIE
MARK HARFIELD
ANDREW HARRIS
JOHN HASLAM
ANTHEA HELLIWELL
SUE HILLWOOD
BUSH HOLLYHEAD
PETER HORRIDGE
DAVID HUGHES
CLARE JARRETT
SANDY LAING
PAUL LEITH
KIKI LEWIS
IAN MASSEY
IAN McALISTER
IAN McCULLOUGH
CHRIS McEWAN
SHANE McGOWAN
DAVID MELDRUM
JOHNATHAN MERCER
RODERICK MILLS
RUSSELL MILLS
MARIO MINICHIELLO
ANDREW MOCKETT
MARK MORAN
DANIEL MORGENSTERN
MARTIN ORME
MICHAEL
O'SHAUGHNESSY
ALAN PARKER
MARY ROBERTS
JULIA ROBINSON
WIL ROWLANDS
WILLIAM ROWSELL
IAN SAXTON
SATWINDER SCHMI
DAVID SEMPLE
ROBERT SHADBOLT
NICK SHARRATT
MICHAEL SHEEHY
SUE SHIELDS
WENDY SINCLAIR
JANE SMITH
EMMA SUTHERLAND
MADELEINE THOMPSON
DENNIS TINKLER
TRACY WILSON
JANET WOOLLEY

Design Director
BEN CASEY

Designers
LISE WARBURTON
ANDY BAINBRIDGE

Copywriter
BEN CASEY

Typographers
LISE WARBURTON
LIONEL HATCH

Design Group
THE CHASE CREATIVE
CONSULTANTS
LIMITED

Client Marketing Executive
NICK BOWYER

Client
THE CO-OPERATIVE
BANK

*Best use of
Illustration*

Illustrator
NICK BELL

Design Director
MARITA LASHKO

Photographers
ANDY RUMBALL
NICK BELL

Client
THE PARTNERS
DESIGN
CONSULTANTS

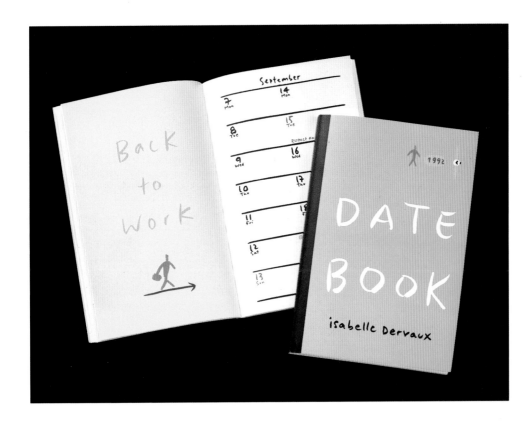

*Best use of
Illustration*

Illustrator
ISABELLE DERVAUX

Creative Director
KENJI KAWAMOTO

Art Director
HIDERO HORIO

Designer
KOHICHI
YOSHIIZUMI

Author
ISABELLE DERVAUX

Design Group
FORUM CORP

Client
PARCO
MERCHANDISING
DIVISION

ic

ad₃₀

SILVER AWARD
for the most outstanding
Radio Commercial

Copywriter
DION HUGHES

Agency Producer
LISA HOROWITZ

Recording Engineer
IAN HADLEY

Agency
CHIAT/DAY/MOJO-NY

Production Company
JOHN CRAWFORD
RADIO

Director of Marketing
BERNARD A
BLOOMFIELD

Client
NYNEX
INFORMATION
RESOURCES

TITLE: DENTAL DISCOUNTS

Mike: It's absolutely true, you can find anything and everything
          in your NYNEX Yellow Pages, and today under 'Dentists', I
          found Dr. Joseph Tam of the Dental Discounters. Joe, I see
          from your ad that you stock off-the-rack dentures.

Joe: (A whistley, clacky voice gives away a badly fitting pair of
          dentures)
          Thith ith correct, Michael. We manufacture them thmall,
          medium, largthe, and metric.

Mike: And is that an example of your work?

Joe: You're referring to my dentureth?

Mike: Yes, they, umm, they don't seem to fit very well.

Joe: What you thacrifithe in the thithe, you more than make up in
          convenienthe and prithing.

Mike: Now, do people really buy these things.

Joe: Thure. Many people keep them ath a thecond pair.

Mike: You mean spares?

Joe: Well, back upths, yeah. Thome clienth buy many pairth. Mikth
          and match. It'th a very original and inekthpenthive fashion
          statement. Aaaayee...

Mike: What's the matter, Dr.?

Joe: My teeth, they're locked, Michael.

Mike: Oh no, does this happen often?

Joe: M. Everytime you thay an 'm' you run the danger of them
          locking.

Mike: Can I help you?

Joe: Do you have a ball point pen I could borrow?

Mike: No, not really. Well, there you have it. Further proof that
          if it's out there, it's in your NYNEX Yellow Pages.

Joe: Ith thith the model with the withdom teeth or without?

Mike: Looks like some wisdom teeth back there.

Joe: Oh, even worth.

Mike: Why would anyone need another?

SILVER AWARD
for the most outstanding
Radio Campaign

Copywriter
DION HUGHES

Agency Producer
LISA HOROWITZ

Recording Engineer
IAN HADLEY

Agency
CHIAT/DAY/MOJO-NY

Production Company
JOHN CRAWFORD
RADIO

Director of Marketing
BERNARD A
BLOOMFIELD

Client
NYNEX
INFORMATION
RESOURCES

TITLE: DENTAL DISCOUNTS

Mike: It's absolutely true, you can find anything and everything
            in your NYNEX Yellow Pages, and today under 'Dentists', I
            found Dr. Joseph Tam of the Dental Discounters. Joe, I see
            from your ad that you stock off-the-rack dentures.

Joe: (A whistley, clacky voice gives away a badly fitting pair of
            dentures)
            Thith ith correct, Michael. We manufacture them thmall,
            medium, largthe, and metric.

Mike: And is that an example of your work?

Joe: You're referring to my dentureth?

Mike: Yes, they, umm, they don't seem to fit very well.

Joe: What you thacrifithe in the thithe, you more than make up in
            convenienthe and prithing.

Mike: Now, do people really buy these things.

Joe: Thure. Many people keep them ath a thecond pair.

Mike: You mean spares?

Joe: Well, back upths, yeah. Thome clienth buy many pairth. Mikth
            and match. It'th a very original and inekthpenthive fashion
            statement. Aaaayee...

Mike: What's the matter, Dr.?

Joe: My teeth, they're locked, Michael.

Mike: Oh no, does this happen often?

Joe: M. Everytime you thay an 'm' you run the danger of them
            locking.

Mike: Can I help you?

Joe: Do you have a ball point pen I could borrow?

Mike: No, not really. Well, there you have it. Further proof that
            if it's out there, it's in your NYNEX Yellow Pages.

Joe: Ith thith the model with the withdom teeth or without?

Mike: Looks like some wisdom teeth back there.

Joe: Oh, even worth.

Mike: Why would anyone need another?

Copywriter
DION HUGHES

Agency Producer
LISA HOROWITZ

Recording Engineer
IAN HADLEY

TITLE: AMAZING MR ANDY

Mike: You know, it really is true you can find anything in the
           NYNEX Yellow Pages. For instance,today under 'Entertainers'
           I found the amazing Mr Andy, and your ad says you're a man
           of thousand voices.

Andy: (Weird voice)
           That's right, Michael.

Mike: Hey, that's really funny. Who's it supposed to be?

Andy: Whaddya mean? This is my real voice.

Mike: Oh...uhhh...I'm sorry. I just thought...

Andy: You find this amusing, pencil neck? You think I'm a clown.

Mike: No, really, I ahhh...

Andy: (Normal voice)
           Just kidding, that was my big tough guy voice. Had you going
           though, didn't I?

Mike: (A touch shaken)
           I, well, uh, what other voices do you do?

Andy: Listen to this.

SFX: Throat clearing.

Andy: (Brooklyn)
           Morning Andy. Can I borrow your hedge clippers?

Mike: Gee, I can't seem to place that one.

Andy: That's Jacky, my next door neighbor. You don't know Jacky?

Mike: No.

Andy: Aw, that's a shame. Sounds exactly like him.

Mike: Oh, I bet it does.

Andy: Okay, get this.

SFX: Throat clearing.

Andy: (Sounding exactly like Mike)
           They say you can find anything in the NYNEX Yellow Pages.

Mike: Now that would be...

Andy: That's you Mike. Yeah, I even called your girlfriend this
           morning and proposed to her. I used your voice.

Mike: What?

Andy: (As Mike)
           Well, there it is, more proof that if it's out there, it's
           in your NYNEX Yellow Pages.

Mike: Boy, you have an awesome power, Andy. I hope you use it
           responsibly.

Andy: (As Mike)
           Why would anyone need another?

Mike: Oooh, spooky.

Copywriters
DION HUGHES
IAN HADLEY
JOHN CRAWFORD
MICHAEL O'BRIEN

Agency Producer
LISA HOROWITZ

Recording Engineer
IAN HADLEY

TITLE: GENEALOGY

Mike: As they say you can find anything in the NYNEX Yellow Pages
           and today under the heading, 'Genealogist', we found
           Dr. Ian Hadley.

Ian: Michael.

Mike: Dr. Hadley, you trace family roots, I guess.

Ian: Yes, as a matter of fact, we traced your family roots as far
           back as the Battle of Hastings.

Mike: What? That sounds pretty interesting.

Ian: Your ancestor Ethelred the Fleet, led the retreat from the
           battle to the forest.

Mike: Probably just regrouping, I guess...

Ian: ...Spent the next one hundred years living as vassals and
           indentured servants and they reappear interestingly at the
           time of the American Revolution...

Mike: Oh.

Ian: ...Where the battle of Lexington was fought on their land.

Mike: Minute men fighting for the young country...

Ian: Well, no, they had left a week earlier to disappear into the
           forest.

Mike: To fight on as guerillas.

Ian: Uh, that's speculation.

Mike: I guess this is the family coat of arms?

Ian: Yes, this is your family crest.

Mike: The mighty oak tree.

Ian: And if you look carefully you'll notice a small man cowering
          behind the mighty oak tree.

Mike: Well, if it's out there, it's in your NYNEX Yellow Pages. We
          can't vouch for the accuracy of all these services...

Ian: And the Latin inscription — Festina Ad Silva.

Mike: ·   Why would anyone need another?

Ian: Or 'Make haste to the woods'.

Copywriter
DION HUGHES

Agency Producer
LISA HOROWITZ

Recording Engineer
IAN HADLEY

TITLE: INFLATABLE FURNITURE

Mike: You know how they say you can find just about anything in
          the Nynex Yellow Pages? Today, I found the Inflatable
          Furniture Warehouse and with me is sales manager Rick
          Slovitt.

Rick: Mike, welcome to the largest inventory of inflatable home
          furnishings on the eastern seaboard.

Mike: So, I'm curious, why would anyone want an inflatable file
          cabinet?

Rick: Well, Mike, inflatable means deflatable. So if you ever get
          a surprise IRS audit you just pull the plug here; it
          deflates into a briefcase and you're out the back door.

Mike: That's clever. Okay. This table looks kind of lopsided.

Rick: That's a pressure thing, that's easily fixed.

SFX: Hand pump.

Rick: There we go. Part of our Louis XIV collection.
          Hand painted vinyl.

Mike: Are leaks a problem?

Rick: No, we offer a one year warranty provided you don't own cats
          or knit.

Mike: Right, yeah.

Rick: You can't beat our inflatables for comfort. Ever experience
          an inflatable chaise lounge, Mike?

Mike: Not that I know of.

Rick: Sit down here.

Mike: Well, you sink right in.

Rick: Floating on air. Hey, that isn't a pin, uh?

SFX: Balloon burst, followed by a rubber balloon rapidly
            deflating. The sofa starts to fly around the room,
            deflating.

Mike: Whooooaaaahhhh.

Rick: Hold on, Mike, we'll have you down in no time.

Mike: (In pain)
            Well, there you have it. If it's out there, it's in your
            NYNEX Yellow Pages.

Rick: I'll get you some air into this ladder.

SFX: Pumping sound.

Mike: Why would anyone need another?

Rick: If you're going to fall, fall onto the inflatable coffee
            table, okay?

Singles

Concept Creator
STEVE CALLEN

Copywriter
STEVE CALLEN

Agency Producer
STEVE CALLEN

Recording Engineer
JAMES CLARK

Producer
MARK RIVETT

Music Composer/Arranger
MARK RIVETT

Agency
YOUNG & RUBICAM
ADELAIDE

Production Company
RIVETT'S
RECORDING STUDIO

Public Relations Officer
DOREEN BATE

Client
ROYAL ZOOLOGICAL
SOCIETY OF SOUTH
AUSTRALIA INC

TITLE: ZOO POO SONG

Zoo Keeper: Okay, okay, listen up all you animals
                I'm the man they call your keeper
                The one with all the demure
                But I'm much, much more that just the
                Guy that feeds ya
                I also collect your manure.

                Every monkey, every Peacock, every Armadillo
                Can help everybody's garden grow
                If you keep on pooin'
                Just keep doin'
                That Zoo Poo that you do so well.

                Green fingered gardeners try every potion
                So let's give them our best
                Let's all pass a motion
                To keep on pooin'
                All keep doin'
                That Zoo Poo that you do so well.

                $5.95's not so much to ask
                When so much good can come
                From such a simple task
                It don't come from the horses mouth
                But if he's facin' north, it comes from the south.

                So if you want a better Zoo
                And I know you all do
                And gardners too, really love our Zoo Poo.

                Every poo, you do, helps you and the Zoo
                And everything'll be swell
                Do that Zoo Poo that you do so well
                Do that Zoo Poo that you do so well.

Singles

Concept Creator
PAUL PAECH

Copywriters
PAUL PAECH
LUKE WHITE

Agency Producer
CHIPPIE McLEOD

Director
PAUL PAECH

Recording Engineer
JOHN WORRELL

Producer
PAUL PAECH

Music Composer/Arranger
JOHN WORRELL

Agency
SUDLER &
HENNESSEY

Marketing Director
KURIAN VERGHESE

Client
PFIZER AUSTRALIA

TITLE: MUSIC TO YOUR REAR

MVO: (The tone is erudite but quietly confiding)
              If you suffer from haemorrhoids,
              you'll know about the pain...

SFX: Single violin effect to suggest pain, continues under...

MVO: and the swelling...

SFX: Joined by another violin effect to suggest swelling,
              continues under...

MVO: and the itching.

SFX: Joined by a third violin effect to suggest itching...

SFX: (Ends abruptly)

MVO: But you may not know about Rectinol.

MUSIC: The sweeping cliched theme from Tchaikovsky's 'Waltz of The
              Flowers' fades up under voice and continues...

MVO: Rectinol is available from chemists and unlike some other
              haemorrhoid treatments, it works in three ways. A local
              anaesthetic temporarily relieves the pain...then it reduces
              the swelling...and eases the itch.

              Use Rectinol ointment and suppositories only as directed and
              if pain continues, see your doctor.

MUSIC: Waltz reaches a triumphant climax and ends.

MVO: Tone abruptly changes from personal intimacy to proud public
              achievement.

              Rectinol. It'll be MUSIC TO YOUR REAR.

Campaigns

Concept Creator
DON BARCLAY

Copywriter
KEVIN KNEALE

Agency Producer
SANDI BENNETT

Recording Engineers
PETER LEGGETT
MATTHEW ROBERTS

Music Composer/Arranger
SAINT-SAENS

Agency
LOWE HOWARD-SPINK

Client
TESCO STORES
LIMITED

TITLE: PIRANHAS

SFX: Tesco theme music under announcer and as a reprise.

VO 1:   (Pompous intellectual announcer)
           Today's poem is in celebration of bananas being reduced by
           14p to just 45p per lb loose this week at Tesco.

VO 2:   Green piranhas,
           In pink pyjamas,
           Reciting Shakespearian dramas,
           I seem to have gone bananas.

TITLE: UP A TREE

SFX: Tesco theme music under announcer and as a reprise.

VO 1:   (Pompous intellectual announcer)
           Today's poem is in celebration of bananas being reduced by
           14p to just 45p per lb loose this week at Tesco.

VO 2:   Recently you were up a tree,
           As part of a big bunch,
           Now you're in my basket,
           And you're going to be my lunch.

TITLE: CARRIBEAN

SFX: Tesco theme music under announcer and as a reprise.

VO 1:   (Pompous intellectual announcer)
           Today's poem is in celebration of bananas being reduced by
           14p to just 45p per lb loose this week at Tesco.

VO 2:   Oh, sundrenched Carribean,
           Oh, islands as hot as the Med,
           Where bananas gently ripen,
           And I just go bright red.

TITLE: BARBEQUE

SFX: Tesco theme music under announcer and as reprise.

VO 1:   (Pompous intellectual announcer)
            Today's poem is in celebration of fresh, whole medium sized
            chicken being reduced by 26p to just 69p per lb this week at
            Tesco.

VO 2:   I've brought a chicken for a barbeque,
            But I've got no garden furniture,
            I'd be grateful if you'd lend me some,
            And I promise to returniture.

and cin
em
a advertis

elevision

ng³⁰

SILVER AWARD
for the most outstanding
Television Commercial
up to 40 seconds

Director
MATT FORREST

Copywriter
ALAN YOUNG

Art Director
TREVOR ROBINSON

Creative Director
STEVE HENRY

Producer
STORR REDMAN

Agency Producer
JANE FULLER

Lighting Cameraman
NIC MORRIS

Production Company
LIMELIGHT
COMMERCIALS

Agency
HOWELL HENRY
CHALDECOTT LURY
LIMITED

Director of Brand Marketing
TONY HILLYER

Client
BRITVIC SOFT
DRINKS LIMITED

ORANGE MAN

We open on 3 ordinary looking bloke
opposed to street wise) in their late t
They are stood on a street corner cas
chatting. One bloke takes a drink fr
can of Tango then gulps with
satisfaction. We hear two commenta
talk, one's a Geordie, one's a Londo

Ralph:
Hello Gordie, I think we might us
video replay here.

Tony:
Super Ralph, let's do that.

The event is rewound and played b
faster than real time. As the guy dri
from the can, an orange, semi-nake
bald genie type runs up behind th
drinker and taps him on the should
The drinker turns his head and th
orange man runs round and gives hin
enormous two handed Eric Morecor
slap on the cheeks. He then turns a
runs back out of shot. our two
commentators react.

Ralph:
Whoa! we could be in for a
quintessential Tango taste sensation h

(slap)

Whyyy-aayy! yes, Tony! Lets look ag

The film is rewound and replayed ag
to show the orange man running in f
a different angle, still playing faster t
real time.

Tony:
Yes Ralph, the big orange fella run
from the left and he gives him a good
slapping.

Ralph:
It just illustrates the bite and buzz of
oranges in Tango!

Tony:
Yes Ralph, super taste sensation,
smashing drink, lovely.

We cut back to the drinker in real tir
He eyes the can slightly suspiciously a
to say what was that, that hit me ?
Finally we cut to a shot of the back of
orange man's head with a can of Tan
on top of it and a super on his head
saying: "You know when you've bee
Tango'd".

VO:
You know when you've been Tango'

SHOES IN ACTION

Across a grey screen, runs a single white line. It represents, we will come to see, the line around which sporting excellence always seems to revolve.

It will become in succession the touchline, the high jump bar, the baseline, etc, etc. It never moves its position on the screen.

The perspective only reveals itself when a sportsman or woman appears.

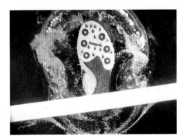

SILVER AWARD
*for the most outstanding
Television Commercial
up to 60 seconds*

Director
DAVID GARFATH

Copywriter
CHRIS HERRING

Art Director
JOHN MERRIMAN

Creative Director
PAUL WEINBERGER

Producer
MARY FRANCIS

Set Designer
MIKE HALL

Agency Producer
AMANDA DICKS

Editor
SIMON WILLCOX

Lighting Cameraman
ROGER PRATT

Music Composer/Arranger
CHRIS BLACKWELL

Production Company
PAUL WEILAND FILM
COMPANY

Agency
LOWE HOWARD-SPINK

Client
REEBOK UK

SILVER AWARD
*for the most outstanding
Cinema Commercial Single*

Director
FRANK BUDGEN

Copywriter
JOHN PALLANT

Art Director
MATT RYAN

Creative Director
PAUL ARDEN

Producer
PAUL ROTHWELL

Agency Producer
MARK HANRAHAN

Editor
CYRIL METZGER

Lighting Cameraman
CHRIS DUFFY

Production Company
PAUL WEILAND FILM
COMPANY

Agency
SAATCHI & SAATCHI

*Director of Products &
Marketing*
ROGER HEAPE

Head of Marketing
TIFFANY HALL

Client
BRITISH AIRWAYS
HOLIDAYS

SURPRISE SURPRISE

*On the screen, a young couple are
walking arm in arm in various rom
Parisian locations.*

*Just as their faces become recognisa
actress actually planted in the cine
audience stands up and interacts u
them. The man, it transpires, is h
boyfriend who had told her he was
away on business. After giving him a
of her mind, the girl storms off – as
the girl on screen too. Abandoned, th
looks for sympathy from a French
watching from a park bench. She giv
a withering look and buries her hea
newspaper.*

THE SWIMMER

Soundtrack:
Dinah Washington 'Mad about the boy'

A boy from the wrong side of the tracks swims across several swimming pools to get to his girlfriend, who is celebrating her 18th birthday. He whisks her off and they dive into the great wide yonder. Proving along the way, that...

Super:
The more you wash them the better they get.

Levi's (logo).

SILVER AWARD
NOMINATION
*for the most outstanding
Television Commercial
up to 60 seconds*

Director
TARSEM

Copywriter
LARRY BARKER

Art Director
ROONEY CARRUTHERS

Creative Director
JOHN HEGARTY

Producer
ROBERT CAMPBELL

Set Designer
ALEX McDOWELL

Agency Producer
PHILIPPA CRANE

Editor
ANDREA McARTHUR

Lighting Cameraman
PAUL LAUFER

Music Composer/Arranger
NOEL COWARD

Production Company
SPOTS FILMS

Agency
BARTLE BOGLE
HEGARTY

Senior Marketing Manager
LARRY RUFF

Client
LEVI STRAUSS UK

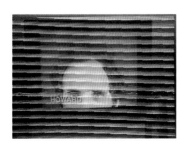

VIDEO DATING

*We see a woman at home
expectantly and hopefully about to
watch her dating video.*

*We see her prospective dates on
the TV.*

Gregor:
*I want a woman who wants to
hunt.*

Rajiv:
(Gurgles then chants religiously)

Jonathon:
*I'm rich, successful and good-
looking.*

Another:
*I don't do drugs...OK, I take
lithium.*

Lenny:
*I want a woman who's HOT
phew, wowsa wowsa wowsa.*

The woman looks horrified.

VO over HBO logo:
*When life gets rough laugh it off
with the new comedy channel.*

*24 hours a day we're there when
you need us.*

Lenny:
Hi! It's Lenny Tepper again!

SINGER

Music:
Guitar strumming.

Singer:
Wake up this morning and the sun smiled down on me.

Sun smiled on me, that ain't the blues.

Wife:
Oh honey, that's cute.

Singer:
Woe...woe, woe, woe the boat happily down the stream.

Dam that ain't the blues either.

Wife:
What is this lipstick doing on your collar?

Singer:
Honey, that ain't no lipstick.

Wife:
Honey or nothing.

Singer:
I was shaving.

Wife:
You're lying.

Repo. Man:
We repossessing your car.

SFX:
Thunderclap.

Wife:
And I ain't never coming back.

SFX:
Guitar, harmonica.

Singer:
Sadness is my first name, last name is misery, I lost my woman, and the rain is coming down...

Oh...yer.

SILVER AWARD
NOMINATION
*for the most outstanding
Television Commercial
up to 60 seconds*

Director
PAUL WEILAND

Copywriter
MARK WNEK

Art Director
ALAN WALDIE

Creative Director
ADRIAN HOLMES

Producer
ALICIA BERNARD

Set Designer
LESLIE POPE

Agency Producer
SARAH HORRY

Editor
IAN WEIL

Lighting Cameraman
ALEXANDER WITT

Music Composers/Arrangers
PAUL HART
LONI BROOKS

Production Company
PAUL WEILAND FILM
COMPANY

Agency
LOWE HOWARD-SPINK

Marketing Director
STEVE PHILPOTT

Client
THE WHITBREAD
BEER COMPANY

SILVER AWARD
NOMINATION
for the most outstanding
Cinema Commercial Single

Director
TARSEM

Copywriter
LARRY BARKER

Art Director
ROONEY CARRUTHERS

Creative Director
JOHN HEGARTY

Producer
ROBERT CAMPBELL

Set Designer
ALEX McDOWELL

Agency Producer
PHILIPPA CRANE

Editor
ANDREA McARTHUR

Lighting Cameraman
PAUL LAUFER

Music Composer/Arranger
NOEL COWARD

Production Company
SPOTS FILMS

Agency
BARTLE BOGLE
HEGARTY

Marketing Manager
LARRY RUFF

Client
LEVI STRAUSS UK
LIMITED

THE SWIMMER

Soundtrack:
Dinah Washington 'Mad about the boy'

A boy from the wrong side of the tracks swims across several swimming pools to get to his girlfriend, who is celebrating her 18th birthday. He whisks her off and they dive into the great wide yonder. Proving along the way, that...

Super:
The more you wash them the better they get.

Levi's (logo).

TONGUE TWISTER

Billy Connolly:
*I'm not a pheasant plucker I'm a
pheasant plucker's son and I'm
only plucking pheasants till the
pheasant plucker comes.*

...And I've been drinking.

*Television
Commercials up to
10 seconds*

Director
SIMON DELANEY

Copywriter
IAN FRANKS

Art Director
MARK RILEY

Creative Director
ANDREW
RUTHERFORD

Producer
ADAM LYNE

Agency Producer
LIZZIE O'CONNELL

Editor
PIERS DOUGLAS

Lighting Cameraman
ROGER PRATT

Production Company
DELANEY HART

Agency
FCO LIMITED

Marketing Manager
STEPHEN DAY

Client
KALIBER FROM
GUINNESS

*Television
Commercials up to
20 seconds*

Director
THEO DELANEY

Copywriter
TREVOR BEATTIE

Art Director
STEVE CHETHAM

Creative Director
MURRAY PARTRIDGE

Producer
SIMON TURTLE

Set Designer
MICHELLE CALVERT

Agency Producer
RACHEL PERRY

Editor
PIERS DOUGLAS

Lighting Cameraman
STEVEN BERNSTEIN

Music Composer/Arranger
RICHARD KIRSTEIN

Production Company
SPOTS FILMS

Agency
TBWA/HOLMES
KNIGHT RITCHIE

Marketing Director
CLIVE SMITH

Client
DYNO-ROD PLC

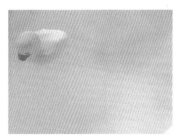
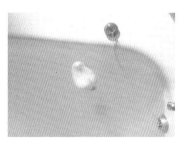

BATH

Soundtrack:
Eerie music

MVO:
*If there is one thing worse than a
blocked bath, it's the absurd quote
that can come with it...*

Cowboy plumber:
*It's not the men in my life, it's the
life in my men that counts.*

Soundtrack:
William Tell overture

MVO:
*For a more sensible, affordable
quote and an unblocked blockage
before you can say "who was that
masked man" call Dyno-Rod.*

The Lone Drainer and Pronto!

DRAIN

Soundtrack:
Eerie music.

MVO:
*If there is one thing worse than a
blocked drain it's the horrendous
quote that can come with it...*

Cowboy plumber:
*But soft, what light through
yonder window breaks? Tis the
east and Juliet is the sun.*

Soundtrack:
William Tell Overture.

MVO:
*For a more sensible, affordable
quote and an unblocked blockage
before you can say "who was that
masked man?" call Dyno-Rod.*

The Lone Drainer and Pronto!

*Television
Commercials up to
20 seconds*

Director
THEO DELANEY

Copywriter
TREVOR BEATTIE

Art Director
STEVE CHETHAM

Creative Director
MURRAY PARTRIDGE

Producer
SIMON TURTLE

Set Designer
MICHELLE CALVERT

Agency Producer
TIGGY GATFIELD

Editor
PIERS DOUGLAS

Lighting Cameraman
STEVEN BERNSTEIN

Music Composer/Arranger
RICHARD KIRSTEIN

Production Company
SPOTS FILMS

Agency
TBWA/HOLMES
KNIGHT RITCHIE

Marketing Director
CLIVE SMITH

Client
DYNO-ROD PLC

Television
Commercials up to
20 seconds

Director
GRAHAM ROSE

Copywriter
SIMON CARBERY

Art Director
CHARLES INGE

Creative Director
ADRIAN HOLMES

Producer
JOHN HACKNEY

Agency Producer
CHARLES CRISP

Editor
DAVE GARLAND

Lighting Cameraman
ADRIAN BIDDLE

Music Composer/Arranger
JOHN ALTMAN

Production Company
ROSE HACKNEY
PRODUCTIONS

Agency
LOWE HOWARD-SPINK

Marketing Director
STEVE PHILPOTT

Client
THE WHITBREAD
BEER COMPANY

RUDOLPH

Open on Rudolph the red-nosed reindeer.

He is sitting at home on Xmas day, watching the telly. Unfortunately, sound and picture on his TV are terrible.

Slightly annoyed, he takes a sip of Heineken, which allows him to adjust his antlers as if they were a TV aerial.

The picture comes back beautifully, complete with sound. Close in on the TV. We catch the end of a Heineken commercial.

Super:
Only Heineken can do this.

SOUTH POLE

Video:
The commercial opens with a close up of a man wearing Bonds Grand Slam briefs. We see the excellent fit and style of the briefs.

MVO:
Now, from the makers of Grand Slam Shirts, come Grand Slam Briefs.

Video:
Suddenly we see something in the underwear move! For the rest of the commercial the front of the briefs moves left and right and up and down in an hilarious way.

MVO:
They're modern, sleek, more stylish than your average briefs. Grand Slam briefs come in a huge range of colours and styles, too.

How can you tell if they're Grand Slam?

Video:
Suddenly the cause of the commotion hops out! A cute little Penguin!

*We now cut to the penguin Logo and Super:
Grand Slam Briefs from Bonds.*

MVO:
New Grand Slam Briefs from Bonds.

*Television
Commercials up to
30 seconds*

Director
CHRIS GODFREY
MARRCUS JAACSON

Copywriter
SIIMON REYNOLDS

Art Director
MARRCUS JAACSON

Creative Director
MARRCUS JAACSON

Producer
ZAREH NALBANDIAN

Agency Producer
DARCEY

Lighting Cameraman
DAVID WAKELY

Production Company
ANIMAL LOGIC

Agency
OMON ADVERTISING
AGENCY

Marketing Managing
STEVE KOPP

Client
BONDS INDUSTRIES

*Television
Commercials up to
30 seconds*

Director
BARRY MYERS

Copywriter
PETER SMITH

Art Director
CAB RICHARDSON

Creative Director
CAB RICHARDSON

Producer
OLIVIA BENDON

Set Designer
DAVID BILL

Agency Producer
LINDSAY HUGHES

Editor
TERRY JONES

Lighting Cameraman
PHIL MEHEUX

Music Composer/Arranger
BRIAN BENNETT

Production Company
SPOTS FILMS

Agency
BSB DORLAND

Marketing Director
BILL WHITING

Client
B & Q PLC

THE VOTE

Soundtrack:
Heartbeat.

SFX:
Rustling of paper.

Foreman: (reads)
Guilty.

Guilty.

Guilty.

Guilty.

Guilty.

Blue Hawk Plaster Coving.

Pack of 6.

£9.99 at B&Q?

VO:
*B&Q. Prices so low you just have
to tell somebody.*

RESTAURANT

Soundtrack:
Romantic orchestral piece.

Man:
(summons waiter to deliver
message)
Gino.

Music:
Romantic theme builds...

and builds...

and builds...

*...to a crescendo as the woman
opens the napkin with the message
on it.*

MVO:
*B&Q. Prices so low you just have
to tell somebody.*

*Television
Commercials up to
30 seconds*

Director
BARRY MYERS

Copywriter
PETER SMITH

Art Director
CAB RICHARDSON

Creative Director
CAB RICHARDSON

Producer
OLIVIA BENDON

Set Designer
DAVID BILL

Agency Producer
ANGELA ZABALA

Editor
TERRY JONES

Lighting Cameraman
ADRIAN BIDDLE

Music Composer/Arranger
COLIN TOWNS

Production Company
SPOTS FILMS

Agency
BSB DORLAND

Marketing Director
BILL WHITING

Client
B & Q PLC

*Television
Commercials up to
30 seconds*

Director
JON FRANCIS

Copywriter
DON AUSTEN

Art Director
BRUCE HURWIT

Creative Directors
CLIFF FREEMAN
DONNA WEINHEIM

Producer
SVEN SHELGREN

Agency Producer
MELANIE KLEIN

Editor
IAN McKANZIE

Production Company
STIEFEL & COMPANY

Agency
CLIFF FREEMAN &
PARTNERS

Marketing Director
ROB ELLIOTT

Client
LITTLE CAESARS
ENTERPRISES

HIGH CHAIR

SFX:
*Sounds from another room –
banging rattle, loud squirt of a
water gun, and cat meows.*

*Cheese stretching.
Cheese stretch gets louder.*

*High chair dragging on the floor.
Cartoon rocket sound.
Baby giggles.*

Grampa:
Well...look who's here!

SFX:
*Crash off-camera of high chair
returning to house.*

Announcer:
*Little Caesars' Cheeser! Cheeser!
Not one but two pizzas with extra
cheese, up to 4 toppings, and free
Crazy Bread for $8.98.*

Little Caesar:
Cheeser! Cheeser!

SWAN LAKE

Music:
Swan Lake.

Supers:
His mother wanted him married and out of the house.

So he meets somebody.

Nice girl. Lives on a lake.

And then, this other girl comes along.

He's all confused.

But not as confused as his mother.

She just wanted him to meet a nice girl.

He brings home a swan.

"Swan Lake"

Boston Ballet

For tickets, call 931-2000.

His mother wanted him
married and out of the house.

So he meets somebody.

And then, this other
girl comes along.
He's all confused.

But not as confused
as his mother.

She just wanted him to
meet a nice girl.

He brings home a swan.

*Television
Commercials up to
30 seconds*

Copywriters
MARK NARDI
TODD RIDDLE

Art Directors
TODD RIDDLE
MARK NARDI

Creative Director
JAY WILLIAMS

Agency Producer
DIANE CARLIN

Editor
ANDRE BETZ

Music Composers/Arrangers
RICK SWEETZER
BILL BOOKHEIM

Agency
HILL HOLLIDAY
CONNORS
COSMOPULOS INC

Marketing Director
JOANNE SCHEUBLE

Client
BOSTON BALLET

SWAN LAKE
April 30 – May 17

BOSTON BALLET
For tickets, call 931-2000

*Television
Commercials up to
30 seconds*

Director
GREG WINTER

Copywriter
JOSH DENBERG

Art Director
JAC COVERDALE

Creative Director
JAC COVERDALE

Producer
RIDGE HENDERSON

Agency Producer
JENEE SCHMIDT

Editor
GARY 'CRASH' MEDIN

Lighting Cameraman
GREG WINTER

Music Composer/Arranger
HANK WILLIAMS SNR

Production Company
WILSON GRIAK

Agency
CLARITY COVERDALE
RUEFF ADVERTISING
INC

Director of Marketing
DENNIS REISNOUR

Client
THE UNITED
RECOVERY CENTER

TEAR IN MY BEER

Soundtrack:
Hank Williams Snr. "Tear In My Beer" plays throughout.

SFX:
Crackle of an old record album.

Super:
Hank Williams Snr. wrote this song at the age of 28.

Sung:
I'm gonna keep drinking until I'm petrified

Super:
One year later, he died of alcoholism.

Sung:
Then maybe dear this tear will leave my eyes

Super:
If someone you care about has a problem with alcohol,

Sung:
There's a tear in my beer

Super:
singing about it won't help.

Sung:
'cause I'm cryin' for you dear

Super:
Talking about it just might.

Sung:
you are on my lonely mind.

Super:
*United Recovery Center
780-5900*

PILLOWS

SFX:
Music and sfx up and throughout.

Title card:
180

Title card scroll from right:
'by Alex Proyas Australia'

Cut to medium close-up of moving fans.

Cut to close-up of individual wearing goggles and tight cap.

Cut to medium close-up side view of person running with fans in background.

Shot of person passing behind post.

Cut to medium close-up of fan with rings around stands.

Side close-up of person with cap on.

Cut to moving shot of person running on pillows in background. In foreground circle with swirl on it on stand.

Person running toward camera.

Medium close-up of person's foot landing on pillow.

Cut back shot of person running away from camera on pillows.

Stakes with 1,2,3 on them in background.

Cut close-up of moving fans.

Overhead shot of person running on pillows in foreground, a stake with number six on it, and power lines.

Cut to moving fans.

Cut to person running toward camera with line of pillows in background.

Back shot of person standing looking to their left, right, left and right again at Y in pillow formation. Fan in foreground on right.

Cut to close-up of Nike shoe as heel is lifting off the floor.

Title card:
Orange Nike logo 180.

Television Commercials up to 30 seconds

Director
ALEX PROYAS

Copywriters
JAMIE BARRETT
PETER WEGNER

Art Director
WARREN EAKINS

Creative Directors
DAN WIEDEN
DAVID KENNEDY

Producer
MARGOT FITZPATRICK

Set Designer
STEVE MARR

Agency Producer
ELLEN ISRAEL

Lighting Cameraman
ALEX PROYAS

Music Composer/Arranger
PETER MILLER

Production Company
M.E.C./LIMELIGHT COMMERCIALS

Agency
WIEDEN & KENNEDY

International Marketing Director
TIM O'KENNEDY

Client
NIKE INC

Television Commercials up to 30 seconds

Director
DOMINIC SENA

Copywriter
BOB MOORE

Art Director
SUSAN HOFFMAN

Creative Directors
DAN WIEDEN
DAVID KENNEDY

Producer
AVIS McGARRY

Set Designer
TEREZ KREISZ

Agency Producer
TRISH REEVES

Lighting Cameraman
DOMINIC SENA

Production Company
PROPAGANDA

Agency
WIEDEN & KENNEDY

Director of Advertising
SCOTT BEDBURY

Client
NIKE INC

BOUNCING TV

SFX:

SFX (only) up and throughout

Open to title card: 'Tennis with Andre Agassi U.S.A.'

Cut to Andre Agassi playing solo tennis while the TV set is animating the exaggerated movements of each radical shot played by Agassi.

Close-up shot of Nike shoe in TV screen.

TV screen scrambles.

Julia Child:

...the one exception is the artichoke...

TV screen scrambles and continues to show Agassi playing radical tennis while the TV set reacts to each shot.

Cuts back to TV set with Agassi who hits another radically hard tennis shot that flips the TV set upside down.

The TV screen cuts to an upside down shot of the Air Tech Challenge tennis shoe.

Cut to the Nike Air logo and words: 'air tech challenge'.

STRANGE TASTE

Music:
*Incidental music 'Colin the
Elephant' – arranged by Jenkins
Ratledge.*

*John Cleese indulges in some
fashionable black and white
introspection about the meaning of
life and relationships with a lizard
and a lady friend. The latter gets
so angry she provides him with an
unusual opportunity to taste the
product.*

Echoing whisper:
Straight Schweppes

John Cleese:
*Why do we walk like one dancer
in a dream?*

Woman:
*Because when I dance in your
shadow it is I that feels the pain.*

John Cleese:
I am both of us and so are you.

Woman:
What was that shot of a lizard?

John Cleese:
*When I talk to you I talk to
myself.*

Woman:
I asked you a question.

John Cleese:
*And when I am with you I am on
my own.*

Woman:
*On your own! Try this, this is on
its own.*

John Cleese:
*Schweppes Tonic...on its own so
dry and yet so wet.*

Hello Colin.

Title:
*The grown-up soft drink. (Well
quite).*

The grown-up soft drink. (Well, quite).

*Television
Commercials up to
30 seconds*

Director
PAUL WEILAND

Copywriter
JAMES LOWTHER

Art Director
ALEXANDRA TAYLOR

Creative Director
JAMES LOWTHER

Producer
MARY FRANCIS

Set Designer
ROD McCLEAN

Agency Producer
FIONA WINBURN

Editor
RICHARD LEAROYD

Lighting Cameraman
DAVID WATKIN

Music Composers/Arrangers
CARL JENKINS
MIKE RATLEDGE

Production Company
PAUL WEILAND FILM
COMPANY

Agency
SAATCHI & SAATCHI

Marketing Manager
DAVID WHELAN

Client
SCHWEPPES

*Television
Commercials up to
30 seconds*

Director
JEFF GORMAN

Copywriter
TOM GABRIEL

Art Director
GUY TOM

Creative Director
TOM GABRIEL

Producer
LILLY WEINGARTEN

Set Designer
MICHAEL GAW

Agency Producer
DIANNE BROWN

Lighting Cameraman
BILL BENNETT

Production Company
JOHNS & GORMAN
FILMS

Agency
MILICI VALENTI
GABRIEL/DDB
NEEDHAM

*Vice President of Marketing
& Services*
NEIL TAKEKAWA

Client
ALOHA AIRLINES

UNIVERSAL MAN

Video:
*Open on inside of airplane, lighted
panel. Animation man goes
through various phases of
frustration.*

Pilot:
*Ladies and gentlemen, please
prepare for take-off...*

*This is Captain Peterson... we'll be
experiencing a little
delay...shouldn't be long...*

*Captain Peterson again, we're still
a little behind schedule...*

*This is Captain Peterson, well it
looks like it will be a little longer
than expected...*

Just sit back and relax...

Announcer:
*Next time, fly Aloha. The airline
you haven't been waiting for.*

EARLY WORDS

SFX:
Toddler gurgles.

Toddler calls.

Toddler:
Ma...

Ma. Ma.

Mother:
Ma. Ma.

Toddler:
Ma. Ma.

Mother:
Ma. Ma.

Toddler:
Ma. Ma. Ma.

Mother:
Ma. Ma. Ma. Ma.

Toddler:
Marmite.

MVO:
Marmite is made with yeast, one of the richest natural sources of B vitamins.

Marmite. Her mate, your mate, mates for life.

SFX:
Toddler laughs.

Television Commercials up to 30 seconds

Director
SIMON DELANEY

Copywriter
DAVID RYLAND

Art Director
TONY GILLAN

Creative Directors
ALAN MIDGLEY
JOHN BACON

Producer
ADAM LYNE

Set Designer
MARTIN JOHNSON

Agency Producers
JOHN MONTGOMERY
BEVERLY WATSON

Editor
PIERS DOUGLAS

Lighting Cameraman
MIKE GARFATH

Production Company
DELANEY & HART

Agency
OGILVY & MATHER

Marketing Manager
JULIAN FROST

Client
CPC UK LIMITED

*Television
Commercials up to
30 seconds*

Director
NICK PARK

Copywriters
PAUL CARDWELL
NICK PARK

Art Directors
NICK PARK
PAUL CARDWELL

Creative Director
PAUL CARDWELL

Producer
CHRIS MOLL

Set Designer
STUART ROSE

Animator
NICK PARK

Agency Producers
SAMANTHA PAYNE
DEBBIE TURNER

Editor
ROD HOWICK

Lighting Cameraman
TRISTAN OLIVER

Production Company
AARDMAN
ANIMATIONS
LIMITED

Agency
GGK LONDON
LIMITED

Chairman
DR DOUG SWINDEN

Client
SELSE & CONSORTIUM

PENGUINS 1

*The Penguin family at a table in a
modern kitchen.*

*Kitchen units in the background.
An electric cooker with ceramic
hob is visible.*

*They walk into a microphone,
labelled ELECTRIC.*

Mr Penguin:
*Oh yeah, we've got a new electric
cooker.*

Mrs Penguin:
*Ceramic hob? Oh yes, we've got
that,*

Baby Penguin:
Very efficient.

Mrs Penguin:
*Very efficient. You just turn it on
and within seconds it's red, just
turn it down slightly...*

Mr Penguin:
And it is very quick...

Mrs Penguin:
Instantly controllable.

Mr Penguin:
*Instant, yes that's a good word.
Instantly yes, it is really.*

Baby Penguin:
And it goes bing when it's finished.

Super:
*Graphic representation of a cooker
animates into COOK ELECTRIC
(logo) and endline.*

MVO:*For all your creature
comforts – COOK ELECTRIC.*

PANDAS 2

The Panda family in a modern kitchen.

Kitchen units in the background. A dishwasher is visible.

They talk into a microphone, labelled ELECTRIC.

Mrs Panda:
Oh it's essential now. It was a luxury before we got it, but it's definitely an essential now.

Mr Panda:
I used to do the washing up, before we had a dishwasher and it took an hour and a half, it was hellish.

Yeah well, these days we don't fight about it. We used to always argue about who was doing the dishes.

Mrs Panda:
Now I've got a complete monopoly.

Mr Panda:
So we spend our time arguing about other issues rather than who does the dishes.

Graphic representation of dishwasher animates into DISHWASH ELECTRIC (logo) and endline.

MVO:
For all your creature comforts – DISHWASH ELECTRIC.

Television Commercials up to 30 seconds

Director
PETER LORD

Copywriters
PAUL CARDWELL
NICK PARK

Art Directors
NICK PARK
PAUL CARDWELL

Creative Director
PAUL CARDWELL

Producer
CHRIS MOLL

Set Designer
TIM FARRINGTON

Animator
PETER LORD

Agency Producers
SAMANTHA PAYNE
DEBBIE TURNER

Editor
ROD HOWICK

Lighting Cameraman
TRISTAN OLIVER

Production Company
AARDMAN
ANIMATIONS
LIMITED

Agency
GGK LONDON
LIMITED

Chairman
DR DOUG SWINDEN

Client
SELSE & CONSORTIUM

Television
Commercials up to
30 seconds

Director
SYD MACARTNEY

Copywriter
STEVE GRIME

Art Director
STEVE GRIME

Creative Director
STEVE GRIME

Producer
ALISON MAYO

Agency Producer
JUDY ROSS

Editor
MARTIN SMITH

Lighting Cameraman
IAN WILSON

Music Composer/Arranger
JOHN ALTMAN

Production Company
RAWI MACARTNEY
LIMITED

Agency
AYER LIMITED

Marketing Director
ALAN PALMER

Client
TREBOR BASSETT
LIMITED

FOR A FEW BERTIES MORE

Open on young couple in an apartment. The young man is very well groomed and the woman is very pretty but frumpily dressed. They both seem to be in a state of panic.

Man:
They should have known.

The young woman (over-acting) holds on to the man's arm.

Woman:
It's got so out of control.

The man takes out a packet of Liquorice Allsorts from his pocket. Stares at them and angrily throws them onto a table.

Man:
Putting Bassetts Liquorice Allsorts into a handy size bag.

He walks over to the window, pulls back the curtain and looks out.

Man:
This was bound to happen.

From his point of view we see the street below. It seems the world has gone Bertie mad. People at bus stops, riding bikes, policemen, sitting on park benches, all with Bertie heads and packets of Liquorice Allsorts.

Cut back to our man by the window, without looking he talks to the woman.

Man:
Looks as though we're the only ones left.

Camera pulls back to show the girl by the table, pack in hand and she's turned Bertie.

Cut to pack.

MVO:
Bassetts Liquorice Allsorts

One too many and you might turn Bertie.

BARBER SHOP

Soundtrack:
Old Norwegian folk tune.

General story:
After having his beard shaven off, the client hands his Visa card to the barber who compares the photo on the back of the card with his client. After everyone has scrutinized the photo and the newly shaven man, the barber refuses to accept the card.

Pay-off:
The new Visa-card has got your picture on it.

Television Commercials up to 40 seconds

Director
JOHAN GULBRANSON

Copywriters
LISBETH AMUNDSEN
JOHAN GULBRANSON

Art Directors
BENTE AMUNDSEN
STEIN LEIKANGER

Producer
ROLF PEDERSEN

Set Designer
KALLE BOMAN

Editor
JOHAN GULBRANSON

Lighting Cameraman
THOMAS BOMAN

Production Company
LEO FILM

Agency
N & T LEO BURNETT
A / S

Marketing Director
TOMMY BERGLUND

Client
SPAREBANKKORT

*Television
Commercials up to
40 seconds*

Director
ANDREW STAVELEY

Copywriter
DAVID SHANE

Art Director
LYNN KENDRICK

Creative Directors
JON GREENHALGH
KES GRAY

Producer
MARTIN GREAVES

Animator
ANDREW STAVELEY

Agency Producer
HEATHER REID

Lighting Cameraman
GRAHAM PETIT

Music Composer/Arranger
K REHFIELD

Production Company
3 PEACH ANIMATION

Agency
CHIAT/DAY

Managing Director
ROBIN BINES

Client
FULL MOON

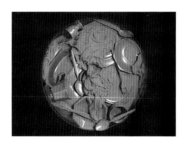

LARGE GLASS THINGYS

Soundtrack:
Chirrupy music throughout.

Super:
Recycled advertising.

Video:
*We open on some grainy, black
and white 50's footage of a soap
powder commercial. A chronically
perky woman is standing by a sink,
addressing the camera. As she
talks, an Ecover washing up liquid
bottle is crudely superimposed over
the pack she is holding.*

Overdubbed: (woman)
*Oh, I see. I'm in one of those
recycled commercials for Ecover.
Well then, take a good look at this
bottle. See that line there? (pause).
You'll notice it doesn't say for
people who kind of, sort of care
about the environment, or for
people who would like to care
about the environment if they had
more time. If you're one of those
people, well...well, I think that's
very very naughty. Because Ecover
is for people who care that its
active ingredients are fully
biodegradable, that it contains
camomile and marigold extracts,
and of course, that it really, really
cleans large...glass...thingys...*

Video:
*Cue to blue and green clothes
spinning behind the glass of a
washing machine. The words
"Washes Righter" are
superimposed" underneath.*

EDMUND DUDLEY

VO Edmund:

To the Tower of London, in chains and disgrace, the year of 1510.

By Traitors Gate I came in.

And will not go out again.

And I can tell of deeds blacker than a raven's wing.

Of princes in their prime snuffed out.

Of Lady Jane, Guy Fawkes and Anne Boleyn.

Where now I tread, I tread on ancient bones.

Where history brimful with blood spilled and seeped into the stones.

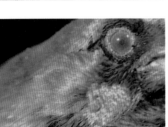

Television Commercials up to 40 seconds

Director
TONY KAYE

Copywriter
JOHN O'DONNELL

Art Director
GARRY HORNER

Creative Director
JOHN O'DONNELL

Producer
EUGENIA KAYE

Set Designer
JENNY SELDEN

Agency Producer
MARK ANDREWS

Editor
SAM SNEADE

Lighting Cameraman
TONY KAYE

Music Composer/Arranger
JEFF McCORMACK

Production Company
TONY KAYE FILMS
LIMITED

Agency
COLLETT DICKENSON
PEARCE & PARTNERS
LIMITED

Marketing Director
DYLAN HAMMOND

Client
HISTORIC ROYAL
PALACES

*Television
Commercials up to
40 seconds*

Director
NICK PARK

Copywriters
PAUL CARDWELL
NICK PARK

Art Directors
NICK PARK
PAUL CARDWELL

Creative Director
PAUL CARDWELL

Producer
CHRIS MOLL

Set Designer
JONATHAN LEE

Animator
NICK PARK

Agency Producers
SAMANTHA PAYNE
DEBBIE TURNER

Editor
ROD HOWICK

Lighting Cameraman
DAVE SPROXTON

Production Company
AARDMAN
ANIMATIONS
LIMITED

Agency
GGK LONDON
LIMITED

Chairman
DR DOUG SWINDEN

Client
SELSE & CONSORTIUM

TERRY 2

Terry the tortoise in the hallway of a flat.

A storage heater is visible against the wall.

He talks into a microphone, labelled ELECTRIC.

Terry:
An athlete like me has to be able to come in from doing a training run and be warm in all the rooms.

If you are going to replace your existing heating you've got to go for something that's economical, worry free,

Um...I'm a bit of a worrier.

I like to cuddle...I like to cuddle up in my own home. I don't...it's not nice to get out of bed and be freezing. I need to be warm.

One thing about installing new electric heating is that you've got no kind of worries like that...

...and that's magic.

Super:
Graphic representation of heater animates into HEAT ELECTRIC (logo) and endline.

MVO:
For all your creature comforts – HEAT ELECTRIC.

RIDER

Soundtrack:
Elvis Presley "The wonder of you".

Sung:
When no one else can understand me...

When everything I do is wrong...

You give me hope and consolation...

You give me strength to carry on... And you're always there to lend a hand...

In everything I do...

That's the wonder...

The wonder of you.

Television Commercials up to 40 seconds

Director
STEVE LOWE

Copywriter
PETE LEWTAS

Art Director
JON PRIME

Creative Director
TONY COX

Producer
RONNIE WEST

Agency Producer
MAGGIE BLUNDELL

Editor
ADAM CROSSLAND

Lighting Cameraman
GEOFF BOYLE

Rostrum Cameraman
TONY JACKSON

Production Company
GUARD PHILLIPS
HUGHES & LOWE

Agency
BMP DDB NEEDHAM

Marketing Manager
JULIAN FROST

Client
C P C UK LIMITED

*Television
Commercials up to
40 seconds*

Director
DAVID GARFATH

Copywriter
PAUL HODGKINSON

Art Director
KEVIN JONES

Creative Director
PAUL WEINBERGER

Producer
MARY FRANCIS

Agency Producer
TRACEY JOHNSTON

Editor
KATHY O'SHEA

Lighting Cameraman
PETER HANNAN

Music Composers/Arrangers
EDWIN ASLER
JOE CAMPBELL
PAUL HART

Production Company
PAUL WEILAND FILM
COMPANY

Agency
LOWE HOWARD-SPINK

Sales & Marketing Director
LES COMPEY

Client
WEETABIX LIMITED

NOT SO MERRYMEN

Music:
Robin Hood 'Fanfare'

Song: *(heroic voice)*
Robin Hood, robin Hood,
Riding through the glen.

Robin Hood, Robin Hood,
With his band of men.

Feared by the bad,
Loved by the good,

Robin Hood, Robin Hood, Robin
Hood.

Robin Hood, Robin Hood,
Could be in a fix.

Robin Hood, Robin Hood,
Spies the Weetabix.

Does he retreat, back to
Sherwood?

(brief pause)

Merrymen:
'Course he should,
'course he should,
'course he should.

SURVIVAL

Soundtrack:

Music track throughout, overlaid with items of news, weather forecasts, clauses from insurance policies, evangelical preachers etc, in the manner of David Byrne, particularly "My life in the bush of ghosts".

Video:

Open on a girl's face. Superimposed on it and filling the rest of the screen is b/w footage of a stressful city street.

We cut to b/w footage of smokey factory chimneys. We cut to b/w footage of people eating and drinking.

We cut to b/w footage of wind and rain lashing a coastal town.

We cut to b/w footage of exhaust fumes in traffic.

We cut to b/w footage on empty reservoir cracking in the harsh sun.

As we progress through these cuts the footage fades, and the girl's face progressively becomes clearer. As it does so she washes her face, rubs away cleansing lotion, wipes make-up from her eyes and applies moisturiser.

Soundtrack:

Music fades out.

Video:

When she has finished, the superimposed footage has gone completely and only her pure and beautiful face remains.

We cut to four Visage packs and super the line:

Visage by Nivea.

Protect and Survive.

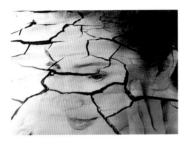

Television Commercials up to 40 seconds

Director
GERARD DE THAME

Copywriter
PETER RUSSELL

Art Director
ROB OLIVER

Creative Director
DAVID ABBOTT

Producer
ANITA OVERLAND

Agency Producer
FRANCINE LINSEY

Editor
PETER GODDARD

Lighting Cameraman
PASCAL LEBEGUE

Music Composer/Arranger
BARRY ADAMSON

Production Company
HELEN LANGRIDGE
ASSOCIATES

Agency
ABBOTT MEAD
VICKERS.BBDO
LIMITED

Marketing Controller Toiletries
ANDREW FROST

Client
SMITH & NEPHEW
CONSUMER PRODUCTS

*Television
Commercials up to 40
seconds*

Director
LESTER BOOKBINDER

Copywriter
CECILY CROKE

Art Director
PAUL ARDEN

Creative Director
PAUL ARDEN

Producer
AMANDA TURVEY

Agency Producer
MATTHEW FAULK

Editor
ROSS SIMMONS

Lighting Cameraman
ANDY ANDREWS

Music Composer/Arranger
MATTHEW FAULK
JONATHAN HARVEY

Production Company
RSA FILMS

Agency
SAATCHI & SAATCHI

Director of Marketing
DEBBIE MALMO

Client
SARA LEE
CORPORATION

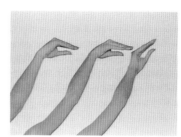

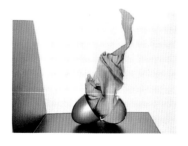

L'EGGS

Soundtrack:
'L'Eggs' music throughout.

Video:
*Open on a medium close-up of 2
pairs of legs. They move to reveal
a third.*

*Cut to 3 arms shaped like ostrich
heads, moving in various
directions.*

*Cut to 'birds' crossing the frame
from left to right, the last one
freezes centre frame.*

*Cut to abstract angle of chair in
close-up.*

*Cut to 'bird' sitting on chair, it
crosses its legs.*

*Cut to close-up of legs crossed, a
hand strokes the leg.*

*Cut to 'bird' getting up to reveal it
has laid an egg on the chair.*

*Cut to close-up of the egg as it
opens and tights float out of it up
into the air.*

*Cut to leg folding out from the top
of the frame to form the 'L' of the
logo 'L'Eggs'.*

Cut to pack shot of L'Eggs tights.

INTENSIVE

SFX:
Speeding trains. Graphic sequence of trains criss-crossing the screen in close-up. (Sequence is repeated throughout).

Network SouthEast tannoy:
Network SouthEast, take 1.

Network SouthEast employee:
What makes this network different?

SFX:
Speeding trains.

Network SouthEast employee:
Is the sheer amount of traffic we handle in the rush hour.

SFX:
Trains speeding by.

Network SouthEast employee:
Every 7 minutes on this line.

SFX:
Trains speeding by.

Network SouthEast employee:
Every 5 minutes on some.

SFX:
Trains speeding by.

Network SouthEast employee:
Eight thousand trains a day.

Network SouthEast employee:
In this one little corner of the country.

SFX:
Trains speeding by.

Network SouthEast employee:
Almost 2 million passenger trips.

Every day.

It takes a lot of teamwork.

Network SouthEast.

All for one and one for all.

SFX:
Trains speeding by.

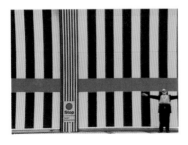

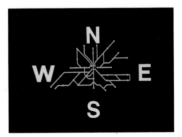

Television Commercials up to 40 seconds

Directors
SIMON COLE
ADAM CAMERON

Copywriter
JEFF STARK

Art Director
PAUL ARDEN

Creative Director
PAUL ARDEN

Producers
MARTHA GREENE
CHRIS STEVENSON

Animator
MIKE McGEE

Agency Producer
ARNOLD PEARCE

Editor
SAM SNEADE

Lighting Cameraman
JIM ALLOWAY

Production Company
STARK FILMS

Agency
SAATCHI & SAATCHI

Marketing Director
DAVID WALKER

Client
NETWORK SOUTHEAST

Television
Commercials up to
40 seconds

Directors
SIMON COLE
ADAM CAMERON

Copywriter
JEFF STARK

Art Director
PAUL ARDEN

Creative Director
PAUL ARDEN

Producers
MARTHA GREENE
CHRIS STEVENSON

Animator
MIKE McGEE

Agency Producer
ARNOLD PEARCE

Editor
SAM SNEADE

Lighting Cameraman
JIM ALLOWAY

Production Company
STARK FILMS

Agency
SAATCHI & SAATCHI

Marketing Director
DAVID WALKER

Client
NETWORK
SOUTHEAST

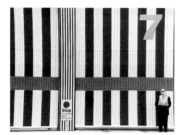

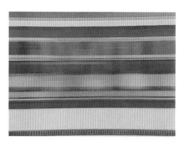

11 SECONDS PEOPLE

This commercial features Network SouthEast employees only. Throughout the commercial numbers (1-11) appear on the top right hand side of screen in grey colour.

David:
Ladies and Gentlemen, every day, every morning, during the rush hour a train arrives in Central London every 11 seconds.

Felix:
Every 11 seconds.

David:
What was that again?

Felix:
Every 11 seconds.

Dominic:
No other railway in Europe has a turnaround like that and a lot of people know that.

They say he does it.

David:
What do you think of that?

Felix:
That's sharp.

Dominic:
We do try you know.

David:
There are a lot of trains and a lot of people.

David:
Every 11 seconds.

I thank you.

Network SouthEast logo.

59 CLUB

Music:
ou're undecided' – Charlie Burnett.

en on swinging sign of the 59 Club.

Cut to cub interior.

*'ut between numerous shots of club
mbers, discussing bikes, drinking tea,
etc.*

it to exterior shots with motorcycles.

*it to 75 year old vicar amongst other
bikers.*

*'e is the Rev William Shergold. The
ginal 'Leather Vicar' and founder of
the club.*

He dons his helmet.

A motorcycle roars into the night.

*it to close-up of woven patch on the
rm of a leather jacket which reads:
W – BE MORE THAN JUST A
NUMBER.*

Super:
Wrangler logo.

*Television
Commercials up to
40 seconds*

Director
ALEX ZSARZSY

Copywriter
CHRIS PALMER

Art Director
MARK DENTON

Creative Directors
CHRIS PALMER
MARK DENTON

Producer
STEPHEN ADAMS

Agency Producer
JANE FITCH

Editor
JOEY PAZANO

Music Composer/Arranger
CHARLIE BURNETT

Production Company
INFERNO/
STEVE ADAMS
PRODUCTIONS

Agency
SIMONS PALMER
DENTON CLEMMOW &
JOHNSON LIMITED

Marketing Director
ROBIN DILLEY

Client
WRANGLER UK
LIMITED

*Television
Commercials up to 40
seconds*

Directors
VAUGHAN & ANTHEA

Copywriter
CHRIS PALMER

Art Director
MARK DENTON

Creative Directors
CHRIS PALMER
MARK DENTON

Producer
ROSIE MUCH

Agency Producer
PAUL FENTON

Editor
DUNCAN SHEPHERD

Lighting Cameraman
JOSEPH YACOE

Music Composer/Arranger
RONIN

Production Company
PMC

Agency
SIMONS PALMER
DENTON CLEMMOW &
JOHNSON LIMITED

Marketing Director
JOHN HART

Managing Director
FRANK DIMECH

Client
WRANGLER UK
LIMITED

DJ

*An L.A.P.D. squad car searches for
pirate DJ transmitting across an L..
neighbourhood.*

DJ:

*Word up, this is K-Baz about to pum
some more bass...We're gonna get
fly...This is coming at you from the
underground...Doing it with the big
40...Stupid! Funky! We're gonna do
divine! Hard! Word up!*

*Word is bond...You know what I'm
saying...This is going out to my
boys...You know what I'm saying th
four hoods...You know what I'm
saying...Pumping me over your big l
inch woofers...*

*...You know my girl is just so fly...M
we're gonna get together and
er...yeah...This is the baz and I'm ju
about to drop the science...Kick the
ballistics in Compton...You know wh
I'm saying...'Cos this is the real deal.*

SFX:
Telephone rings.

DJ:
You're on...

Girl:
*K Baz, I just want to let you know th
you're the sexiest man alive, and ooo
Baby...*

DJ:
*Doing the right thing to your
eardrums...Pumping holes in them...S
something to the five O's out there...V
know the deal...I'm the Baz, ain't go
job, but that's cool though...If you do
like it come see me...*

*I'm not a gas or liquid but a solid
substance...*

*The police break down the door of th
makeshift studio. K-Baz is long gone,
tape recorder plays the show into th
microphone.*

DJ:
*I'm getting down with the groove 'co
I'm smoother than the cream in a
Twinkie – Word up!*

*Cut to close up of DJ's 'W' ring as h
caresses his girl's shoulder.*

Super:

BE MORE THAN JUST A NUMBE

Wrangler logo.

COCKTAIL

...n on Don behind a small cocktail bar.
...the bar are two extremely attractive
women.

Don:
Tonight we look at compatibility.

...saunters in and chats up the first girl.

Stan:
...an's the name, romance is my game.

The girl slaps him around the face.

SFX:
Smack!!!

Cut to Don.

Don:
(shaking head)
...Incompatible.

...n recovers enough to start chatting up
the next girl.

Stan:
...ney, what makes love like a tiger and
winks?

He winks.

She thumps him in the stomach

Don:
(wincing and shaking head)
Uh-oh.

...walks round to the front of the bar. the
girls respond favourably to his chat.

Don:
Tammy Baby...some outfit!

Tammy:
Well thanks Don.

Don:
Cindy Honey...dinner Thursday?

Cindy:
Ooh, yes Donny poos.

Don turns to camera.

Don:
...Now we're compatible...just like this
...mputer which can talk to virtually all
others.

Cut to beauty shot of a Tandon.

SFX:
Heavenly choirs.

...t back to Don. His teeth sparkle as he
smiles.

Don:
Isn't that incredible?

...t to Stan & Don 2 shot. Stan covers the
...'S' on his sweater to create the word
Tandon.

MVO:
...dies and Gentlemen. Stan and Don are
brought to you courtesy of Tandon
computers.

Television
Commercials up to
40 seconds

Director
STEVE LOWE

Copywriters
SEAN DOYLE
CHRIS PALMER

Art Director
MARK DENTON

Creative Directors
CHRIS PALMER
MARK DENTON

Producer
RONNIE WEST

Agency Producer
JANE FITCH

Editors
ADAM CROSSLAND
TERRY BROWN

Lighting Cameraman
CHRIS ASHBROOK

Music Composers/Arrangers
M. CARTLAND
COLIN TOWNS
R. SHARPLES

Production Company
GUARD McMILLAN &
HUGHES

Agency
SIMONS PALMER
DENTON CLEMMOW &
JOHNSON LIMITED

Marketing Director
JAMIE MINOTTO

Client
TANDON COMPUTERS

*Television
Commercials up to
40 seconds*

Director
STEVE LOWE

Copywriters
SEAN DOYLE
CHRIS PALMER

Art Director
MARK DENTON

Creative Directors
CHRIS PALMER
MARK DENTON

Producer
RONNIE WEST

Agency Producer
JANE FITCH

Editors
ADAM CROSSLAND
TERRY BROWN

Lighting Cameraman
CHRIS ASHBROOK

Music Composer/Arranger
R SHARPLES

Production Company
GUARD McMILLAN &
HUGHES

Agency
SIMONS PALMER
DENTON CLEMMOW &
JOHNSON LIMITED

Marketing Director
JAMIE MINOTTO

Client
TANDON COMPUTERS

YO GUYS

Open on close-up of Stan.

Stan:
Hi I'm Stan.

Cut to close-up of Don.

Don:
And I'm Don.

Stan & Don:
We're Stan & Don.

Don:
*And now a simple demonstration to
show how this computer can talk to
virtually all others.*

Cut to beauty shot of Tandon computer

SFX:
Heavenly choirs.

Don:
*...In which Stan plays the
computer...Take it away Stan!*

*Cut to Stan on a pedestal. He braces
himself and speaks into a 'bullhorn'.*

Stan:
Yo guys!

*Whip pan to a group of people wearing
'OTHER COMPUTER' sweaters.*

Other guys:
Yo Stan!

Whip pan back to Stan on the pedestal.

SFX:
Applause.

Don:
*And there you have it. In a
word...compatible...right Stan?*

Stan:
Right Don!

*Cut to Stan and Don 2 shot. Stan covers
the 'S' on his sweater to create the word
TANDON.*

MVO:
*Ladies & Gentlemen, Stan & Don are
brought to you courtesy of Tandon
computers.*

NELLIE

Open on the Stan & Don Show.

MVO:
*Ladies & Gentlemen, it's Stan &
Don!*

Don:
*Thank you...Stan, if I suggested this
computer was incompatible...*

*Cut to beauty shot of Tandon
computer.*

SFX:
Heavenly choirs.

Cut back to Don.

Don:
...What would you say?

*Cut to Stan holding a model
elephant with piece of string tied in a
knot around it.*

Stan:
Not on your Nellie.

*Stan cuts the string on a pair of furry
dice.*

Stan:
No dice.

*A Mexican appears. Stan stops him
with a 'NO ENTRY' sign.*

Stan:
No way – Jose!

*Stan picks up an armful of footballs,
tennis balls, etc.*

Stan:
An absolute load of b...

Don cuts off Stan mid sentence.

Don:
Thank you Stan. Yes, you were right.

Don:
*This computer...is indeed compatible
with virtually all others.*

Cut to beauty shot of computer.

SFX:
Heavenly choirs.

Don turns to Stan.

Don:
*But tell me Stan. Why didn't you
just say no.*

*Don holds up a small bush which he
hits lightly with a stick.*

Don:
*...Instead of 'beating around the
bush'?*

*Cut to Stan & Don 2 shot. Don
covers the 'S' on Stan's sweater to
create the word TANDON.*

MVO:
*Ladies & Gentlemen, Stan and Don
are brought to you courtesy of
Tandon computers.*

*Television
Commercials up to
40 seconds*

Director
STEVE LOWE

Copywriters
SEAN DOYLE
CHRIS PALMER

Art Director
MARK DENTON

Creative Directors
CHRIS PALMER
MARK DENTON

Producer
RONNIE WEST

Agency Producer
JANE FITCH

Editors
ADAM CROSSLAND
TERRY BROWN

Lighting Cameraman
CHRIS ASHBROOK

Music Composer/Arranger
R SHARPLES

Production Company
GUARD McMILLAN &
HUGHES

Agency
SIMONS PALMER
DENTON CLEMMOW &
JOHNSON LIMITED

Marketing Director
JAMIE MINOTTO

Client
TANDON COMPUTERS

*Television
Commercials up to
40 seconds*

Director
JOHN O'DRISCOLL

Copywriter
LINDA MORGAN

Art Director
JOANNA DICKERSON

Creative Directors
NICK WELCH
BILLY MAWHINNEY

Producer
ANDY McCLEAN

Set Designer
MIKE HALL

Agency Producer
ALISTAIR FRYER

Editor
RICHARD LEAROYD

Lighting Cameraman
MOSTYN ROWLANDS

Production Company
PAUL WEILAND FILM
COMPANY

Agency
J WALTER THOMPSON

Production Manager
DAVE HALL

Client
SWADDLERS

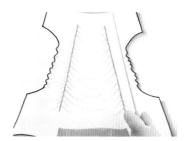
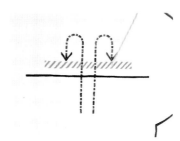

HOW YA DOING?

Soundtrack:
Half a second silence.

Video:
Open on a baby wearing Togs nappy

Prof. Togs puppet: *(humming)*
Doo, doo, doo, doo, doo, doo, doo, doo, doo

He walks over to the baby:
Hello baby.

Doo, doo's. what to do.

*Wear the new Ultra Absorbent Togs nappy
course.*

Humming as he walks over to wall chart
Let's take a closer look shall we.

*As you can see the amazing Ultra Togs leak
shields – here and here.*

Keep the doo doo here.

He walks back to baby:
Cos a babys gotta do, what a babys got to do

Oh, how ya doing?

Cut to togs pack

MVO:
New Ultra Togs – with amazing leak shields

Prof. Togs puppet:
Stay dry. Stay happy.

Toodle – oo.

LADYBIRDS

VO:

Hello there all you John Smith's drinkers, yes it's treat-time again, thirty mouth-watering seconds to look at the great stuff itself. Only today, look out for the naughty scene.

SFX:

"Je t'aime"

(At the end of commercial break)

Ladybird:

Ahh – I've had enough I fancy a pint of John Smith's.

Television Commercials up to 40 seconds

Director
TONY MAY

Copywriter
JOHN WEBSTER

Art Director
JOHN WEBSTER

Creative Directors
JOHN WEBSTER
TONY COX

Producer
ANDREW SHELTON

Set Designers
JAMIE LEONARD
TIM DANN

Animator
BEN CAIN

Agency Producer
LUCINDA KER

Editor
PETER BESTON OBE

Lighting Cameraman
KEITH GODDARD

Rostrum Cameraman
DAVID WYNN-JONES

Music Composer
SERGE GAINSBOURG

Music Arranger
GRAHAM PRESKETT

Production Company
ALEX MYERS &
ASSOCIATES

Agency
BMP DDB NEEDHAM

Group Manager Brand Marketing
CHRIS DEATHE

Client
COURAGE LIMITED

*Television
Commercials up to
40 seconds*

Director
TONY MAY

Copywriter
JOHN WEBSTER

Art Director
JOHN WEBSTER

Creative Directors
JOHN WEBSTER
TONY COX

Producer
ANDREW SHELTON

Set Designers
JAMIE LEONARD
TIM DANN

Agency Producer
LUCINDA KER

Editor
PETER BESTON OBE

Lighting Cameraman
KEITH GODDARD

Rostrum Cameraman
DAVID WYNN-JONES

Production Company
ALEX MYERS &
ASSOCIATES

Agency
BMP DDB NEEDHAM

*Group Manager Brands
Marketing*
CHRIS DEATHE

Client
COURAGE LIMITED

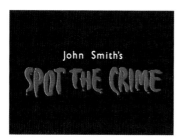

SERIOUS CRIME

VO:
*Today for our John Smith's
presentation, it's 'Spot-The-
Crime'. Watch carefully the
following images and see if you
can spot the serious crime.*

Is it A?

B?

C?

D?

Or E?

*Well did you spot it? 'Course you
did, it was D – short measure on a
pint of John Smith's and you can't
get more serious than that.*

*Well we can't go out on such a
dismal picture so we'll put it right
for you...*

SFX:
Drip.

VO:
...there that's better isn't it?

SAFETY CAR CRASH

Announcer VO:

This Mercedes-Benz was travelling on a highway outside Melbourne at 9 o'clock on a Tuesday evening.

Inside were the Nies family – husband, wife, and two teenagers,on the way to their farm.

As they crested a hill, another car on the wrong side of the road, and travelling at high speed in a 100 kilometre zone, speared into the Mercedes.

In all, 120 safety features are built into every Mercedes-Benz and in that split second of the accident, many of them saved the family's lives.

The driver's pedals droppped to the floor, away from his feet. The electronic seat belt pre-tensioning device pressed the occupants deep into their seats.

And despite the horrifying impact, the Mercedes safety passenger cell did not collapse.

Survival space remained intact.

This is the Nies family. To them, a Mercedes-Benz is not a luxury.

Television Commercials up to 60 seconds

Director
PAUL CLYDESDALE

Copywriter
DAVID BLACKLEY

Art Director
MAURICE DOWD

Creative Director
DAVID BLACKLEY

Producer
BILL REGAN

Agency Producer
PAUL CLYDESDALE

Lighting Cameraman
ADRIAN VAN VALEN

Music Composer/Arranger
RIC FORMOSA

Production Company
PORT PRODUCTIONS

Agency
CLEMENGER MELBOURNE PTY LIMITED

Senior Executive National Car Sales
DIETMAR HAUG

Client
MERCEDES-BENZ (AUST) PTY LIMITED

*Television
Commercials up to
60 seconds*

Director
JOE PYTKA

Copywriter
JIM RISWOLD

Art Director
DARRYL McDONALD

Creative Directors
DAN WIEDEN
DAVID KENNEDY

Producer
BRENDA
HAVERSTOCK

Set Designer
GEOFFREY KIRKLAND

Agency Producer
DEREK RUDDY

Lighting Cameraman
JOE PYTKA

Production Company
PYTKA PRODUCTIONS

Agency
WIEDEN & KENNEDY

Director of Advertising
SCOTT BEDBURY

Client
NIKE INC

BO SHOW

VO:
A-one, two, three, four!

Chorus: *(singing)*
Bo know it's got the air thing!

Bo: *(singing)*
Nice shoes!

Chorus:
Bo knows it works!

Bo: *(singing)*
Bo knows it's got the air thing!

Chorus:
Bo knows they...

Bo:
Stop!

Bo:
This is ridiculous. I'm an athlete not an actor.

Bo: *(from TV)*
Let me out of this thing. I've got rehab to do. Gimme those shoes.

Guy:
Bo?

Bo: *(to the family)*
Excuse me. You watch too much Tv, kid.

(Music up)
Cuts to Bo working out.

Chorus:
*Bo knows it's got...
...the air thing.*

Bo:
Hey! Where's that music coming from ?

Chorus:
Bo knows it's...

Bo:
You know I don't have time for this!

George:
But I do! hit it!

(Music up)

Chorus:
George knows it's got the air thing

DAYBREAK

Music:
An arrangement of 'Dawn Patrol'.

Milkman:
Two semi-skimmed...

...one Silver Top...

*Number eighteen. Ah, rice
pudding tonight.*

Music: *(Stops)*

Milkman:
*Lads, lads. What are you playing
at? You know they're away for a
fortnight. But next door want two
extra. Go on then.*

VO:
Whatever your order...

*...your milkman can deliver...all
the milk you'll ever need.*

Milkman:
Empties!

*Television
Commercials up to
60 seconds*

Director
BILL MATHER

Copywriter
DAVE BUCHANAN

Art Director
MIKE HANNETT

Creative Director
TONY COX

Producer
KEITH VALENTINE

Set Designer
JAMIE LEONARD

Animators
DAVE THROSSEL
LINDA JOHNSON

Agency Producer
LUCINDA KER

Editor
KEVIN WHEELAN

Lighting Cameraman
ROGER PRATT

Rostrum Cameraman
PETER TAYLOR

Music Composer/Arranger
GRAHAM PRESKETT

Production Company
REDWING FILM
COMPANY

Agency
BMP DDB NEEDHAM

Marketing Manager
JULIAN NOLAN

Client
NATIONAL DAIRY
COUNCIL

*Television
Commercials up to
60 seconds*

Director
MANDIE FLETCHER

Copywriter
JOHN O'DONNELL

Art Director
GARRY HORNER

Creative Director
JOHN O'DONNELL

Producer
ALAN TAYLOR

Set Designer
VOYTEK

Agency Producer
MARK ANDREWS

Editor
TERRY JONES

Lighting Cameraman
DAVID WALSH

Production Company
PHOENIX FILMS

Agency
COLLETT DICKENSON
PEARCE & PARTNERS
LIMITED

Marketing Director
IAN DICKENS

Client
OLYMPUS

MR RADIATOR MAN

Dawn:
Coo-eee

I'm here for the portrait luv.

Excuse me Mr Radiator Man...

But could we chill out a bit please.

Oh yes...

*Course he's done them all you
know.*

The Everley Brothers.

Herman Hermit.

*Oh wow. It's art. It's sculptor.
It's...it's...what is it?*

Bailey:
It's the latest Olympus. The MJU.

Dawn: *(feigning instant
recognition)*

Oh the MJU.

Bailey:
Automatic everything.

*Even a new kind of flash, helps
stop red eye.*

Chirpy:
Trouble with the radiator Guv?

Dawn:
Bailey!

*Radiator...wicked sense of
humour...love it.*

Now how do you want me?

MVO:
From Olympus, the new MJU.

It helps say goodbye...to red eye.

RIVER

Soundtrack:
'Sweet Thunder' by Yello.

Video:
*We open on a little boy drinking
from a pump by the side of a river
somewhere in Africa. He then runs
from the pump to the water's edge
and relieves himself in the river.
The camera pans on to reveal a lot
of activity going on by the river.*

*We see some women carrying
water pitchers on their heads, a
man paddling his canoe across the
river. On the other side there are
people walking, loading and
unloading boats, generally
carrying about their daily business.*

*On this side of the river the camera
continues to pan past some women
washing their clothes, some cattle
drinking and bathing in the river,
a steam boat passes whilst the
cattle drivers watch on. We then
come back to the same little boy
drinking at the same pump.*

*This action repeats exactly twice
more.*

*Dissolve through to ICI end
device.*

Title:
World Class.

MVO:
*Water is the source of all life.
But who washes the water?*

*Who has the technology to develop
a filter fine enough to wash the
water even of bacteria?*

World problems. World solutions.

World Class.

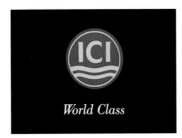

*Television
Commercials up to
60 seconds*

Director
HUGH JOHNSON

Copywriter
SIMON DICKETTS

Art Director
PAUL ARDEN

Creative Director
PAUL ARDEN

Producer
PHILIPPA THOMAS

Agency Producer
JIM BAKER

Editor
BRIAN DYKE

Lighting Cameraman
HUGH JOHNSON

Music Composer/Arranger
YELLO

Production Company
RSA FILMS

Agency
SAATCHI & SAATCHI

Head of Group Communications
ANNE FERGUSON

Client
ICI

*Television
Commercials up to
60 seconds*

Director
MIKE STEPHENSON

Copywriters
TIM DELANEY
MIKE STEPHENSON

Art Director
STEVE DUNN

Creative Director
TIM DELANEY

Producer
GLYNIS SANDERS

Set Designer
JOHN BEARD

Agency Producer
NICKY GREGOROWSKI

Editor
CYRIL METZGER

Lighting Cameraman
TONY
PIERCE-ROBERTS

Music Composer
GEOFF MACK

Music Arrangers
JOE CAMPBELL
PAUL HART

Production Company
PAUL WEILAND FILM
COMPANY

Agency
LEAGAS DELANEY

Head of Marketing Services
PETER RANDALL

*Marketing Communications
Controller*
GAUTAM DATAR

Client
NATIONWIDE
BUILDING SOCIETY

OUR CUSTOMERS

MVO:
*From cooks in Cookham.
Bakers in Burnham.*

*Don't leave the loaves long,
Don't forget to turn 'em.*

*Players from Rugby,
Plumbers from Bath.*

*Polishers from East Sheen.
Keep your television clean.*

*Painters from Gainsborough,
Try not to shake 'em,
Better check the signature,
Or you might have a Fakenham.*

*Babies from Crawley,
Tailors from Coatbridge,
If they haven't got your size,*

*You can let it out an inch.
Potters from Potter's Bar,*

*Carpenters from Wood Green,
Builders from Hammersmith,
Anyone whose name is Smith.*

*Farmers from Cowes, Oxford and
Barnsley,
Please close the Ramsgate,
Keep 'em outta Harm's Way...*

*Pet shops in Pett's Wood,
Tilers from Tylehurst,
Photographers from Ilford,
Don't forget to smile first...*

Nationwide.

*With more branches than anyone else
We're the nation's Building Society.*

Super:
The nation's Building Society.

Nationwide

The Nation's Building Society.

Nationwide Building Society

PRINCESS

(Music under)

MVO:
Once upon a time there was a beautiful princess.

SFX:
Mmm!

MVO:
Once upon a time, there was a princess.

SFX:
Mmm!

MVO:
Once upon a time, there was a girl called Mary.

SFX:
Ding!

MVO:
Mary travelled everywhere in a beautiful golden coach.

SFX:
Mmm!

MVO:
Mary travelled everywhere in a chauffeur driven limousine.

SFX:
Mary drove a Volkswagen Polo.

Ding!

MVO:
And, of course, she was worshipped and adored by a handsome prince.

SFX:
Mmm!

MVO:
She was worshipped and adored by a cost account called Ernie. Whom she loved as much as he loved her.

SFX:
Ding!

MVO:
And, this being a true story, Mary and Ernie lived happily ever after.

SFX:
Mmm!

Bickering voices: "I said turn right!" etc.

MVO:
Okay, so they fell out now and again. What are you looking for here? Perfection? I mean come on, gimme a break...

*Television
Commercials over
60 seconds*

Director
ROSS CRAMER

Copywriter
TONY COX

Art Director
TONY COX

Creative Director
TONY COX

Producer
CAMILA BOWRING

Animator
STEVE SMALL

Agency Producer
HOWARD SPIVEY

Editor
IAN WEIL

Lighting Cameramen
JOHN CRAWFORD
TREVOR WRENN

Music Composer/Arranger
RACHEL PORTMAN

Production Company
ROSE HACKNEY
PRODUCTIONS

Agency
BMP DDB NEEDHAM

Marketing Director
MIKE CORNISH

Client
VAG UK LIMITED

*Television
Commercials over
60 seconds*

Director
RICHARD DEAN

Copywriter
TIM MELLORS

Art Director
GRAHAM FINK

Creative Director
TIM MELLORS

Producer
MATTHEW JUSTICE

Set Designer
BRYCE WALMSLEY

Agency Producer
DIANE CROLL

Editors
ANDY KEMP
ROB HODGSON

Lighting Cameraman
CHRIS PARKER

Production Company
THE MOVING
PICTURE
PRODUCTION
COMPANY

Agency
GGT

Managing Director
GIULIANO
GNAGNATTI

Marketing Director
NIGEL GRASHAM

Client
ARISTON

CYCLE

Open on a kitchen.

*A series of people enter and
perform various mundane
functions in a cycle of repeats.*

DRAMA

...wan Atkinson voice over reads out a 'school register' style list of famous people's names to which they all answer 'Yes'.

...he list of actors and actresses have all ...ppeared in BBC dramas. The film is ...made up of existing BBC film clips.

MVO:
The BBC. Drama at its best.

*Television
Commercials over
60 seconds*

Copywriter
DOMINIC GETTINS

Art Director
TONY HARDCASTLE

Creative Director
ANDREW
RUTHERFORD

Producer
SIMON WINCHESTER

Editors
SIMON WINCHESTER
JEREMY DEAR
DOMINIC GETTINS

Production Company
BBC TELEVISION
CENTRE

Agency
FCO LIMITED

Marketing Director
HOWELL JAMES

Client
BBC

*Television
Commercials over
60 seconds*

Director
BRIAN GRIFFIN

Copywriters
PAUL ARDEN
EUGENE RUANE

Art Directors
PAUL ARDEN
BOB GABRIEL

Creative Director
PAUL ARDEN

Producer
LEWIS
MORE O'FERRALL

Agency Producer
FIONA WINBURN

Editor
IAN WEIL

Lighting Cameraman
CURTIS CLARK

Production Company
PHOENIX FILMS

Agency
SAATCHI & SAATCHI

*Head of Corporate
Communications*
MICHAEL DENT

Client
FORTE PLC

FOR THE WORLD

Soundtrack:
'Le Lac De Come' by Galos.

(Music throughout)

*Shot in France, America, Morocco,
Bahamas and the UK, this commerc
features a series of vignettes depicting a
of the group's activities. Each vignett
linked with a caption stating 'For......*

Video:
Man in Little Chef.
Title: *'For Him'.*
Elegant Lady.
Title: *'For Her'.*
Family in rubber rings.
Title: *'For Fun'.*
Four Admirals.
Title: *'Formality'.*
Two tennis players.
Title: *'For Service'.*
Ladies cleaning staircase.
Title: *'For polish'.*
Chambermaid on bed.
Title: *'Fourposter'.*
Valet.
Title: *'For Style'.*
Pianist.
Title: *'Fortissimo'.*
Boardroom meeting.
Title: *'For Business'.*
Man jumping from springboard.
Title: *'For Pleasure'.*
Bicycle upside down, passing Little C
Title: *'For the Road'.*
Car with Travelodge sign reflected
Title: *'For the Night'.*
Couple enter Bear Hotel.
Title: *'For the Weekend'.*
Wine bottle.
Title: *'For Quality'.*
Eiffel Tower and wine glass.
Title: *'4 AM'.*
View of Manhattan.
Title: *'For America'.*
Harvester scene.
Title: *'For the Family'.*
Casablanca Hotel front.
Title: *'For All the World'.*
Nuns jumping on beds.
Title: *'For the Time of Your Life'.*
Wedding on the beach.
Title: *'For Ever'.*
Ice Swan.
End Title: *'Forte, Host to the Worl*

RUDOLPH

Open on Rudolph the red-nosed reindeer.

He is sitting at home on Xmas day, watching the telly.

Unfortunately, sound and picture on his TV are terrible.

Slightly annoyed, he takes a sip of Heineken, which allows him to adjust his antlers as if they're a TV aerial.

The picture comes back beautifully, complete with sound. Close in on the TV. We catch the end of a Heineken commercial. We see a Super:

Super:
ONLY HEINEKEN CAN DO THIS.

Television Commercials campaigns

Directors
GRAHAM ROSE
PAUL WEILAND

Copywriters
SIMON CARBERY
MARK WNEK

Art Directors
CHARLES INGE
ALAN WALDIE

Creative Director
ADRIAN HOLMES

Producers
JOHN HACKNEY
ALICIA BERNARD
MARY FRANCIS

Set Designers
LESLIE POPE
ROD McCLEAN

Agency Producers
CHARLES CRISP
SARAH HORRY

Editors
DAVE GARLAND
IAN WEIL

Lighting Cameramen
ADRIAN BIDDLE
ALEXANDER WITT
ROGER PRATT

Music Composers/Arrangers
JOHN ALTMAN
PAUL HART

Production Companies
ROSE HACKNEY
PRODUCTIONS
&
PAUL WEILAND FILM
COMPANY

Agency
LOWE HOWARD-SPINK

Marketing Director
STEVE PHILPOTT

Client
THE WHITBREAD
BEER COMPANY

SINGER

Music:
Guitar strumming.

Singer:
Wake up this morning and the sun smiled down on me.

Sun smiled on me, that ain't the blues.

Wife:
Oh honey, that's cute.

Singer:
Woe...woe, woe, woe the boat happily down the stream.

Dam that ain't the blues either.

Wife:
What is this lipstick doing on your collar?

Singer:
Honey, that ain't no lipstick.

Wife:
Honey or nothing.

Singer:
I was shaving.

Wife:
You're lying.

Repo. Man:
We repossessing your car.

SFX:
Thunderclap.

Wife:
And I ain't never coming back.

SFX:
Guitar, harmonica.

Singer:
Sadness is my first name, last name is misery, I lost my woman, and the rain is coming down...

Oh...yer.

THE PROBE

Editor:
Sorry, sunbeam, I'm gonna have to tell you: you just ain't got a nose for the gutter -

Woman:
Proofs, Sir.

Editor:
Not now! I knocked off half an hour ago!

SFX:
The phone rings.

Editor:
Grab the dog, son!

Young Man: *(into phone)*
No, he's tied up...totally trapped in a throbbingly torrid tangle with titillating...

Editor:
Go on my son.

Young Man:
...Theresa the tousle-haired temptress from typing. (Pause)

Certainly.

Your wife, Sir.

Editor:
Desiree -

Wife:
Don't you Desiree me!

Editor:
Top tipple titillates tongues lesser liquids can't.

*Television
Commercials
campaigns*

Directors
IAN SINGLE
BARRY LEITH

Copywriters
KEVIN KNEALE
KEVIN JONES
JOHN SILVER

Art Directors
DON BARCLAY
KEVIN JONES
KEVIN THOMAS

Creative Director
PAUL WEINBERGER

Producers
YVONNE CHALKLEY
MICK FOLEY

Set Designer
STEVE COOPER

Animator
BARRY LEITH

Agency Producers
AMANDA DICKS
SARAH HORRY

Editors
MARTIN SMITH
PIERS DOUGLAS

Lighting Cameramen
FRANK GELL
MICHEL GEMMEL
ALEX THOMAS

Production Companies
THE IAN SINGLE
FILM COMPANY
&
PUPPETOON
PRODUCTIONS
LIMITED

Agency
LOWE HOWARD-SPINK

*Divisional Director of Corporate
Marketing*
ED OWEN

Client
TESCO STORES
LIMITED

LAMB

Music:
*Tesco theme music throughout.
(possibly a mix a whistles, woofs
and baa baa's)*

*Open on overhead shot of the
Tesco script – 'Fresh leg of Lamb
0.001b' – printed on a green
background. From top left of the
screen a sheep dog runs into frame.
He is rounding up a small flock of
numbers which are the reduced
price.*

*The numbers, chased by the dog,
exit frame. They reappear and are
herded into position.*

*The dog lies down across the old
price.*

Super:
Tesco logo.

FROZEN PRAWNS

Music:
Tesco Theme.

SFX:
Teeth chattering.

Open on a backdrop with the lettering:
TESCO FROZEN PRAWNS
400g pack

Below the words we see two 'Spitting Image' type prawns complete with scarfs and ear muffs, sat shivering in front of a two bar electric fire.

Super:
Tesco logo.

TEA UP

Music:
Tesco music.

Open on the top of some scaffolding against a backdrop.

A man in painter's overalls is painting words on the backdrop.

We can read:
TESCO PREMIUM TEABAGS

Another workman enters from screen right with mugs of tea.

Workman:
Tea up!

The painter moves aside, revealing the final part of what he has written.

TESCO PREMIUM TEABAGS.

Painter:
No it isn't.

TRAFFIC LIGHTS

Video:
Open on close-up of traffic lights.

Jeff is sitting in his pick-up truck at the lights, elbow on the window, tapping his fingers impatiently. He keeps looking to see if the traffic lights have changed.

Identical men are mowing the lawn. All the lawns of the houses are beautifully kept, and each house has an identical white picket fence and an identical estate car in each drive.

Every time Jeff starts to move, he is held up by another set of red traffic lights.

He looks to camera.

Jeff:
You know, I could have sworn I saw 2.2 kids back there.

But I haven't seen a Holsten Pils anywhere.

The sooner I get out of here the better.

Video:
He holds a remote control, points it and all the sets of lights change to green.

Cut to the woman. She is stringing a banner across the street. On the banner is written:
STOPS IN HELL.

Television Commercials campaigns

Director
JOHN LLOYD

Copywriter
TIM HEARN

Art Director
KATE STANNERS

Creative Director
TIM MELLORS

Producer
CAROLINE WARNER

Agency Producer
DIANE CROLL

Editors
RICHARD LEAROYD
STEVE GANDOLFI

Lighting Cameraman
JOHN STANIER

Production Company
LIMELIGHT
COMMERCIALS

Agency
GGT

Marketing Director
CAROL FISHER

Client
HOLSTEN
DISTRIBUTORS
LIMITED

DENTIST

Video:
Open on foot dangling.

Cut to Jeff in black tuxedo walking along a long stretch of sand. He is drinking from a glass of Pils.

Jeff:
I've been out with an old flame, Ulrika, my little German dentist.

Video:
He looks dreamily ahead, obviously nostalgic.

Jeff:
It was five years ago she fixed my crown. I took her out for a drink the same night...

Video:
He sighs reminiscently, slightly sad.

Jeff:
Gee, seeing her again brought back all those old feelings...

Video:
He raises the glass to drink. He slooshes the Pils then spits it out. He realises what he's done and looks shocked.

Jeff:
My gosh!

Video:
He takes another sip.

Jeff:
Mmmm Mmmm.

Video:
Quick cuts to a lifeguard's chair. On it is the woman dressed as a lifeguard. She looks towards us and on the front of her bathing hat is written:
SPLOSH INLET.

CHARITY

Video:
Open on Jeff standing at the door as if seeing the last guests out of his house.

Jeff:
Goodbye. And don't worry about it...I'm just sorry you couldn't stay longer...Auf wiedersehen!

Video:
He closes the door and leans against it. He speaks to the camera.

The entire room is full of flowers. There are vases of them and bunches of them on every available surface.

Jeff:
I like to help the afflicted. Every year right around this time, I like to throw a party in aid of charity.

Video:
He walks to table in the middle of the room which has dozens of unopened bottles of Holsten Pils on it.

Jeff:
This year it was a bring a bottle fundraiser for some delightful folks from Hamburg representing the Association of Hayfever Sufferers...

Video:
Jeff picks up a bottle of Pils from the table and eyes the rest appreciatively.

We see Jeff starting to stack up the bottles in a fridge. the cupboard is divided into sections, each marked with the name of a different month: January, February, etc.

He surveys the flowers with wicked satisfaction and opens the Pils.

Cut to him eyeing the bottles smugly. He pours and sips from his.

We see looking up at the woman.

Cut to the woman placing the final flower into a wall of flowers.

Cut to full view of the wall of flowers. They are arranged to spell the words:
SH...IT'S POLLEN.

Cut back to Jeff sniffing a flower with a wicked grin. He sniggers.

Director
JOHN LLOYD

Copywriter
MARK COLLIS

Art Director
JOHN CLIFFORD

Creative Director
TIM MELLORS

Producer
CAROLINE WARNER

Agency Producer
DIANE CROLL

Editors
RICHARD LEAROYD
STEVE GANDOLFI

Lighting Cameraman
JOHN STANIER

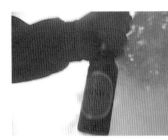

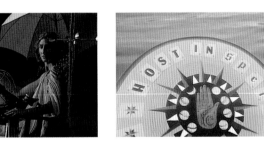

HOST

Video:
Open on an idyllic lake surrounded by woodland.

We see Jeff walking past a tree.

Jeff:
It's strange you know. Last night I had an out of body experience.

I felt my spirit leave my body and go down to the off-license.

Sometime later it returned.

Video:
He comes into a clearing where camp has been set up. He picks up a bottle of Holsten Pils and opens it. He then takes a glass from a bucket of ice.

Jeff:
I knew it had. I felt a sudden chill and a voice said 'I'm back would you hand me that bottle opener?'

I felt somehow...purified.

Video:
An enigmatic woman watches from a floating platform.

Jeff sips from the glass.

Cut back to the enigmatic woman. Cut to a close-up of ouji board type arrangement of letters. Woman puts last card down to spell: HOST IN SPELL.

Cut to Jeff sipping Pils.

ACTION REPLAY

VO:

Have you noticed these days commercials are full of trendy people in exotic locations, usuallly accompanied by an old sixtie's hit.

Leaving the product to appear only fleetingly at the end. Well this one for John Smith's is reversed, giving you the chance to get a good look at the great stuff itself.

There - isn't it gorgeous?

OK here comes the boring bit.

SFX:

Rock and Roll soundtrack.

Television Commercials Campaigns

Director
TONY MAY

Copywriters
JOHN WEBSTER
NICK GILL

Art Director
JOHN WEBSTER

Creative Directors
JOHN WEBSTER
TONY COX

Producer
ANDREW SHELTON

Set Designers
JAMIE LEONARD
TIM DANN

Animator
BEN CAIN

Agency Producer
LUCINDA KER

Editor
PETER BESTON OBE

Lighting Cameraman
KEITH GODDARD

Rostrum Cameraman
DAVID WYNN-JONES

Music Composer/Arranger
JOHN BARRY

Production Company
ALEX MYERS &
ASSOCIATES

Agency
BMP DDB NEEDHAM

Group Manager Brand Marketing
CHRIS DEATHE

Client
COURAGE LIMITED

Director
TONY MAY

Copywriter
JOHN WEBSTER

Art Director
JOHN WEBSTER

Creative Directors
JOHN WEBSTER
TONY COX

Producer
ANDREW SHELTON

Set Designers
JAMIE LEONARD
TIM DANN

Animator
BEN CAIN

Agency Producer
LUCINDA KER

Editor
PETER BESTON OBE

Lighting Cameraman
KEITH GODDARD

Rostrum Cameraman
DAVID WYNN-JONES

REVERSE

VO:
We've had a letter from a Mr Armitage of Hull complaining of 'lack of action' in our last John Smith's commercial.

Well I don't know what you were watching Mr Armitage but watch again and this time keep your eye on that bubble near the bottom of the glass.

SFX:
James Bond music.

VO:
What do you want Mr Armitage...blood?

SERIOUS CRIME

VO:

Today for our John Smith's presentation it's 'Spot-the-Crime'.

Watch carefully the following images and see if you can spot the serious crime.

Is it A?

B?

C?

D?

Or E?

Well did you spot it? 'Course you did, it was D – short measure on a pint of John Smith's and you can't get more serious than that.

Well we can't go out on such a dismal picture so we'll put it right for you...

SFX:
Drip.

VO:
...there that's better isn't?

Director
TONY MAY

Copywriters
JOHN WEBSTER
NICK GILL

Art Director
JOHN WEBSTER

Creative Directors
JOHN WEBSTER
TONY COX

Producer
ANDREW SHELTON

Set Designers
JAMIE LEONARD
TIM DANN

Animator
BEN CAIN

Agency Producer
LUCINDA KER

Editor
PETER BESTON OBE

Lighting Cameraman
KEITH GODDARD

Rostrum Cameraman
DAVID WYNN-JONES

Music Composer/Arranger
JOHN BARRY

Director
TONY MAY

Copywriter
JOHN WEBSTER

Art Director
JOHN WEBSTER

Creative Directors
JOHN WEBSTER
TONY COX

Producer
ANDREW SHELTON

Set Designer
JAMIE LEONARD

Set Designer
TIM DANN

Animator
BEN CAIN

Agency Producer
LUCINDA KER

Editor
PETER BESTON OBE

Lighting Cameraman
KEITH GODDARD

Rostrum Cameraman
DAVID WYNN-JONES

Music Composer
SERGE GAINSBOURG

Music Arranger
GRAHAM PRESKETT

LADYBIRDS

VO:
Hello there all you John Smith's drinkers, yes it's treat-time again, thirty mouth-watering seconds to look at the great stuff itself. Only today, look out for the naughty scene.

SFX:
'Je t'aime'

(At the end of commercial break)

Ladybird:
Ahh – I've had enough I fancy a pint of John Smith's.

DAYBREAK

Music:
An arrangement of 'Dawn Patrol'.

Milkman:
Two semi-skimmed...

...one Silver Top...

*Number eighteen. Ah, rice
pudding tonight.*

Music: *(Stops).*

Milkman:
*Lads, lads. What are you playing
at? You know they're away for a
fortnight. But next door want two
extra. Go on then.*

VO:
Whatever your order...

*...your milkman can deliver...all
the milk you'll ever need.*

Milkman:
Empties!

*Television
Commercials
Campaigns*

Director
BILL MATHER

Copywriter
DAVE BUCHANAN

Art Director
MIKE HANNETT

Creative Director
TONY COX

Producer
KEITH VALENTINE

Set Designer
JAMIE LEONARD

Animators
DAVE THROSSEL
LINDA JOHNSON

Agency Producer
LUCINDA KER

Editor
KEVIN WHEELAN

Lighting Cameraman
ROGER PRATT

Rostrum Cameraman
PETER TAYLOR

Music Composer/Arranger
GRAHAM PRESKETT

Production Company
REDWING FILM
COMPANY

Agency
BMP DDB NEEDHAM

Marketing Manager
JULIAN NOLAN

Client
NATIONAL DAIRY
COUNCIL

GARDEN PATH

Music:
An arrangement of 'Dawn Patrol'.

VO:
What's all this fuss about being green?

You've been returning our bottles for years.

THREESOME

Music:
An arrangement of 'Dawn Patrol'.

VO:
Whole milk...

...Semi-skimmed.

...Skimmed...

Your milkman delivers them all.

CARRIER BAGS

Music:
*Appropriate ploddy arrangement
of 'Dawn Patrol'.*

VO:
*It's a lot easier to get all your
weekend milk from your milkman.*

SNOW

Music:
A muted version of 'The
Grasshopper Dance'.

No matter how bad the weather
is...

...we always do our best to get
through.

DON'T FORGET

Music:
An arrangement of 'Dawn Patrol'.

VO:
When you put the cat out tonight...

...don't forget the emp-ties!

DINGHY

Music:
Latham theme.

Bough:
This is it, Sir.

Latham:
Excellent. Nine minutes, then.

Bough:
Nice pair of binoculars, Sir.

Latham:
Hmmm.

Bough:
They're not service issue?

Latham:
Certainly not! They're Austrian.

Bough:
Barclaycard, was it, Sir?

Latham: *(Icily)*
What?

Bough:
*d you get them on your Barclaycard,
Sir?*

Latham:
*why should I want to do a thing like
that /*

Bough:
, sir, you get 100 days free insurance.

Latham:
Yes...?

Bough:
Well, in case...

Latham:
*ase they get stolen? And who's going
eal them exactly? Are we about to be
mugged by a gang of delinquent
haddock?*

Bough:
You could always lose them, Sir.

Latham:
*se them? In a five-foot dinghy? 'Oh-
-I've-lost-my-binoculars-oh-no-they-
are-under-the-seat'.*

Bough:
You got your damage, sir...

Latham: *(angrily)*
*ill you shut up about Barclaycard,
ugh. You couldn't damage a pair of
binoculars in here if you tried.*

*et's hear no more about Barclaycard.
 see, a man of my experience knows
 when he's got a pair of binoculars...*

AAAAAAAARGGGHH!

*Television
Commercials
Campaigns*

Director
JOHN LLOYD

Copywriter
JON MATTHEWS

Art Director
PETER GATLEY

Creative Director
TONY COX

Producer
CAROLINE WARNER

Set Designer
DAVID BROCKHURST

Agency Producer
SARAH POLLITT

Editor
IAN WEIL

Lighting Cameraman
CLIVE TICKNER

Music Composer/Arranger
HOWARD GOODALL

Production Company
LIMELIGHT
COMMERCIALS

Agency
BMP DDB NEEDHAM

Head of Barclaycard Marketing
ALAN SILVERMAN

Client
BARCLAYCARD

SNAKEBITE

Bough:
Still no answer, Sir...

Latham:
Right, Bough, we're going in!

Wendy:
Urrgh!

Latham:
Wendy!

Wendy:
Snakebite!

Latham:
Right, Bough, you loosen his clothin
I'll get the local doctor.

(into the phone) Ao medico a qui per
Taban. Adios! Blast!

Bough:
What is it, Sir?

Latham:
Apparently he is the local doctor. Th
enough loosening now, Bough.

Bough:
I'm looking for his Barclaycard, Si

Latham:
His Barclaycard? This man is in no s
to go shopping!

Bough:
I'm going to phone them up for medi
advice, Sir.

Latham:
You're going to phone Barclaycard f
medical advice?

Bough:
Barclaycard International Rescue, S
They can send doctors and...

Latham:
Look, we're wasting time here, Boug
this man has a serious case of snakeb
and there's only one thing that's going
save him. I'm going to have to locate
wound and suck out the poison!

SFX:
Flies buzzing.

Latham:
Yes, perhaps you'd better phone
Barclaycard, Bough, I'm not sure I'
got the ppphwwtt...my lips are a litt
shwwhhooohh...

Latham: *(to doctor)*
Well, I thought I had the solution,
then...pphwwt...

NATURAL HISTORY

David Attenborough voice over:

The biggest nature reserve in the world. 5,000 miles long and 16 mm wide. A place where lizards lie next to lamas and whales lie wherever they like. 9,000 species of exotic animals, each of them rolled up tightly then packed in a can and kept in a darkened room.

MVO:
The BBC. Natural History at its best.

Television Commercials Campaigns

Copywriter
DOMINIC GETTINS

Art Director
TONY HARDCASTLE

Creative Director
ANDREW RUTHERFORD

Producer
SIMON WINCHESTER

Editors
SIMON WINCHESTER
JEREMY DEAR
DOMINIC GETTINS

Production Company
BBC TELEVISION CENTRE

Agency
FCO LIMITED

Director of Corporate Affairs
HOWELL JAMES

Client
BBC

DRAMA

Rowan Atkinson voice over reads out a 'school register' style list of famous people's names which they all answer 'Yes'.

The list of actors and actresses have all appeared in BBC Dramas.

The film is made up of existing BBC clips.

MVO:
The BBC. Drama at its best.

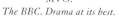

DRAMA AT ITS BEST

BBC

FOREIGN SALES

According to Nigel Hawthorne's voice over, the Russians have adopted our politics, and the Indians just can't resist our cowboys.

On screen are clips selected from the 20,000 hours of BBC television sold abroad, from 'Yes Minister' dubbed into Russian, to 'Only Fools and Horses'.

Copywriter
JUSTIN ROGERS

Art Director
PHIL REEDY

Creative Director
ROBIN WIGHT

Producer
SIMON WINCHESTER

Animator
SUE WORTHY

Editor
PERRY WIDOWSON

Copywriter
JUSTIN ROGERS

Art Director
PHIL REEDY

Creative Director
ROBIN WIGHT

Producer
SIMON WINCHESTER

Animator
SUE WORTHY

Editor
PERRY WIDOWSON

COMEDY

The titles that appear to be introducing some extremely serious topics (Drama, Foreign Affairs and Education among them), are really referring to clips of some of the most popular BBC comedy programmes.

Griff Rhys-Jones voice-over points out that 7 of the top 10 comedy programmes come from the BBC.

SPORT

A tennis rally with a difference: although the ball is hit from one side of the screen to another in time-honoured fashion, only the first shot is taken from a tennis match.

The rest of the rally is made up of BBC clips from other sports.

The voice-over explains that 2 out of 3 people prefer the BBC's sport's coverage to anyone else's.

Copywriter
JUSTIN ROGERS

Art Director
PHIL REEDY

Creative Director
ROBIN WIGHT

Producer
SIMON WINCHESTER

Animator
SUE WORTHY

Editor
PERRY WIDOWSON

Television
Commercials
Campaigns

Director
NICK PARK

Copywriters
PAUL CARDWELL
NICK PARK

Art Directors
NICK PARK
PAUL CARDWELL

Creative Director
PAUL CARDWELL

Producer
CHRIS MOLL

Set Designer
JONATHAN LEE

Animator
NICK PARK

Agency Producers
SAMANTHA PAYNE
DEBBIE TURNER

Editor
ROD HOWICK

Lighting Cameraman
DAVE SPROXTON

Production Company
AARDMAN
ANIMATIONS
LIMITED

Agency
GGK LONDON
LIMITED

Chairman
DR DOUG SWINDEN

Client
SELSE & CONSORTIUM

TERRY 2

*Terry the tortoise in the hallway of
a flat.*

*A storage heater is visible against
the wall.*

*He talks into a microphone,
labelled ELECTRIC.*

Terry:
*An athlete like me has to be able to
come in from doing a training run
and be warm in all the rooms.*

*If you are going to replace your
existing heating you've got to go
for something that's economical,
worry free,*

Um...I'm a bit of a worrier.

*I like to cuddle...I like to cuddle
up in my own home. I don't...it's
not nice to get out of bed and be
freezing. I need to be warm.*

*One thing about installing new
electric heating is that you've got
no kind of worries like that...*

...and that's magic.

Super:
*Graphic representation of heater
animates into HEAT ELECTRIC
(logo) and endline.*

MVO:
*For all your creature comforts –
HEAT ELECTRIC.*

PENGUINS 1

The Penguin Family at a table in a modern kitchen.

Kitchen units in the background. An electric cooker with ceramic hob is visible.

They walk into a microphone, labelled ELECTRIC.

Mr Penguin:
Oh yeah, we've got a new electric cooker.

Mrs Penguin:
Ceramic hob? Oh yes, we've got that,

Baby Penguin:
Very efficient.

Mrs Penguin:
Very efficient. You just turn it on and within seconds it's red, just turn it down slightly...

Mr Penguin:
And it is very quick...

Mrs Penguin:
Instantly controllable.

Mr Penguin:
Instant, yes that's a good word. Instantly yes, it is really.

Baby Penguin:
And it goes bing when it's finished.

Super:
Graphic representation of a cooker animates into COOK ELECTRIC (logo) and endline.

MVO:
*For all your creature comforts –
COOK ELECTRIC.*

Director
NICK PARK

Copywriters
PAUL CARDWELL
NICK PARK

Art Directors
NICK PARK
PAUL CARDWELL

Creative Director
PAUL CARDWELL

Producer
CHRIS MOLL

Set Designer
STUART ROSE

Animator
NICK PARK

Agency Producers
SAMANTHA PAYNE
DEBBIE TURNER

Editor
ROD HOWICK

Lighting Cameraman
TRISTAN OLIVER

Director
PETER LORD

Copywriters
PAUL CARDWELL
NICK PARK

Art Directors
NICK PARK
PAUL CARDWELL

Creative Director
PAUL CARDWELL

Producer
CHRIS MOLL

Set Designer
TIM FARRINGTON

Animator
PETER LORD

Agency Producers
SAMANTHA PAYNE
DEBBIE TURNER

Editor
ROD HOWICK

Lighting Cameraman
TRISTAN OLIVER

PANDAS 2

The Panda Family in a modern kitchen.

Kitchen units in the background. A dishwasher is visible.

They talk into a microphone, labelled ELECTRIC.

Mrs Panda:
Oh it's essential now. It was a luxury before we got it, but it's definitely an essential now.

Mr Panda: I used to do the washing up, before we had a dishwasher and it took an hour and a half, it was hellish.

Yeah well, these days we don't fight about it. We used to always argue about who was doing the dishes.

Mrs Panda:
Now I've got a complete monopoly.

Mrs Panda:
So we spend our time arguing about other issues rather than who does the dishes.

Graphic representation of dishwasher animates into DISHWASH ELECTRIC (logo) and endline.

MVO:
For all your creature comforts – DISHWASH ELECTRIC.

LOADS OF MONET

Music:
'La Forza del Destino' by Verdi.

Painter: *(in French)*
*Hello, I was wondering, would
you accept my painting in return
for a beer?*

Barman:
It's pretty but...

...Oh alright.

Painter:
Thank you.

Stella Artois. Reassuringly expensive.

*Cinema Commercials
Singles*

Director
MICHAEL SERESIN

Copywriter
JANE GARLAND

Art Director
CHARLES INGE

Creative Director
ADRIAN HOLMES

Producer
MICHAEL HAYES

Set Designer
MARIANNE FORD

Agency Producer
SUE BRALEY

Editor
NICK DISS

Lighting Cameraman
MICHAEL SERESIN

Music Composer
VERDI

Music Arranger
JOHN ALTMAN

Production Company
BFCS

Agency
LOWE HOWARD-SPINK

Marketing Director
STEVE PHILPOTT

Client
THE WHITBREAD
BEER COMPANY

Cinema Commercials
Singles

Director
KEITH ROSE

Copywriter
MATTHEW BULL

Art Director
TONY GRANGER

Creative Director
JOHN HUNT

Producers
HOWARD BULKIN
BARRY MUNCHICK

Agency Producer
GUIA IACOMIN

Editor
GUY SPILLER

Lighting Cameraman
KEITH ROSE

Production Company
VELOCITY FILMS

Agency
HUNT LASCARIS
TBWA

Marketing Manager
IVAN HONEYBORNE

Client
BMW SOUTH AFRICA

MOUSE

Video:
*Opening shot of small cage
situated on BMW dashboard. Door
swings open and small white
mouse peers out. He then exits
cage and runs across BMW
dashboard. The mouse then looks
over edge of dashboard at the
steering wheel, and walks onto it.*

*Wheel begins to turn and mouse
runs on top of it, changing
direction after several seconds.*

MVO:
*The BMW 318i. Now with power
steering.*

Video:
*Mouse then stops and stands up on
hind legs to receive applause.*

SFX:
Loud applause.

Super:
BMW (logo).

Title:
Sheer Driving Pleasure.

THE TRUTH

*In this commercial we see stills of
various famous people and hear
their voices denying things.
During each denial the screen the
truth- is stretched like the rubber
skin of a balloon.*

Nixon:
*There will be no white wash at the
White House.*

Bush:
Read my lips...no new taxes.

Ben Johnson:
*People who know me know I
would never take drugs.*

Jim Bakker:
*And I come out today still
innocent of the charges against me.*

Waldheim:
*It has nothing to do with
intelligence. I was not an umphia
officer as the Jewish Congress
pretends I was. It is just not true.*

Gary Hart:
*Did I do anything immoral? I
absolutely did not.*

Geoffrey Howe:
*I'm very happy serving under
Margaret Thatcher's leadership.*

Major:
*The Prime Minister is leader of the
Conservative Party. She will
remain leader of the Conservative
Party up to and through and after
the General Election.*

*Cinema Commercials
Singles*

Directors
TIM DELANEY
STEVE DUNN

Copywriter
TIM DELANEY

Art Director
STEVE DUNN

Creative Director
TIM DELANEY

Special Effects
DEREK HENDEN

Agency Producer
NICKY GREGOROWSKI

Editor
DAVE FORDHAM

Lighting Cameraman
JOHN SWINNERTON

Motion Control
MARTIN BODY

Production Company
PEERLESS CAMERA
COMPANY

Agency
LEAGAS DELANEY

Marketing Director
DAVID BROOK

Client
THE GUARDIAN

Cinema Commercials
Singles

Director
ROGER LYONS

Copywriter
KIM PAPWORTH

Art Director
TONY DAVISON

Creative Director
TONY COX

Producer
FABYAN DAW

Agency Producer
SARAH POLLITT

Editor
DAVID MOORE

Lighting Cameraman
ALEXANDER WITT

Rostrum Cameraman
TIM OLLIVE

Opticals
ANDY JEFFERY

Music Composer/Arranger
CHUCK BERRY

Production Company
THE BOYS OWN
PICTURE COMPANY

Agency
BMP DDB NEEDHAM

Senior Brand Director
STEPHEN THORPE

Client
CADBURY BEVERAGES
EUROPE

CHUCK BERRY

Cal:
Twenty seven dollars?

Gaffer:
Less deductions.

Cal's VO:
So one summer I packed my bags. And me and Chuck Berry hit the road...

Music:
Chuck Berry's 'No particular Place to Go'.

Cal's VO:
...Stupid name for a dog but I kinda like it. Now this place ain't exactly small,

Cal's VO:
*So I figured there'd be plenty of interesting things to see...
...And people to meet.*

DJ VO:
We interrupt this broadcast for an important news bulletin.

Farmer:
My prize pig's just had triplets.

Cal's VO:
*I'm telling you, if it hadn't been for the drink...
...I'd have headed out years ago.*

EVO:
Canada Dry. This is the best thing to come out of Canada since...since...

1st Old man:
Ed?

2nd Old Man:
Yep!

1st Old man:
Just checkin'

DJ

An L.A.P.D. squad car searches for a pirate DJ transmitting across an L.A neighbourhood.

DJ:
Word up, this is K-Baz about to pump some more bass...We're gonna get fly...This is coming at you from the underground...Doing it with the big fat 40...Stupid! Funky! We're gonna do it divine! Hard! Word up!

Word is bond...You know what I'm saying...This is going out to my boys...You know what I'm saying the four hoods...You know what I'm saying...Pumping me over your big 15 inch woofers...

...You know my girl is just so fly...Man we're gonna get together

and er...yeah...This is the baz and I'm just about to drop the

science...Kick the ballistics in Compton...You know what I'm saying...'Cos this is the real deal...

SFX:
Telephone rings.

DJ:
You're on...

GIRL:
K-Baz, I just want to let you know that you're the sexiest man alive, and ooooh Baby...

DJ:
Doing the right thing to your eardrums...Pumping holes in them...Say something to the five O's out there...We know the deal...I'm the Baz, ain't got a job, but that's cool though...If you don't like it come see me...

I'm not a gas or liquid but a solid substance...

The police break down the door of the makeshift studio. K-Baz is long gone, a tape recorder plays the show into the microphone.

DJ:
...I'm getting down with the grove 'cos I'm smoother than the cream

in a Twinkie – Word up!

Cut to close up of DJ's 'W' ring as he caresses his girl's shoulder.

Super:
BE MORE THAN JUST A NUMBER.

Wrangler logo.

Cinema Commercials Singles

Director
VAUGHAN & ANTHEA

Copywriter
CHRIS PALMER

Art Director
MARK DENTON

Creative Directors
CHRIS PALMER
MARK DENTON

Producer
ROSIE MUCH

Agency Producer
PAUL FENTON

Editor
DUNCAN SHEPHERD

Lighting Cameraman
JOSEPH YACOE

Music Composer/Arranger
RONIN

Production Company
P M C

Agency
SIMONS PALMER
DENTON CLEMMOW &
JOHNSON LIMITED

Managing Director
FRANK DIMECH

Client
WRANGLER UK
LIMITED

*Cinema Commercials
Campaigns*

Director
DANIEL KLEINMAN

Copywriter
DANIEL KLEINMAN

Art Director
DANIEL KLEINMAN

Creative Director
MICHAEL PREISWERK

Producers
DAVID BOTTERELL
SIOBHAN BARRON

Set Designer
ALISON DOMINETZ

Agency Producer
JERRY CAMMISA

Editors
DAVID YARDLEY
TIM WEBBER

Lighting Cameraman
CLIVE TICKNER

Music Composer/Arranger
RACHEL PORTMAN

Production Company
LIMELIGHT
COMMERCIALS

Agency
McCANN-ERICKSON

*Group Product Manager –
Camel*
HANS JOSEF
BALMANT

Client
R J REYNOLDS

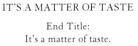

IT'S A MATTER OF TASTE

End Title:
It's a matter of taste.

IT'S A MATTER OF TASTE

End Title:
It's a matter of taste.

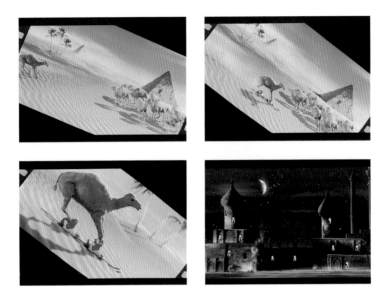

tele
vision and
tising cra
30

cine
ma ad
ver

fts

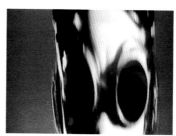

PILLOWS

SFX:
Music and sfx up and throughout.

Title card:
180

Title card scroll from right:
'by Alex Proyas Australia'

Cut to medium close-up of moving fans.

Cut to close-up of individual wearing goggles and tight cap.

Cut to medium close-up side view of person running with fans in background.

Shot of person passing behind post.

Cut to medium close-up of fan with rings around stands.

Side close-up of person with cap on.

Cut to moving shot of person running on pillows in background.

In foreground circle with swirl on it on stand.

Person running toward camera.

Medium close-up of person's foot landing on pillow.

Cut back shot of person running away from camera on pillows.

Stakes with 1,2,3 on them in background.

Cut close-up of moving fans.

Overhead shot of person running on pillows in foreground, a stake with number six on it, and power lines.

Cut to moving fans.

Cut to person running toward camera with line of pillows in background.

Back shot of person standing looking to their left, right, left and right again at Y in pillow formation. Fan in foreground on right.

Cut to close-up of Nike shoe as heel is lifting off the floor.

Title card:
Orange Nike logo 180.

SILVER AWARD
for the most outstanding
Use of Music

Directors
MATT FORREST
MIKE HANNETT
DAVE BUCHANAN

Copywriter
DAVE BUCHANAN

Art Director
MIKE HANNETT

Creative Director
TONY COX

Producer
STORR REDMAN

Set Designer
TEMPLE CLARKE

Animator
BRUCE STELE

Agency Producer
MAGGIE BLUNDELL

Editor
JEZ GIBSON

Lighting Cameraman
ADRIAN WILDE

Music Composer/Arranger
TONY GIBBER

Production Company
LIMELIGHT
COMMERCIALS

Agency
BMP DDB NEEDHAM

*Group Manager Brands
Marketing*
CHRIS DEATHE

Client
COURAGE LIMITED

GLAD

Sung:

Shiny new shoes...
...and old jeans...
...baking days...
...and baked beans.

Peking duck...
...stir-fry...
...'65 E-Type...
...sci-fi.

Clean, white sheets...
...blue notes..

...Auntie Dot..
...anecdotes.

Long, slim legs...
...and long blonde hair...

...Ginger Rogers...
...Camembert.

Brilliant shades...
...and brilliant pass...
...smooth, clean Miller...
...low on gas.

All of these things make me
happy...

...all of these things make me glad.

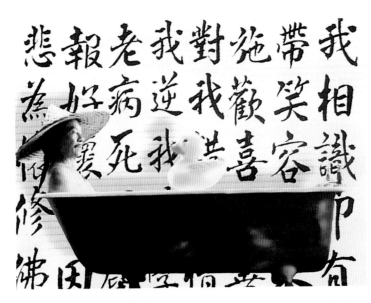

SILVER AWARD
NOMINATION
for the most outstanding
Direction

Director
DAVID GARFATH

Copywriter
CHRIS HERRING

Art Director
JOHN MERRIMAN

Creative Director
PAUL WEINBERGER

Producer
MARY FRANCIS

Set Designer
MIKE HALL

Agency Producer
AMANDA DICKS

Editor
SIMON WILLCOX

Lighting Cameraman
ROGER PRATT

Music Composer/Arranger
CHRIS BLACKWELL

Production Company
PAUL WEILAND FILM
COMPANY

Agency
LOWE HOWARD-SPINK

Client
REEBOK UK

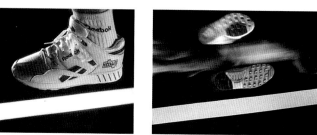

SHOES IN ACTION

Across a grey screen, runs a single white line. It represents, we will come to see, the line around which sporting excellence always seems to revolve.

It will become in succession the touchline, the high jump bar, the baseline, etc, etc. It never moves its position on the screen.

The perspective only reveals itself when a sportsman or woman appears.

SHOES IN ACTION

Across a grey screen, runs a single white line. It represents, we will come to see, the line around which sporting excellence always seems to revolve.

It will become in succession the touchline, the high jump bar, the baseline, etc, etc. It never moves its position on the screen.

The perspective only reveals itself when a sportsman or woman appears.

SILVER AWARD
NOMINATION
*for the most outstanding
Use of Music*

Director
DAVID GARFATH

Copywriter
CHRIS HERRING

Art Director
JOHN MERRIMAN

Creative Director
PAUL WEINBERGER

Producer
MARY FRANCIS

Set Designer
MIKE HALL

Agency Producer
AMANDA DICKS

Editor
SIMON WILLCOX

Lighting Cameraman
ROGER PRATT

Music Composer/Arranger
CHRIS BLACKWELL

Production Company
PAUL WEILAND FILM
COMPANY

Agency
LOWE HOWARD-SPINK

Client
REEBOK UK

Direction

Director
TONY KAYE

Copywriter
JOHN O'DONNELL

Art Director
GARRY HORNER

Creative Director
JOHN O'DONNELL

Producer
EUGENIA KAYE

Set Designer
JENNY SELDEN

Agency Producer
MARK ANDREWS

Editor
SAM SNEADE

Lighting Cameraman
TONY KAYE

Music Composer/Arranger
JEFF McCORMACK

Production Company
TONY KAYE FILMS
LIMITED

Agency
COLLETT DICKENSON
PEARCE & PARTNERS
LIMITED

Marketing Director
DYLAN HAMMOND

Client
HISTORIC ROYAL
PALACES

EDMUND DUDLEY

VO Edmund:
*To the Tower of London,
in chains and disgrace,
the year of 1510.*

*By Traitors Gate I came in.
And will not go out again.*

*And I can tell of deeds
blacker than a raven's
wing.*

*Of princes in their prime
snuffed out.*

*Of Lady Jane, Guy Fawkes and
Anne Boleyn.*

*Where now I tread, I tread on
ancient bones.*

*Where history brimful with blood
spilled and seeped into the stones.*

ARE YOU TUNED IN?

People move in rythm but no music is heard, just the whirr of the projector.

Suddenly, shouts are heard. sound! Sound!

A unique quadrophonic track gives the impression that the shouts are coming from the audience.

A title now appears: If you want the sound for this commercial tell the projectionist.

Inspired by this and the shouts, the audience joins in.

The commercial is visually rewound. It restarts with the music (Salt 'n' Pepa's 'Let's Talk About Sex'), but not quite at full volume.

A voice asks the projectionist to 'turn it up'.

The crowd becomes more rowdy and finally the music is heard at full blast.

Title:
Kiss 100 FM

Direction

Director
PATRICIA MURPHY

Copywriter
TOM CARTY

Art Director
WALTER CAMPBELL

Creative Director
DAVID ABBOTT

Producer
JENNY SELBY

Set Designer
PATRICIA MURPHY

Agency Producer
FRANCINE LINSEY

Editor
RICK RUSSELL

Lighting Cameraman
ANTONY STANIER

Music Composer/Arranger
SALT 'N' PEPA

Production Company
TONY KAYE FILMS
LIMITED

Agency
ABBOTT MEAD
VICKERS.BBDO
LIMITED

Marketing Director
GORDON MAC

Client
KISS 100 FM

Direction

Director
TONY KAYE

Copywriter
MALCOLM GREEN

Art Director
GARY BETTS

Creative Director
TONY COX

Producer
EUGENIA KAYE

Agency Producer
ROGER SHIPLEY

Editor
GEOFF PAYNE

Lighting Cameraman
TONY KAYE

Music Composer/Arranger
PETER LAWLOR

Production Company
TONY KAYE FILMS
LIMITED

Agency
BMP DDB NEEDHAM

Marketing Manager
DAVID WHELAN

Client
SCHWEPPES

WHERE'S GINI

Music throughout

SFX:
Cars racing towards each other.

Charles:
Gini est partie
(Subtitles: Gini's gone)

Maurice:
Ou?
(Subtitle: Where to?)

Charles:
Grande-Bretagne

Girl:
Gini est partie en Grande-Bretagne
(Subtitles: Gini's gone to Britain)

Mayor:
Les Britaniques ont Gini
(Subtitle: The British have got Gini)

SFX:
Galloping hooves.

Girl on horse:
Gini

Young man:
(In local language) I know

SFX:
Band, dancing etc.

MVO:
Gini, the lemon drink of the
Mediterranean, is now available in
Britain.

Super:
Gini is made in Britain

Old man:
Bon boit les Britaniques
(Subtitle: Good taste, the British)

FREEZE

Open on a kitchen.

*A series of people enter and
perform various mundane
functions in a cycle of repeats.*

Direction

Director
RICHARD DEAN

Copywriter
TIM MELLORS

Art Director
GRAHAM FINK

Creative Director
TIM MELLORS

Producer
MATTHEW JUSTICE

Set Designer
BRYCE WALMSLEY

Agency Producer
DIANE CROLL

Editors
ANDY KEMP
ROB HODGSON

Lighting Cameraman
CHRIS PARKER

Production Company
THE MOVING
PICTURE COMPANY

Agency
GGT

Managing Director
GIULIANO
GNAGNATTI

Marketing Director
NIGEL GRASHAM

Client
ARISTON

DJ

*An L.A.P.D. squad car searches for a
DJ transmitting across an L.A
neighbourhood.*

DJ:
*Word up, this is K-Baz about to pump
more bass...We're gonna get fly...Th
coming at you from the
underground...Doing it with the big
40...Stupid! Funky! We're gonna do
divine! Hard! Word up!*

*Word is bond...You know what I'm
saying...This is going out to my boys..
know what I'm saying the four hoods.
know what I'm saying...Pumping me
your big 15 inch woofers...*

*...You know my girl is just so fly...M
we're gonna get together
and er...yeah...This is the baz and I'm
about to drop the science...Kick th
ballistics in Compton...You know wha
saying...'Cos this is the real deal..*

SFX:
Telephone rings.

DJ:
You're on...

GIRL:
*K Baz, I just want to let you know t
you're the sexiest man alive, and ooe
Baby...*

DJ:
*Doing the right thing to your
eardrums...Pumping holes in them...
something to the five O's out there...
know the deal...I'm the Baz, ain't got
but that's cool though...If you don't l
come see me...
I'm not a gas or liquid but a solid
substance...*

*The police break down the door of
makeshift studio. K-Baz is long gone,
recorder plays the show into the
microphone.*

DJ:
*...I'm getting down with the grove 'co
smoother than the cream in a Twink
Word up!*

*Cut to close up of DJ's 'W' ring as
caresses his girl's shoulder.*

Super:
BE MORE THAN JUST A NUMB

NOT SO MERRYMEN

Music:
Robin Hood 'Fanfare'

Song:
(heroic voice)

Robin Hood, Robin Hood,
Riding through the glen.

Robin Hood, Robin Hood,
With his band of men.

Feared by the bad,
Loved by the good,
Robin Hood, Robin Hood, Robin
Hood.

Robin Hood, Robin Hood,
Could be in a fix.

Robin Hood, Robin Hood,
Spies the Weetabix.

Does he retreat, back to
Sherwood?

(brief pause)

Merrymen:
'Course he should,
'course he should,
'course he should.

Direction

Director
DAVID GARFATH

Copywriter
PAUL HODGKINSON

Art Director
KEVIN JONES

Creative Director
PAUL WEINBERGER

Producer
MARY FRANCIS

Agency Producer
TRACEY JOHNSTON

Editor
KATHY O'SHEA

Lighting Cameraman
PETER HANNAN

Music Composers/Arrangers
EDWIN ASLER
JOE CAMPBELL
PAUL HART

Production Company
PAUL WEILAND FILM
COMPANY

Agency
LOWE HOWARD-SPINK

Sales & Marketing Director
LES COMPEY

Client
WEETABIX LIMITED

Direction

Director
PAUL WEILAND

Copywriter
MARK WNEK

Art Director
ALAN WALDIE

Creative Director
ADRIAN HOLMES

Producer
ALICIA BERNARD

Agency Producer
SARAH HORRY

Editor
IAN WEIL

Lighting Cameraman
ALEXANDER WITT

Music Composers/Arrangers
PAUL HART
LONI BROOKS

Production Company
PAUL WEILAND FILM
COMPANY

Agency
LOWE HOWARD-SPINK

Marketing Director
STEVE PHILPOTT

Client
THE WHITBREAD BEER
COMPANY

SINGER

Music:
Guitar strumming.

Singer:
*Wake up this morning and the sun
smiled down on me.*

*Sun smiled on me, that ain't the
blues.*

Wife:
Oh honey, that's cute.

Singer:
*Woe...woe, woe, woe the boat
happily down the stream.*

Dam that ain't the blues either.

Wife:
*What is this lipstick doing on your
collar?*

Singer:
Honey, that ain't no lipstick.

Wife:
Honey or nothing.

Singer:
I was shaving.

Wife:
You're lying.

Repo. Man:
We repossessing your car.

SFX:
Thunderclap.

Wife:
And I ain't never coming back.

SFX:
Guitar, harmonica.

Singer:
*Sadness is my first name, last name
is misery, I lost my woman, and
the rain is coming down...*

Oh...yer.

STRANGE TASTE

Music:
*Incidental music 'Colin the
Elephant' – arranged by Jenkins
Ratledge.*

*John Cleese indulges in some
fashionable black and white
introspection about the meaning of
life and relationships with a lizard
and a lady friend. The latter gets
so angry she provides him with an
unusual opportunity to taste the
product.*

Echoing whisper:
Straight Schweppes

John Cleese:
*Why do we walk like one dancer
in a dream?*

Woman:
*Because when I dance in your
shadow, it is I that feels the pain.*

John Cleese:
I am both of us and so are you.

Woman:
What was that shot of a lizard?

John Cleese:
*When I talk to you I talk to
myself.*

Woman:
I asked you a question.

John Cleese:
*And when I am with you I am on
my own.*

Woman:
*On your own! Try this, this is on
its own.*

John Cleese:
*Schweppes Tonic...on its own so
dry and yet so wet.*

Hello Colin.

Title:
*The grown-up soft drink. (Well
quite).*

Direction

Director
PAUL WEILAND

Copywriter
JAMES LOWTHER

Art Director
ALEXANDRA TAYLOR

Creative Director
JAMES LOWTHER

Producer
MARY FRANCIS

Set Designer
ROD McCLEAN

Agency Producer
FIONA WINBURN

Editor
RICHARD LEAROYD

Lighting Cameraman
DAVID WATKINS

Music Composers/Arrangers
CARL JENKINS
MIKE RATLEDGE

Production Company
PAUL WEILAND FILM
COMPANY

Agency
SAATCHI & SAATCHI

Client
SCHWEPPES

Direction

Director
DAVID GARFATH

Copywriter
ALISTAIR WOOD

Art Director
TOM NOTMAN

Creative Director
ANDREW CRACKNELL

Producer
PAUL ROTHWELL

Set Designer
MIKE HALL

Agency Producer
BARRY STEPHENSON

Editor
SIMON WILLCOX

Lighting Cameraman
MIKE GARFATH

Production Company
PAUL WEILAND FILM
COMPANY

Agency
BSB DORLAND

Marketing Director
JOHN COE

Client
BASS BREWERIES
LIMITED

YEAST

We open as two men enter a busy pub watched by the pub landlord, who is looking up into a mirror behind the bar, his back to the door. A series of strange and unusual things follows:

SFX:
Mysterious, suspense music.

Barman:
gentlemen ?

Man 1:
We have come to see your famous dog.

Barman:
Dog ?

Man 2:
And to enjoy a pint of Tennent's Pilsner.

Barman:
Notice anything...unusual?

Man 1:
Yes, it's Pilsner, brewed to taste a bit different.

Barman: *(laughs)*
But do you know why? Czechoslovakian yeast.

Man 2:
You have nothing to fear. Your secret is safe.

Barman:
Down boy, down.

MVO:
Is someone pulling your Pilsner?

MUSICIAN

*Open on the words 'MIND THE
STEP' printed at the foot of a
flight of stairs. Pulling back we see
our two men descending the stairs.*

SFX:
*Piano playing backwards
(producing a ghastly cacophony).*

Man 1:
You'd think they'd complain.

Man 2:
Complain? Complain ?

When he's wearing that hat ?

*And when they serve Tennent's
Pilsner here.*

Waitress:
*Brewed with Czechoslovakian
yeast to taste a bit different.*

Man 1: *(to waitress)*

That's right.

Waitress:
Thank you!

Man 1, Man 2:
Mind the step.

MVO:
Is someone pulling your Pilsner?

Direction

Director
DAVID GARFATH

Copywriter
ALISTAIR WOOD

Art Director
TOM NOTMAN

Creative Director
ANDREW CRACKNELL

Producer
PAUL ROTHWELL

Set Designer
MIKE HALL

Agency Producer
BARRY STEPHENSON

Editor
SIMON WILLCOX

Lighting Cameraman
MIKE GARFATH

Production Company
PAUL WEILAND FILM
COMPANY

Agency
BSB DORLAND

Marketing Director
JOHN COE

Client
BASS BREWERIES
LIMITED

Use of Music

Directors
TIM DELANEY
STEVE DUNN

Copywriter
TIM DELANEY

Art Director
STEVE DUNN

Creative Director
TIM DELANEY

Producer
MIKE STONES

Agency Producer
NICKY GREGOROWSKI

Editor
BOBBY HOLMES

Lighting Cameraman
KEITH GODDARD

Music Composer/Arranger
ARIEL RAMIREZ

Production Company
PARK VILLAGE
PRODUCTIONS

Agency
LEAGAS DELANEY

Managing Director
KEITH TUBBY

Marketing Manager
CHRISTINE PARSONS

Client
CITIZEN WATCH UK
LIMITED

SCHOOL

Open on a close-up of a medieval clocktower which rises above the pantile roofs and sunbathed village square of a Tuscan hill town.

Bells strike to announce five o'clock.

A group of school girls aged about 16 as they leave a convent under the strict supervision of a mother superior with a Priest and Monseigneur in background, crossing the courtyard. One of the prettiest of the girls falls behind to meet her young boyfriend who is anxiously waiting for her in the cloisters. They embrace.

Dissolve to red. cut to see the clock face in close-up at 5 o'clock. It is another day. Cut to see the couple rendez-vous at a small bench.

The bells strike. Then cut to the clock tower which shows the time at 5 o'clock. We match dissolve to the same clock face showing the time to be 7.10 pm. The light has turned to dusk.

Cut to a fist knocking at the oak door of the convent. A small grill in the door opens and a nun furtively hands the boy a letter. He reads it in disbelief. He tries to hold back the tears as he drops the letter to his side.

We close in on the letter and pan up to reveal our young man is now years older. Dissolve to red.

Cut to the older man alone in his apartment.

Cut to the old maid who hands him a small and lovingly wrapped parcel. Cut to close-up of the parcel unwrapped to reveal a watch.

Super:
Citizen. Because a watch should know more than seconds, minutes and hours.

SINGER

Music:
Guitar strumming.

Singer:
Wake up this morning and the sun smiled down on me.

Sun smiled on me, that ain't the blues.

Wife:
Oh honey, that's cute.

Singer:
Woe...woe, woe, woe the boat happily down the stream.

Dam that ain't the blues either.

Wife:
What is this lipstick doing on your collar?

Singer:
Honey, that ain't no lipstick.

Wife:
Honey or nothing.

Singer:
I was shaving.

Wife:
You're lying.

Repo. Man:
We repossessing your car.

SFX:
Thunderclap.

Wife:
And I ain't never coming back.

SFX:
Guitar, harmonica.

Singer:
Sadness is my first name, last name is misery, I lost my woman, and the rain is coming down...

Oh...yer.

Use of Music

Director
PAUL WEILAND

Copywriter
MARK WNEK

Art Director
ALAN WALDIE

Creative Director
ADRIAN HOLMES

Producer
ALICIA BERNARD

Set Designer
LESLIE POPE

Agency Producer
SARAH HORRY

Editor
IAN WEIL

Lighting Cameraman
ALEXANDER WITT

Music Composers/Arrangers
PAUL HART
LONI BROOKS

Production Company
PAUL WEILAND FILM
COMPANY

Agency
LOWE HOWARD-SPINK

Marketing Director
STEVE PHILPOTT

Client
THE WHITBREAD
BEER COMPANY

Use of Music

Director
BARRY KINSMAN

Copywriter
STEVE HOOPER

Art Director
DENNIS LEWIS

Creative Director
JOHN HEGARTY

Producer
JOANNE HOLLAND

Set Designer
ANDREW DRUMMOND

Agency Producer
KATE O'MULLOY

Editor
DAVID SKETCHLEY

Lighting Cameraman
MIKE MOLLOY

Music Composers/Arrangers
JAMES BROWN
BOBBY BYRD
RONALD LENHOFF
MARENZIO

Production Company
KINSMAN & COMPANY

Agency
BARTLE BOGLE
HEGARTY

Senior Marketing Manager
BRENDA JONES

Client
SONY UK LIMITED

MONSEIGNEUR

Soundtrack:
'Sex Machine' by James Brown.

Open on a black screen.

Title:
The hidden pleasure. Sony.

Video:
Mix to spacious interior of large, ornate Italian villa. A middle-aged maid is polishing the floor and singing along in English to the lyrics.

She shakes the dust out of the window. The courtyard below is filled with monseigneurs who turn, as music fills the courtyard, to look at the maid who is singing the words to 'Sex Machine'.

Suddenly aware of her audience, she looks for the source of music. It is nowhere in sight.

One of the monseigneurs is walking sternly towards the house.

Panicking, she searches everywhere for the music. Finally, as the monseigneur is almost at the door, she shrieks and runs off past him. He finds the MHC and flicks a switch.

SFX:
Choral music.

Looking out, he smiles as the woman runs off through the crowd of monseigneurs.

Super:
Sony. Why compromise?

VO:
Sony mini hi-fi system. Music that's heard, and not seen.

WINTER WONDERLAND

Open on a pick-up truck driving through a desert landscape. In the back of the truck we see a 30 year-old Bohemian Irish traveller sitting with a battered suitcase.

As the truck pulls up outside a bar at the edge of the road, the Irish traveller leaps out and enters the bar.

The camera remains outside locked-off on the bar.

Above it a solitary cloud appears and passes over.

He orders a pint of Murphy's and puts on a thick overcoat.

Cut to the beer being poured. Cut outside to snow on cactus.

Cut to our hero drinking. Cut outside to see bar covered in snow.

VO:
A pint of Murphy's should always be served at 46 degrees Fahrenheit. Wherever you are.

Super:
Murphy's. A lore unto itself. Brewed in cork since 1856.

Use of Music

Director
BRIAN GRIFFIN

Copywriter
STEVE HOOPER

Art Director
DENNIS LEWIS

Creative Director
JOHN HEGARTY

Producer
ALAN TAYLOR

Set Designer
JEFF STAGGS

Agency Producer
REBECCA ATKINSON

Editor
TERRY JONES

Lighting Cameraman
CURTIS CLARK

Music Arrangers
BERNARD/SMITH/
DAY/HUNTER

Production Company
PHOENIX FILMS

Agency
BARTLE BOGLE
HEGARTY

Marketing Director
STEVE PHILPOTT

Client
THE WHITBREAD
BEER COMPANY

Use of Music

Directors
VAUGHAN & ANTHEA

Copywriter
CHRIS PALMER

Art Director
MARK DENTON

Creative Directors
CHRIS PALMER
MARK DENTON

Producer
ROSIE MUCH

Agency Producer
PAUL FENTON

Editor
DUNCAN SHEPHERD

Lighting Cameraman
JOSEPH YACOE

Music Composer/Arranger
RONIN

Production Company
P M C

Agency
SIMONS PALMER
DENTON CLEMMOW &
JOHNSON LIMITED

Managing Director
FRANK DIMECH

Client
WRANGLER UK
LIMITED

DJ

*An L.A.P.D. squad car searches for a p
DJ transmitting across an L.A
neighbourhood.*

DJ:

*Word up, this is K-Baz about to pump
more bass...We're gonna get fly...Th
coming at you from the
underground...Doing it with the big
40...Stupid! Funky! We're gonna do
divine! Hard! Word up!*

*Word is bond...You know what I'r
saying...This is going out to my boys...
know what I'm saying the four hoods..
know what I'm saying...Pumping me
your big 15 inch woofers...*

*...You know my girl is just so fly...M
we're gonna get together*

*and er...yeah...This is the baz and I'm
about to drop the*

*science...Kick the ballistics in
Compton...You know what I'm
saying...'Cos this is the real deal...*

SFX:
Telephone rings.

DJ:
You're on...

GIRL:

*K Baz, I just want to let you know th
you're the sexiest man alive, and ooo
Baby...*

DJ:

*Doing the right thing to your
eardrums...Pumping holes in them...S
something to the five O's out there...W
know the deal...I'm the Baz, ain't got a
but that's cool though...If you don't lik
come see me...*

*I'm not a gas or liquid but a solid
substance...*

*The police break down the door of th
makeshift studio. K-Baz is long gone
tape recorder plays the show into th
microphone.*

DJ:
*...I'm getting down with the grove 'cos
smoother than the cream*

in a Twinkie – Word up!

*Cut to close up of DJ's 'W' ring as h
caresses his girl's shoulder.*

Super:
BE MORE THAN JUST A NUMBE

Wrangler logo.

OUR CUSTOMERS

MVO:
From cooks in Cookham.
Bakers in Burnham.

Don't leave the loaves long,
Don't forget to turn 'em.

Players from Rugby,
Plumbers from Bath.

Polishers from East Sheen.
Keep your television clean.

Painters from Gainsborough,
Try not to shake 'em,
Better check the signature,
Or you might have a Fakenham.

Babies from Crawley,
Tailors from Coatbridge,
If they haven't got your size,

You can let it out an inch.
Potters from Potter's Bar,

Carpenters from Wood Green,
Builders from Hammersmith,
Anyone whose name is Smith.

Farmers from Cowes, Oxford and
Barnsley,
Please close the Ramsgate,
Keep 'em outta Harm's Way...

Pet shops in Pett's Wood,
Tilers from Tylehurst,
Photographers from Ilford,
Don't forget to smile first...

Nationwide.

With more branches than anyone
else,
We're the nation's Building
Society.

Super:
The nation's Building Society.

Nationwide Building Society

Use of Music

Director
MIKE STEPHENSON

Copywriters
TIM DELANEY
MIKE STEPHENSON

Art Director
STEVE DUNN

Creative Director
TIM DELANEY

Producer
GLYNIS SANDERS

Set Designer
JOHN BEARD

Agency Producer
NICKY GREGOROWSKI

Editor
CYRIL METZGER

Lighting Cameraman
TONY
PIERCE-ROBERTS

Music Composer
GEOFF MACK

Music Arrangers
JOE CAMPBELL
PAUL HART

Production Company
PAUL WEILAND FILM
COMPANY

Agency
LEAGAS DELANEY

Head of Marketing Services
PETER RANDALL

Marketing Communications
Controller
GAUTAM DATAR

Client
NATIONWIDE
BUILDING SOCIETY

Use of Music

Director
HUGH JOHNSON

Copywriter
SIMON DICKETTS

Art Director
PAUL ARDEN

Creative Director
PAUL ARDEN

Producer
PHILIPPA THOMAS

Agency Producer
JIM BAKER

Editor
BRIAN DYKE

Lighting Cameraman
HUGH JOHNSON

Music Composer/Arranger
YELLO

Production Company
RSA FILMS

Agency
SAATCHI & SAATCHI

Head of Group Communications
ANNE FERGUSON

Client
ICI

RIVER

Soundtrack:
'Sweet Thunder' by Yello.

Video:
*We open on a little boy drinking
from a pump by the side of a river
somewhere in Africa. He then runs
from the pump to the water's edge
and relieves himself in the river.
the camera pans on to reveal a lot
of activity going on by the river.*

*We see some women carrying
water pitchers on their heads, a
man paddling his canoe across the
river. On the other side there are
people walking, loading and
unloading boats, generally
carrying about their daily business.*

*On this side of the river the camera
continues to pan past some women
washing their clothes, some cattle
drinking and bathing in the river,
a steam boat passes whilst the
cattle drivers watch on. We then
come back to the same little boy
drinking at the same pump.*

*This action repeats exactly twice
more.*

*Dissolve through to ICI end
device.*

Title:
World Class.

MVO:
*Water is the source of all life.
But who washes the water?*

*Who has the technology to develop
a filter fine enough to wash the
water even of bacteria?*

*World problems.
World solutions. World Class.*

FOR THE WORLD

Soundtrack:
'Le Lac De Come' by Galos.

(Music throughout)

*n France, America, Morocco, the Bahamas
he UK, this commercial features a series of
·ignettes depicting aspects of the group's
·ties. Each vignette is linked with a caption
stating 'For............'.*

Video:
Man in Little Chef.
Title: *'For Him'.*

Elegant Lady.
Title: *'For Her'.*

Family in rubber rings.
Title: *'For Fun'.*

Four Admirals.
Title: *'Formality'.*

Two tennis players.
Title: *'For Service'.*

Ladies cleaning staircase.
Title: *'For Polish'.*

Chambermaid on bed.
Title: *'Fourposter'.*

Valet.
Title: *'For Style'.*

Pianist.
Title: *'Fortissimo'.*

Boardroom meeting.
Title: *'For Business'.*

Man jumping from springboard.
Title: *'For Pleasure'.*

·cycle upside down, passing Little Chef.
Title: *'For the Road'.*

Car with Travelodge sign reflected.
Title: *'For the Night'.*

Couple enter Bear Hotel.
Title: *'For the Weekend'.*

Wine bottle.
Title: *'For Quality'.*

Eiffel Tower and wine glass.
Title: *'4 AM'.*

View of Manhattan.
Title: *'For America'.*

Harvester scene.
Title: *'For the Family'.*

Casablanca Hotel front.
Title: *'For All the World'.*

Nuns jumping on beds.
·itle: *'For the Time of Your Life'.*

Wedding on the beach.
Title: *'For Ever'.*

Ice Swan.

End title:
'Forte, Host to the World'.

FOR HIM

FOR HER

FOR FUN

FORMALITY

FOUR POSTER

FOR THE TIME OF YOUR LIFE

FORTE
HOST TO THE WORLD

Use of Music

Director
BRIAN GRIFFIN

Copywriters
PAUL ARDEN
EUGENE RUANE

Art Directors
PAUL ARDEN
BOB GABRIEL

Creative Director
PAUL ARDEN

Producer
LEWIS
MORE O'FERRALL

Agency Producer
FIONA WINBURN

Editor
IAN WEIL

Lighting Cameraman
CURTIS CLARK

Music Arrangers
CARL JENKINS
MIKE RATLEDGE

Production Company
PHOENIX FILMS

Agency
SAATCHI & SAATCHI

*Head of Corporate
Communications*
MICHAEL DENT

Client
FORTE PLC

Use of Animation

Director
CHUCK GAMMAGE

Copywriter
DEREK APPS

Art Director
VINCE SQUIBB

Creative Director
PAUL WEINBERGER

Producer
ANDREW RUHEMANN

Art Director
TONY NOBLE

Animators
CHUCK GAMMAGE
DUNCAN
MARJORIBANKS

Agency Producer
TRACEY JOHNSTON

Editor
ROD HOWICK

Lighting Cameraman
DAVID WALSH

Rostrum Cameramen
PETER JONES
SAM JAMES

Production Companies
PASSION PICTURES/
ROSE HACKNEY
PRODUCTIONS

Agency
LOWE HOWARD-SPINK

Client
WEETABIX LIMITED

BIG SHOTS

Video:
Night time in New York. A black Sedan pulls up outside a restaurant in Little Italy.

Three hoods jump out – a boss and two henchmen. They quickly check the bullets in their guns, then burst into the restaurant.

They raise their guns and fire.

Track with the bullets who become animated caricatures of famous Hollywood gangsters.

Boss Bullet: *(Edward G. Robinson-type)*
Let's get'em boys!

2nd Bullet: *(James Cagney-type)*
Sure boss.

3rd Bullet: *(Peter Lorre-type)*
Evil laugh.

Video:
Cut to a bullet eye view of their targets – a group in the corner, spoons raised and a large pack of Weetabix prominent on the table in front of them.

The Boss Bullet holds the other two back, in alarm.

Edward G. Bullet:
Weetabix! They've had their Weetabix!

James Cagney Bullet:
Those dirty rats!

Video:*The James Cagney Bullet makes his excuses and leaves. He shoots off to the right, cutting a path through a waiter's hair. He then punctures a steaming expresso coffee maker at the bar, disappears up a pipe and pokes his head up warily through a flap on top.*

Peter Lorre Bullet:
I guess I'll give it a miss.

Video:*The Peter Lorre Bullet shoots off to the left. He ricochets off the wall, smashes a wine bottle out of the way and by cunningly removing his hat hides himself amongst the salt and pepper pots in the centre of the table.*

Taking a swift look at his pocket watch the boss bullet does a sharp U-turn.

Edward G. Bullet:
Waaa...Home time!

Video:
From the Boss Bullet's POV we see the head gangster's shocked face as the bullet heads straight back towards the muzzle of his still outstretched gun.

*Cut to pack shot and Super:
Have you had your Weetabix?*

DAYBREAK

Music:
An arrangement of 'Dawn Patrol'.

Milkman:
Two semi-skimmed...

...one Silver Top...

Number eighteen. Ah, rice pudding tonight.

Music: *(Stops)*

Milkman:
Lads, lads. What are you playing at? You know they're away for a fortnight. But next door want two extra. Go on then.

VO:
Whatever your order...

...your milkman can deliver...all the milk you'll ever need.

Milkman:
Empties!

Use of Animation

Director
BILL MATHER

Copywriter
DAVE BUCHANAN

Art Director
MIKE HANNETT

Creative Director
TONY COX

Producer
KEITH VALENTINE

Set Designer
JAMIE LEONARD

Animators
DAVE THROSSEL
LINDA JOHNSON

Agency Producer
LUCINDA KER

Editor
KEVIN WHEELAN

Lighting Cameraman
ROGER PRATT

Rostrum Cameraman
PETER TAYLOR

Music Composer/Arranger
GRAHAM PRESKETT

Production Company
REDWING FILM
COMPANY

Agency
BMP DDB NEEDHAM

Marketing Manager
JULIAN NOLAN

Client
NATIONAL DAIRY
COUNCIL

Use of Animation

Director
BARRY LEITH

Copywriter
KEVIN JONES

Art Director
KEVIN JONES

Creative Director
PAUL WEINBERGER

Producer
MICK FOLEY

Animator
BARRY LEITH

Agency Producer
SARAH HORRY

Editor
MARTIN SMITH

Lighting Cameraman
MICHEL GEMMEL

Music Composer/Arranger
SAINT SAENS

Production Company
PUPPETOON
PRODUCTIONS
LIMITED

Agency
LOWE HOWARD-SPINK

*Divisional Director of
Corporate Marketing*
ED OWEN

Client
TESCO STORES
LIMITED

FROZEN PRAWNS

Music:
Tesco Theme.

SFX:
Teeth chattering.

*Open on a backdrop with the
lettering:*
TESCO FROZEN PRAWNS
400g pack

*Below the words we see two
'Spitting Image' type prawns
complete with scarfs and ear
muffs, sat shivering in front of a
two bar electric fire.*

Super:
Tesco logo.

ARE YOU TUNED IN?

People move in rhythm but no music is heard, just the whirr of the projector.

Suddenly, shouts are heard: Sound! Sound!

A unique quadrophenic track gives the impression that the shouts are coming from the audience.

A title now appears: If you want the sound for this commercial tell the projectionist.

Inspired by this and the shouts, the audience joins in.

The commercial is visually rewound. It restarts with the music (Salt 'n' Pepa's 'Let's Talk About Sex'), but not quite at full volume.

A voice asks the projectionist to 'turn it up'.

The crowd becomes more rowdy and finally the music is heard at full blast.

Title:
Kiss 100 FM

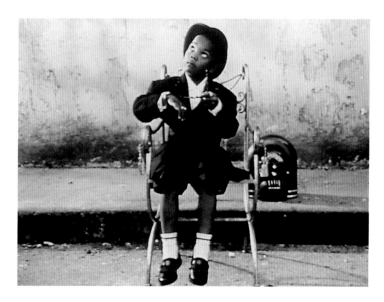

Editing

Director
PATRICIA MURPHY

Copywriter
TOM CARTY

Art Director
WALTER CAMPBELL

Creative Director
DAVID ABBOTT

Producer
JENNY SELBY

Set Designer
PATRICIA MURPHY

Agency Producer
FRANCINE LINSEY

Editor
RICK RUSSELL

Lighting Cameraman
ANTONY STANIER

Music Composer/Arranger
SALT 'N' PEPA

Production Company
TONY KAYE FILMS
LIMITED

Agency
ABBOTT MEAD
VICKERS.BBDO
LIMITED

Marketing Director
GORDON MAC

Client
KISS 100 FM

Editing

Director
TONY KAYE

Copywriter
JEAN RHODE

Art Director
JOHN MORRISON

Creative Director
TOM McELLIGOTT

Producer
EUGENIA KAYE

Agency Producer
VINCE DI GABRIELE

Lighting Cameraman
TONY KAYE

Production Company
TONY KAYE FILMS
LIMITED

Agency
McELLIGOTT WRIGHT
MORRISON WHITE

VP Marketing
TOM McNULTY

Client
VILLAGE INN

 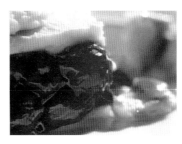

FAMILY

Super:
The Itsy Bitsy Spider.

Kid:
*I don't know if I like this new family me
thing.*

Mom:
*Someday you'll be glad we spent more tir
together.*

Dad:
*When I was your age I felt the same way
Maybe we should make this a weekly thir
– just the three of us.*

Kid:
I have no ears.

Mom:
(Laughs).

Dad:
Well, this is our family.

Mom:
*She's getting too used to the baby-sitter –
think she thought it was her mother.*

Montage of babysitters:
Hi, Hi, Hi there, Bye.

Kid:
OK, now let me do this.

Mom:
It's really been fun hasn't it?

Kid:
I know...

Dad:
But those family reunions, they're great f

Mom:
People that you haven't seen for years..

Dad:
The whole clan.

Mom:
Isn't that wonderful?

Dad:
You betcha.

Mom:
*To get everybody together with no
appointments, and no rushing around..*

Dad:
Well, that's more important really.

Kid: *(sings)*
*The Itsy Bitsy Spider went up the wate
spout. Down came the train and washed
spider out.*

Dad:
*The best decision we ever made was to
spend more time together.*

Kid:
I'm getting out of here.

Super:

Village Inn. The Time. The Place.

REUNION

Music throughout

MVO:
*Sgt. Stan Jackson's last minute
decision to attend his unit's
anniversary reunion was only made
possible by Barclays' on the spot help.*

*It was an occasion he will never
forget.*

Barclays. When it matters most.

Editing

Director
GERARD DE THAME

Copywriter
BOB STANNERS

Art Director
NORMAN ICKE

Creative Director
GILES KEEBLE

Producer
ANITA OVERLAND

Agency Producer
DAVID MANSON

Editor
PETER GODDARD

Lighting Cameraman
PASCAL LEBEGUE

Music Composer/Arranger
JOHN ALTMAN

Production Company
HELEN LANGRIDGE
ASSOCIATES

Agency
LEO BURNETT
ADVERTISING

*Advertising Group Account
Director*
ROS KING

Client
BARCLAYS BANK PLC

Editing

Director
TONY KAYE

Copywriter
JEAN RHODE

Art Director
JOHN MORRISON

Creative Director
TOM McELLIGOTT

Producer
EUGENIA KAYE

Agency Producer
VINCE DI GABRIELE

Editor
RICK RUSSELL

Lighting Cameraman
TONY KAYE

Production Company
TONY KAYE
FILMS LIMITED

Agency
McELLIGOTT WRIGHT
MORRISON WHITE

VP Marketing
TOM McNULTY

Client
VILLAGE INN

CAREERS

Super:
Maybe.

Man:
How about a piece of pie?

Woman:
Maybe.

Man:
You wanna see a movie?

Woman:
Maybe.

Man:
I can see you as a lawyer – you never give a straight answer.

Woman:
And I can see you as an architect.

Man:
I don't know if I can see myself being an architect for the rest of my life.

Woman:
Why not?

Man:
Life is short – I wanna have fun.

Woman: *(laughs)*
Maybe when I look back, I'll be happy I was a good lawyer.

Man:
Maybe you'll look back and be glad you split a sundae.

Woman:
Maybe.

Super:
Village Inn. The Time. The Place.

DJ

*a L.A.P.D. squad car searches for a
rate DJ transmitting across an L.A
neighbourhood.*

DJ:
*ord up, this is K-Baz about to pump
some more bass...We're gonna get
y...This is coming at you from the
derground...Doing it with the big fat
..Stupid! Funky! We're gonna do it
divine! Hard! Word up!*

*Vord is bond...You know what I'm
saying...This is going out to my
ys...You know what I'm saying the
four hoods...You know what I'm
ing...Pumping me over your big 15
inch woofers...*

*You know my girl is just so fly...Man
we're gonna get together*

*d er...yeah...This is the baz and I'm
just about to drop the*

*science...Kick the ballistics in
Compton...You know what I'm
saying...'Cos this is the real deal...*

SFX:
Telephone rings.

DJ:
You're on...

GIRL:
*Baz, I just want to let you know that
u're the sexiest man alive, and ooooh
Baby...*

DJ:
*Doing the right thing to your
drums...Pumping holes in them...Say
ething to the five O's out there...We
ow the deal...I'm the Baz, ain't got a
, but that's cool though...If you don't
like it come see me...*

*I'm not a gas or liquid but a solid
substance...*

*he police break down the door of the
akeshift studio. K-Baz is long gone, a
ape recorder plays the show into the
microphone.*

DJ:
*I'm getting down with the grove 'cos
I'm smoother than the cream*

in a Twinkie – Word up!

*Cut to close up of DJ's 'W' ring as he
caresses his girl's shoulder.*

Super:
MORE THAN JUST A NUMBER.

Editing

Directors
VAUGHAN & ANTHEA

Copywriter
CHRIS PALMER

Art Director
MARK DENTON

Creative Directors
CHRIS PALMER
MARK DENTON

Producer
ROSIE MUCH

Agency Producer
PAUL FENTON

Editor
DUNCAN SHEPHERD

Lighting Cameraman
JOSEPH YACOE

Music Composer/Arranger
RONIN

Production Company
P.M.C

Agency
SIMONS PALMER
DENTON CLEMMOW &
JOHNSON LIMITED

Managing Director
FRANK DIMECH

Client
WRANGLER UK
LIMITED

Special Effects

Director
MIKE STEPHENSON

Copywriters
TIM DELANEY
MIKE STEPHENSON

Art Director
STEVE DUNN

Creative Director
TIM DELANEY

Producer
GLYNIS SANDERS

Set Designer
JOHN BEARD

Agency Producer
NICKY GREGOROWSKI

Editor
CYRIL METZGER

Lighting Cameraman
TONY
PIERCE-ROBERTS

Music Composer
GEOFF MACK

Music Arrangers
JOE CAMPBELL
PAUL HART

Production Company
PAUL WEILAND FILM
COMPANY

Agency
LEAGAS DELANEY

Head of Marketing Services
PETER RANDALL

Communication Controller
GAUTAM DATAR

Client
NATIONWIDE
BUILDING SOCIETY

The Nation's Building Society.

Nationwide Building Society

OUR CUSTOMERS

MVO:
*From cooks in Cookham.
Bakers in Burnham.*

*Don't leave the loaves long,
Don't forget to turn 'em.*

*Players from Rugby,
Plumbers from Bath.*

*Polishers from East Sheen.
Keep your television clean.*

*Painters from Gainsborough,
Try not to shake 'em,
Better check the signature,
Or you might have a Fakenham.*

*Babies from Crawley,
Tailors from Coatbridge,
If they haven't got your size,*

*You can let it out an inch.
Potters from Potter's Bar,*

*Carpenters from Wood Green,
Builders from Hammersmith,
Anyone whose name is Smith.*

*Farmers from Cowes, Oxford and
Barnsley,
Please close the Ramsgate,
Keep 'em outta Harm's Way...*

*Pet shops in Pett's Wood,
Tilers from Tylehurst,
Photographers from Ilford,
Don't forget to smile first...*

Nationwide.

*With more branches than anyone
else,
We're the nation's Building
Society.*

Super:
The nation's Building Society.

TALKING TENNIS BALLS

SFX:
Balls are making noises, 'You'll never call me anymore', etc.

Woman preparing for the first ball to shoot from ball machine. Images of people haranguing her as she approaches. (Her boss, a police officer, a dog barking, etc.). Everytime she connects with the ball the image dissipates.

Bossball: *(rapidly)*
Listen Smith, you want to make it this corporation you gotta give up your weekends, you gotta push...

SFX:
Thwap.Raquet hits ball.

Dogball: *(Dog yiping)*

Yap yap yap yap yap...

SFX:
Thwap.Raquet hits ball.

Leering man who's waiting for the court talks to player.

Lounge Lizard:
Hey baby, are you gonna hog the court forever ?

She pumps up her Reeboks. The man, who just approached the court, now has his face on the tennis ball, haranguing the player.

Lounge Lizard Ball:
Hey baby, are you gonna hog the court forever ?

SFX:
Thwap. Raquet hits ball.

Super:
LIFE IS SHORT.

Super:
PLAY HARD.

Super:
REEBOK

Special Effects

Director
BARRY SONNENFELD

Copywriters
DICK SITTIG
BOB RICE

Art Director
STEVE SWEITZER

Creative Director
DICK SITTIG

Agency Producer
KATHI CALEF

Editor
CHRISTOPHER
WAIGIN

Production Company
LUCAS FILMS

Agency
CHIAT/DAY/MOJO

Director of Advertising
KELLY SHERIDAN

Client
REEBOK UK

Special Effects

Director
RICHARD DEAN

Copywriter
TIM MELLORS

Art Director
GRAHAM FINK

Creative Director
TIM MELLORS

Producer
MATTHEW JUSTICE

Set Designer
BRYCE WALMSLEY

Agency Producer
DIANE CROLL

Editor
ANDY KEMP
ROB HODGSON

Lighting Cameraman
CHRIS PARKER

Production Company
THE MOVING
PICTURE
PRODUCTION
COMPANY

Agency
GGT

Managing Director
GIULIANO
GNAGNATTI

Marketing Director
NIGEL GRASHAM

Client
ARISTON

WASH

Open on a kitchen.

A series of people enter and perform various mundane functions in a cycle of repeats.

SURPRISE SURPRISE

*the screen, a young couple are seen
king arm in arm in various romantic
Parisian locations.*

*s their faces become recognisable, an
ress actually planted in the cinema
dience stands up and interacts with
em. The man, it transpires, is her
riend who had told her he was going
on business. After giving him a piece
r mind, the girl storms off – as does
rl on screen too. Abandoned, the man
ks for sympathy from a French girl
ing from a park bench. She gives him
thering look and buries her head in a
newspaper.*

Special Effects

Director
FRANK BUDGEN

Copywriter
JOHN PALLANT

Art Director
MATT RYAN

Creative Director
PAUL ARDEN

Producer
PAUL ROTHWELL

Agency Producer
MARK HANRAHAN

Editor
CYRIL METZGER

Lighting Cameraman
CHRIS DUFFY

Production Company
PAUL WEILAND FILM
COMPANY

Agency
SAATCHI & SAATCHI

*Director of Products &
Marketing*
ROGER HEAPE

Head of Marketing
TIFFANY HALL

Client
BRITISH AIRWAYS
HOLIDAYS

Special Effects

Director
BILL MATHER

Copywriter
DAVE BUCHANAN

Art Director
MIKE HANNETT

Creative Director
TONY COX

Producer
KEITH VALENTINE

Set Designer
JAMIE LEONARD

Animators
DAVE THROSSEL
LINDA JOHNSON

Agency Producer
LUCINDA KER

Editor
KEVIN WHEELAN

Lighting Cameraman
ROGER PRATT

Rostrum Cameraman
PETER TAYLOR

Music Composer/Arranger
GRAHAM PRESKETT

Production Company
REDWING FILM
COMPANY

Agency
BMP DDB NEEDHAM

Marketing Manager
JULIAN NOLAN

Client
NATIONAL DAIRY
COUNCIL

DAYBREAK

Music:
An arrangement of 'Dawn Patrol'.

Milkman:
Two semi-skimmed...

...one Silver Top...

*Number eighteen. Ah, rice
pudding tonight.*

Music: *(Stops)*

Milkman:
*Lads, lads. What are you playing
at? You know they're away for a
fortnight. But next door want two
extra. Go on then.*

VO:
Whatever your order...

*...your milkman can deliver...all
the milk you'll ever need.*

Milkman:
Empties!

COOK

Open on a kitchen.

*A series of people enter and
perform various mundane
functions in a cycle of repeats.*

Special Effects

Director
RICHARD DEAN

Copywriter
TIM MELLORS

Art Director
GRAHAM FINK

Creative Director
TIM MELLORS

Producer
MATTHEW JUSTICE

Set Designer
BRYCE WALMSLEY

Agency Producer
DIANE CROLL

Editors
ANDY KEMP
ROB HODGSON

Lighting Cameraman
CHRIS PARKER

Production Company
THE MOVING
PICTURE
PRODUCTION
COMPANY

Agency
GGT

Managing Director
GIULIANO
GNAGNATTI

Marketing Director
NIGEL GRASHAM

Client
ARISTON

Special Effects

Director
MARTIN CAMPBELL

Copywriter
GORDON GRAHAM

Art Director
NEIL SULLIVAN

Creative Director
ADRIAN HOLMES

Producer
SHEILA SIMPSON

Agency Producer
TRACEY JOHNSTON

Editor
JOHN SMITH

Lighting Cameraman
TOM McDOUGAL

Music Composers/Arrangers
BILL CONTI
CARL JENKINS
MIKE RATLEDGE

Production Company
CHALLENGE

Agency
LOWE HOWARD-SPINK

Marketing Director
PETER VEY

Client
NATIONAL POWER
COMPANY

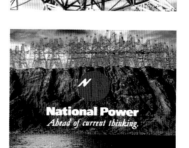

CCGT

MVO:
In the future, where will we generate cleaner and cheaper electricity?

SFX:
Dramatic use of music throughout.

Electric charge.
Buzz.

MVO:
National Power are building a new type of power station...

...that will burn not coal or oil, but gas.

To generate electricity 30% more efficiently...

...with less than half the emissions.

MVO:
National Power.

Ahead of current thinking.

ele
vision and
30

cinema g

raphics

Brand Identity

Director
ROB KELLY

Producer
CELIA CHAPMAN

Modelmaker
STUART MURDOCH

Music Composer/Arranger
ROGER JACKSON

Animator
ANDY GOFF

Lighting Cameraman
DOUG FOSTER

Harry Editor
ROB HARVEY

Production Company
LAMBIE-NAIRN
& COMPANY

Marketing Director
WENDY MARTIN
YONI COHEN

Client
BRAVO
(UNITED ARTISTS
PROGRAMMING)

BRAVO

Bravo is a channel dedicated to classic movies and television series. The style of the identity is nostalgic, its design borrows familiar icons from the early days of film and television adapted for the needs of modern day presentation and promotion.

SCREEN ONE

The titles were a generic sequence introducing 8 new plays. Each scene is part of a puzzle. The scenes were shown in 8 combinations of 4 images. In each case the last image ends with the unicorn. The viewer had to have seen all 8 sequences to work out the puzzle.

Brand Identity

Graphic Designer
ROSALIND DALLAS

Director
ROSALIND DALLAS

Producer
ROSALIND DALLAS

Set Designers
ROSALIND DALLAS
DIGBY HOWARD

Music Composer/Arranger
JOHN STEHALEY

Modelmaker
RAYMOND
EVANGELISTA

Lighting Cameraman
KARL WATKINS

Editor
ROB HARVEY

Production Company
BBC TELEVISION
GRAPHIC DESIGN
DEPARTMENT

Client
BBC TELEVISION

Brand Identity

Graphic Designer
CHARLOTTE CASTLE

Director
CHARLOTTE CASTLE

Producer
MICHELLE JAFFE

Model Maker
MICHAEL GEISSLER

Lighting Cameraman
GEORGE TIFFIN

Harry Editor
CHRIS LEONARD

Post Production Company
COMPLETE VIDEO

Music Composer/Arranger
WILL WOOLF

Production Company
PASSION PICTURES

Client
BBC TELEVISION

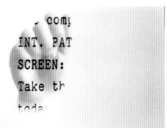

SCREENPLAY

A screenplay is being typed out on paper. The writer's hand pulls back and dissolves away with the script leaving the behind the first part of the title.

The writer's hand then returns, punching through what is now a screen leaving the second part of the title behind.

CHRISTMAS ON BBC 2

As a result of the touring exhibition of George Mellie's films around the country at the moment, designer/directors Brendon Norman-Ross and Sue Worthy thought the opportunity too good to miss for the basis of a theme 'George Mellie meets Christmas on BBC 2'

The naive filming of puff explosions and amateur theatrics based on original ideas from the design team lent a warm quirky charm to programming on BBC2. The ideas are based on mishaps that one experiences during Christmas. The first idea is the concept of Christmas tree lights never working. The second is one awaiting the arrival of presents.

The shoot was developed on the basis of filming everything a George Mellie would have done in 1898, and only using Harry to composite opticals and tint layers.

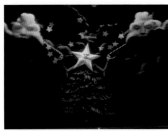

Brand Identity

Graphic Designers
BRENDON
NORMAN-ROSS
SUE WORTHY

Directors
BRENDON
NORMAN-ROSS
SUE WORTHY

Producer
MARK WILSON

Set Designer
BRIAN SYKES

Lighting Cameraman
DOUG FOSTER

Harry Editor
ROB HARVEY

Production Company
BBC GRAPHIC DESIGN

Client
BBC TELEVISION

THE

DESIGN AND ART DIRECTION

STUDENT AWARDS SCHEME

In 1992 the projects set for the Awards Scheme included
a campaign for 'Polo Mints' and 'Say Yes/No To Sunday Trading'
and work for 'Manchester 2000', 'Mencap' and 'Eye Magazine'.
There were 361 individual projects submitted from 36 colleges
and the winning pieces are featured here. No prizes were awarded
for the 'Eye Magazine' brief.

WINNER &
OVERALL WINNER

Student
SUIMAN WONG

Tutor
MIKE LUXTON

College
BUCKINGHAMSHIRE
COLLEGE

MENCAP

Creative requirements
The brief is to convince showbusiness personalities to devote a day of their time, to help raise funds to open 10 new hostels for mentally handicapped children and adults. Mencap has set very high targets – one new hostel opened every year, for the next ten years. To make this dream a reality, Mencap is planning a fundraising, marketing and promotional campaign which will be launched in August 1992.

The task
To devise a launch mailing which exploits the benefits of the medium and generates enough enthusiasm for the recipient to feel happy to give up a day of their time to help Mencap.

The item should allow for a 200 word introduction, the rest of the content is up to you.

Your design must be able to travel through the post and conform to to current Royal Mail regulations.

The second part of the brief is to design two support mailings that will reinforce the request and motivate a positive response.

JAMES BEVERIDGE
The Partners

POLO MINTS

What is the problem the advertising must address?
Polo occupies a very small space in people's minds. It's been around for so long it's easy to take for granted and all the action seems to come from extra strong and chewy mints. Polo is in danger of being forgotten.

What is the opportunity?
To use advertising to make Polo seem big and famous once more.

What is the single most important point we want people to take from the advertising?
Only Polo gives refreshment with interest.

Other useful information
Polo needs to seem big. It doesn't have the budget to achieve this on TV, so we need to think laterally, about <u>owning</u> a particular medium. Is it bus sides, posters, topical press or some other medium? You should also consider targeting the trade with direct mail to launch the campaign, so that they don't forget how unique Polo is.

BILLY MAWHINNEY
J. Walter Thompson

WINNER
Students
DAVID MASTERMAN
IAN EDWARDS
Tutor
DAVE MORRIS
College
BUCKINGHAMSHIRE
COLLEGE

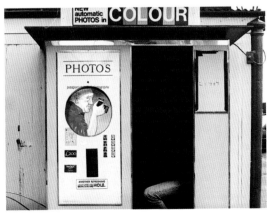

WINNER
Student
HELEN J NEIL
Tutor
SIMON BAILEY
College
LANCASHIRE
POLYTECHNIC

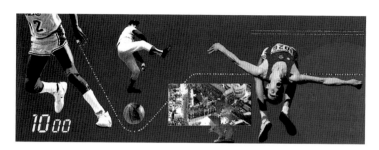

THE BRITISH OLYMPIC BID MANCHESTER 2000

It would seem the unsuccessful 1996 bid was not entirely wasted, on the strength of all the material originally created, Manchester successfully beat London earlier this year to secure itself the privilege of representing Britain's bid to be the host nation for the year 2000 Olympics.

What are the requirements?

A brochure (3 sample spreads and cover) to be sent to all local authorities in an attempt to drum up their support for the bid emphasising the benefits to Britain as a whole.

A storyboard for the title sequence of a TV programme about the bid.

A signage system. Or anything else that you feel would be appropriate.

ALEX MARANZANO
Minale, Tattersfield & Partners

TRADING ON A SUNDAY

Why are we advertising?
To put the case as to why stores should be allowed to trade on Sundays.

Who are we talking to?
Everyone – but particularly those influential groups who are in a position to lobby hard for a change in the law, e.g. MPs, retail management and newspaper/TV editors and journalists.

What must the advertising say?
Stores should be free to trade on Sundays.

What tone of voice?
Dr George Carey: concerned guardian of the nation's moral well-being. <u>Or</u> Maggie Thatcher: champion of the freedom to choose.

What are the requirements?
3 full page black and white press advertisements. A direct mail shot aimed at influential groups

GRAHAM WATSON
Bartle Bogle Hegarty

Mary had a wonderful day with her daughters even though her shorts were too tight

Set Sunday aside for yourself
———————————
The Campaign Against Sunday Trading

WINNER
Student
CATHERINE
FLETCHER

Tutors
SIMON BAILEY
MARTIN
CHATTERTON

College
LANCASHIRE
POLYTECHNIC

HOW TO
BECOME A MEMBER

To be eligible for Full Membership of
Design and Art Direction, you must have had your work
accepted for exhibition by a Design and Art Direction jury,
and must also be working professionally as one of the following: Art
Director, Designer, Copywriter, Illustrator, Photographer, Model
Maker, Typographer, Television Director, Television Graphics
Designer, Art Editor, Television Producer, Agency Producer, Film
Editor, Lighting Cameraman, Animator, Set Designer or
Music Arranger/Composer.

From 1993 D&AD will be introducing a tiered membership scheme.
This will allow people to join as Associate Members, people, who in
the opinion of Full Members, are supportive of the aims and ideals of
the Association. Such members, after acceptance by the Executive
Committee, will be eligible to attend the AGM or have a role in the
running of the Association. It is expected that Associate Membership
will comprise of those who buy, sell, print or promote creative
excellence as well as agencies who may not have won a
D&AD Award.

Included in the tiered system is a programme to promote Student
Membership and to encourage International Membership.
Further information on membership categories is available from
the D&AD office.

D & A D

LIST OF MEMBERS

A

David Abbott • *Copywriter*
Fraser Adamson • *Art Director*
Frank Ainscough • *Design Director*
Roger Akerman • *Art Director*
Douglas Alexander • *Designer*
JuliaAlldridge • *Designer*
Jim Allen • *Art Director*
Christopher T Allen • *Art Director*
John Altman • *Composer*
Stak Alvaliotis • *Photographer*
Ethan Ames • *Graphic Designer*
Jim Andrews • *Managing Director*
Mark Andrews • *Agency Producer*
Geoffrey Appleton • *Illustrator*
Derek Apps • *Copywriter*
Jim Archer • *Copywriter*
Robert Archer • *Graphic Designer*
Paul Arden • *Creative Director*
Andy Arghyrou • *Art Director*
Rosemary Arnold • *Art Director*
Will Awdry • *Copywriter*

B

John Bacon • *Copywriter*
Jim Baker • *Director*
Jack Bankhead • *Photographer*
Zafer Baran • *Photographer*
Don Barclay • *Concept Creator*
Chris Bardsley • *Copywriter*
Sally Bargman • *Art Director*
David Barker • *Copywriter*
Stuart Baron • *Creative Director*
Peter Bates • *Designer*
John Bateson • *Designer*
Harold Batten • *Designer*
Ann Baxendale • *Art Director*
Kate Baxter • *Designer*
Flo Bayley • *Designer*
Roger Beattie • *Copywriter*
Mike Bell • *Art Director*
Nick Bell • *Copywriter*
Madeleine Bennett • *Designer*
Noel Bennett • *Producer*
Bruce Beresford • *Designer*
Steve Bernstein • *Lighting Cameraman*
Gary Betts • *Art Director*
James Beveridge • *Designer*
Steve Bicknell • *Photographer*
John Blackburn • *Designer*
Ruth Blair • *Copywriter*
Anthony Blake • *Photographer*
Alan Blake • *Director*
Nick Bleasel • *Copywriter*
Karen Blincoe • *Graphic Designer*
Laurence Blume • *Creative Director*
Roland Blunk • *Graphic Designer*
Hans Bockting • *Designer*
Tony Bodinetz • *Creative Director*
Edward Booth-Clibborn • *Art Director*
Julia Bostock • *Creative Director*
David Bourne • *Copywriter*
Chris Bourne • *Art Director*
Graham Bowes • *Designer*
Anthony Bowran • *Photographer*
George Boyter • *Art Director*
Chris Bradley • *Designer*
Timothy Braybrooks • *Copywriter*
Paul Brazier • *Designer*

John Brewer • *Creative Director*
Paul Briginshaw • *Art Director*
Peter Bristow *Creative Director*
Mike Brooking • *Copywriter*
Alan Brooking • *Photographer*
Simon Brotherson • *Art Director*
Warren Brown • *Art Director*
David Brown • *Director*
Ron Brown • *Art Director*
Bryan Brown • *Copywriter*
Richard Bryan • *Director*
Gary Bryan • *Film Director/Photographer*
David Buchanan • *Copywriter*
Frank Budgen • *Director*
Sheila Bull • *Copywriter*
Terry Bunton • *Director*
Doug Buntrock • *Art Director*
Paul Burke • *Concept Creator*
Alan Burles • *Art Director*
Cliff Butler • *Typographer*
Dan Butterfill • *Art Director*
Ian Butterworth • *Art Director*
Brian Byfield • *Director*

C

Andrew Cade • *Creative Director*
Aziz Cami • *Designer*
Maggie Campbell • *Head Of Tv*
Robert Campbell • *Copywriter*
Walter Campbell • *Art Director*
Simon Carbery • *Copywriter*
Paul Cardwell • *Copywriter*
Richard Carman • *Copywriter*
Fiona Carpenter • *Designer*
Jeremy Carr • *Art Director*
Robin David Carroll • *Creative Director*
Cameron Carruthers • *Designer*
Terry Carter • *Art Director*
Peers Carter • *Copywriter*
Philip Carter • *Designer*
Tom Carty • *Copywriter*
Ben Casey • *Designer*
Iain Cassie • *Director*
Mario Cavalli • *Animator*
Michael Cavers • *Creative Director*
Peter Celiz • *Art Director*
Derek Chambers • *Designer*
Andrew Chappin • *Art Director*
Charity Charity • *Copywriter*
Barry Chattington • *Director*
Chloe Cheese • *Illustrator*
Peter Cherry • *Art Director*
Joanne Lee Chevlin • *Typographer*
John Cigarini • *Producer*
John Claridge • *Photographer*
Curtis Clark • *Cinematographer*
John S Clarke • *Director*
Rob Cleary • *Typographer*
Ed Cleary • *Typographer*
Stafford Cliff • *Creative Director*
John Clifford • *Art Director*
Tom Climpson • *Art Director*
John P Clive • *Director*
Paul Collis • *Art Director*
Patrick Collister • *Copywriter*
Thomas Connaughton • *Copywriter*
Gary Cooke • *Designer*
Roger Cooper • *Designer*
Ric Cooper • *Copywriter*
Graham Cornthwaite • *Art Director*
James Cotier • *Photographer*

Michael Court • *Creative Director*
Michael Courthold • *Designer*
Tony Cox • *Creative Director*
Michael Cozens • *Director*
Andrew Cracknell • *Creative Director*
Colin Craig • *Art Director*
Jeremy Craigen • *Copywriter*
Robert Cramp • *Photographer*
Lol Creme • *Director*
Jonathan Crisp • *Creative Director*
Cyril Cronin • *Creative Director*
Clive Crook • *Art Director*
Andrew Cross • *Designer*
Bruce Crouch • *Copywriter*
Michael Crozier • *Editor*
Alan Curson • *Copywriter*

D

Vernon Daglish • *Director*
Michael Darby • *Art Director*
Ashted Dastor • *Designer*
Peter Davenport • *Designer*
Tony Davidson • *Art Director*
Ian Davidson • *Art Director*
Glynn Scott Davidson • *Art Director*
Steve Davies • *Designer*
Gill Davies • *Director*
Nigel Dawson • *Typgrapher*
Derek Day • *Designer*
Will De L'ecluse • *Designer*
Trevor De Silva • *Copywriter*
Phillip Dearman • *Copywriter*
Simon Delaney • *Director*
Tim Delaney • *Creative Director*
Gregory Delaney • *Creative Director*
Paul Delaney • *Creative Director*
Barry Delaney • *Copywriter*
Mike Dempsey • *Art Director*
Rita Dempsey • *Copywriter*
Michael Denny • *Designer*
Jonathan Dent • *Designer*
Mark Denton • *Art Director*
Stephen Denton • *Copywriter*
Bryan Denyer • *Designer*
Michael Devito-French • *Art Director*
Martin Devlin • *Designer*
Shaun Dew • *Director*
Nigel Dicker • *Art Director*
Simon Dicketts • *Creative Director*
Rachael Dinnis • *Graphic Designer*
John Donnelly • *Copywriter*
Robert Dowling • *Photographer*
Terry Dowling • *Graphic Designer*
Nick Downes • *Art Director*
Steve Dowson • *Designer*
Ian Ducker • *Art Director*
Bruce Duckworth • *Designer*
Malcolm Duffy • *Copywriter*
Belinda Duggan • *Designer*
Gert Dumbar • *Designer*
Geoff Dunbar • *Director*
Steve Dunn • *Art Director*
Iain Dunn • *Copywriter*
Paul Durbin • *Designer*

E

Antony Easton • *Art Director*
Paul Eastwood • *Creative Director*

Barney Edwards • *Photographer*
Garnet Edwards • *Art Director*
Michael Elliot • *Art Director*
Simon Esterson • *Designer*
Nicholak Evans • *Art Director*
Trevor Evans • *Producer*
Andy Ewan • *Graphic Designer*

F

Will Farquhar • *Copywriter*
Mark Farrow • *Designer*
Neil Fazakerly • *Creative Director*
Graham Featherstone • *Art Director*
Paul Fella • *Art Director*
Sandy Field • *Graphic Designer*
Alan Field • *Art Director*
Paul Fielding • *Designer*
Graham Fink • *Art Director*
Clinton Firth • *Art Director*
Kate Fishenden • *Designer*
Jeffrey Fisher • *Illustrator*
Rodney Fitch • *Designer*
Alistair Fleming • *Designer*
Alan Fletcher • *Designer*
Howard Fletcher • *Copywriter*
Adrian Flowers • *Photographer*
Graham Ford • *Photographer*
Max Forsyth • *Photographer*
John Foster • *Art Director*
Richard Foster • *Copywriter*
Nigel Foster • *Producer*
Nancy Fowler • *Director*
Cliff Francis • *Copywriter*
Stephen Franks • *Graphic Designer*
Eddy French • *Editor*
John French • *Copywriter*
Terry Fry • *Agency Producer*
Jane Fuller • *Producer*

G

Bill Gallacher • *Art Director*
Jerry Gallaher • *Copywriter*
Cara Gallardo • *Graphic Designer*
Martin Galton • *Art Director*
Surrey Garland • *Copywriter*
Peter Garrett • *Art Director*
Paul Garrett • *Art Director*
Malcolm Gaskin • *Creative Director*
Peter Gatley • *Art Director*
Peter Gausis • *Art Director*
Paul Gay • *Art Director*
Harry Georgiades • *Art Director*
Peter Gibb • *Designer*
Steve Gibbons • *Designer*
Ginger Gibbons • *Producer*
Nick Gill • *Art Director*
Peter Gill • *Designer*
Neil Godfrey • *Art Director*
Jo Godman • *Producer*
Ian Golding • *Designer*
John Gorham • *Designer*
Bernard Gormley • *Director*
Lee Goulding • *Art Director*
Carl Gover • *Executive Producer*
Mark Graham • *Creative Director*
Kes Gray • *Copywriter*
Antony Green • *Designer*
Malcolm Green • *Copywriter*

Barry Greensted • *Copywriter*
Eddy Greenwood • *Art Director*
Mark Greenwood • *Art Director*
Andrew Greetham • *Designer*
Michael Griffin • *Producer*
Brian Griffin • *Photographer*
Kenneth Griffiths • *Photographer*
Oscar Grillo • *Animation Director*
Steven Grime • *Creative Director*
Ken Grimshaw • *Art Director*
Ian Grindle • *Designer*
Steven Grounds • *Copywriter*

H

John Hackney • *Producer*
Nigel Hadley • *Editor*
Karen Hagemann • *Art Director*
Jeremy Haines • *Art Director*
Jonathan Hall • *Art Director*
Michael Hall • *Producer*
Robin Hall • *Designer*
Ralph Hall • *Photographer*
Geoff Halpin • *Typgrapher*
Mike Hannett • *Art Director*
George Hardie • *Designer*
Chips Hardy • *Copywriter*
Peter Harold • *Designer*
Tony Harris • *Creative Director*
John Harris • *Art Director*
Robert Harris • *Art Director*
Adrian Harrison • *Producer*
Wendy Harrop • *Art Director*
Caroline Hart • *Producer*
Chris Hartwill • *Director*
John Harvey • *Designer*
Derrick Hass • *Art Director*
Ian Hay • *Designer*
Richard Haydon • *Art Director*
John Hegarty • *Creative Director*
Alexander Hemming • *Director*
David Henderson • *Copywriter*
Cathy Heng • *Art Director*
Max Henry • *Creative Director*
Susie Henry • *Copywriter*
Jan Heron • *Copywriter*
Chris Herring • *Copywriter*
Margie Hetherington • *Designer*
Andres Heumann • *Photographer*
Jerry Hibbert • *Animator*
Bob Hinks • *Animator*
Paul Hiscock • *Designer*
Derek Hodgetts • *Copywriter*
Gillian Hodgson • *Graphic Designer*
Michael Hodgson • *Art Director*
Kenneth Hodgson • *Art Director*
Kenneth Hoggins • *Art Director*
Roger Holdsworth • *Copywriter*
Geoff Hollington • *Designer*
Adrian Holmes • *Creative Director*
David Holmes • *Art Director*
Robert Hook • *Art Director*
Steve Hooper • *Copywriter*
Geoff Horne • *Copywriter*
Garry Horner • *Art Director*
Sue Horner • *Designer*
Dave Horry • *Art Director*
Michael Horseman • *Art Director*
John Horton • *Art Director*
Keren House • *Graphic Designer*
Stewart Howard • *Art Director*
Michael Howard • *Designer*

Alun Howell • *Art Director*
Joe Hoza • *Typographer*
Graham Hughes • *Photographer*
David Hughes • *Art Director*
Simon Hunt • *Art Director*
Barrie Hunt • *Creative Director*
Andrew Hunter • *Art Director*
Sam Hurford • *Art Director*
Chris Hutchinson • *Creative Director*
Ian Hutton • *Copywriter*

I

Christopher Impey • *Designer*
Charles Inge • *Art Director*
Darrell Ireland • *Graphic Designer*
Jon Isherwood • *Art Director*
Paul Izard • *Designer*

J

David James • *Photographer*
Liz James • *Graphic Designer*
Rob Janowski • *Creative Director*
Thomas Jenkins • *Copywriter*
David Jennings • *Copywriter*
Jonathan John • *Copywriter*
Simon John • *Director*
Timothy Johnson • *Copywriter*
Brian Johnson • *Designer*
Michael Johnson • *Designer*
David Johnson • *Art Director*
Barrie Joll • *Director*
Christine Jones • *Designer*
Ed Jones • *Copywriter*
Monica Jones • *Designer*
David Jones • *Director*
Peter Jones • *Producer*
Penny Jones • *Designer*
Michael Joseph • *Photographer*
Rod Josey • *Designer*
Jerry Judge • *Art Director*

K

Nadav Kander • *Photographer*
Michael Kaufman • *Editor*
Tony Kaye • *Director*
Adam Kean • *Copywriter*
Michael Keane • *Art Director*
Siobhan Keaney • *Designer*
John Kelley • *Executive Creative*
Steve Kelsey • *Designer*
Adrian Kemsley • *Art Director*
Kiki Kendrick • *Art Director*
Malcolm Kennard • *Designer*
Trevor Kennedy • *Art Director*
Roger Kennedy • *Typographer*
Nigel Kent • *Typographer*
Lucinda Ker • *Producer*
Paul Kilvington • *Design Director*
Ashley King • *Art Director*
Rodney Kinsman • *Art Director*
Barry Kinsman • *Director*
Richard Knight • *Chairman*
Jilly Knight • *Animator*
Mervyn Kurlansky • *Designer*
Ray Kyte • *Designer*

L

Kate Lackie • *Designer*
Martin Lambie-Nairn • *Designer*
Sean Langford • *Designer*
John Larkin • *Creative Director*
Barry Lategan • *Photographer*
Peter Lavery • *Photographer*
Bob Lawrie • *Graphic Designer*
Andy Lawson • *Art Director*
Sandra Leamon • *Creative Director*
Paul Leeves • *Creative Director*
Stephen Legate • *Typographer*
Adrianne Leman • *Managing Director*
Alan Lerner • *Art Director*
Peter Levelle • *Film Director*
Barbara Levett • *Producer*
Dan Levin • *Copywriter*
Mitch Levy • *Art Director*
Janetta Lewin • *Art Director*
John Lewis • *Copywriter*
Dennis Lewis • *Art Director*
Maggie Lewis • *Typographer*
Mary Lewis • *Art Director*
Frank Lieberman • *Agency Producer*
Graham Lincoln • *Art Director*
Mario Lippa • *Art Director*
Rami Lippa • *Designer*
Tony Liston • *Creative Director*
David Little • *Creative Director*
Lewis Lloyd • *Art Director*
John Lloyd • *Designer*
David Lock • *Designer*
Linda Loe • *Designer*
Alan Lofthouse • *Art Director*
Ian Logan • *Designer*
Richard Loncraine • *Director*
John Londei • *Photographer*
Rod Lord • *Animator*
Peter Lorimer • *Copywriter*
Terry Lovelock • *Director*
Frank Lowe • *Creative Director*
Barry Lowenhoff • *Graphic Designer*
Chris Lower • *Designer*
James Lowther • *Director*
Roger Lunn • *Director*
David Lyle • *Copywriter*

M

Ian Macdonald • *Executive Producer*
Wendy Macdonald • *Executive Producer*
Arthur Maddams • *Designer*
David Magee • *Designer*
Peter Maisey • *Art Director*
Tony Malcolm • *Copywriter*
Lyndon Harcourt Mallett • *Creative Director*
Theodora Mantzaris • *Designer*
Alex Maranzano • *Designer*
Alfredo Marcantonio • *Copywriter*
Pearce Marchbank • *Designer*
John Maries • *Director*
Giles Marking • *Director*
Colin Marr • *Creative Director*
Kit Marr • *Art Director*
John Marsh • *Designer*
Gary Marshall • *Art Director*
Paul Marshall • *Copywriter*
Paul Martin • *Designer*
Chris Martin • *Copywrier*

Dominic Martin • *Art Director*
Steven Martin • *Advertising Agency*
Greg Martin • *Art Director*
Phillip Mason • *Art Director*
Jon Matthews • *Copywriter*
Roger Mavity • *Art Director*
Billy Mawhinney • *Creative Director*
Joanna Mawtis • *Art Director*
David May • *Art Director*
Ros McClellan • *Agency Producer*
John McConnell • *Designer*
Stewart McEwan • *Animator*
David McGrath • *Creative Director*
Ian McIlroy • *Designer*
Aird McKinstrie • *Designer*
Brigid McMullen • *Designer*
Barry Meekums • *Photographer*
Richard Mellor • *Designer*
Tim Mellors • *Creative Director*
Debby Mendoza • *Producer*
Frederick Mergeridchian • *Copywriter*
Jeff Merrells • *Head Of Typography*
John Merriman • *Art Director*
Alan Midgley • *Creative Director*
Peter Mill • *Copywriter*
Gerry Miller • *Creative Director*
Robert Miller • *Art Director*
Kathy Miller • *Copywriter*
Greg Mills • *Producer*
Colin Millward • *Creative Director*
Howard Milton • *Designer*
Marcello Minale • *Designer*
Tracy Mitchell • *Copywriter*
Marola Mitotich • *Graphic Designer*
Maxwell Modray • *Lighting Cameraman*
Gerry Moira • *Creative Director*
David Montgomery • *Photographer*
Guy Moore • *Art Director*
Robert Morris • *Art Director*
Brian Morrow • *Director*
Anna Moult • *Copywriter*
Kim Mukerjee • *Copywriter*
Ken Mullen • *Copywriter*
Chris Munds • *Copywriter*
Tony Muranka • *Art Director*
Patricia Murphy • *Director*
Michael Murphy • *Art Director*
Lorna Murrell • *Copywriter*
Robin Murtough • *Copywriter*
Richard Myers • *Copywriter*

N

Minaz Nanji • *Graphic Designer*
Quentin Newark • *Graphic Designer*
Frances Newell • *Creative Director*
David Newton • *Art Director*
George Niklas • *Creative Director*
Roger Noakes • *Creative Director*
Barbara Nokes • *Copywriter*
Tilly Northedge • *Designer*
Michael Northey • *Art Director*
Jim Northover • *Designer*

O

Nicholas O'Bryan-Tear • *Copywriter*
Lizzie O'Connell • *Agency Producer*
John O'Donnell • *Copywriter*
John O'Driscoll • *Art Director*

Gerard O'Dwyer • *Director*
Sean O'Flynn • *Designer*
John O'Keefe • *Copywriter*
Kate O'Mulloy • *Agency Producer*
Chris O'Shea • *Copywriter*
Steven Oates • *Art Director*
Jerry Oke • *Photographer*
Robert Oliver • *Art Director*
Mark Osborne • *Director*
Roger Owen • *Film Editor*
Rosemary Oxley • *Art Director*

P

Alan Page • *Copywriter*
John Pallant • *Copywriter*
David Palmer • *Creative Director*
Chris Palmer • *Copywriter*
Kim Papworth • *Copywriter*
Malcolm Park • *Creative Director*
Larry Parker • *Copywriter*
John Parker • *Photographer*
John Pasche • *Creative Director*
Richard Patterson • *Art Director*
Derek Payne • *Copywriter*
Arnold Pearce • *Producer*
Mark Pearce • *Designer*
Jack Pearce • *Designer*
David Pearce • *Designer*
Alex Pearl • *Copywriter*
John Pearson-Taylor • *Director*
Jeremy Pemberton • *Creative Director*
Simon Pemberton • *Designer*
Sarah Perry • *Graphic Designer*
Michael Peters • *Director*
Tor Pettersen • *Designer*
Kia Boon Phoa • *Designer*
John Pickering • *Designer*
David Pocknell • *Designer*
Liz Pollard • *Copywriter*
Jeanna Polley • *Producer*
Nick Pollitt • *Designer*
Jay Pond-Jones • *Creative Director*
Colin Porter • *Illustrator*
Gerry Poulson • *Director*
Barry Poulter • *Typographer*
Keith Priest • *Designer*
Tim Purvis • *Designer*

Q

Malachy Quinn • *Creative Director*

R

Andy Ray • *Copywriter*
Tom Rayfield • *Copywriter*
Carolyn Reed • *Designer*
Nigel Reed • *Copywriter*
Steven Reeves • *Copywriter*
Hugh Ribbans • *Graphic Designer*
Steven Richards • *Copywriter*
Darren Richardson • *Designer*
Chris Ridley • *Photographer*
Tim Riley • *Copywriter*
Ian Ritchie • *Designer*
Mike Rix • *Typographer*
Mark Roalfe • *Art Director*
Sidney Roberson • *Director*

Michael Robinson • *Illustrator*
Frederick Robinson • *Producer*
Colin Robinson • *Designer*
Paul Rodger • *Designer*
Simon Rodway • *Copywriter*
Joe Roman • *Director*
Graham Rose • *Director*
Nigel Rose • *Art Director*
Peregrine Roskilly • *Illustrator*
Michael Ross • *Art Director*
Michael Rossi • *Creative Director*
David Rossiter • *Copywriter*
Adrian Rowbotham • *Producer*
John Rushton • *Director*
Jonathan Russell • *Designer*
Peter Russell • *Copywriter*
Richard Russell • *Copywriter*
Andrew Rutherford • *Copywriter*
Matt Ryan • *Art Director*
Phil Rylance • *Art Director*

S

John Salmon • *Creative Director*
Martin Sampson • *Director*
Colin Sands • *Designer*
Mike Sands • *Art Director*
Kenneth Sara • *Art Director*
Su Sareen • *Art Director*
Richard Saunders • *Copywriter*
Peter Saville • *Designer*
Richard Scholey • *Designer*
Nick Schon • *Art Director*
Klaus Schultheis • *Art Director*
William Scott • *Art Director*
Kenneth Scott • *Designer*
Graham Scott • *Design Associate*
Derek Seaward • *Photographer*
Richard Selbourne • *Copywriter*
Geoff Senior • *Photographer*
Geoffrey Seymour • *Director*
Ruth Shabi • *Copywriter*
Charles Shand • *Copywriter*
Harry Shaw • *Copywriter*
Tony Sherwood • *Director*
Brian Shields • *Director*
Roger Shipley • *Producer*
John Shuttleworth • *Designer*
Peter Silk • *Graphic Designer*
John Silver • *Copywriter*
Graham Simpson • *Designer*
Loz Simpson • *Copywriter*
Jeremy Sinclair • *Copywriter*
Ian Single • *Director*
Indra Sinha • *Copywriter*
Ian Sizer • *Art Director*
David Smith • *Director*
Gordon Smith • *Art Director*
Richard Smith • *Creative Director*
Roy Smith • *Lighting Cameraman*
Jay Smith • *Designer*
Rick Smith • *Creative Director*
David Smith • *Director*
John Sorrell • *Art Director*
Peter Souter • *Copywriter*
Stephen Spence • *Copywriter*
Alan Spencer • *Director*
Vince Squibb • *Art Director*
Michael Staniford • *Designer*
Lora Starling • *Graphic Designer*
Mike Stephenson • *Director*
Brian Stewart • *Cocept Creator*

Anthony Stileman • *Designer*
Graham Storey • *Art Director*
Celia Stothard • *Graphic Designer*
Mark Stothert • *Producer*
Terry Stratton • *Designer*
David Stuart • *Designer*
Frank Sully • *Art Director*
James Surridge • *Designer*
Jeff Suthons • *Art Director*
Linda Sutton • *Art Director*
Rupert Sutton • *Copywriter*

T

Amanda Tatham • *Graphic Designer*
Brian Tattersfield • *Designer*
Steven Taylor • *Art Director*
Richard Taylor • *Typographer*
Graham Terry • *Producer*
Michael Thierens • *Designer*
Nick Thirkell • *Designer*
Vyvyan Thomas • *Designer*
Allen Thomas • *Copywriter*
Andrew Thomas • *Designer*
Steve Thomas • *Designer*
Gordon Thompson • *Creative Director*
Martin Thompson • *Photographer*
Bill Thompson • *Art Director*
John Thornton • *Director*
Mark Thrush • *Designer*
Alan Tilby • *Creative Director*
Richard Tilley • *Designer*
Sean Toal • *Copywriter*
Tony Toller • *Creative Director*
Alison Tomlin • *Designer*
Tony Tonkin • *Art Director*
Peter Townsend • *Creative Director*
John Townshend • *Copywriter*
Lynn Trickett • *Designer*
Peter Trickett • *Designer*
Chen Tsoi • *Design Director*
David Turner • *Designer*
Geoff Turner • *Art Director*
Joyce Turner • *Copywriter*
Kenneth Turner • *Director*
Christopher Turrall • *Art Director*
Claire Tuthill • *Designer*
Glenn Tutssel • *Designer*
Alan Tyers • *Art Director*

V

Christopher Vane • *Designer*
Louise Vanstone • *Copywriter*
Andy Vargo • *Designer*
Judy Veal • *Designer*
Pierre Vermeier • *Art Director*
Paul Vester • *Animator*
Jackie Vicary • *Creative Director*
Cedric Vidler • *Creative Director*

W

Russell Wailes • *Art Director*
Christopher Waite • *Copywriter*
David Wakefield • *Typographer*
Alan Waldie • *Art Director*
Tim Walker • *Art Director*
Mitch Walker • *Director*

Martyn Wallwork • *Designer*
Martyn Walsh • *Art Director*
Gary Walton • *Art Director*
Richard Ward • *Designer*
Rod Waskett • *Art Director*
Eric Watson • *Director*
Graham Watson • *Art Director*
Denis Waugh • *Photographer*
Graham Webb • *Designer*
Brian Webb • *Designer*
Peter Webb • *Photographer*
John Webster • *Copywriter*
Paul Weiland • *Director*
Paul Weinberger • *Creative Director*
Len Weinreich • *Creative Director*
Mark Welby • *Designer*
Nicholas Welch • *Creative Director*
Joanna Wenley • *Art Director*
Michael Werkmeister • *Designer*
Ken Wheat • *Copywriter*
Paul White • *Art Director*
Paul White • *Copywriter*
Richard Whitmore • *Designer*
Lynn Whyte • *Graphic Designer*
Mark Wickens • *Designer*
Valerie Wickes • *Design Director*
Robin Wight • *Copywriter*
Ian Wight • *Designer*
Mark Wilkins • *Copywriter*
Karen Wilks • *Graphic Designer*
Greg Willcox • *Director*
Don Williams • *Designer*
Nancy Williams • *Designer*
Gary Willis • *Art Director*
Dennis Willison • *Art Director*
Ian Wills • *Designer*
Logan Wilmont • *Art Director*
Peter Windett • *Art Director*
Mark Wnek • *Copywriter*
Michael Wolf • *Designer*
David Wombwell • *Creative Director*
Phillip Wong • *Designer*
Peter Wood • *Photographer*
John Wood • *Creative Director*
David Woodall • *Art Director*
Patrick Woodward • *Copywriter*
Nick Wootton • *Art Director*
David Worthington • *Designer*
Susan Worthy • *Director*
Barry Wrightson • *Creative Director*
Matthew Wurr • *Model Maker*
Klaus Wuttke • *Designer*
Jack Wyper • *Creative Director*

Y

Clive Yaxley • *Art Director*
Ruth Yee • *Art Director*

INDEX

CONCEPT CREATORS

COPYWRITERS

D & A D

SPONSORS

WORRY ABOUT AWARDS. NOT MONEY.

Touche Ross

Deloitte Touche Tohmatsu International

REALTIME STUDIO

real time

What every studio may be like in the new millennium

studio

Services include

- Concept/Design
- Creative typography
- Presentations
- Rubdowns
- Marker visuals/Illustration
- Apple Mac graphics and type
- Over 3500 PostScript typefaces
- Scantext 2000 typesetting
- Finished mechanicals

For a full presentation or for further information please contact Phil Jones or Annie Eaves

15 Vine Hill London EC1R 5DX
Telephone 071 814 9494
Facsimile 071 814 9480
Modem 071 814 9481

KENDALL TARRANT PARTNERSHIP

83 CHARLOTTE STREET LONDON W1P 1LB
TELEPHONE: 071-636 1633 FAX: 071-631 4671

IF SAATCHI'S WEREN'T HAPPY, IT WOULD HAVE COST US A XXXX FORTUNE.

We've always claimed to be the best pre-press production company in the world, so we're now putting our money where our mouth is.

So confident are we to be able to live up to our promise we're making you this unique offer. If you're not completely satisfied with the quality of our work, you don't pay a thing. Not a bean. Zilch. Nought.

Proof that there's at least one pre-press company where you really do get what you pay for. Or put another way, if you ever say 'no way' you no pay.

MAYDAY • TRUMPET • WACE BLACK & WHITE • BORKEY'S • STYLE/STUDIO 10 • INLINE COLOUR

Wace Agency Division, Wace House, Shepherdess Walk, London N1 7LH. Telephone: 071 250 3055 Fax: 071 490 4916

TO SEE HOW WELL DIRECT MAIL CAN WORK, HAND OUT SOME OF THESE.

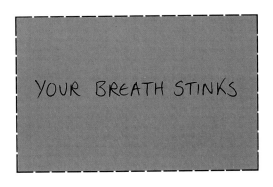

As you can see, the messages above are simple, clear and arresting. They will get a response.

If you match the message to the person.

Direct mail is the only advertising medium which can do this. Because you can split up your target market and talk to each different group in their own language.

This is done with the help of postcodes and other targeting techniques. So your message is directed with pin-point accuracy to the right people.

Write to Neville Holland, Royal Mail Streamline, FREEPOST, Beaumont House, OXFORD OX4 5BR or call

0800 378 671. He'll send you a free copy of the new Guide to Successful Direct Mail.

With it, you'll see why direct mail is Britain's fastest growing advertising medium.

NAME MR/MRS/MS

JOB TITLE

COMPANY

ADDRESS

POSTCODE   TELEPHONE   DDZ1

If you'd like one of our account managers to contact you, tick here. ☐
If you do not wish to receive information on other Royal Mail products and services, please tick here. ☐

DIRECT MAIL

Official sponsor of the
British Olympic Team

Royal Mail

STREAMLINE

IT'LL BE ALRIGHT ON THE NIGHT

THE ONE TO WATCH

Daily *an* Mail

Supporting D&AD by sponsoring the
Best Press Advertisement - Public Service Category.

"Errm..."

BOWATER

Print and Packaging

Bowater plc

Bowater House, Knightsbridge

London SW1X 7NN

Telephone 071 584 7070

Fax 071 581 1149

{Joe & Co music Ltd ▯: Telephone 071-439 1272 *mf*ax: 071 437 5504

Very best, best wishes.

M A S

MEDIA & AIRTIME SALES LTD

We're always very happy to fill spaces.

This space was
reserved for an ad for
the Tape Gallery,
but they've been too
busy to write it.

AWARD FOR BEST DIRECTION IN TELEVISION AND CINEMA

SPONSORED BY SHEPPERTON STUDIOS · PANAVISION SHEPPERTON
LEE ELECTRIC LIGHTING LTD

Inflated egos, acute paranoia, megalomania.

Even we haven't found a cure.

In fact, we're making things worse by sponsoring the illustration and 20 second TV categories.

Claude Monet : Sunrise.

We'll make sure sunrise over Paris doesn't become sunset over Peckham.

PEOPLE WITH AN EYE
FOR COLOUR

LUMIS COLOUR 1-2 HARDWICK STREET LONDON EC1R 4RB TELEPHONE: 071-833 2661

REMEMBER THOSE DAYS WHEN YOU GOT JOBS JUST BY TAKING PEOPLE OUT TO LUNCH? WE WERE TALKING TO GRAHAM ALLEMAN ABOUT IT ONLY THE OTHER DAY AT L'ETOILE.

O B S C U R A

**Colour Photocomposition Retouching and Electronic Imagery for Graham
Alleman at Leagas Delaney, Linsey Winton at
Saatchi and Saatchi and Peter Carrow at The Partners amongst others.
Contact: John Stanley. Telephone: 071 723 1487.**

IT'S NOT
JUST ANDY WARHOL
WHO'S MADE
CAMPBELLS FAMOUS.

VOGUE

*Vogue, sponsors of the 1992
best photographic campaign category.*

Like **hundreds of bartenders, doormen and cab drivers we're pleased to have supported Jeffrey Bernard.**

The Guardian, sponsors of the 1992 best individual copy category, would like to congratulate
C.D.P. on their award winning advertisement, 'Jeffrey Bernard is unwell.'

The **Guardian**

"Right, let's cut the crap."

Nothing if not forthright (some might say nothing if not Welsh), Lowe Howard-Spink art director, Jeff Curtis, had begun his retouching brief.

"Not too clean, mind" he went on. "These bulls are prop-forwards, y'know, not stand-offs."

They looked more like mud wrestlers to us, but we got the drift.

It would need one of our Graphic Paintbox XLs, one of our Dalims, in fact practically every piece of space age wizardry at our disposal, not to mention extra coffee for the night shift, yet it had to look realistic.

Interesting.

We weren't helped by the fact that because fighting bulls are as keen on their personal space being invaded as they are on their personal hygiene, they had to be shot separately.

Making no less than eighteen separate trannies.

It would take a book thicker than this one to catalogue every stage of the operation – the balancing of colour variations and light sources, the individual retouching requirements,

the various masking and distortion techniques.

It would also give away a few trade secrets.

But we are rather proud of the fact that some of the bulls are standing on legs that didn't exist on the origination.

(Yes, we do have the technology.)

And the fact that the white bull is, in real life, brown.

(Eat your heart out, T. Steele.)

And the fact that we brought it in on time, under budget and to our client's satisfaction.

"Magic, that." He said.

No, Jeff, that costs extra.

VISUAL NETWORK

For further information contact Jeff Saisi at Visual Network, 3-7 Ray Street, London EC1R 3DJ. Telephone: 071-833 8541.

CARLTON

Television designed for London

THE MILL

Flexible and efficient, The Mill is a digital post-production house
built with the advertising community in mind. With editors and production advisors
working to achieve top quality results at realistic prices.
All housed in an airy purpose-designed complex.

The Mill's facilities include an Ursa digital telecine
with selective colour correction, digital editing,
Harry, Harriet, Alias, T-Morph and SoftImage
computer animation, Avid non-linear editing
and multi-format dubbing facilities.

A central machine area, controlled by digital matrix,
allows different resources to be routed
to different suites as needed. This ensures
that each task is tackled in the right
suite with the right combination of equipment –
charged at the right price.

Please ask for a copy of our showreel. Or, better still,
drop in and see us in West Soho, London.

40-41 great marlborough st london w1v 1da
telephone + 44 71 287 4041
fax + 44 71 287 8393